ASIA

The Ultimate Cookbook

Asia: The Ultimate Cookbook

13-Digit ISBN: 978-1-64643-241-7
10-Digit ISBN: 1-64643-241-X

This book may be ordered by mail from the publisher. Please include $5.99 for postage and handling.
Please support your local bookseller first!

Books published by Cider Mill Press Book Publishers are available at special discounts for bulk purchases in the United States by corporations, institutions, and other organizations. For more information, please contact the publisher.

Cider Mill Press Book Publishers
"Where good books are ready for press"
PO Box 454
12 Spring Street
Kennebunkport, Maine 04046
Visit us online
cidermillpress.com

Typography: Adobe Garamond, Brandon Grotesque, Lastra, Sackers English Script
Front cover image: Beef Pho, page 254
Back cover image: General Tso's Pork Belly Steam Buns, page 461
Front endpaper image: Vietnamese Crepe, page 315; Satay, page 39; Yellow Chicken Curry, page 300
Back endpaper image: Beef Pho, page 254; Pho Ga, page 257

Printed in China

1 2 3 4 5 6 7 8 9 0

First Edition

ASIA

The Ultimate Cookbook

BRIAN HUSKEY

with VANESSA CECENA

Photographs by JIM SULLIVAN

CIDER MILL PRESS

BOOK
PUBLISHERS
KENNEBUNKPORT, MAINE

CONTENTS

PROLOGUE

As a Korean American Chef born and raised in Los Angeles, I grew up in a household where most of our family traditions revolved around delicious, shared meals, whether they were home cooked by my mom or relatives, or served at our favorite restaurants. I can vividly remember the smell of garlic and chili spices permeating our home when I was a child, as I watched my halmoni, "grandmother" in Korean, prepare different banchan (Korean side dishes), kimchi, stir frys, or stews. Sometimes I even got to help her fold dumplings.

Growing up, we were blessed to have a mother who would cook four to five meals a week, mostly Korean dishes. On occasion she would prepare tacos, spaghetti, meatloaf, or turkey dinners, all with an Asian twist. Even her non-Korean dishes are still some of my favorite home-cooked meals.

My mom learned most of her Korean cooking from my grandmother and non-Korean dishes by trial and error—she was focused on perfectly replicating new dishes. My mom had three sisters and four brothers; every visit would turn into a party in the kitchen. All the different dishes they prepared and cooked sparked my interest because of the unique ingredients they used; my palate was curious at a young age.

I always enjoyed spending time with my mom, watching and helping her cook. This was our way of connecting and spending quality time with each other. My grandma and mom expressed their love for the family through their food. At a young age I didn't understand this and took it for granted; I thought everyone ate as well as we did.

My parents were foodies, and they exposed us to the many different cuisines Los Angeles had to offer. Most Sundays, Mom and Dad would load my two brothers and me into the car and take us to a restaurant. It was never the same restaurant; it could be Korean, Chinese, Mexican, Thai, Japanese, Italian, Middle Eastern, French, or Vietnamese. I always looked forward to our Sunday family dinner adventures, because I liked trying something new; however, my favorite restaurants were usually the Asian ones.

While attending UCLA, I started cooking out of necessity, to help pay my bills. My earliest cooking jobs were at an American diner and a Korean fast casual restaurant, both at the Farmers Market at The Grove in Los Angeles. These experiences made me realize I wanted to cook professionally. Once I graduated, I moved to San Francisco for culinary school and to start my cooking journey. Throughout my career, I worked my way up the ranks of fine dining kitchens, which led to me competing on Bravo's *Top Chef* and the opportunity to operate my own restaurants.

Along the way, I have become close friends with so many wonderful cooks and people in the hospitality industry. The family meals at restaurants and intimate conversations with coworkers after work helped me gain further appreciation and exposure to different ethnic flavor profiles and cultures. When it was their turn to cook a family meal, many cooks would prepare dishes that shared their culture and identity. One cook in particular has really made an impact on me: my "right hand" in the kitchen, Chris Le. His Vietnamese background and culinary expertise from this region have taught me new ways of preparing and executing Asian-inspired food.

Cooking, which started as a way to spend time with my mom and family, turned into a means to survive during college, and it has become my passion, craft of choice, and identity. It has even led the way to my own family. Food has always been what connects us regardless of our background, and for me, cooking has always been one of my love languages—I believe it's the most universal language of all. My partner, Aly, and I met because of our mutual love of food. Our daughter, Lola, has found her own passion in the kitchen, and like my childhood, this is our way of connecting and creating memories together.

This book is a compilation of Asian recipes from some of my earliest and fondest food memories, as well as ones I've learned during my travels and through my fellow hospitality peers, friends, and family. Always remember that there is never really a right or wrong when it comes to cooking. Everyone's palate is food, the same as the stories we tell through the food we make are different. The key to executing a delicious meal, and my life philosophy, is to take every step with purpose and intention. The love you put into preparing a dish will always be noticed and appreciated.

Enjoy making these dishes alongside your family and friends, and use them as a road map to replicate some of my favorite memories and create some that are uniquely your own.

Brian Huskey

INTRODUCTION

*L*arge metropolitan cities across the United States, and the rest of the world, have an extensive concentration of Asian communities, primarily Japanese, Chinese, Vietnamese, and Korean. New York's and San Francisco's Chinatowns are inconic. In Southern California, Little Tokyo mirrors the streets of Japan, with small, hidden ramen and sushi restaurants. San Diego's Convoy District has blocks of Japanese, Chinese, and Korean barbeque restaurants. A few miles south is Little Saigon, a community that received the majority of Vietnamese refugees after the war and is now a destination for exquisite, traditional pho.

Asian communities popped up across America as people migrated to cities and towns that would offer them opportunities to work and sustain their families. In the American South, we have Vietnamese and Chinese communities that work in the fishing industry, and in the Midwest, there are workers in meat factories and poultry farms.

In the agricultural industry on the West Coast, Filipinos partnered with Mexicans during the historic Delano grape strike that began in 1965 in California; the two separate labor organizations went on strike in solidarity, and they also shared with one another the food of their home countries in solidarity. This era also witnessed a change to US federal immigration policies, allowing for more migration from China.

Japanese food began to get notoriety in America in the 1990s, when the Japanese economy struggled and there was a shift toward branding and marketing as a tool to showcase their cuisine on a global scale. But even before that, the story of the iconic California roll is the perfect example of how the popularity of Asian food outside of Asia was achieved by catering to local ingredients and tastes. Reportedly invented by Ichiro Mashita at Tokyo Kaikan in Little Tokyo in Los Angeles in the 1960s, the California roll's use of avocado was due to a lack of tuna and an abundance of avocados, and the rice on the outside of the roll was used to essentially hide the nori on the inside, since eating seaweed was not common in the United States at the time.

Today, Chinese cuisine is known as the most popular ethnic cuisine in America. About 30,000 to 40,000 restaurants across the country serve noodle dishes like chow mein and General Tso's chicken, which aren't commonly cooked in households in China.

This is a cursory explanation for how Asian diasporas brought the food of their homelands to the rest of the world. Through these events and circumstances, Asian dishes were present, feeding workers, families, and anyone else looking for what is undeniably delicious food. Middle-class Americans were the first to begin exploring Chinese food, making it a trend. Being able to pay someone to cook for you was a luxury and an indicator of socioeconomic status. The desire to consume the luxury of not cooking for oneself influenced the beginning of the take-out and delivery food culture. Small-business owners running Chinese food restaurants were the first to deliver food to their customers' doorsteps.

ESSENTIAL FLAVORS
& INGREDIENTS

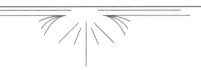

Asian cuisine in its entirety shares commonalities; however, each country has a rich and complex history that has shaped and shifted dishes throughout time. The French, Dutch, Portuguese, and Spanish colonized countries in the region. Through this process, various spices and cooking methods were introduced and woven into the traditional cuisine and cooking styles.

Asian cuisine shares a close relationship with using all parts of the animals is a way to pay respect to nature and the sustenance it provides. Even fish, chicken, and beef bones are used and are integral to making rich and savory stocks that are the foundation of many revered dishes. It is no surprise, then, that meals are traditionally enjoyed with family and friends, and food is plated "family style."

CHINA

The six regions of China—North, Northwest, Northeast, East, South Central, and Southwest—offer varying dishes that center around the cultural histories and food staples of those areas, which are determined by climate and geography. Chinese food is a combination of eight traditional culinary cuisines: Anhui, Cantonese, Fujian, Hunan, Jiangsu, Shandong, Szechuan, and Zhejiang.

Wheat is the predominant grain used to make dumplings and noodles in regions with low rainfall and freezing winters, which make rice difficult to cultivate. The use of rice in dishes is more common in southern China,

where it rains and the climate is warm. Southern cuisine is the opposite of the food from the north—it is spicy and incorporates fruit, vegetables, animal protein, and mushrooms.

Cantonese cuisine is from Guangdong Province near the South China Sea, and its proximity to the ocean is reflected in the seafood found in dishes. Lamb and goat are rarely added to dishes; instead, chicken feet, snails, and duck tongues are present. Dim sum, dumplings stuffed usually with ground pork, were created in this region. Dishes are prepared mainly using a wok for stir-frying and steaming.

Szechuan food is characterized by the volumes of garlic, chilies, and Szechuan peppers, along with food that has been pickled, dried, or salted. Cabbages, radishes, and other vegetables that have been pickled are served alongside rice, porridge, and bread. The idea is that the pickles will help push down the rice and other plain foods. In China, this is called xiafan, which means "to send the rice down."

Anhui food is cooked by the people from the Huangshan Mountain region and includes locally sourced herbs and vegetables, with little use of seafood. Fujian dishes are light and have an umami flavor profile. Wild mushrooms, bamboo shoots, fish, shellfish, and turtles are found in dishes from this coastal and mountainous region.

The flavors of Hunan dishes are like Szechuan food; however, the chilies used don't give off a numbing spice that can be overpowering to some.

Zhejiang cuisine is lighter and includes a lot of fresh produce. Xiao long bao, the stuffed buns from the Shanghai region, are found in Zhejiang cuisine.

Shangdong is a cuisine from the coastal region in the northern part of the country, but it appears in other areas as well. The two styles that make up this regional cuisine are Jiaodong, consisting of light seafood dishes, and Jinan, which includes soups as the main course. Shangdong-style food is considered the most influential style of cooking in the history of Chinese culinary traditions.

Jiangsu cuisine, native to Eastern China, is influenced by its various bodies of water, including rivers, lakes, and the sea. This food is light, sweet, and salty. The preparation of dishes requires frying, stewing, and braising proteins and other ingredients.

Tibet is an area in Western China that experiences harsh weather, limiting the availability of fresh vegetables, herbs, and animal protein. Many residents are yak farmers and enjoy foods like yak tea. Tibetan food is a mixture of Indian, Nepalese, and Szechuan cuisines, due to its geographic location.

The use of food staples including pork, ginger, and scallions is found in each of the seven cuisines. Ginger, known for its health benefits that support a healthy immune system, is an addition to almost every Chinese dish. The root is spicy and adds heat to dishes. Nonanimal protein sources, including tofu, are diverse and plentiful. Sea cucumbers and scallops are dried, rehydrated, and added to soups in coastal areas where the seafood is plentiful.

SOUTH KOREA

Korean cuisine is known to be well-balanced, and the dishes present spicy, salty, sweet-and-sour, and acidic notes. Farmers made up most of the population until the twentieth century. The members of the farming society took the art of cultivating their land seriously. They valued the abundance of their surroundings, and they gathered and stored the food they found in nature. The close relationship they created with the land allowed for the creation of hearty foods that were unique from other cuisines in the region.

The introduction of chilies to Korea by Europeans paved the way for the iconic gochujang, Korean red chili paste. Chilies then began to be folded into traditional dishes. Now we cannot imagine Korean soups and noodle dishes like tteokbokki, a popular dish that contains rice cakes and slices of fish, without this wonderful spice. Tteokbokki began as a side dish served to the royal family, and it was made with soy sauce instead of the modern street food version that has a hefty amount of gochujang. A variation that includes ramen noodles and rabokki has become popular as well.

Every Korean meal is served with banchan, side dishes. It's a visual, noteworthy display of flavors of the kitchen and what is available in any given season. Kimchi, soybeans (kong-

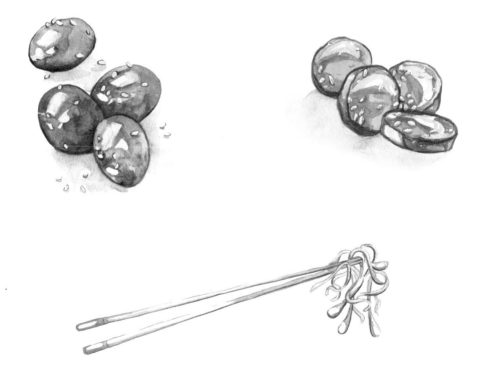

namul muchim), oi muchim (spicy cucumbers), and gamja jorim (braised potatoes) are typical side dishes.

Korean food has existed outside of the peninsula for decades, yet it took much longer than other Asian cuisines to become known, and appreciated, by Western diners. This is because Korean cooks were not interested in creating versions of their food that would be more palatable for others and preferred to maintain the pungent and bold flavors that define this cuisine. Dining out to enjoy Korean favorites like bulgogi or samgyupsal isn't inexpensive, a factor that also shaped the rate at which non-Koreans were exposed to this food.

A recent increase in the popularity of Korean pop music and soap operas has further exposed the international community, especially the younger generations, to popular dishes and street food.

JAPAN

The prestige of Japanese food reflects its access to fresh ingredients, whether they be seafood or vegetables. The quality of all the ingredients used in dishes is imperative to the cuisine. The islands that make up the country are surrounded by the Pacific Ocean, the East China Sea, and the Sea of Okhotsk, home to vibrant marine life. Wild vegetation from the forest highlands is referred to as sansai. It was imperative in combating famine during World War II.

Dashi, a fish broth made from kelp and bonito, is used in practically every dish, adding the distinct umami flavor.

Rice is the primary food staple in Japan. Dishes revolve around the fluffy and light grain, with local wild vegetables and seafood accompanying it. Rice is always served for dinner and may also be enjoyed during breakfast and lunch.

Beef and chicken made their way into Japanese kitchens when the country opened to Western influences. The protein in dishes prior to this period came from seafood, tofu, and vegetables, and reflected long-held Buddhist values. Because of the geography of the islands, they did not have the land necessary to raise large amounts of cattle. Therefore, when the demand for beef increased, they had to begin importing the product. Even so, Japanese beef, wagyu, is one of the most prized types of meat. Its fat content creates a beautifully marbled red-and-white beef. Wagyu beef has grown in popularity in recent years, with the rise in international chefs and restaurants using tender meat in their elevated fusion dishes.

Sushi, nigirizushi, as we know it today is prepared very differently from when the dish emerged at the beginning of the nineteenth century. The earlier sushi did not include sliced raw fish; instead, the fish was fermented and pickled. The length of fermentation for the fish

would range from a few days to a year. Fish that was fermented for a shorter amount of time was referred to as "fresh matured sushi." It is claimed that Hanaya Yohei came up with the idea of pressing fish on top of rice, calling it nigirizushi.

Sushi is served with an optional side of wasabi and sliced ginger and can be gently dipped in soy sauce. In Japan, there are three different types of soy sauce, the most accepted Asian food condiment worldwide. Tamari soy sauce has a strong taste that is acquired during the long fermentation process. Light soy sauce requires a shorter fermentation period and is saltier. Dark soy sauce is the most common in Japan, due to its balanced sweet-and-salty smell and flavor.

THAILAND

Thai cuisine can be described as the perfect ratio of sweet, spicy, bitter, salty, and sour. Customary meals are well-balanced and will include soup, curry, and rice.

Originally, Thai food mainly consisted of aquatic animals, plants, and herbs, a reflection of Thais' close relationship to their rivers and coastal regions. And, of course, one cannot imagine Thai cuisine existing without the taste and smell of spicy chilies. However, chilies did not arrive in Thailand until the 1600s, thanks to Portuguese missionaries. Prior to outside influences, Thai people did not consume large quantities of meat, given that they were predominantly Buddhist.

Traditional cooking methods include steaming, stewing, baking, and grilling. Stir-frying, frying, and deep-frying were introduced by southern Chinese immigrants.

Food in the northern region is influenced by its Burmese and Chinese neighbors to the north. Southern cuisine is typically spicier and reflects a Malaysian influence. The use of coconut is more prevalent in the western region, even though it can be found in many dishes throughout the country. Seafood can be found in every region.

Thai curry dishes are an adaptation of the Indian curry, the first version created, but the Thai version has fewer spices (some spices were replaced by fresh herbs) and uses coconut milk. The red, green, and yellow curries use coconut milk instead of ghee, adding a light, creamy taste that balances out the fiery Thai chilies.

VIETNAM

The most common spices and flavors found in Vietnamese cuisine are chilies, lime, ginger, lemongrass, garlic, and shallots.

The food is similar to dishes in Thailand in the sense that it is also well-balanced. However, it is the combination of specific categories of ingredients that makes the food of Vietnam whole and balanced. A dish will typically include rice, in either grain or noodle form, a protein (seafood, meat, or tofu), and fresh greens like mint, which add complex aromas and flavor to the already elaborate taste of the dishes. The fat in dishes comes from the addition of coconut and nuts.

Vietnamese food is meant to provide all essential nutrients in a bowl, making it satisfying each time.

Like in all cultures and regions of the world, food represents and mirrors society and its people. New dishes are birthed during times of crisis, and often during times of war. A sought-after native Hanoi dish, chả cá, was first cooked in a clandestine restaurant that functioned as a meeting place for people to plot against the French colonizers. The plate of pieces of fried fish served with bun—vermicelli noodles, shallots, peanuts, and dill—is still served today in the same restaurant.

Dishes were also created during the US embargo, which drastically limited access to food, especially meat. Efforts to make do with what was readily available led to the emergence of dishes like bún đậu mắm tôm, cold noodles with fermented shrimp paste and fried tofu.

Phở bò, beef noodle soup served with a basket of mint, bean sprouts, chilies, and lime wedges on the side, was first prepared near Hanoi. Northern Vietnam's version of pho does not customarily come with a basket full of fresh herbs, but instead it is served with garlic vinegar. Some believe that it was inspired by French beef stews or by Chinese noodle dishes, but regardless of which food combinations led to the dish, pho has become the international poster child of Vietnamese cuisine.

RICE

A warm and humid environment is required to achieve a flourishing rice harvest, making regions like Southeast Asia ideal for rice cultivation. It is believed that rice was domesticated in Vietnam and later adopted by the Chinese. It's estimated that around ninety percent of the worldwide consumption of rice comes from Asia.

Rice can grow on different types of soil, including the ones found in Thailand and China. A large quantity of water is required, and so it's cultivated in areas that receive a lot of rainfall annually.

Japan's mountainous geography is used mainly for harvesting rice in paddies. It is difficult to harvest other foods or to raise large quantities of cattle for consumption; therefore, rice was, and continues to be, the center of Japanese cuisine and culture. Before rice became the focal point of meals in Japan, rice was reserved for the elite, and it was used as a form of taxation and payment up until the middle of the nineteenth century. Wealth was measured based on how much rice one had. In ancient times, Japanese people revered the rice god, Inari. There are around 300 varieties of rice in Japan alone.

The typical, most consumed rice is koshihikari (koshi) rice. This short-grain variety is sweet and fluffy, ideal for sushi.

The long-grain jasmine rice is grown in the Southeast Asian countries of Thailand, Cambodia, Laos, and Vietnam. When it is cooked, it gives off a sweet taste and maintains moisture, making it a flawless accompaniment to curries and grilled fish dishes.

Jasmine rice is also the preference for Thai fried rice.

Broken rice, com tam, is a type of white rice that is served topped with a fried egg or with a deep-fried patty in Vietnam. It was created by workers who would collect the small pieces of rice that fell off the mill during the milling process. Now it's eaten throughout the country and used in popular street food dishes.

CHILIES

Chilies have a compound, capsaicin, that causes the burning heat sensation we get when we eat them. This also helps to preserve chilies. It is common to find spicier dishes in warmer climates, which can indicate the preservation quality.

China is the largest consumer and producer of chilies, providing over forty-five percent of the total production worldwide. They were brought from the Americas in the 1500s, and now there are around 2,000 seed landraces in Beijing. Chilies not only play the main role in many Chinese dishes, but they also made their way into popular culture. Chairman Mao was a superfan of the hot flavors and claimed: "No chilies, no revolution!"

The quintessential Chinese chili is the Tien Tsin chili, also known as the Chinese red pepper, Chinese hot pepper, and chao tian jiao, which translates to "facing heaven." It was given that nickname because of the way that it grew—facing up, toward the sky and heaven. The Tien Tsin chili is native to the Tianjin province and

is the pepper used in Szechuan cooking, giving the regional cuisine its medium heat and kick. Dried hot claw peppers are also used in Szechuan dishes. The Szechuan seven star pepper is a purple variety native to the Szechuan region. It also grows facing up and is one of the spiciest chilies of Southern China.

The bonnet pepper (named for its shape), or the Hainan yellow lantern chili, has an intense level of spice and is predominantly used for making hot sauce to be used sparingly on food, because it is so spicy. This yellow chili is from the Hainan region in Southern China.

In the southwest region bordering Myanmar (Burma), the Yunnan shuan shuan chili grows wildly. These chilies are extremely hot; wearing gloves while handling them is highly recommended. The bright lime-green Yunnan wrinkled skin pepper packs a mild heat that intensifies with each bite.

In Thailand, the bright yellow-green prik yuak chili is on the lower end of the heat spectrum, making it ideal for stuffing and battering.

Prik mun chilies are long and come in hues of red and green. One can find them in vinegar and fish sauce condiments.

Prik kee noo suan is a small, green chili that gives tom yum soup and green curry their warmth. While it is one of the spiciest in Thailand, it's the most used—a testament to the culture's love for spice.

Chilies are also consumed in a dry format and used for curries. Dried prik chee fah is used to make red curry. There are green and red varieties, and they are also served fresh or pickled.

Sweet chili peppers are popular in Japan and are enjoyed grilled or fried. The best-known pepper is the shishito pepper, because of its medium and sweet taste, though spicy ones pop up every now and again. Fushimi peppers have little to no heat when they are cooked and are also sweet. They are long, green, thin, and ideal for frying. Manganji peppers, also known as the king of Japanese chilies, have hearty flesh, making them perfect for grilling, sautéing, and frying.

Yatsufusa chilies are like cayenne or Thai peppers. They are also known as Japones chilies ("Japones" in Spanish means Japanese).

Santaka chilies are red and present a medium heat.

In Korea, eating chilies is thought to help relieve stress, one of the explanations behind why Korean food is spicy. But chilies were introduced to Korea and Japan by Portuguese settlers in the seventeenth century, with the peppers arriving in Korea coming specifically from Bolivia. "Gochu" is the Korean word for chili. Gochujang, red chili pepper paste, can easily be spotted in Asian markets by its red lid or red container.

Put-gochu is young green chilies served fresh. Slices are placed in lettuce wraps along with sizzling bulgogi, or eaten alone dipped in jang, a fermented sauce. Hong-gochu, red, ripe, and mature chilies, is used to make kimchi or gochugaru (red chili pepper flakes). In Korea, you can see people sun-drying hong-gochu outside on pieces of cloth that are laid down on the ground.

Gwari-gochu is the Korean version of a shishito pepper and it packs little to no heat. These have more of a pepper flavor and aren't as crunchy when they're fresh. One way to enjoy them in Korea is to sauté them with dried shrimp or anchovies.

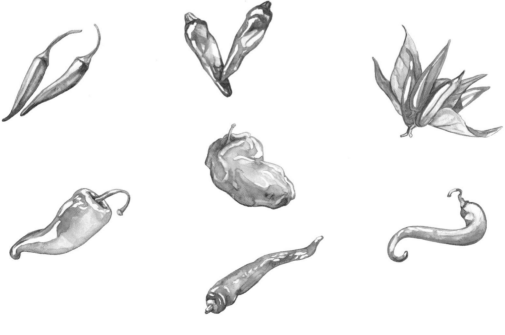

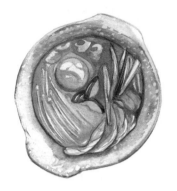

TOFU AND SOYBEANS

The plant-based foods that have made their way onto fast-food menus worldwide wouldn't be possible without the creation of tofu in China 2,000 years ago. There are a few tofu creation myths, and one that even involves a prince's attempt to find immortality. Some scholars believe that the creation of tofu was made by applying cheese-making techniques to soy milk. These methods are thought to have been learned from Mongolia. Others think that tofu is a result of an accidental creation in a kitchen by a cook.

Tofu consists of water, soybeans, and a coagulant. In ancient times, people had access to a natural coagulant, nigari, which is found in unrefined salt. This means that soybeans could have been accidentally boiled with salt, producing tofu.

Tofu traveled from China to Korea, arriving in Japan by the eighth century. This spread was primarily due to Buddhism and its preference for a meatless diet. The nutrient-rich food provided people with protein, iron, and magnesium.

Regardless of its origin, tofu is the central ingredient in dishes found throughout Asia, even in dishes that also include animal protein, like mapo tofu, which traditionally includes pork. The variations of tofu include soft and silken, ideal for soups, and firm, or extra firm, for stir-fry dishes. Nonsilken tofu is considered the "regular" version.

The firmer the tofu, the more protein and fat it holds, because of its method of preparation. To create the square tofu blocks we're accustomed to, water must be pressed out to achieve the desired level of firmness. This variation of tofu is preferred for dishes that require frying or sautéing, because it can take heat for longer periods of time without crumbling.

Soft tofu is perfect for making comforting soups like the Korean soondubu jjigae, and even to make smoothies.

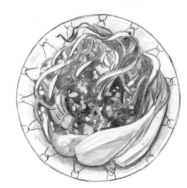

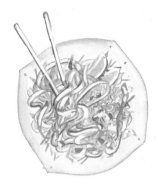

NOODLES

A 4,000-year-old bowl of noodles made from millet was discovered in Northwestern China along the Yellow River. Millet is native to China and was used to make the first noodles. Later, with the cultivation of wheat, noodles were mainly made with wheat.

The length of noodles symbolizes longevity—the longer your noodles, the longer you'll live.

Movies and TV shows sometimes have a comedic scene that shows characters slurping noodles. But slurping in Asian culture is a way to let the cook know that one is enjoying the meal.

Chinese wheat noodles, or mein, are the most common noodles in the region; they are bright yellow and round. These are the types of noodles that many would recognize in Westernized noodle dishes like chow mein and lo mein.

The egg noodle is another typical noodle variation that is frequently used in Chinese and Thai cooking, as well as other cuisines. Crispy egg noodles are deep-fried and served with seafood with a marinade and sauce that resembles gravy, but lighter. Egg noodles are also boiled and used in dishes like dan dan noodles, spicy pork with pickled mustard greens and peanuts. As exposure to Asian food continues to increase globally, dan dan noodles are becoming more recognized and craved.

Ramen noodle soup is easily the second-most popular Japanese dish in the world, next to sushi, and hands down the most quintessential noodle dish. The over 200,000 ramen shops throughout Japan attest to its popularity and cultural importance.

The instant noodle was created by Momofuku Ando in 1958. He was determined to transform noodles into food that could be consumed anywhere, that was nonperishable, and that was accessible to everyone regardless of their socioeconomic status. The years after

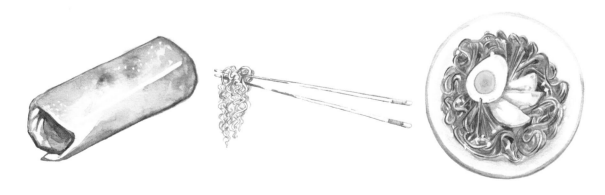

World War II brought food insecurity to Japan, and instant noodles provided ease, ensuring that people wouldn't go hungry.

Regardless of the functionality aspect of instant noodles, they did not hit the world stage until the 1970s. Momofuku developed a Styrofoam cup that would make it even easier for noodle fanatics to quickly prepare their noodle soup. This clever innovation rebranded the original instant noodle into the versions in cups now found in almost every supermarket.

Thin white rice noodles dominate Southeast Asian cuisine, with dishes like pad thai and pho.

Glass noodles are thin, like angel hair pasta. When people dine at a Vietnamese restaurant, they will most likely order fresh spring rolls as an appetizer. These rice paper rolls are made with pork or shrimp, thinly sliced noodles, cilantro, and glass noodles, which add an airy, light texture to the dish.

Naengmyeon, Korean buckwheat noodles, are thin, chewy noodles that are the focal point of bibim (spicy) naengmyeon or mul naengmyeon, a flavorful but not spicy version, and are

served with a chilled beef broth. Both versions are traditionally eaten during hot and humid months, since the noodles are served cold and the broth is served with ice.

FERMENTATION & PICKLING

The fermentation process dates back to the Stone Age, where it is thought to have originated. In essence, it's a historic way of preserving fresh food to last the winter months. While fermenting is practiced across cultures, in Asia it is predominant in a plethora of dishes and condiments.

Fermented soybeans are the main ingredient in the traditional Japanese dish natto. Its taste resembles salty cottage cheese, brie, or foie gras.

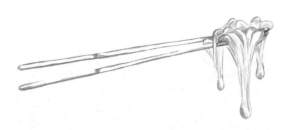

Fish sauce, a staple condiment found widely in Asian cuisine, is made by fermenting fish in brine. It can be used to cook or be mixed with chilies and lime juice to make a popular condiment. In Vietnamese cuisine, it is referred to as nuoc mam. Thai restaurants and food stalls will always serve sliced Thai chilies in fish sauce to add acid and heat to dishes.

Kimchi has been named an "intangible cultural heritage" by UNESCO and is the cornerstone of Korean cuisine. It was essential to helping people survive the freezing months. This delicacy consists of gochujang and other ingredients, like spices and salt, that are rubbed into cabbage and fermented for months. Chinese cabbage gained popularity in the nineteenth century and is the most typical variety used in kimchi. In southern Korea, seafood like shrimp is added.

The main difference between kimchi and other pickled foods is that it's technically brined, not pickled. Vegetables like radishes are pickled and served as side dishes, banchan, with meals. Kimchi jjigae and stuffed cucumber kimchi are other great ways to try kimchi.

Fermentation is also a technique used in Thailand. Fermented pork sausages, naem moo, and khao mak, a fermented alcoholic rice drink like Korea's makgeolli.

TECHNIQUES

Stir-frying was most likely invented by Chinese farmers looking for a quick way to cook, and it required less fuel because of the cooking time. A wok, a cooking vessel made from light carbon steel, is needed to cook the perfect stir-fry dish. A small amount of oil, on high heat, should be used to help vegetables keep their slight crisp. Now, this technique can be seen at food stalls in shopping malls and in kitchens worldwide.

Steaming is another cooking technique that is essential to Asian cooking. Chinese bao buns and vegetables and Southeast Asian fish wrapped in banana leaves are all steamed in traditional woven bamboo baskets that are stackable. Steaming helps to maintain moisture, resulting in a light and flavorful protein or dish.

Deep-frying in vegetable oil is also very common across Asia. Shrimp and vegetable tempura and spring rolls are popular deep-fried preparations. Food that is properly deep-fried is not greasy, but airy and complementary to seafood or vegetables. Many recipes also call for blanching ingredients by deep-frying them for a very short amount of time, so that they can be cooked more later.

ABOUT THIS BOOK

The aromas and complex flavors found in the recipes in this book will take you through the islands and jungles of Thailand, to the rice fields and bustling cities and beaches of Vietnam, to the rows and rows of street food stalls in Osaka, Japan, to the busy city of Seoul, South Korea, with the smells of grilled bulgogi floating through alleys and high-rise buildings, and, of course, all over China, where so many of these traditions originated.

This collection of recipes was compiled to pay homage to Asia, to a region that includes so many distinct countries and cultures. While not all Asian cuisines will be featured in the fol-

lowing pages—that would require more than a few books—Chinese, Korean, Japanese, Thai, and Vietnamese foods are the most recognized Asian cuisines outside of the region, and they form the great majority of this book.

As a celebration of the idea of "Asian food" and how these recipes reflect Chef Brian's upbringing, the individual recipes are presented in no particular order in each chapter. Pretend that you're exploring a fantastic food court with too many options to choose from. Try a little here and there, and then go back again, and again, and again. . . .

STARTERS
& SNACKS

A whole pan-Asian dim sum meal can be made using nothing but the recipes from this chapter. In fact, that is highly encouraged and would be ideal for a party. Your guests would never forget it. But the following pages feature dishes that are typically classified as appetizers.

BLISTERED SHISHITO PEPPERS

YIELD: 4 SERVINGS / ACTIVE TIME: 10 MINUTES / TOTAL TIME: 10 MINUTES

Shishito peppers have quickly become a staple appetizer at all sorts of restaurants. This is a preparation built around Japanese flavors. It's good to keep in mind that most shishito peppers are mild, but every half dozen or so, a spicy one pops up. If you have an aversion to spicy food, replace the peppers with Brussels sprouts.

1. Add the oil to a wok or sauté pan over high heat, and once the oil is smoking, add the peppers, blistering them quickly. Season lightly with the salt and pepper.

2. Once the peppers have blistered, add the sauce, remove the pan from the heat, and stir well to coat the peppers.

3. Place the cooked peppers in a serving bowl and garnish with the Pickled Freson Chilies and bonito flakes, if using.

SOY MAPLE SAUCE

1. Combine all of the ingredients in a bowl, whisk well to combine, and refrigerate in an airtight container.

PICKLED FRESNO CHILIES

1. Soak the chilies in cold water for 15 minutes, strain, and repeat the process 2 or 3 more times if you want them less spicy. Place the strained chilies in a heat-resistant container.

2. Combine the remainder of the ingredients in a saucepan over medium-high heat and bring to a boil, stirring regularly to dissolve the sugar.

3. Pour the boiling pickling liquid over the chilies and cover with plastic wrap or parchment paper to keep the chilies fully submerged, and then cover the container. Let cool at room temperature and refrigerate until needed.

Unlike shishitos, these chilies deliver a consistent sweet heat with every bite. They go great with this recipe, but are also a great go-to condiment for any dish.

INGREDIENTS:

- 3 TABLESPOONS VEGETABLE OIL
- 3 CUPS SHISHITO PEPPERS

  SALT AND PEPPER, TO TASTE
- ¼ CUP SOY MAPLE SAUCE (SEE RECIPE)
- 1–2 TABLESPOONS PICKLED FRESNO CHILIES (SEE RECIPE; OPTIONAL)
- 2–3 TABLESPOONS BONITO FLAKES (OPTIONAL)

SOY MAPLE SAUCE
- ½ CUP SOY SAUCE
- ¼ CUP MAPLE SYRUP
- 1 TABLESPOON WATER

PICKLED FRESNO CHILIES
- 1–2 LBS. FRESNO CHILIES, SLICED INTO THIN RINGS
- ¾ CUP RICE VINEGAR
- ⅔ CUP SUGAR
- ⅔ CUP WATER

SATAY

YIELD: 4 SERVINGS / ACTIVE TIME: 30 MINUTES / TOTAL TIME: 1 HOUR AND 30 MINUTES

Cooking meat, seafood, and poultry on skewers is seen in cuisines worldwide. Here the Southeast Asian version adds the widely used lemongrass to season the meat, and it is served with peanut sauce. Kecap manis is a sweet Indonesian soy sauce that has the consistency of molasses, due to palm sugar. This recipe works for chicken, pork, or beef.

1. In a bowl, combine the soy sauce, salt, lemongrass, shallots, garlic, cumin, coriander, and fish sauce and mix well. Marinate the protein for 1 hour.

2. Skewer the protein, leaving one-quarter of the skewer at the bottom empty to use as a handle.

3. On a hot grill, cook the skewers 3 to 4 minutes per side, or until the meat is cooked through. Baste with the prepared sauce the last 2 to 3 minutes as you cook the skewers.

4. Serve immediately with the Cucumber Relish and Peanut Sauce.

CUCUMBER RELISH

1. In a small pan, combine the salt, sugar, and vinegar and bring to a boil, stirring regularly, and then simmer until the sauce is slightly reduced to a syrup consistency. Remove from heat and let cool.

2. In a bowl, combine the cucumbers, onion, and carrot (if using) and toss with the cooled liquid.

3. Serve immediately.

INGREDIENTS:

¼	CUP KECAP MANIS
1	TABLESPOON SALT
¼	CUP FINELY MINCED LEMONGRASS
2	TABLESPOONS FINELY MINCED SHALLOTS
4-6	GARLIC CLOVES, MINCED
½	TABLESPOON CUMIN
1	TABLESPOON CORIANDER
1	TEASPOON FISH SAUCE (OPTIONAL)
1½	LBS. PORK, CHICKEN, OR BEEF, SLICED INTO 1-INCH-LONG STRIPS
	BAMBOO SKEWERS, SOAKED IN WATER
	SATAY BASTING SAUCE (SEE RECIPE), AS NEEDED
	CUCUMBER RELISH (SEE RECIPE), TO SERVE
	PEANUT SAUCE (SEE RECIPE), TO SERVE

CUCUMBER RELISH

1	TEASPOON SALT
½	CUP SUGAR
½	CUP DISTILLED WHITE VINEGAR
2	CUCUMBERS, SLICED INTO ⅛-INCH HALF-MOONS
⅔	CUP DICED RED ONION
⅔	CUP GRATED CARROTS (OPTIONAL)

Continued . . .

PEANUT SAUCE

1. Using a mortar and pestle, pound the garlic and shallots to form a paste.

2. Add the paste and oil to a small saucepan over low heat and sauté until fragrant and the oil is absorbed.

3. Add the rest of the ingredients and whisk to combine. Once the sauce bubbles, remove from heat. If the sauce is too thick, add water or additional coconut milk. Adjust the seasoning.

4. Cool and refrigerate in an airtight container until needed.

INGREDIENTS:

PEANUT SAUCE

2	GARLIC CLOVES, FINELY MINCED
2	SHALLOTS, FINELY MINCED
2	TABLESPOONS CANOLA OIL
½	CUP COCONUT MILK
¼	CUP CREAMY PEANUT BUTTER
1	TABLESPOON TAMARIND JUICE
1½	TABLESPOONS KECAP MANIS
2	TEASPOONS FISH SAUCE
2	TEASPOONS LIME JUICE
2	TEASPOONS SWEET CHILI DIPPING SAUCE (SEE PAGE 42)

FRIED VIETNAMESE SPRING ROLLS

YIELD: 4 SERVINGS / ACTIVE TIME: 30 MINUTES / TOTAL TIME: 1 HOUR

This is a traditional Vietnamese egg roll wrapped with rice paper. In Vietnam, spring rolls are wrapped in lettuce leaves, with an abundance of fresh herbs.

1. Soak the glass noodles in room-temperature water for 20 to 30 minutes, until pliable. Drain and cut into 3-inch lengths with kitchen scissors. Set aside.

2. In a mixing bowl, combine the noodles with the protein, carrots, mushrooms, shallots, garlic, ginger, egg white, fish sauce, cilantro, white pepper, sugar, and salt and mix well.

3. Prepare a parchment-lined sheet pan.

4. Place the warm water in a bowl and quickly submerge a rice wrapper in the water, being sure not to oversoften the wrapper.

5. Place 3 tablespoons of filling in a log shape on the wrapper. Roll tightly, folding the wrapper over the filling with no air bubbles. Lightly press on each end of the filling to push the filling together and keep it tight. Fold both ends of the wrapper toward the middle, and then roll the spring roll forward to prevent air pockets. Rice paper will stick to itself. Place the roll on the sheet pan and repeat. Make sure not to let the spring rolls stick together before frying.

6. Once all of the spring rolls have been assembled, refrigerate for 2 hours before frying.

7. In a Dutch oven or large pot, bring the oil to 350°F and fry the spring rolls in batches, cooking until golden brown, 4 to 6 minutes. Drain the fried spring rolls on a paper towel–lined plate before serving.

8. Serve with Nuoc Cham and a plate of lettuce and fresh herbs to make wraps.

Continued . . .

INGREDIENTS:

2	OZ. GLASS NOODLES
1	LB. GROUND PORK OR CHICKEN
2	CARROTS, GRATED
½	CUP FINELY CHOPPED WOOD EAR MUSHROOMS
3	TABLESPOONS MINCED SHALLOTS
1	TABLESPOON MINCED GARLIC
2	TEASPOONS MINCED GINGER
1	EGG WHITE
½	TABLESPOON FISH SAUCE
2	TABLESPOONS FINELY CHOPPED CILANTRO
½	TEASPOON WHITE PEPPER
1	TEASPOON SUGAR
1½	TABLESPOONS SALT
20–24	DRIED RICE PAPER WRAPPERS
¼	CUP WARM WATER
	VEGETABLE OIL, FOR FRYING
	NUOC CHAM (SEE PAGE 179), TO SERVE
	GREEN OR RED LEAF LETTUCE, TO SERVE
	THAI BASIL, TO SERVE
	CILANTRO, TO SERVE
	VIETNAMESE PICKLED CARROTS & DAIKONS (SEE PAGE 176), TO SERVE

SWEET CHILI DIPPING SAUCE

1. In a blender, combine the chilies, garlic, vinegar, sugar, salt and 1 cup of water and blend until achieving a smooth but slightly chunky consistency.

2. Add the mixture to a small pot over medium-high heat, bring to a boil, and then simmer for 3 to 4 minutes, stirring regularly, until the garlic is cooked.

3. Meanwhile, in a small bowl, make a slurry by dissolving the starch in 2 tablespoons of water.

4. Add the slurry to the sauce and simmer until the sauce thickens from the slurry, about 1 minute.

5. Remove from heat, let cool, and store in an airtight container in the refrigerator for 1 to 2 months.

INGREDIENTS:

SWEET CHILI DIPPING SAUCE

3	RED THAI LONG CHILIES, STEMMED
4	GARLIC CLOVES
⅓	CUP DISTILLED VINEGAR
½	CUP GRANULATED SUGAR
1	TEASPOON SALT
1	CUP WATER, PLUS 2 TABLESPOONS
1	TABLESPOON CORN OR POTATO STARCH

CHINESE SPRING ROLLS

YIELD: 4 SERVINGS / **ACTIVE TIME:** 1 HOUR / **TOTAL TIME:** 1 HOUR

Fried spring rolls are popular in China, especially in the southern region, and are traditionally cooked to celebrate Chinese New Year. They are also called "spring pancakes" or "thin pancakes" and can be dipped in a sweet-and-sour or spicy sauce.

1. In a bowl, combine the pork, cornstarch, soy sauce, rice wine, and ¼ teaspoon of sesame oil, mix well, and set aside.

2. In a separate bowl, prepare the sauce by combining the light soy sauce, oyster sauce, five-spice powder, and 1 teaspoon of sesame oil and mix well. Set aside.

3. In a sauté pan over medium-high heat, stir-fry the pork until almost done. Add the mushrooms, cook for 1 minute, and then add the remainder of the vegetables and cook for 3 minutes, stirring often and making sure not to overcook the vegetables.

4. Add the prepared sauce to the pan and thicken the filling with the slurry. Cool the thickened filling mix on a sheet pan.

5. Wrap the filling in a spring roll wrapper, being sure not to overfill the wrapper. Seal using the flour paste. Place the wrapped spring rolls on the sheet pan, covered, until needed.

6. In a Dutch oven, heat the canola oil to 350°F. Deep-fry the spring rolls until all sides are golden brown. Remove with a slotted spoon or kitchen spider, drain on a paper towel–lined plate, and serve immediately with the Pineapple Plum Dipping Sauce.

PINEAPPLE PLUM DIPPING SAUCE

1. In a bowl, combine all of the ingredients, mix well, and refrigerate in an airtight container until needed.

INGREDIENTS:

- ¼   LB. PORK SHOULDER/BUTT, THINLY JULIENNED
- ½   TEASPOON CORNSTARCH
- ½   TEASPOON SOY SAUCE
- ½   TEASPOON RICE WINE
- 1¼   TEASPOONS SESAME OIL, DIVIDED
- 2   TABLESPOONS LIGHT SOY SAUCE
- 2   TABLESPOONS OYSTER SAUCE
- ⅛   TEASPOON FIVE-SPICE POWDER
- 8   DRIED SHIITAKE MUSHROOMS, SOAKED, STEMMED, AND FINELY CHOPPED
- ¼   HEAD GREEN CABBAGE, FINELY JULIENNED
- 1   MEDIUM CARROT, FINELY JULIENNED
- 2   CELERY STALKS, THINLY SLICED ON BIAS, THEN JULIENNED
- 1   CUP BEAN SPROUTS
- 3   SCALLIONS, THINLY SLICED ON BIAS
- 1-2   TABLESPOONS CORNSTARCH SLURRY (1:2 RATIO), AS NEEDED

  SPRING ROLL WRAPPERS

  FLOUR PASTE (¼ CUP FLOUR MIXED WITH ENOUGH WATER TO MAKE SEALER)

  CANOLA OIL, FOR FRYING

  PINEAPPLE PLUM DIPPING SAUCE, AS NEEDED (SEE RECIPE)

PIINEAPPLE PLUM DIPPING SAUCE

- ⅔   CUP PINEAPPLE JUICE
- ¼   CUP PLUM SAUCE
- 2   TABLESPOONS SWEET CHILI DIPPING SAUCE (SEE PAGE 42)

PORK POT STICKERS

YIELD: 4 SERVINGS / **ACTIVE TIME:** 1 HOUR / **TOTAL TIME:** 1 HOUR

These stuffed dumplings are cooked with the "fry-steam-fry" method.

1. In a bowl, combine all of the ingredients, except the wrappers, egg, and vegetable oil, and mix well.

2. Set a wrapper on a clean, dry surface and, using a brush or finger, apply the egg wash along half of the wrapper's circumference. Place a teaspoon of the pork mixture in the center—do not overfill—fold over, and seal by pinching the edges together. Repeat, placing the dumplings on a plate until all of the pot stickers are assembled. Refrigerate until needed, or freeze for future use.

3. Add the vegetable oil to a large nonstick pan over medium-high heat. Once the oil begins to shimmer, carefully add the pot stickers one at a time in a single layer until the pan is full. Cook for 2 to 3 minutes, or until lightly browned and most of the oil is absorbed.

4. Add ¼ cup the water and immediately cover the pan, lower heat to medium, and steam the pot stickers for 3 to 4 minutes.

5. Remove the lid and cook for another 1 to 2 minutes, or until the bottoms of the pot stickers are darker brown and crisp, and the water has evaporated. Use more oil if necessary to develop a nice bottom crisp.

6. Serve immediately with dipping sauce.

POT STICKER DIPPING SAUCE

1. In a bowl, combine all of the ingredients, mix well, and let the flavor develop for at least 30 minutes before serving with pot stickers, dumplings, or anything else you like.

INGREDIENTS:

1	LB. GROUND PORK
3	CUPS FINELY MINCED NAPA CABBAGE
2	TABLESPOONS FINELY MINCED GINGER
1	TABLESPOON FINELY MINCED GARLIC
2	TABLESPOONS FINELY MINCED SCALLIONS
2	TABLESPOONS LIGHT SOY SAUCE
1	TEASPOON SUGAR
1	TEASPOON SESAME OIL
1	TEASPOON SALT
½	TEASPOON BAKING SODA
24-30	POT STICKER WRAPPERS
1	EGG, BEATEN
2	TABLESPOONS VEGETABLE OIL, PLUS MORE AS NEEDED
	POT STICKER DIPPING SAUCE, AS NEEDED (SEE RECIPE)

POT STICKER DIPPING SAUCE

2	TABLESPOONS SOY SAUCE
1	TABLESPOON SAMBAL (OPTIONAL)
1	TABLESPOON WHITE WINE VINEGAR
1	TABLESPOON CHINKIANG VINEGAR
1	TABLESPOON SUGAR
1	TABLESPOON FINELY MINCED GARLIC
1	TABLESPOON FINELY MINCED SCALLION
1	TABLESPOON FINELY MINCED CILANTRO
1	TEASPOON SESAME OIL
1	TEASPOON CHILI OIL

SCALLION PANCAKES

YIELD: 4 SERVINGS / **ACTIVE TIME**: 30 MINUTES / **TOTAL TIME**: 1 HOUR

These savory Chinese pancakes, which are really unleavened flatbreads, can be used as a vessel to make Asian-style "wraps" or sandwiches.

1. In a bowl, slowly combine the hot water with the flour, and mix until the hot water is fully absorbed. Slowly add the cold water and continue to mix by hand until dough flakes form. Turn out the mixture onto a floured work surface and knead until a firm dough ball forms. Use a little extra water if needed. Cover with plastic and let rest for 30 minutes at room temperature.

2. Portion the dough into golf ball–size pieces and keep covered. On a floured work surface, roll out each dough ball to a very thin pancake, about ⅙ inch thick.

3. Spread a thin layer of the shortening or lard on the rolled-out dough and sprinkle with the salt, paprika, and scallions.

4. Roll up each pancake into a cylinder, so the scallions are absorbed into the dough. Then coil the scallion dough and roll it out again into a 3-inch circle. Set the formed scallion pancake aside and repeat the steps. To store for later use, place and stack between parchment paper and cover.

5. Heat enough oil to cover the pan so the onion cakes will slightly float as you fry both sides over medium heat, until both sides are golden brown.

6. Cut into 6 pieces and serve with dipping sauce as an appetizer, or use to make Asian-style wraps or sandwiches.

INGREDIENTS:

- ½   CUP HOT WATER
- 2   CUPS ALL-PURPOSE FLOUR, PLUS MORE AS NEEDED
- ¼   CUP COLD WATER
- 2   TABLESPOONS VEGETABLE SHORTENING OR LARD
-      SALT, TO TASTE
-      PAPRIKA, TO TASTE
- ½   CUP MINCED SCALLIONS
-      CANOLA OIL, AS NEEDED

PA JUN

YIELD: 4 SERVINGS / **ACTIVE TIME:** 30 MINUTES / **TOTAL TIME:** 30 MINUTES

This is a savory Korean battered pancake that is commonly enjoyed with a glass of ice-cold beer or a makgeolli, a milky, carbonated alcoholic rice beverage.

1. In a bowl, combine the flour, salt, pepper, eggs, mirin, 1 teaspoon of soy sauce, and soda water and mix well to form a batter.

2. Make the dipping sauce in a bowl by combining ¼ cup of soy sauce with the rice vinegar, sesame oil, and toasted sesame seeds and mixing well.

3. Add a tablespoon of the canola oil to a nonstick pan over medium heat and ladle enough batter into the pan to form a thick, 3-inch round cake.

4. Scatter the scallions, pepper strips, and sesame seeds on top—sprinkle on the batter only when it is starting to set, or the seeds will sink into the batter—and cook for 2 to 3 minutes, or until the bottom of the pancake is golden. Flip the pancake over and cook the other side until golden brown. Continue making pancakes, repeating the steps.

INGREDIENTS:

2	CUPS ALL-PURPOSE FLOUR
2	TEASPOONS SALT
½	TEASPOON BLACK PEPPER
2	EGGS
¼	CUP MIRIN
¼	CUP SOY SAUCE, PLUS 1 TEASPOON
1	CUP SODA WATER
¼	CUP RICE VINEGAR
1	TABLESPOON SESAME OIL
2	TEASPOONS TOASTED SESAME SEEDS, LIGHTLY CRUSHED
	CUP CANOLA, AS NEEDED
2	BUNCHES SCALLIONS, CUT DIAGONALLY INTO 2-INCH PIECES
1	RED BELL PEPPER, THINLY JULIENNED INTO 2-INCH PIECES
2	TABLESPOONS SESAME SEEDS

SHRIMP TOAST

YIELD: 4 SERVINGS / ACTIVE TIME: 30 MINUTES / TOTAL TIME: 30 MINUTES

This classic Hong Kong dim sum option of fried toast is coated with a flavorful minced-shrimp paste.

1. Trim the crusts off the bread and reserve for another use. Let each piece of bread air dry until cooking.

2. In a bowl, combine the remainder of the ingredients, except the sesame seeds, paprika, and oil, and mix well.

3. Cut each slice of bread into 3 or 4 pieces, in whatever shape you prefer. Spread the filling on each piece of bread from end to end. Sprinkle the sesame seeds and paprika (if using) on top.

4. Add the oil to a large nonstick pan over medium heat. Once the oil begins to shimmer, add the shrimp toasts to the pan, shrimp side down. Cook for 1 minute, flip, and cook for another minute, or until the bread is golden. Drain on a paper towel–lined plate. Repeat until all of the toasts are cooked.

5. Garnish with the chives and serve.

INGREDIENTS:

10–12	SLICES WHITE SANDWICH BREAD
1	LB. SHRIMP, SHELLED, DEVEINED, AND MINCED
1–2	GARLIC CLOVES, FINELY MINCED
¼	CUP WATER CHESTNUTS (OPTIONAL)
1	TABLESPOON FINELY MINCED LEMONGRASS (OPTIONAL)
2	TABLESPOONS CORNSTARCH
2	TEASPOONS SALT
2	TABLESPOONS RICE WINE
1	EGG, BEATEN
3	TABLESPOONS MINCED CHIVES, PLUS MORE FOR GARNISH
3	TABLESPOONS SESAME SEEDS
1	TABLESPOON PAPRIKA (OPTIONAL)
2	TABLESPOONS VEGETABLE OIL, PLUS MORE AS NEEDED

SIU MAI

YIELD: 4 SERVINGS / **ACTIVE TIME:** 30 MINUTES / **TOTAL TIME:** 45 MINUTES

O riginating in Northern China but popularized in Cantonese cuisine, this dumpling is considered to be the most popular dim sum.

1. In a bowl, combine all of the ingredients, except the wrappers and tobiko, and mix well.

2. Place about 1 tablespoon of filling in the center of a wrapper, and bring the wrapper up the sides of the filling, making an open "purse." Make sure to push down the filling into the gap formed in the middle of the purse. Create an "o" shape in the middle, and check to see that the filled dumpling can stand upright without leaning.

3. Garnish the middle of the exposed filling with a little tobiko.

4. Repeat until all of the filling has been used up.

5. Once all the dumplings have been formed, using a bamboo steamer lined with lightly oiled parchment paper, steam for about 15 minutes.

6. Serve immediately with your favorite dipping sauce.

INGREDIENTS:

½	LB. GROUND PORK
¼	LB. PORK FAT BACK, MINCED
4	LARGE SHRIMP, SHELLED, DEVEINED, AND COARSELY CHOPPED
2	TABLESPOONS FINELY DICED WATER CHESTNUTS
1	TEASPOON MINCED GINGER
1	TEASPOON CORNSTARCH
¼	TEASPOON BAKING SODA
1	TABLESPOON SUGAR
½	TABLESPOON SALT
½	TABLESPOON SOY SAUCE
2	TEASPOONS RICE WINE
1	TEASPOON SESAME OIL
1	PACKAGE SIU MAI WRAPPERS
	TOBIKO, FOR GARNISH

MARBLE EGGS

This Chinese-style marinated egg is a great snack or condiment for a meal.

1. Lightly crack each hard-boiled egg all around with the back of a spoon. Immerse the eggs in the Master Sauce for 12 to 24 hours, turning the eggs often to ensure even coloring.

2. Peel the cracked, marinated eggs and serve sliced.

INGREDIENTS:

6   HARD-BOILED EGGS

       MASTER SAUCE (SEE PAGE 347), AS NEEDED

FRESH SPRING ROLLS WITH SHRIMP

YIELD: 4 SERVINGS / ACTIVE TIME: 30 MINUTES / TOTAL TIME: 30 MINUTES

Traditional Vietnamese spring rolls are fresh, light, and healthy. They can be made with shrimp or pork, or with tofu for a vegetarian option.

1. Lay a damp, clean kitchen towel over the work surface to help prevent the rice paper from sticking to the work surface.

2. Fill a bowl with lukewarm water. Quickly dip the rice paper in the water and lay it on the work surface. The rice paper will continue to soften.

3. Lay a leaf of butter lettuce toward the lower edge of the rice paper. On top of the lettuce, place the noodles, vegetables, and herbs. Place 3 pieces of halved shrimp in a line about 1½ inches from the top edge.

4. Grab the lower edge of the rice paper with your thumbs and, using your fingers, roll the paper over the lettuce and continue to roll forward until reaching the shrimp; if desired, add the pork at this step.

5. Fold both sides of the spring roll toward the center, and then roll it over on itself, so the rice paper seals itself. Repeat the steps until all spring rolls are assembled.

6. Serve with the Peanut Hoisin Dipping Sauce.

PEANUT HOISIN DIPPING SAUCE

1. In a bowl, combine all of the ingredients, except the peanuts, and mix well.

2. Refrigerate in an airtight container until needed.

3. Before serving, sprinkle the chopped peanuts on top.

INGREDIENTS:

12	SHEETS RICE PAPER
12–14	BUTTER LETTUCE LEAVES
½	CUP JULIENNED CUCUMBER
½	CUP JULIENNED CARROTS
1	CUP BEAN SPROUTS
4	OZ. THIN RICE VERMICELLI NOODLES, COOKED
24	THAI BASIL LEAVES
24	WHOLE MINT LEAVES
24	ASIAN CHIVES
12–24	CILANTRO SPRIGS, CUT INTO 2-INCH PIECES
18	POACHED SHRIMP, CLEANED, DEVEINED, AND HALVED LENGTHWISE
	CHAR SIU PORK (SEE PAGE 336; OPTIONAL), SLICED INTO THIN STRIPS
	PEANUT HOISIN DIPPING SAUCE (SEE RECIPE)

PEANUT HOISIN DIPPING SAUCE

¼	CUP HOISIN SAUCE
¼	CUP UNSEASONED RICE VINEGAR
2	TABLESPOONS SUGAR
2	TABLESPOONS SOY SAUCE
2	TABLESPOONS SWEET CHILI DIPPING SAUCE (SEE PAGE 42)
3	TABLESPOONS COARSELY CHOPPED, DEEP-FRIED PEANUTS

SHRIMP & CRAB CAKES
WITH SWEET CHILI DIPPING SAUCE

YIELD: 4 SERVINGS / ACTIVE TIME: 30 MINUTES / TOTAL TIME: 30 MINUTES

Seafood cakes make delicious appetizers, yet they are satisfying and filling enough to be served as a main course. The dipping sauce is great to have on hand, since it pairs well with other appetizers like Crab Rangoon (see page 69).

1. Using a mortar and pestle, pound the garlic, chilies, and sugar to make a paste. In a bowl, combine the paste with the lemon juice and fish sauce, mix well, and set aside until needed.

2. For the shrimp and crab cakes, in a large bowl, combine all of the ingredients, except the panko, oil, lettuce, and herbs, mix well, and then form the mixture into cakes, about 2 inches long and ½ inch tall.

3. Once all the cakes are formed, coat them with panko on both sides.

4. Add 2 tablespoons of the oil to a skillet over medium heat and panfry the cakes until golden brown on both sides. Drain on a rack to keep extra crispy.

5. Serve the cakes on a lettuce-lined plate and garnish with the torn fresh herbs. On the side, serve the with Sweet Chili Dipping sauce or your favorite sauce.

INGREDIENTS:

SWEET CHILI DIPPING SAUCE

1	GARLIC CLOVE, MINCED
3	THAI CHILIES, MINCED
¼	CUP SUGAR
½	CUP FRESH LEMON JUICE
¼	CUP FISH SAUCE

SHRIMP & CRAB CAKES

1	LB. SHRIMP, CLEANED, DEVEINED, AND CHOPPED
1	LB. CRAB MEAT, CLEANED
1	TABLESPOON MINCED GARLIC
1	TABLESPOON MINCED SHALLOTS
1	TABLESPOON CHOPPED CILANTRO
1	TABLESPOON CHOPPED MINT
1	TABLESPOON FINELY MINCED LEMONGRASS STALK
2	TEASPOONS SALT
1	TEASPOON FISH SAUCE
¼	TEASPOON WHITE PEPPER
3	TABLESPOONS MAYONNAISE
1	EGG, BEATEN
1-2	CUPS PANKO
2	TABLESPOONS CANOLA OIL, PLUS MORE AS NEEDED
6-8	LETTUCE LEAVES
	FRESH HERBS, FOR GARNISH

STEAMED DAIKON CAKE

YIELD: 4 SERVINGS / **ACTIVE TIME:** 30 MINUTES / **TOTAL TIME:** 1 HOUR AND 30 MINUTES

The daikon cake is another dim sum staple and can be served chilled or warm with any favored dipping sauce. Lap cheong is Chinese sausage.

1. In a pot, combine the daikon with the stock, bring to a boil, and cook until the daikon is tender. Strain and reserve the cooking liquid.

2. Add the oil, shrimp, sausage, and turnip to a sauté pan over medium heat and, once, warm, add most of the scallions and cilantro and mix well. Remove from heat and set aside.

3. In a bowl, combine the rice flour with the daikon water and mix well. Then add the shrimp-and-sausage mixture. Add additional daikon water to achieve a medium-thin batter.

4. Line an 8-inch cake pan with parchment paper and lightly coat with the oil. Pour the batter into the cake pan and steam for 30 to 45 minutes, or until set.

5. Cool for 20 minutes, and then run a knife around the inside of the cake pan and invert onto another serving parchment. Remove the parchment that was at the bottom of the cake pan.

6. Slice and serve as is, serve topped with the remaining scallions and cilantro, or slice and panfry to crisp the cake.

INGREDIENTS:

- 3   CUPS GRATED DAIKON
- 2   CUPS CHICKEN STOCK (SEE PAGE 680)
- 2   TABLESPOONS CANOLA OIL, PLUS MORE AS NEEDED
- 1   TABLESPOON DRIED SHRIMP, SOAKED UNTIL SOFT AND COARSELY CHOPPED
- ½   CUP FINELY CHOPPED LAP CHEONG
- 1   TABLESPOON DICED CHOAN CHOY (SALTED TURNIP)
- 1   TEASPOON SALT
- ¼   CUP CHOPPED SCALLIONS
- ¼   CUP COARSELY CHOPPED CILANTRO
- 1½   CUPS RICE FLOUR
- 1½   CUPS DAIKON WATER (RESERVED COOKING WATER)

CRAB RANGOON

YIELD: 4 SERVINGS / **ACTIVE TIME:** 45 MINUTES / **TOTAL TIME:** 45 MINUTES

These are Chinese-style fried wontons filled with crab and cream cheese. They're also called crab puffs and can be found in American Chinese restaurants.

1. In a bowl, combine all of the ingredients, except the wrappers, egg, and oil, and mix well.

2. Place 1 tablespoon of the crab mixture in the center of a wrapper and wet the edges with the egg.

3. Bring together the corners and seal. Repeat until all of the filling has been used.

4. In a Dutch oven, heat the oil to 350°F and deep-fry until golden brown. Remove with a slotted spoon or kitchen spider and drain on a paper towel–lined plate.

5. Serve with the Sweet Chili Dipping Sauce on the side.

INGREDIENTS:

½   LB. CRAB MEAT, CLEANED

½   LB. CREAM CHEESE

2   TABLESPOONS SWEET CHILI DIPPING SAUCE (SEE PAGE 42), PLUS MORE TO SERVE

1   TABLESPOON MINCED SCALLIONS

1½ TEASPOONS RICE VINEGAR

    CHILI FLAKES, TO TASTE (OPTIONAL)

    SALT, TO TASTE

1   PACKAGE WONTON WRAPPERS

1   EGG, BEATEN

    CANOLA OIL, FOR FRYING

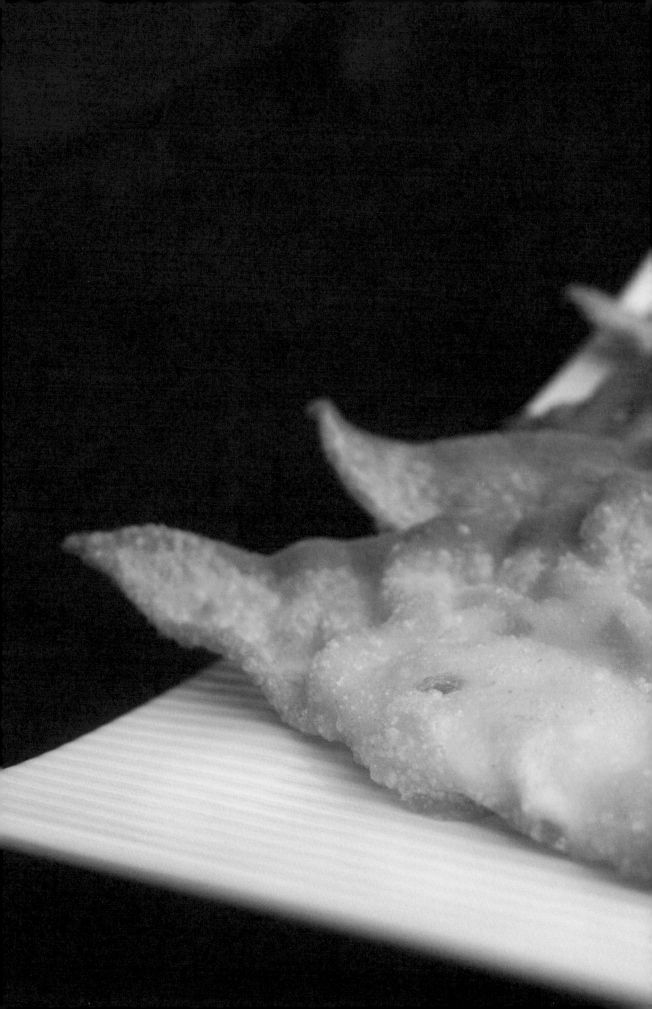

PERKEDEL JAGUNG

YIELD: 4 SERVINGS / **ACTIVE TIME:** 45 MINUTES / **TOTAL TIME:** 45 MINUTES

These easy-to-prepare Indonesian corn fritters are sweet and savory, with a slight spice from the jalapeños.

1. Using a mortar and pestle or blender, combine the galangal, cilantro, shallots, garlic, jalapeño, nuts, salt, and sugar and form a paste. Set aside.

2. In a bowl, coarsely pound the corn kernels and add the scallions, eggs, flour, and baking powder. Mix with the ground paste. The mixture should resemble a thick batter. If needed, add more flour.

3. In a Dutch oven, heat the oil to 325°F. Do a taste test by frying a small spoonful of the batter until golden brown. Remove, cool, and eat, then adjust the seasoning if needed.

4. Working in batches so as not to overcrowd the pot, carefully drop a ladleful of fritter batter and fry each side for 2 to 3 minutes, until golden brown. Remove with a slotted spoon or kitchen spider, drain the excess oil on a wire rack or paper towel–lined plate, and immediately season with salt.

INGREDIENTS:

- 2 TABLESPOONS FINELY MINCED GALANGAL
- ½ CUP MINCED CILANTRO
- 4 SHALLOTS, MINCED
- 4 GARLIC CLOVES, MINCED
- 1 RED JALAPEÑO, SEEDED AND MINCED
- 4 MACADAMIA NUTS, SOAKED 10 MINUTES
- ½ TABLESPOON SALT, PLUS MORE TO TASTE
- 2 TEASPOONS SUGAR
- 4-6 EARS OF CORN, KERNELS REMOVED
- ¼ CUP MINCED SCALLIONS
- 2 EGGS, BEATEN
- ¾ CUP ALL-PURPOSE FLOUR
- 1 TEASPOON BAKING POWDER
- CANOLA OIL, FOR FRYING

STEAMED DUMPLINGS

YIELD: 4 SERVINGS / **ACTIVE TIME:** 1 HOUR AND 30 MINUTES / **TOTAL TIME:** 1 HOUR AND 30 MINUTES

This style of dumplings is found in Chinese, Korean, and Japanese cuisines with various types of fillings. They are great to snack on or to be served as a side to a main course.

1. Make the filling in a bowl by combining the meat with the garlic, 2 teaspoons of sesame oil, 1 teaspoon of salt, and the black pepper and mixing well. Refrigerate until ready to use.

2. In a pot, bring 4 cups of water to a boil and blanch the bean sprouts for 1 minute. Drain, rinse in cold water, and squeeze out excess water. Transfer to a bowl and add the chives.

3. In a separate bowl, toss the zucchini with the remainder of the salt and let stand for 15 minutes. Then squeeze out the the excess water.

4. Add a little oil to a pan over medium-high heat and sauté the zucchini slightly soft. Transfer to the bowl with the sprouts and chives.

5. Add a little more oil to the same pan over medium heat and sauté the onion until semitranslucent and fragrant. Transfer to the bowl with the other vegetables.

6. Squeeze the excess water from the tofu and add to the vegetables.

7. Remove the meat from the refrigerator.

8. Add a little oil to a clean skillet over medium-high heat and cook until the meat is no longer pink, about 3 minutes; the meat will not be fully cooked at this point. Remove from heat and cool on a sheet pan.

9. Transfer the cooled, cooked meat to the bowl with the vegetables and tofu. Add ½ teaspoon of salt and the remainder of the sesame oil to the dumpling filling and mix well.

10. Prepare to make the dumplings: have a small bowl of water nearby to wet the edges in order to seal the dumpling wrappers, and a parchment–lined sheet pan to hold formed dumplings before steaming.

INGREDIENTS:

½	LB. GROUND PORK, BEEF, OR CHICKEN
3	GARLIC CLOVES, MINCED
4	TEASPOONS SESAME OIL, DIVIDED
1½	TEASPOONS SALT, DIVIDED
½	TEASPOON BLACK PEPPER
⅔	CUP MUNG BEAN SPROUTS
¼	CUP CHOPPED ASIAN CHIVES
1	SMALL ZUCCHINI, CUT INTO MATCHSTICKS
	CANOLA OIL, AS NEEDED
½	CUP FINELY MINCED ONION
4	OZ. MEDIUM-FIRM TOFU
	DUMPLING SKINS
	SESAME SOY VINEGAR SESAME SOY VINEGAR DIPPING SAUCE (SEE RECIPE)

SESAME SOY VINEGAR DIPPING SAUCE

¼	CUP SOY SAUCE
1½	TABLESPOONS WHITE VINEGAR
1	TEASPOON GOCHUGARU
1	TABLESPOON TOASTED SESAME SEEDS
2	TABLESPOONS SCALLIONS, FINELY CHOPPED

11. Lay a dumpling skin flat in the palm of your hand. Using your other hand, wet a finger and wet the edges of the wrapper. Place a generous tablespoon of filling into the center of the wrapper. Fold the dumpling wrapper skin over the filling and press the edges to seal, creating a half moon.

12. Make 6 to 8 pleats across the sealed dumpling edges to seal the dumpling tighter; this serves an aesthetic purpose, but the folds also help to gather the dipping sauce. Place on the lined sheet pan and repeat the steps until all the filling is used.

13. Fill a steamer with 3 inches of water and bring to a boil. Remove the bamboo basket from the steamer and line it with cheesecloth, cotton cloth, or parchment paper. Place the dumplings in the lined bamboo basket and put back on top of the steamer. Cover and steam over medium-high heat for 10 to 15 minutes, until the dumpling skins are shiny and translucent and the filling is cooked through.

14. Remove from heat and serve immediately in the bamboo basket, or transfer to a plate. Serve with the Sesame Soy Vinegar Dipping Sauce or any favorite dipping sauce.

SESAME SOY VINEGAR DIPPING SAUCE

1. In a small bowl, combine the soy sauce, vinegar, and chili flakes and mix well. Add the sesame seeds and scallions.

2. Store until needed, up to three days. Serve with dumplings, savory pancakes, fried tofu, or anything else you desire.

SHRIMP & VEGETABLE TEMPURA

YIELD: 4 SERVINGS / **ACTIVE TIME:** 30 MINUTES / **TOTAL TIME:** 30 MINUTES

This is a hugely popular appetizer in Japan and everywhere else. There are so many vegetables with textures that lend themselves to tempura, so experiment based on your tastes and whatever is in season or readily available. Some suggestions include: green beans, trimmed; lotus root, peeled and sliced into ¼-inch-thick rounds; carrots, peeled and cut into diagonal slices; Japanese eggplant, sliced thin lengthwise into 3-inch pieces; sweet potatoes, peeled and sliced into ¼-inch rounds; zucchini, cut into 3-inch lengths and sliced thin lengthwise; onions, cut into ¼-inch rings; cauliflower and broccoli, cut into florets; okra, whole with stem removed; mushrooms, whole; and bell peppers, cut into ¼-inch rings.

1. Preheat a fryer or oil in a Dutch oven to 350°F.

2. Clean the shrimp. Make 3 small slits with a knife on the underside of the shrimp. Squeeze the body of the shrimp in three different places along the length of the body to straighten it. This will help keep the shrimp from curling when frying, as well as elongate the shrimp.

3. Prepare the chosen vegetables as directed above.

4. Working in batches so as not to overcrowd the fryer, dip the shrimp or vegetables in the tempura batter, shake off the excess batter, and slowly place in the fryer away from you.

5. Fry until golden crispy. Remove with a slotted spoon or kitchen spider and drain on a rack.

6. Serve hot with the tempura sauce.

TEMPURA SAUCE

1. Add the sake to a small saucepan over high heat. Bring to a boil, flambee, and remove from heat.

2. Once the fire goes out, add the Dashi stock, soy sauce, mirin, sugar, and lemon juice and stir to dissolve the sugar. Cool and store until needed.

3. When ready to serve the tempura, place the sauce in a small bowl and garnish with the daikon and ginger.

INGREDIENTS:

- 1-2 LBS. SHRIMP, SHELLED, DEVEINED, TAIL ON
- 1-2 LBS. VEGETABLES OF YOUR CHOOSING
- TEMPURA BATTER, AS NEEDED (SEE RECIPE)
- TEMPURA SAUCE, TO SERVE (SEE RECIPE)

TEMPURA SAUCE

- ¼ CUP SAKE
- ¼ CUP DASHI (SEE PAGE 293)
- ¼ CUP SOY SAUCE
- ¼ CUP MIRIN
- ¼ TEASPOON SUGAR
- 1 TABLESPOON FRESH LEMON JUICE
- 2 TABLESPOONS GRATED DAIKON, FOR GARNISH
- 1 TEASPOON GRATED GINGER, FOR GARNISH

TEMPURA BATTER

1. In a bowl, combine all of the dry ingredients and mix well.

2. In a separate bowl, whisk together the egg yolks and the cold liquids of your choosing.

3. Add the wet ingredients to the dry ingredients and combine, being sure not to overmix the batter; it should still be slightly lumpy, like a muffin batter.

4. If not using immediately, store covered in the refrigerator or over ice.

TEMPURA BATTER

2	CUPS ALL-PURPOSE FLOUR
1	TEASPOON BAKING POWDER
1	TEASPOON BAKING SODA
1	TEASPOON SALT
⅛	TEASPOON TURMERIC (FOR BATTER COLOR)
2	EGG YOLKS
1¼	CUPS ICE-COLD WATER OR SODA WATER
1¼	CUPS CHILLED SAKE OR COLD LIGHT BEER

SOY-GLAZED SPAM MUSUBI

YIELD: 6 SERVINGS / **ACTIVE TIME**: 30 MINUTES / **TOTAL TIME**: 30 MINUTES

Spam gets a bad rap. So don't knock this Hawaiian fusion snack inspired by Japanese flavors until you try it. If you don't have a musubi mold, use the Spam can to mold the rice blocks, but be sure to rinse it out first.

1. In a bowl, combine the soy sauce, brown sugar, and mirin, whisking well until the sugar dissolves. Set aside for later.

2. Add the oil to a large skillet over medium-high heat and fry the Spam slices until browned and crispy on both sides, about 2 to 3 minutes per side.

3. Pour the prepared sauce over the crispy Spam and turn off the heat, letting the residual heat glaze the Spam. Coat the Spam evenly and then transfer to a plate. Make sure not to burn the glaze.

4. Using a musubi mold or a cleaned, plastic wrap–lined Spam can, fill the mold with the cooked rice and press down. Add more rice if necessary to create a nice rectangular rice block. Remove the formed rice from the mold and repeat until all of the rice has been molded.

5. Using a clean work surface, place the nori shiny side down. Place the Spam in the middle and sprinkle the Furikake over the Spam. Place the molded rice on top of the Spam

6. Carefully wrap the nori sheet over the rice and enclose the seam. Turn over and serve immediately, or wrap in plastic to enjoy later.

INGREDIENTS:

- 2   TABLESPOONS SOY SAUCE
- 2   TABLESPOONS BROWN SUGAR
- ½   TEASPOON MIRIN
- 2   TEASPOONS CANOLA OIL
- 1   CAN SPAM, CUT HORIZONTALLY INTO 8 SLICES
- 6   CUPS COOKED SHORT-GRAIN WHITE RICE (SEE PAGE 140)
- 3   ROASTED SUSHI NORI SHEETS, CUT INTO THIRDS
- 2   TEASPOONS FURIKAKE (SEE PAGE 146)

BOILED PEANUTS

YIELD: 8 SERVINGS / **ACTIVE TIME:** 30 MINUTES / **TOTAL TIME:** 24 HOURS

The most important thing to remember when you serve these addictive peanuts is to make sure to have enough cold beer on hand.

1. Wash and rinse the peanuts well.

2. In a large pot, combine the water, sea salt, star anise, bay leaves, and peppercorns, if using, and stir well.

3. Add the rinsed peanuts to the pot and place something heavy over the peanuts to keep them submerged. Let the pot stand at room temperature overnight or up to 24 hours.

4. Bring the pot to a boil, lower the heat, and simmer for roughly 1½ hours covered. After 1 hour, check for doneness. The peanuts should be tender, with a slight crunch.

5. Once the peanuts are cooked, remove the lid and remove the pot from heat. Let the peanuts cool in the cooking liquid for 1 hour before straining.

6. Serve the peanuts warm, or store in resealable bags to eat later. They keep in the refrigerator for 4 to 5 days.

INGREDIENTS:

2	LBS. RAW SHELL-ON PEANUTS
3	QUARTS WATER
2-3	TABLESPOONS SEA SALT
2	STAR ANISE
2	BAY LEAVES
½	TABLESPOON SZECHUAN PEPPERCORNS (OPTIONAL)

LUMPIA

YIELD: 4 SERVINGS / **ACTIVE TIME**: 1 HOUR / **TOTAL TIME**: 1 HOUR

These Filipino deep-fried, crepe-like pastries are stuffed with pork and finely sliced vegetables. They are often served as an appetizer and appear in large quantities at celebrations.

1. Make a dipping sauce by adding 2 tablespoons of oil to a pan over medium heat and slowly cooking 2 tablespoons of garlic without browning it. Add the vinegar and 3 tablespoon of fish sauce, bring to a boil, and then gently simmer for 4 minutes. Remove from heat, cool, and set aside.

2. Add the remaining 2 tablespoons of oil to a wok or skillet over medium-high heat and stir-fry the pork, ginger, onion, and remaining garlic until the meat is cooked through. Add the cabbage, carrot, celery, jicama, and mushrooms and cook for another 3 minutes before adding the pepper, salt, sugar, and remaining fish sauce and mixing well.

3. If the liquid hasn't fully cooked out, sprinkle a little cornstarch and mix well to tighten the filling mixture.

4. Cool the filling mixture completely before the next step.

5. Cut a lumpia wrapper in half. Place the filling on the short end of the wrapper and roll up tightly like a cigar. Use the flour paste to seal the seam. Repeat until all of the filling is used up.

6. In a Dutch oven, heat the canola oil to 325°F. Deep-fry the lumpia until golden brown. Remove with a slotted spoon or kitchen spider and drain on a paper towel–lined plate.

7. Serve with the prepared dipping sauce, or your favorite dipping sauce.

INGREDIENTS:

4	TABLESPOONS CANOLA OIL, DIVIDED
4	TABLESPOONS MINCED GARLIC, DIVIDED
¼	CUP RICE VINEGAR
⅔	CUP FISH SAUCE, DIVIDED
1	LB. GROUND PORK
2	TABLESPOONS MINCED GINGER
¼	CUP MINCED ONION
1½	CUPS MINCED CABBAGE
½	CUP MINCED CARROT
½	CUP MINCED CELERY
½	CUP MINCED JICAMA
6	DRY SHIITAKE MUSHROOMS, SOAKED, STEMMED, AND MINCED
1	TEASPOON BLACK PEPPER
½	TABLESPOON SALT
½	TEASPOON SUGAR
	CORNSTARCH, AS NEEDED
	LUMPIA WRAPPERS
	FLOUR PASTE (¼ CUP ALL-PURPOSE FLOUR MIXED WITH ENOUGH WATER TO FORM A THICK PASTE)
	CANOLA OIL FOR DEEP-FRYING

CRISPY SPICY POTATOES

YIELD: 6 SERVINGS / **ACTIVE TIME**: 20 MINUTES / **TOTAL TIME**: 1 HOUR AND 30 MINUTES

This is a favorite Chinese side dish or snack that can be enjoyed with rice.

1. Preheat the oven to 350°F.

2. Toss the potatoes in 1 tablespoon of oil on a sheet pan and roast for roughly 1 hour, or until tender and roasted golden brown. Make sure to rotate the sheet pan after 30 minutes.

3. Meanwhile, in a bowl, combine all of the dry ingredients, mix well, and set aside.

4. Add 1 tablespoon of oil to a large skillet over medium-high heat. Once the oil begins to shimmer, quickly stir-fry the garlic and ginger for 20 seconds, then add the onion and cook for 30 seconds.

5. Turn down the heat to medium and add the dry spice mixture to the skillet and stir for 30 seconds.

6. Add the cooked potatoes to the skillet and coat with the spice mixture.

7. Remove from heat and finish with the scallions. Serve immediately.

INGREDIENTS:

1½ LBS. BABY POTATOES

2 TABLESPOONS CANOLA OIL, DIVIDED

1 TEASPOON TOASTED SESAME SEEDS

1 TEASPOON CHILI POWDER

1 TEASPOON CUMIN

½ TEASPOON GROUND SZECHUAN PEPPERCORNS

1 TEASPOON LIGHT BROWN SUGAR

1 TEASPOON SMOKED PAPRIKA

½ TEASPOON SEA SALT

5 GARLIC CLOVES, MINCED

1-INCH PIECE GINGER, PEELED AND GRATED

½ RED ONION, FINELY SLICED

2 SCALLIONS, FINELY SLICED

CHILLED TOFU
WITH GOCHUJANG GINGER SCALLION SAUCE

YIELD: 4 SERVINGS / **ACTIVE TIME:** 10 MINUTES / **TOTAL TIME:** 10 MINUTES

Tofu with a spicy mixture of scallions and Korean red chilies is often a side dish when eating barbeque. This can also be made with silken tofu for a creamier consistency.

1. Arrange the tofu on a serving platter and top each tofu steak with the Gochujang Ginger Scallion Sauce.

2. Drizzle with the sesame oil and garnish with the scallions and toasted sesame seeds.

INGREDIENTS:

1   PACKAGE EXTRA-FIRM TOFU, CUT INTO RECTANGLES OR SQUARES

3   TABLESPOONS GOCHUJANG GINGER SCALLION SAUCE (SEE PAGE 194)

1   TABLESPOON SESAME OIL

1   TABLESPOON THINLY SLICED SCALLIONS, FOR GARNISH

½   TABLESPOON TOASTED SESAME SEEDS, FOR GARNISH

SOY SAUCE EGGS

YIELD: 8 SERVINGS / **ACTIVE TIME:** 15 MINUTES / **TOTAL TIME:** 10 HOURS

This Japanese-style egg is great as a snack, but also works well as a side, or as a topping for ramen.

1. In a saucepan, combine all of the ingredients, except the eggs, bring to a boil, and then lower the heat and simmer for 3 to 4 minutes, stirring to dissolve the sugar.

2. Transfer the mixture to a container large enough to also fit the eggs, and cool completely.

3. Once the mixture is cool, add the peeled soft-boiled eggs, making sure they are submerged. Marinate the eggs for 8 to 10 hours. Do not marinate for longer; the eggs will become rubbery.

4. Remove the eggs from the marinade and refrigerate until ready to use.

INGREDIENTS:

1½	CUPS SOY SAUCE
1	CUP SAKE
½	CUP MIRIN
1	CUP WATER
1½	TABLESPOONS SUGAR
2	TEASPOONS CHOPPED GINGER
12	6-MINUTE SOFT-BOILED EGGS

BACON-WRAPPED RICE CAKE
SKEWERS WITH PONZU

YIELD: 4 SERVINGS / **ACTIVE TIME**: 30 MINUTES / **TOTAL TIME**: 45 MINUTES

This is a riff on the South Korean street food so-tteok, glazed skewers of rice cakes and sausage. Since bacon makes everything better, this version wraps the rice cakes.

1. In a bowl, toss the rice cakes with the sesame oil to coat; this both seasons the rice cakes and prevents them from sticking.

2. Cut the bacon slices in half and wrap each half around a piece of rice cake. Spear 2 bacon-wrapped rice cakes onto a skewer. Repeat until all of the skewers are assembled.

3. Cook each skewer over medium heat in a nonstick pan or on a grill over medium heat. Cook both sides 4 to 6 minutes, until the bacon is crispy and the rice cake is cooked through.

4. Transfer the cooked skewers to a serving platter, drizzle with the Ponzu, and garnish with the salt, chives, and jalapeño, if using. Serve with additional Ponzu on the side.

PONZU

1. In a saucepan, combine all of the ingredients, except the bonito, whisk well, and bring to a boil. Lower the heat and simmer for 10 minutes. Turn off the heat, add the bonito, and let steep for 10 to 15 minutes.

2. Strain through cheesecloth, let cool, and store covered until needed.

INGREDIENTS:

12	CYLINDRICAL RICE CAKES, HALVED
1	TABLESPOON SESAME OIL
12	SLICES BACON
	WOODEN SKEWERS, AS NEEDED
	PONZU, TO TASTE (SEE RECIPE)
	SEA SALT, TO FINISH
1	TABLESPOON CHOPPED CHIVES
1	JALAPEÑO, THINLY SLICED, FOR GARNISH (OPTIONAL)

PONZU

1	CUP SOY SAUCE
¼	CUP SEASONED RICE VINEGAR
2	TABLESPOONS MIRIN
2	TABLESPOONS SUGAR
2	ORANGES, JUICED
2	LIMES, JUICED
2	LEMONS, JUICED
⅓	CUP BONITO FLAKES

CURRY SWEET POTATO CROQUETTE

YIELD: 4 SERVINGS / ACTIVE TIME: 30 MINUTES / TOTAL TIME: 2 HOURS

This Japanese appetizer is derived from the traditional French croquette. The use of curry and Fresno chilies adds heat to the dish.

1. Cook the sweet potato until tender, either roasting it in a 375°F oven or microwaving it. Once the sweet potato is soft and tender, remove the flesh from the skin and place in a bowl.

2. Add the peas, curry mixture, ginger, salt, sesame oil, and soy sauce to the sweet potato mix to form a soft mixture.

3. Add 6 tablespoons of panko, mix well, and refrigerate for 30 minutes in order for the filling to firm up. If the mixture is still too wet, add more panko as needed. Adjust the seasoning to taste.

4. Using two large spoons, make quenelles with the sweet potato mixture, creating smooth, oval–shaped patties. Set aside on a parchment-lined sheet pan, and once all the sweet potato mixture is formed, place in the freezer for 30 minutes to make dredging easier.

5. Create a dredging station: one shallow bowl with beaten eggs and another shallow bowl with ⅓ cup of panko mixed with Shichimi Togarashi.

6. Dip each sweet potato patty in egg, then in the seasoned panko to coat well. Repeat until all of the patties are dredged.

7. Add 2 inches of caonla oil to a pot over medium-high heat. Once the oil is hot, fry the croquettes in batches so as not to overcrowd. Cook for 3 to 5 minutes, or until golden brown and heated through.

8. Using a slotted spoon or kitchen spider, remove the cooked croquettes from the oil and set aside on a paper towel–lined plate to remove the excess oil.

9. Transfer to a serving plate and garnish with Fresno chili slices and a side of Katsu Sauce.

INGREDIENTS:

1	SWEET POTATO
3	TABLESPOONS FROZEN PEAS
3	JAPANESE CURRY CUBES, DISSOLVED IN 3 TABLESPOONS WATER
	1-INCH PIECE GINGER, GRATED
1	TEASPOON SALT
2	TEASPOONS SESAME OIL
1	TABLESPOON SOY SAUCE
⅓	CUP PANKO PLUS 6 TABLESPOONS, DIVIDED
2	EGGS, BEATEN
1	TABLESPOON SHICHIMI TOGARASHI (SEE PAGE 146)
	CANOLA OIL, FOR FRYING
1	FRESNO CHILI, SLICED, FOR GARNISH
¼	CUP KATSU SAUCE (SEE PAGE 411)

OKONOMIYAKI

YIELD: 4 SERVINGS / **ACTIVE TIME:** 30 MINUTES / **TOTAL TIME:** 1 HOUR AND 30 MINUTES

Osaka, Japan, is home to this style of okonomiyaki, sometimes referred to as "Japanese pizza." The comparison isn't particularly accurate; but both foods are delicious and incredibly craveable.

1. In a large bowl, combine the flour, baking powder, salt, and sugar and mix well. Next, mix in the grated mountain yam and enough Dashi to create a batter consistency. Refrigerate for 1 hour.

2. Add the eggs and cabbage to the chilled batter and mix well.

3. Add the oil to a nonstick pan over medium-high heat. Once the oil begins to shimmer, ladle in and spread out enough batter to make a 1-inch-thick pancake. Lower the heat to medium and cook for 5 minutes.

4. Add the seafood over the top of the uncooked side and carefully transfer the pancake to a plate, with the uncooked side facing up. Invert the pan over the plate and flip over the pancake into the pan, so the uncooked side is now facing down. Add oil if needed and cook for 3 to 4 minutes with a lid slightly covered. The pancake is ready when it is cooked through and soft while the edges are crispy.

5. Transfer the cooked pancake onto a plate and zigzag drizzle the Okonomiyaki Sauce over the top, then drizzle the mayonnaise over the top in a circular motion.

6. Garnish with the bonito flakes and toasted nori powder, portion into slices, and enjoy immediately.

OKONOMIYAKI SAUCE

1. In a bowl, combine all of the ingredients and whisk well.

2. Store in an airtight container and refrigerate for up to 1 month.

INGREDIENTS:

1	CUP ALL-PURPOSE FLOUR
½	TEASPOON BAKING POWDER
½	TEASPOON SEA SALT
¼	TEASPOON LIGHT BROWN SUGAR
½	CUP PEELED AND GRATED MOUNTAIN YAM OR POTATO
1	CUP DASHI (SEE PAGE 293)
2	EGGS, BEATEN
⅓	NAPA CABBAGE, SHREDDED
1	TABLESPOON CANOLA OIL, PLUS MORE AS NEEDED
½	CUP SQUID OR SHRIMP
2	TABLESPOONS OKONOMIYAKI SAUCE (SEE RECIPE)
1	TABLESPOON KEWPIE MAYONNAISE
	BONITO FLAKES, FOR GARNISH
	TOASTED NORI POWDER, FOR GARNISH

OKONOMIYAKI SAUCE

3	TABLESPOONS WORCESTERSHIRE SAUCE
3½	TABLESPOONS KETCHUP
2	TABLESPOONS OYSTER SAUCE
1½	TABLESPOONS LIGHT BROWN SUGAR

YUKHOE

YIELD: 2 SERVINGS / **ACTIVE TIME:** 20 MINUTES / **TOTAL TIME:** 1 HOUR

The Korean variation of beef tartar calls for a marinade with soy sauce, honey, and sesame oil. Toasted bread, crackers, or rice can be served alongside this delicate plate of raw beef.

1. Freeze the beef for 45 minutes. This makes it easier to cut, but be sure not to freeze it for too long. Using a sharp knife, slice the beef into thin julienne matchsticks.

2. In a bowl, combine the soy sauce, ½ tablespoon of sugar, honey, sesame oil, sesame seeds, garlic, and scallion and mix well. Set aside.

3. In a separate bowl, combine the water with ½ tablespoon of sugar and whisk until the sugar dissolves. Soak the pear in the cold sugar water for 10 minutes. Drain very well and set aside.

4. Mix the cut beef with the sauce mixture and marinate for 1 minute.

5. Plate the marinated beef alongside the pieces of pear and sprinkle the pine nuts and chives over the beef. Make a small well in the middle of the beef and place the egg yolk in it.

6. After admiring the presentation, mix all the ingredients together and enjoy immediately.

INGREDIENTS:

½	LB. FILLET TENDERLOIN
1½	TABLESPOONS SOY SAUCE
1	TABLESPOON SUGAR, DIVIDED
1	TEASPOON HONEY
2	TABLESPOONS SESAME OIL
1	TABLESPOON TOASTED SESAME SEEDS
5	GARLIC CLOVES, MINCED
½	SCALLION, MINCED
1	CUP COLD WATER
½	KOREAN PEAR, PEELED AND CUT INTO MATCHSTICKS
8	PINE NUTS
1	TABLESPOON MINCED CHIVES
1	QUAIL EGG YOLK

BEEF BULGOGI DUMPLINGS

YIELD: 4 TO 6 SERVINGS / ACTIVE TIME: 1 HOUR / TOTAL TIME: 13 HOURS

Stuffing a traditional Korean BBQ recipe into a dumpling is a tremendous idea, especially when it's paired with a spicy aioli.

1. Place the garlic, soy sauce, gochugaru or red pepper flakes, ginger, brown sugar, sesame oil, and steak in a small bowl or resealable plastic bag. Gently shake to combine, place in the refrigerator, and let marinate for 12 hours. Remove approximately 30 minutes before preparing the dumplings and allow to come to room temperature.

2. Warm a sauté pan over medium-high heat until it starts to smoke. Add 1 tablespoon of the vegetable oil and the marinated steak and cook for 1 minute. Turn the meat over and cook for an additional 2 minutes. Remove from the pan and let cool on a baking sheet. When cool enough to handle, chop the meat into small pieces.

3. Dip a finger into the beaten eggs and run it along the edge of a wrapper. Place a tablespoon of meat in the center, fold the circle into a half-moon, and seal tightly. Repeat until all of the dumplings are filled and sealed. Fill a saucepan with 1 inch of water and bring to a boil. Place a steaming tray over the water, add the dumplings, and steam for 6 minutes. Take care not to crowd the steaming tray, and work in batches if necessary. Remove the dumplings and let cool.

4. Place the remaining vegetable oil in a sauté pan or wok and heat over medium heat. When the oil starts to shimmer, add the dumplings in batches and cook until golden brown, about 1 minute on each side. Garnish with the scallion greens and peanuts and serve with the Charred Scallion Aioli.

INGREDIENTS:

- 1   GARLIC CLOVE, MINCED
- 1   TABLESPOON SOY SAUCE
- 2   TEASPOONS GOCHUGARU OR ½ TEASPOON RED PEPPER FLAKES
- 2   TEASPOONS MINCED GINGER
- 2   TEASPOONS LIGHT BROWN SUGAR
- 2   TEASPOONS SESAME OIL
- ½   LB. SIRLOIN STEAK, TRIMMED AND SLICED INTO THIN STRIPS
- 6   TABLESPOONS VEGETABLE OIL, DIVIDED
-     SALT AND PEPPER, TO TASTE
- 2   EGGS, BEATEN
- 24   BASIC DUMPLING WRAPPERS (SEE PAGE 695)
-     SCALLION GREENS, DICED, FOR GARNISH
-     PEANUTS, CRUSHED, FOR GARNISH
-     CHARRED SCALLION AIOLI (SEE RECIPE)

CHARRED SCALLION AIOLI

1. Place the tablespoon of vegetable oil in a large sauté pan and warm over medium-high heat. When the oil starts to shimmer, add the scallion whites and cook until golden brown all over, about 5 minutes. Reduce the heat to medium, add the garlic, peanuts, and hot water, and cook until the garlic and peanuts are golden brown, about 5 minutes. Turn off the heat and let cool.

2. Transfer the contents of the pan to a food processor and puree until smooth. Add the mustard, gochugaru or red pepper flakes, lemon juice, soy sauce, and eggs and blitz until incorporated. Reduce the speed to low and add the sesame oil and remaining vegetable oil in slow streams. When all of the oils have been incorporated, transfer the aioli to the refrigerator and chill for 1 hour before using.

CHARRED SCALLION AIOLI

¾	CUP VEGETABLE OIL, PLUS 1 TABLESPOON
6	SCALLION WHITES
2	GARLIC CLOVES
¼	CUP PEANUTS
1	TABLESPOON HOT WATER (125°F)
1	TEASPOON DIJON MUSTARD
1	TABLESPOON GOCHUGARU OR RED PEPPER FLAKES
	JUICE OF ½ LEMON
1	TABLESPOON SOY SAUCE
2	EGGS
¼	CUP SESAME OIL

MOMOS

The meat of choice in Tibet, where these dumplings are beloved, is yak, but ground beef or lamb will also work.

1. Place the ground beef, garlic, onion, scallion whites, ginger, and a couple pinches of salt in a mixing bowl and stir to combine. Place the peppercorns in a small, dry skillet and toast over medium heat until fragrant, 2 to 3 minutes. Using a spice grinder or a mortar and pestle, crush the peppercorns into a fine powder. Place the powder in a bowl, add the oil, water, and a couple of pinches of salt, and stir to combine. Pour over the ground beef mixture and stir to incorporate.

2. Place a wrapper in a cupped hand and place about 1 tablespoon of filling in the center, leaving about ¾ inch of open wrapper around the edge. Moisten the edge with a wet finger, fold the wrapper into a half-moon, and press down to seal, trying to remove as much air as possible. Make small folds in the wrapper and press them flat as you work along the edge. Place the sealed dumpling on a parchment-lined baking sheet and repeat with the remaining wrappers and filling.

3. Place 1 inch of water in a large pot and bring it to a boil. Line a steaming tray with the cabbage leaves and then add the momos in batches, leaving ½ inch between each of the dumplings. Place the steaming tray over the boiling water, cover, and steam until the dumplings have puffed up slightly, about 8 minutes. Transfer to a warmed plate, tent loosely with foil to keep warm, and repeat with the remaining dumplings. Serve immediately with the chili sauce.

MOMO DOUGH

1. In a large bowl, combine the flour, oil, water, and salt and mix well.

2. Knead until the dough is smooth, about 8 to 10 minutes. If the dough seems dry, add water a tablespoon at a time.

3. Cover and let sit at room temperature for at least 30 minutes. Knead well again for about 5 minutes. Set aside.

INGREDIENTS:

¾	LB. GROUND BEEF
3	GARLIC CLOVES, MINCED
½	LARGE YELLOW ONION, MINCED
5	SCALLION WHITES, SLICED THIN
	2-INCH PIECE GINGER, MINCED
	SALT, TO TASTE
¾	TEASPOON SZECHUAN PEPPERCORNS
2	TABLESPOONS SAFFLOWER OR PEANUT OIL
5	TABLESPOONS WATER
	BASIC DUMPLING WRAPPERS (SEE PAGE 695)
	CABBAGE LEAVES, FOR STEAMING (OPTIONAL)
	CHILI GARLIC SAUCE (SEE PAGE 180), FOR SERVING

MOMO DOUGH

4	CUPS ALL-PURPOSE FLOUR, PLUS MORE FOR DUSTING
1	TABLESPOON CANOLA OIL
1¾	CUPS WATER, PLUS MORE AS NEEDED
1	PINCH SALT

BANSH

YIELD: 4 SERVINGS / ACTIVE TIME: 1 HOUR AND 30 MINUTES / TOTAL TIME: 2 HOURS

In Mongolia, you'd find the stronger-tasting mutton in these small dumplings, which are so delicious that no dipping sauce is required.

1. Place the lamb, onion, garlic, coriander, parsley, salt, and pepper in a mixing bowl and stir to combine. Place a small piece of the mixture in a skillet and cook it through. Taste and adjust the seasoning if necessary. Add the water 1 teaspoon at a time and stir until the filling is smooth.

2. Cup a wrapper in a hand and add about a teaspoon of filling. Wet a finger and moisten the edge of the wrapper. Pinch one-quarter of the wrapper and fold it over itself to create a pleat. Pinch to seal and then repeat with the rest of the wrapper, so that the sealed dumpling resembles a rose about to bloom. Place the sealed dumplings on a parchment-lined baking sheet and repeat with the remaining wrappers and filling.

3. Bring a large pot of salted water to a boil and add the dumplings. Cook, while stirring to prevent sticking, until the dumplings float to the surface, 8 to 10 minutes. Place the cooked dumplings on a warm platter and serve with the cucumber and radish.

INGREDIENTS:

- ¾ LB. GROUND LAMB
- 1 YELLOW ONION, MINCED
- 2 LARGE GARLIC GLOVES, MINCED
- 1 TABLESPOON GROUND CORIANDER
- HANDFUL OF PARSLEY LEAVES, MINCED
- SALT AND PEPPER, TO TASTE
- 3–5 TEASPOONS WATER
- BASIC DUMPLING WRAPPERS (SEE PAGE 695)
- CUCUMBER, SLICED THIN, FOR SERVING
- RADISH, SLICED THIN, FOR SERVING

CHICKEN GYOZA

YIELD: 4 TO 6 SERVINGS / **ACTIVE TIME:** 25 MINUTES / **TOTAL TIME:** 40 MINUTES

This dish is adapted from one of the standards that Chef Ming Tsai built his glittering reputation upon.

1. Place the cabbage, salt, chicken, ginger, carrot, scallions, and garlic in a large bowl and stir until thoroughly combined. Add the soy sauce, sesame oil, sesame seeds, red pepper flakes, and egg and stir to incorporate.

2. Spoon 2 teaspoons of the filling into the center of a wrapper and run a wet finger along the wrapper's edge. Fold into a half-moon and press down on the edge to seal. Repeat until all of the filling and wrappers have been used.

3. Place a large skillet over medium-high heat and add 1 tablespoon of the vegetable oil. Place as many gyoza in the pan as will fit without touching. Add about ½ cup of the water, cover the pan, and cook until the water has evaporated, about 6 minutes. Turn the gyoza over and cook until crispy, about 1 minute. Transfer to a paper towel–lined plate and repeat with any remaining gyoza, replenishing the vegetable oil and water as needed. Serve immediately.

INGREDIENTS:

2	CUPS SHREDDED NAPA CABBAGE
1	TEASPOON KOSHER SALT
⅓	LB. GROUND CHICKEN
1	TABLESPOON MINCED FRESH GINGER
1	CARROT, PEELED AND SHREDDED
2	SCALLIONS, TRIMMED AND CHOPPED
2	GARLIC CLOVES, MINCED
2	TABLESPOONS SOY SAUCE
2	TEASPOONS SESAME OIL
1	TABLESPOON SESAME SEEDS
1	LARGE PINCH RED PEPPER FLAKES
½	EGG, LIGHTLY BEATEN
30	WONTON WRAPPERS (SEE PAGE 699)
3	TABLESPOONS VEGETABLE OIL, DIVIDED
	WATER, AS NEEDED

PORK & SHIITAKE GYOZA

YIELD: 4 TO 6 SERVINGS / **ACTIVE TIME:** 30 MINUTES / **TOTAL TIME:** 45 MINUTES

The emphasis on the freshness and umami flavor that Japanese cuisine is famous for is on full display here.

1. Place the cabbage and salt in a mixing bowl, stir to combine, and let sit for 30 minutes. After 30 minutes, squeeze the cabbage to remove as much liquid as possible. Place it in a bowl with the pork, garlic, mushrooms, ginger, soy sauce, and half of the sesame oil and use your hands to combine the mixture. Season with the salt and pepper.

2. Place 1 tablespoon of the pork-and-mushroom mixture in the center of a wrapper, wet a finger, and brush it around the wrapper's edge. Fold the wrapper closed and pinch to seal. Repeat with the remaining wrappers.

3. Place the remaining sesame oil in a skillet and warm over medium heat. Place as many gyoza in the pan as will fit without touching. Add 1 cup of water, cover the pan, and cook until the water has evaporated, about 6 minutes. Turn the gyoza over and cook until crispy, about 1 minute. Transfer to a paper towel–lined plate and repeat with any remaining gyoza, replenishing the sesame oil and water as needed. Serve with the Szechuan Peppercorn Oil.

SZECHUAN PEPPERCORN OIL

1. Place the oil, star anise, cinnamon stick, bay leaves, and peppercorns in a skillet and cook over the lowest possible heat for 20 minutes, taking care not to let anything burn.

2. Place the red pepper flakes in a bowl and strain the oil over them. Let cool and then season with the salt.

INGREDIENTS:

1	CUP DICED GREEN CABBAGE
1	TEASPOON KOSHER SALT, PLUS MORE TO TASTE
1	LB. GROUND PORK
1	GARLIC CLOVE, MINCED
4	SHIITAKE MUSHROOM CAPS, SLICED THIN
1	TABLESPOON MINCED GINGER
1	TABLESPOON SOY SAUCE
2	TABLESPOONS SESAME OIL, DIVIDED
	PEPPER, TO TASTE
24	WONTON WRAPPERS (SEE PAGE 699)
	WATER, AS NEEDED
	SZECHUAN PEPPERCORN OIL (SEE RECIPE), FOR SERVING

SZECHUAN PEPPERCORN OIL

1½	CUPS VEGETABLE OIL
5	STAR ANISE PODS
1	CINNAMON STICK
2	BAY LEAVES
3	TABLESPOONS SZECHUAN PEPPERCORNS
¾	CUP RED PEPPER FLAKES
1	TEASPOON KOSHER SALT

SHENGJIAN BAOZI

YIELD: 4 SERVINGS / ACTIVE TIME: 1 HOUR / TOTAL TIME: 2 HOURS

Traditionally, these pan-fried pork buns have been found all over Shanghai, though today they're popular the world over.

1. Place the pork, ginger, and scallions in a mixing bowl and stir to combine. Place the remaining ingredients, except for the wrappers and vegetable oil, in a separate bowl and stir until the salt and sugar have dissolved. Pour the liquid mixture over the pork mixture and stir to incorporate. Cover the mixing bowl and let sit for 30 minutes.

2. Place a wrapper in the palm of one hand and add about 1 tablespoon of the pork mixture. Cup the wrapper and close it over the filling. Squeeze it so that it is tightly sealed, and twist to remove any excess dough. Place the filled dumplings, seam side down, on a parchment-lined baking sheet and let them rise until doubled in size, about 30 minutes.

3. Warm half of the vegetable oil in a skillet over medium heat. Working in batches, add the buns so that they are at least ½" apart. Cook, seam side up, until golden brown on both sides, 1 to 2 minutes. Add hot water until it is ¼" deep, and hold the cover of the pan in front of you to prevent being harmed by any oil splattering. Cover the pan and cook until the water has evaporated, about 6 minutes. Remove the lid and cook until the bottom is crispy, about 2 minutes. Serve immediately with the Baozi Dipping Sauce.

BAOZI DIPPING SAUCE

1. Place 1 tablespoon of the oil in a small saucepan and warm over medium heat. Add the ginger, sauté for 2 minutes, and then add the gochugaru or red pepper flakes and the remaining oil. Let cool.

2. When cool, add the vinegar and soy sauce and place in the refrigerator overnight.

INGREDIENTS:

10	OZ. GROUND PORK
1	TABLESPOON MINCED GINGER
⅓	CUP CHOPPED SCALLIONS
¼	TEASPOON KOSHER SALT
⅛	TEASPOON WHITE PEPPER
1	TEASPOON SUGAR
1	TABLESPOON SOY SAUCE, PLUS 1 TEASPOON
2	TEASPOONS RICE WINE VINEGAR
2	TEASPOONS SESAME OIL
1	TABLESPOON HOT WATER (125°F), PLUS MORE AS NEEDED
	BAOZI WRAPPERS (SEE PAGE 700)
¼	CUP VEGETABLE OIL, DIVIDED
	BAOZI DIPPING SAUCE (SEE RECIPE), FOR SERVING

BAOZI DIPPING SAUCE

¼	CUP VEGETABLE OIL, DIVIDED
2	TABLESPOONS MINCED GINGER
2	TEASPOONS GOCHUGARU OR ½ TEASPOON RED PEPPER FLAKES
⅓	CUP CHINKIANG VINEGAR
1	TABLESPOON SOY SAUCE, OR TO TASTE

HAR GOW

YIELD: 4 TO 6 SERVINGS / **ACTIVE TIME:** 1 HOUR / **TOTAL TIME:** 1 HOUR AND 30 MINUTES

These delicate dumplings are often used to assess the skill of dim sum chefs.

1. Place the shrimp in a bowl, cover with cold water, and stir in the baking soda. Refrigerate for 30 minutes. Drain the shrimp, rinse under cold water, and pat dry. Slice each shrimp into 5 or 6 pieces. Place in a dry mixing bowl and add the garlic, ginger, rice wine or sherry, chili oil, salt, sugar, and cornstarch. Stir until thoroughly combined, and refrigerate as you prepare the Crystal Dumpling Wrappers.

2. Place a wrapper in the palm of one hand and add about 2 teaspoons of filling. Then, working your way around the edge of the wrapper, create pleats by folding a ¼" section of the wrapper over onto itself and then pinching it closed. When you've made your way around the wrapper, pinch the top of the dumpling closed, so that it resembles a crown. Place on a parchment-lined baking sheet and repeat with the remaining wrappers and filling.

3. Place 1" of water in a large pot and bring it to a boil. Line a steaming tray with the cabbage leaves, place it over the boiling water, and place the dumplings in the steaming tray, leaving ½" between each of the dumplings and also between the dumplings and the edge of the tray. Cover and cook until tender but chewy, about 7 minutes. Transfer to a warmed platter, drizzle the vinegar over the top, if using, and serve immediately.

INGREDIENTS:

¾ LB. SHRIMP, PEELED AND DEVEINED

1½ TEASPOONS BAKING SODA

2 GARLIC CLOVES, MINCED

2-INCH PIECE FRESH GINGER, MINCED

1 TEASPOON SHAOXING RICE WINE OR DRY SHERRY

1 TEASPOON CHILI OIL

¾ TEASPOON KOSHER SALT

½ TEASPOON SUGAR

1 TEASPOON CORNSTARCH

CRYSTAL DUMPLING WRAPPERS (SEE PAGE 696)

CABBAGE LEAVES, FOR STEAMING

CHINESE BLACK VINEGAR, FOR SERVING (OPTIONAL)

CHAI KUIH

YIELD: 4 SERVINGS / **ACTIVE TIME:** 1 HOUR / **TOTAL TIME:** 2 HOURS

These "vegetable cakes" are a popular street food in a number of Chinese cities.

1. Place the peanut or grapeseed oil in a wok or large skillet and warm over low heat. When the oil begins to shimmer, add the jicama, mushrooms, and carrot and cook, while stirring frequently, until the jicama is tender but still crunchy, about 15 minutes. Add the soy sauce and sugar, season with the salt and pepper, and stir to combine. Remove from heat and let the mixture cool.

2. Line a baking sheet with parchment paper. Place 1 tablespoon of the jicama mixture in the center of a wrapper. Moisten the wrapper's edge with a wet finger and fold the wrapper over to create a triangle. Take the far edge of the wrapper and gently fold it over the filling to meet the other edge. Using your thumb and index finger, pinch both edges together to create a tight seal, trying to remove as much air as you can. Place the filled dumplings on the baking sheet and repeat with the remaining wrappers and filling.

3. Place 1" of water in a saucepan and bring it to a boil. Line a steaming tray with the cabbage leaves and place the dumplings in the tray, leaving ½" between each of the dumplings and also between the dumplings and the edge of the tray. Place the tray over the boiling water, cover, and steam until the dumplings are tender but still chewy, about 10 minutes. Transfer the dumplings to a warmed platter and serve immediately, accompanied by the chili sauce or Szechuan Peppercorn Oil.

INGREDIENTS:

2 TABLESPOONS PEANUT OR GRAPESEED OIL

1 LB. JICAMA, PEELED AND GRATED

¼ CUP MINCED SHIITAKE MUSHROOM CAPS

1 CARROT, PEELED AND FINELY GRATED

2 TABLESPOONS SOY SAUCE

1 TEASPOON SUGAR

SALT AND PEPPER, TO TASTE

CRYSTAL DUMPLING WRAPPERS (SEE PAGE 696)

CABBAGE LEAVES, FOR STEAMING

CHILI GARLIC SAUCE (SEE PAGE 180) OR SZECHUAN PEPPERCORN OIL (SEE PAGE 112), FOR SERVING

SHIITAKE SIU MAI

YIELD: 6 TO 8 SERVINGS / **ACTIVE TIME:** 45 MINUTES / **TOTAL TIME:** 1 HOUR AND 30 MINUTES

This sweet-and-savory filling will satisfy even the dim sum purist who feels the flavor provided by pork is essential.

1. Place all of the ingredients, except for the wrappers, cabbage leaves, and carrots, in a mixing bowl and stir until well combined.

2. Place a wrapper in a cupped hand and fill it with enough of the mixture to fill the wrapper to the top. Flatten the filling with a butter knife and gently tighten the wrapper around the filling, forming a rough cylindrical shape with a flat bottom. Place the filled dumplings on a parchment-lined baking sheet and repeat with the remaining wrappers and filling.

3. Place 1" of water in a large pot and bring it to a boil. Line a steaming tray with the cabbage leaves and then add the siu mai, leaving ½" between each of the dumplings and also between the dumplings and the edge of the tray. Place the steaming tray over the boiling water, cover, and steam until the dumplings are cooked through, tender, and still chewy, about 10 minutes. Transfer the cooked dumplings to a warmed platter, garnish with the carrots, and serve with additional soy sauce.

INGREDIENTS:

8	SHIITAKE MUSHROOM CAPS, MINCED
4	SCALLIONS, TRIMMED AND SLICED THIN
¼	RED BELL PEPPER, SEEDED AND MINCED
¼	CUP RAISINS
¼	CUP PINE NUTS, TOASTED
¼	CUP CANNED CORN
1	TABLESPOON SOY SAUCE, PLUS MORE FOR SERVING
1	TABLESPOON SHAOXING RICE WINE OR DRY SHERRY
1	TEASPOON FISH SAUCE
1	TEASPOON TOASTED SESAME OIL
2	TEASPOONS CORNSTARCH
½	TEASPOON SUGAR
½	TEASPOON WHITE PEPPER
36	WONTON WRAPPERS (SEE PAGE 699)
	CABBAGE LEAVES, FOR STEAMING
	CARROTS, PEELED AND MINCED, FOR GARNISH

ZUCCHINI & SHIITAKE JIAOZI

YIELD: 4 SERVINGS / ACTIVE TIME: 1 HOUR AND 30 MINUTES / TOTAL TIME: 2 HOURS AND 30 MINUTES

Since their shape resembles an early form of currency in China, these dumplings are thought to promise wealth and longevity in Chinese culture.

1. Place the zucchini in a bowl, add the salt, and stir to combine. Let the mixture stand for 1 hour. Working in batches, place the zucchini in a kitchen towel and wring the towel to remove as much moisture as possible. Transfer the zucchini to a large bowl and set aside.

2. Place the peanut oil in a large skillet and warm over medium-high heat. When the oil starts to shimmer, add the eggs and cook, while stirring continuously, until they just set. Transfer to a plate, cut into very small pieces, and add to the zucchini. Add the mushrooms, ginger, soy sauce, rice wine or sherry, sesame oil, pepper, sugar, and scallions, stir to combine, and season with the salt. Place a small piece of the mixture in the skillet, fry until cooked through, and taste. Adjust the seasoning if necessary.

3. Place a wrapper in a cupped hand and place about 1 tablespoon of the filling in the center, making sure to leave about ¾" of the open wrapper around the edge. Moisten the edge with a wet finger, fold into a half-moon, and press on the edge to seal. Place the filled dumpling on a parchment-lined baking sheet and repeat with the remaining wrappers and filling.

4. Place 1" of water in a saucepan and bring it to a boil. Line a steaming tray with the cabbage leaves and place the dumplings in the tray, leaving ½" between each dumpling and also between the dumplings and the edge of the tray. Place the tray over the boiling water, cover, and steam until the dumplings are tender but still chewy, about 8 minutes. Transfer the dumplings to a warmed platter and serve immediately, accompanied by the Cilantro Chutney.

CILANTRO CHUTNEY

1. Place all of the ingredients, except for the water and salt, in a food processor and puree until smooth, adding water as needed to get the desired consistency. Season with the salt and refrigerate until ready to serve.

INGREDIENTS:

- 4 ZUCCHINI (ABOUT 1½ LBS.), GRATED
- 1½ TEASPOONS KOSHER SALT, PLUS MORE TO TASTE
- 2 TABLESPOONS PEANUT OIL
- 4 LARGE EGGS, LIGHTLY BEATEN
- 8 SHIITAKE MUSHROOM CAPS, MINCED
-   2-INCH PIECE FRESH GINGER, MINCED
- 3 TABLESPOONS SOY SAUCE
- 3 TABLESPOONS SHAOXING RICE WINE OR DRY SHERRY
- 2 TABLESPOONS TOASTED SESAME OIL
- 1 TEASPOON BLACK PEPPER
- ½ TABLESPOON SUGAR
- 5 SCALLIONS, TRIMMED AND SLICED THIN
- 40 BASIC DUMPLING WRAPPERS (SEE PAGE 695)
-   CABBAGE LEAVES, FOR STEAMING
-   CILANTRO CHUTNEY (SEE RECIPE), FOR SERVING

CILANTRO CHUTNEY

- 1 BUNCH CILANTRO
- ¼ CUP GRATED FRESH COCONUT
- 15 MINT LEAVES
- 1 TABLESPOON SEEDED AND MINCED JALAPEÑO PEPPER
- 1 GARLIC CLOVE
- 1 TEASPOON MINCED GINGER
- 1 PLUM TOMATO, CONCASSE (SEE PAGE 749)
- 1 TABLESPOON FRESH LEMON JUICE
-   WATER, AS NEEDED
-   SALT, TO TASTE

TOFU-FILLED MOMOS

YIELD: 4 TO 6 SERVINGS / **ACTIVE TIME:** 1 HOUR / **TOTAL TIME:** 1 HOUR

Pressed tofu, also known as dry bean curd, has a dry, compact texture that lends itself wonderfully to these vegetarian dumplings.

1. Place the mushrooms, a pinch of salt, tofu, spinach, scallion whites, and cilantro in a food processor and pulse until minced and combined. Add the garlic and ginger, pulse to incorporate, and transfer the mixture to a mixing bowl. Add the carrots and soy sauce and work the mixture with your hands until well combined. Place a small amount of the mixture in a skillet, cook it through, and taste. Adjust the seasoning if necessary.

2. Place a wrapper in a cupped hand and place about 1 tablespoon of filling in the center, leaving about ¾" of open wrapper around the edge. Moisten the edge with a wet finger, fold into a half-moon, and press down to seal, trying to remove as much air as possible. To pleat the sealed edge, make small folds in the wrapper and press them flat as you work along the edge. Place the sealed dumpling on a parchment-lined baking sheet and repeat with the remaining wrappers and filling.

3. Place 1" of water in a large pot and bring it to a boil. Line a steaming tray with the cabbage leaves and then add the momos in batches, leaving ½" between each of the dumplings and also between the dumplings and the edge of the tray. Place the steaming tray over the boiling water, cover, and steam until the dumplings have puffed up slightly and become slightly translucent, about 8 minutes. Transfer to a warmed plate, tent loosely with foil to keep warm, and cook the remaining dumplings. Serve immediately with the Tomato & Sesame Dipping Sauce.

TOMATO & SESAME DIPPING SAUCE

1. Place the oils in a small saucepan and warm over medium heat. Add the onion, garlic, red pepper flakes, chili powder, and a pinch of salt and cook until the onion starts to soften, about 6 minutes. Add the tomatoes, water, and soy sauce, bring to a boil, and then reduce the heat to medium-low. Simmer until the tomatoes are soft and the sauce has thickened, about 15 minutes.

2. Stir in the vinegar, season with the pepper, and transfer the mixture to a food processor or blender. Puree until smooth, place the sauce in a bowl, and let cool to room temperature.

INGREDIENTS:

8	SHIITAKE MUSHROOM CAPS
	SALT, TO TASTE
½	LB. PRESSED TOFU, DICED
2	CUPS BABY SPINACH
5	SCALLION WHITES, DICED
2	HANDFULS CILANTRO LEAVES
3	GARLIC CLOVES, MINCED
	2-INCH PIECE GINGER, MINCED
2	CARROTS, PEELED AND GRATED
3	TABLESPOONS SOY SAUCE
	MOMO DOUGH (SEE PAGE 106)
	CABBAGE LEAVES, FOR STEAMING
	TOMATO & SESAME DIPPING SAUCE (SEE RECIPE), FOR SERVING

TOMATO & SESAME DIPPING SAUCE

1	TABLESPOON TOASTED SESAME OIL
1	TABLESPOON PEANUT OIL
1	SMALL RED ONION, DICED
2	GARLIC CLOVES, DICED
½	TEASPOON RED PEPPER FLAKES
¼	TEASPOON CHILI POWDER
	SALT, TO TASTE
3	VERY RIPE PLUM TOMATOES, CONCASSE (SEE PAGE 749)
¼	CUP WATER
1½	TABLESPOONS SOY SAUCE
2	TABLESPOONS RICE VINEGAR
	PEPPER, TO TASTE

KIMCHI MANDU

YIELD: 4 SERVINGS / **ACTIVE TIME:** 1 HOUR / **TOTAL TIME:** 1 HOUR AND 30 MINUTES

Each bite of these delicious dumplings proves salty, sour, savory, spicy, crunchy, and creamy.

1. Place the tofu in a single layer on a paper towel–lined baking sheet. Cover with paper towels and pat dry. Let it sit for 30 minutes, changing the paper towels after 15 minutes. After 30 minutes, mince the tofu and place it in a large mixing bowl.

2. While the tofu drains, bring water to a boil in a saucepan. Place the bean sprouts in a bowl of cold water, discard the hulls that float to the top, and rinse under cold water. Add the sprouts to the boiling water and cook for 2 minutes. Remove with a strainer and run them under cold water. Drain, mince, and place in the mixing bowl with the minced tofu. Place the Kimchi in a kitchen towel and wring the towel to remove as much liquid as possible. Mince and add to the mixing bowl. Add the garlic, shallots, egg, sesame oil, salt, and pepper and stir until combined.

3. Place 1 generous tablespoon of filling in the middle of a wrapper. Moisten the wrapper's edge with a wet finger, fold into a half-moon, and press down on the edge to seal the dumpling, making sure to remove as much air as possible. Place the filled mandu on a parchment-lined baking sheet and repeat with the remaining wrappers and filling.

4. Place a large skillet over medium-high heat and add enough peanut oil to coat the bottom. When the oil starts to shimmer, add the mandu in batches and cook until the bottoms are crisp and golden brown, 2 to 3 minutes. Reduce the heat to medium-low, add 2 tablespoons of water, cover the skillet, and cook until the water has evaporated. Transfer the mandu to a warmed platter and tent loosely with foil to keep warm. Repeat with the remaining mandu. When all of the dumplings have been cooked, serve alongside the Sweet & Spicy Dipping Sauce.

INGREDIENTS:

- 1 LB. EXTRA-FIRM TOFU, DRAINED AND CUBED
- 1½ CUPS MUNG BEAN SPROUTS, PICKED OVER
- 1½ CUPS KIMCHI (SEE PAGE 148)
- 5 GARLIC CLOVES, MINCED
- 2 LARGE SHALLOTS, MINCED
- 1 LARGE EGG
- 1½ TEASPOONS TOASTED SESAME OIL
- 2 TEASPOONS KOSHER SALT
  BLACK PEPPER, TO TASTE
  BASIC DUMPLING WRAPPERS (SEE PAGE 695)
  PEANUT OIL, FOR FRYING
  WATER, AS NEEDED
  SWEET CHILI DIPPING SAUCE (SEE PAGE 42), FOR SERVING

GOAT MOMOS

YIELD: 6 SERVINGS / ACTIVE TIME: 30 MINUTES / TOTAL TIME: 2 HOURS AND 30 MINUTES

These goat momos are absolutely delicious. Pair them with a mint or chili chutney for an amazing spin on a dipping sauce.

1. In a large bowl, combine all of the ingredients, except the dough, and mix well. Cover the bowl with plastic wrap and refrigerate for an hour.

2. Knead the dough for 1 minute and then prepare 1-inch balls by rolling pieces of dough into circles between your palms.

3. Dust your work surface with the flour and gently flatten the ball with your palm to make a 2-inch circle. Make a few semiflattened circles and cover with a bowl.

4. Use a rolling pin to roll out each flattened circle into a wrapper. When rolling out the dough, make sure that the middle of the sphere is a bit thicker than the sides; this will help with the structure.

5. Hold the edges of the semiflattened dough with one hand, and with the other hand begin rolling the edges of the dough out, swirling a bit at a time. Continue until the wrapper has a circular shape. Repeat with the remaining semiflattened dough circles. Cover with a bowl or damp cloth to prevent drying.

6. Hold the wrapper in one palm, put one tablespoon of the filling mixture in the wrapper, and with the other hand bring all edges together to the center, making the pleats. Pinch and twist the pleats to close the stuffed dumpling.

7. Heat up a steamer and oil the steamer rack well. Arrange the uncooked dumplings in the steamer. Close the lid and steam until the dumplings are cooked through, about 10 to 13 minutes.

INGREDIENTS:

2	LBS. GROUND GOAT
1	CUP DICED RED ONION
3	TABLESPOONS CHOPPED FRESH CILANTRO
1	TABLESPOON MINCED GARLIC
1	TABLESPOON MINCED GINGER
¼	TEASPOON FRESHLY GRATED NUTMEG
½	TEASPOON TURMERIC
1	TABLESPOON CURRY POWDER
3	FRESH RED CHILIES, MINCED (OR TO TASTE)
3	TABLESPOONS CANOLA OIL, PLUS MORE AS NEEDED
	SALT AND PEPPER, TO TASTE
	MOMO DOUGH (SEE PAGE 106)

ASIAN MEATBALLS

YIELD: 10 SERVINGS / **ACTIVE TIME**: 15 MINUTES / **TOTAL TIME**: 35 MINUTES

These saucy and delicious meatballs are a perfect appetizer, and super easy to make.

1. Preheat the oven to 400°F.

2. In a large bowl, combine the meat, 2 teaspoons of sesame oil, panko, ½ teaspoon of ginger, eggs, garlic, and scallions.

3. Using your hands, shape the meat into balls and place on a greased sheet pan. Bake for 10 to 12 minutes, or until the meatballs are golden on the outside and cooked throughout.

4. As the meatballs are baking, make the sauce by whisking together the remaining ingredients until well blended.

5. Once the meatballs have finished cooking, place them in a serving dish, pour the sauce over the meatballs, and gently stir them until coated.

HOISIN SAUCE

1. Add the canola oil to a saucepan over medium heat. When the oil begins to shimmer, add the garlic and cook for about 2 minutes, stirring often.

2. Add the soy sauce, honey, vinegar, tahini, and sriracha and stir to incorporate. Cook until the sauce is smooth, about 5 minutes. Set aside.

INGREDIENTS:

2	LBS. GROUND PORK
1	TABLESPOON SESAME OIL, DIVIDED
¾	CUP PANKO
1½	TEASPOONS GRATED GINGER, DIVIDED
2	EGGS
1	TABLESPOON MINCED GARLIC
½	CUP THINLY SLICED SCALLIONS
⅔	CUP HOISIN SAUCE (SEE RECIPE)
¼	CUP RICE VINEGAR
2	GARLIC CLOVES, MINCED
1½	TABLESPOONS SOY SAUCE

HOISIN SAUCE

2	TABLESPOONS CANOLA OIL
4	GARLIC CLOVES, MINCED
¼	CUP SOY SAUCE
3	TABLESPOONS HONEY
2	TABLESPOONS WHITE VINEGAR
2	TABLESPOONS TAHINI
2	TEASPOONS SRIRACHA

SIDES, SALADS
& CONDIMENTS

If there is one culinary component that serves as a through line in Asian cuisines, it's rice. It's used in all sorts of main courses, but it is also a ubiquitous side. And for Chef Brian, being steeped in the traditions of Korean food, kimchi and other banchan were staples on the table. So read on to learn how to make the perfect rice, along with all sorts of other flavor-forward dishes that will add spice, acid, and umami to your meal.

WHITE JASMINE RICE

Long-grain jasmine rice is the preferred variety to be served with Southeast Asian dishes. Rinsing the rice thoroughly removes the starch from the surface of the grains, which results in properly cooked, separated grains.

1. Rinse the rice well under running cold water, changing the water 3 times until it runs fairly clear. Strain well.

2. In a pot, combine the rinsed rice and water and bring to a boil.

3. Reduce the heat to low, cover, and simmer for 20 minutes, until all of the water is absorbed.

4. Remove the pot from heat and let rest, covered, for 10 minutes.

5. Remove the cover, fluff with a fork, and serve.

INGREDIENTS:

2   CUPS WHITE JASMINE RICE

2½   CUPS WATER

BROWN RICE

YIELD: 6 SERVINGS / **ACTIVE TIME:** 10 MINUTES / **TOTAL TIME:** 45 MINUTES

With more fiber and magnesium than white rice, this rice variety is typically offered as an alternative to white rice in Asian restaurants. It can be used to make most dishes, including fried rice.

1. Rinse the rice well under cold running water for 2 minutes, then strain well.

2. In a pot, combine the rinsed rice and water and bring to a boil.

3. Give the rice a swirl, cover with a lid, and immediately lower the heat to low and cook the rice for 30 minutes, until all of the water is absorbed.

4. After 30 minutes, remove the pot from heat and let rest, covered, for 15 minutes.

5. Remove the cover, fluff with a fork, and serve.

INGREDIENTS:

2   CUPS BROWN RICE

3½   CUPS WATER

SUSHI RICE

YIELD: 6 SERVINGS / **ACTIVE TIME:** 20 MINUTES / **TOTAL TIME:** 1 HOUR

Short-grain rice is used to make sushi due to its firm and sticky properties, allowing for the sushi rolls or hand rolls to keep their shape.

1. Rinse the rice well in cold water until the water runs fairly clear. Strain well.

2. In a pot, combine the rinsed rice and water and let steep for 10 minutes before bringing to a boil.

3. Once boiling, immediately cover and lower the heat to low. Continue to cook on low for 20 minutes.

4. Remove the pot from heat after 20 minutes and let rest, covered, for 15 minutes.

5. After 15 minutes, fluff the rice, if serving; if using for sushi, uncover and immediately place the rice into a wooden bowl and let the cooked rice rest for 5 minutes.

6. Slowly drizzle the Sushi Rice Vinegar over the rice while doing a "cutting" and folding motion to the rice to incorporate the vinegar. Make sure not to overwork the rice and smash the kernels.

7. Season the rice to taste, and hold the rice in a well-insulated pot or rice cooker until needed.

INGREDIENTS:

2	CUPS SHORT-GRAIN RICE
2¼	CUPS WATER
2½	TABLESPOONS SUSHI RICE VINEGAR (SEE RECIPE)

SUSHI RICE VINEGAR

	3 X 3–INCH PIECE KOMBU
1½	CUPS UNSEASONED RICE VINEGAR
1	CUP GRANULATED SUGAR
⅔	CUP SALT

SUSHI RICE VINEGAR

1. Gently rinse the kombu and pat dry. Don't overwash.

2. In a small saucepan, combine the vinegar, sugar, and salt over medium heat, whisking to dissolve the sugar and salt.

3. Once dissolved, add the kombu, bring to a gentle simmer, and then turn off the heat and let steep for 30 minutes.

4. Strain before adding to the Sushi Rice.

FIVE-GRAIN RICE

YIELD: 6 SERVINGS / **ACTIVE TIME:** 30 MINUTES / **TOTAL TIME:** 3 HOURS AND 30 MINUTES

This rice variety is a healthier substitute for white rice, which has a higher starch content. In Korea it is prepared with beans, as the recipe indicates below.

1. Rinse the glutinous rice, soak in water for 30 minutes, and strain well.

2. Rinse the black beans, soak in water for 3 hours, and strain well.

3. Rinse the glutinous African millet, rubbing until the water washes clear, soak in water for 1 hour, and strain well.

4. Rinse the glutinous millet in cold water and strain well.

5. Rinse the red beans, strain well, and add to a pot with water. Bring to a boil and boil for 2 minutes. Strain and cover the red beans with new water and bring to a rolling simmer for 20 minutes. Strain well, reserving ½ cup of cooking water.

6. In a pot, combine the reserved red bean water with 2½ cups of water and the salt, and then add the soaked rice, beans, and African millet and bring to a boil for 1 minute.

7. Turn down the heat to low, add the glutinous millet, cover, and simmer for 20 minutes.

8. Remove the pot from heat, and let rest, covered, for 10 minutes.

9. Fluff with a fork and serve.

INGREDIENTS:

2	CUPS GLUTINOUS RICE
½	CUP BLACK BEANS
½	CUP GLUTINOUS AFRICAN MILLET
½	CUP GLUTINOUS MILLET
½	CUP SWEET RED BEANS
3	CUPS WATER (½ CUP RESERVED SWEET RED BEAN COOKING LIQUID PLUS 2½ CUPS WATER)
½	TABLESPOON SALT

GARLIC RICE

YIELD: 6 SERVINGS / **ACTIVE TIME:** 10 MINUTES / **TOTAL TIME:** 45 MINUTES

Cooking rice with garlic originated in the Philippines, but it is also popular in Singapore, Malaysia, and Indonesia. It is the perfect complement to chicken and seafood.

1. Add the oil to a pot over medium heat. Once the oil begins to shimmer, add the rice, garlic, and bay leaves and sauté for 4 minutes, until the rice is well coated with oil and warmed through.

2. Add the Chicken Stock and water and bring the rice to a boil. Immediately cover, turn the down heat to low, and simmer until all of the liquid is absorbed, about 15 to 20 minutes.

3. Remove the pot from heat and let rest for 15 minutes.

4. Fluff with a fork and serve.

INGREDIENTS:

½	CUP CANOLA OIL
4	CUPS JASMINE RICE
⅓	CUP FINELY MINCED GARLIC
2	BAY LEAVES
3	CUPS CHICKEN STOCK (SEE PAGE 680)
1	CUP WATER

TURMERIC RICE WITH COCONUT MILK

YIELD: 6 SERVINGS / **ACTIVE TIME:** 15 MINUTES / **TOTAL TIME:** 1 HOUR

Indonesian cuisine uses primarily long-grain rice, as is the case in Thailand and Vietnam. However, the flavors of the archipelago reflect local ingredients and diverse cultural influences.

1. Rinse the rice well three times, changing the water each time, until the water runs fairly clear.

2. Using a mortar and pestle, pound the turmeric, garlic, and onion to create a paste.

3. In a pot large enough to cook the rice, add the oil and the turmeric mixture and cook slowly over medium heat, until the oil is well absorbed. Add the lemongrass, kaffir leaves, and coconut milk, bring to a boil, and then turn down the heat and simmer for 3 to 4 minutes.

4. Add the rice and the Chicken Stock, return to a boil, and then turn the heat down to low and cover the pot. Cook covered for 15 to 20 minutes, until all of the water is absorbed.

5. Turn off the heat and let rest for 15 minutes.

6. Fluff the rice, remove the lemongrass and kaffir leaves, and serve.

INGREDIENTS:

4	CUPS JASMINE RICE
3	TABLESPOONS MINCED FRESH TURMERIC
4	GARLIC CLOVES, MINCED
½	CUP MINCED ONION
¼	CUP CANOLA OIL
3	LEMONGRASS STALKS, CRUSHED
4	KAFFIR LIME LEAVES
1	CAN COCONUT MILK
4	CUPS CHICKEN STOCK (SEE PAGE 680)
	SALT, TO TASTE

FURIKAKE

YIELD: 1 CUP / **ACTIVE TIME:** 10 MINUTES / **TOTAL TIME:** 10 MINUTES

This Japanese condiment full of umami is widely used throughout Japanese cooking. It transforms a plain bowl of rice and steamed vegetables and pairs well with fish and seafood.

1. Using a mortar and pestle or spice grinder, grind the sesame seeds until partially broken apart.

2. Cut the nori sheets into small, thin strips, and use your hands to crumble them.

3. In a bowl, combine all of the ingredients and mix well.

4. Store in an airtight container until needed. Use silica gel packs to help with moisture during storage. Make sure to shake well before using.

INGREDIENTS:

1	CUP TOASTED SESAME SEEDS
6	NORI SHEETS
½	TABLESPOON FINE SEA SALT
½	TABLESPOON SUGAR
1	TEASPOON CHILI FLAKES (OPTIONAL)
1	TABLESPOON MINCED BONITO FLAKES (OPTIONAL)

SHICHIMI TOGARASHI

YIELD: 1 CUP / **ACTIVE TIME:** 10 MINUTES / **TOTAL TIME:** 10 MINUTES

This is another staple Japanese seasoning that adds a bit of heat to whatever it graces. Feel free to play around with the ingredient ratios to suit your taste.

1. In a bowl, combine all of the ingredients and mix well.

2. Store in an airtight container.

INGREDIENTS:

4	TABLESPOONS CAYENNE PEPPER
2	TABLESPOONS GROUND DRIED ORANGE PEEL
2	TABLESPOONS WHITE AND/OR BLACK SESAME SEEDS
2	TEASPOONS HEMP SEEDS
2	TEASPOONS GROUND SANSHO PEPPERCORNS
2	TEASPOONS FINELY MINCED NORI
1	TEASPOON GROUND GINGER

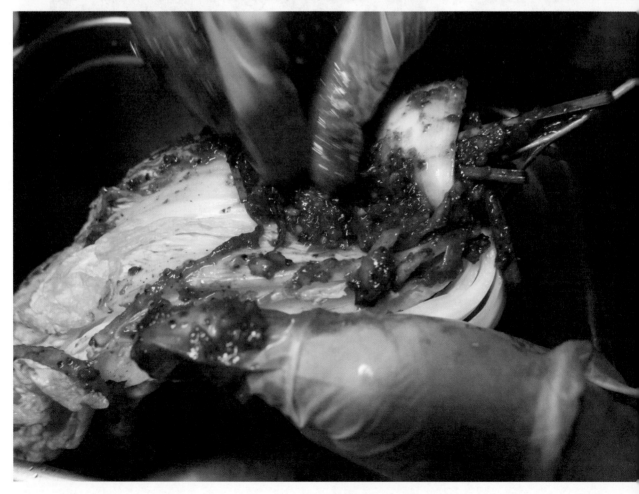

MOMMA'S KIMCHI

YIELD: 24 SERVINGS / ACTIVE TIME: 2 HOURS / TOTAL TIME: 72 HOURS

Korean families have passed down kimchi recipes, generation after generation. This version is Chef Brian's mother's recipe.

1. First, make a rice porridge. Add the rice flour and water to a saucepan over medium-low heat, whisking constantly so the bottom doesn't burn. While cooking, the mixture will start to thicken. Continue to cook until the mixture starts to bubble, stirring continually. Once the rice porridge is fully bubbling, remove from heat and pour the porridge into a bowl in an ice bath. Set aside until ready to make the kimchi marinade.

2. Cut the cabbages in half lengthwise and trim the root at the base if needed. Using a knife, make a slit in the middle of the core; this will help even the marination of the cabbage in the center by the root.

3. Generously massage the salt between each layer of cabbage leaf. Make sure to get the salt down by the core. Place the salted cabbage in a container, cover, and let sit at room temperature for 30 minutes to 2 hours, depending on the size of the cabbage and your preference in its consistency.

4. While waiting on the resting salted cabbage, make the kimchi marinade. Small dice 2½ pounds of daikon; julienne the remainder of the daikon.

5. In a food processor, combine the ginger, diced daikon, onion, and salted shrimp and blend until smooth.

6. Transfer the puree to a large bowl and add the chili flakes, garlic, and julienned daikon and mix well.

7. Add the corn syrup and all the cooled rice porridge and mix well. To finish, fold in the scallions and chives. If needed, adjust the seasoning with the salt.

8. Once the cabbage is done resting, it should be wilted and softer, with water having been pulled out of the cabbage. Rinse the cabbage very well in cold water, making sure to remove all the coarse salt between the leaves; if this salt isn't removed from the cabbage, the kimchi will be salty. Strain well, squeezing out any excess liquid.

INGREDIENTS:

1	CUP SWEET RICE FLOUR
5	CUPS WATER
3-4	NAPA CABBAGES
	COARSE SEA SALT, AS NEEDED
4	LBS. DAIKON
⅓	CUP MINCED GINGER
½	LARGE ONION, CHOPPED
1	TABLESPOON SALTED SHRIMP
2	CUPS KOREAN CHILI FLAKES
1½	CUPS MINCED GARLIC
3	TABLESPOONS CORN SYRUP
1	BUNCH SCALLIONS, FINELY CHOPPED
1	BUNCH ASIAN CHIVES, CUT INTO 1-INCH PIECES
½	CUP FISH SAUCE
1-2	CUPS WATER

9. The kimchi marination process can get messy so work over a large mixing bowl or a large sheet pan. With each salted cabbage, generously massage the kimchi marinade between each layer, leaving the mixture between the layers and making sure to get the mixture to the core of the cabbage.

10. Using the outermost end leaves, wrap these leaves around the front of the cabbage, to keep the mixture from falling out.

11. Once all the half cabbage heads have been marinated with the kimchi mixture, place them tightly in a glass or plastic container in a single layer. If needed, stack them as well. Do not use a metal container.

12. Add 1 to 2 cups of water to the mixing bowl you worked in. mix with the remaining kimchi marinade, and then pour over the stacked marinated cabbage to barely cover.

13. Cover the container with plastic wrap and set aside in a cool, dark place for 1 to 3 days, or longer, depending on your preference in fermentation. Check each day, and gently let gas out if needed by peeling back the plastic wrap and then resealing.

14. Store in the refrigerator once ready, and slice into portions to serve.

STUFFED CUCUMBER KIMCHI

YIELD: 6 SERVINGS / **ACTIVE TIME:** 30 MINUTES / **TOTAL TIME:** 72 HOURS

Kimchi, the wonderfully funky and fiery Korean side dish, doesn't always have to be made with cabbage. This is a great recipe if you find yourself with a bumper crop of Kirby cucumbers, also known as pickling cucumbers.

1. Quarter each cucumber lengthwise, leaving ¼ inch at the end intact and connected.

2. Season the cucumbers with the salt, being sure to get inside each one. Cover and set aside for 1 hour.

3. Rinse off the salted cucumbers with cold water and gently pat dry.

4. In a bowl, combine the remainder of the ingredients and mix well.

5. Stuff the mixture into the cucumbers and then place the stuffed cucumbers in an airtight jar. Leave the jar at room temperature for 24 hours before refrigerating. If you prefer more fermentation, keep the jar at room temperature for 2 days before refrigerating.

INGREDIENTS:

10	KIRBY CUCUMBERS
3	TABLESPOONS KOSHER SALT
1	CUP ASIAN CHIVES, CUT INTO ½-INCH SLICES
4	GARLIC CLOVES
1	TEASPOON MINCED GINGER
¾	CUP JULIENNED CARROT
½	CUP YELLOW ONION, THINLY SLICED
½	CUP KOREAN CHILI FLAKES
1	TABLESPOON SUGAR
¼	CUP WATER
1½	TABLESPOONS MINCED SALTED SHRIMP
1½	TABLESPOONS FISH SAUCE
1	TABLESPOON TOASTED SESAME SEEDS

SPICY BEAN SPROUT SALAD

YIELD: 4 SERVINGS / ACTIVE TIME: 10 MINUTES / TOTAL TIME: 15 MINUTES

This umami-rich, crunchy salad can be served as banchan or used to top rice or ramen.

1. In a bowl, combine the soy sauce, oil, Shichimi Togarashi, and salt and whisk well.

2. Bring a pot of water to a boil. Add the bean sprouts and blanch for 1 minute, and then drain well.

3. Add the warm bean sprouts and the sesame seeds to the dressing and mix to combine. Season with the pepper, to taste, and adjust the seasoning if needed.

4. Serve immediately, or refrigerate covered for up to 3 days.

INGREDIENTS:

2   TEASPOONS SOY SAUCE

2   TABLESPOONS SESAME OIL

1   TEASPOON SHICHIMI TOGARASHI (SEE PAGE 146)

½   TEASPOON KOSHER SALT

12   OZ. BEAN SPROUTS

1   TABLESPOON TOASTED SESAME SEEDS

    BLACK PEPPER, TO TASTE

SMASHED CUCUMBER SALAD

YIELD: 2 SERVINGS / ACTIVE TIME: 15 MINUTES / TOTAL TIME: 15 MINUTES

Using the technique of smashing the cucumbers makes it possible for the soy sauce and other seasonings to permeate the vegetables, making this dish more flavorful. Rayu is Japanese chili oil, and a worthy addition to your pantry if you like spicy oils.

1. Place the cucumbers in a resealable plastic bag. Press out as much air as possible. Using a rolling pin or the bottom of a pan, whack the cucumbers to smash them.

2. Add the soy sauce, oil, vinegar, and chili flakes to the bag and massage all of the ingredients together. Taste to adjust the seasoning.

3. Transfer the seasoned cucumbers to a serving plate, garnish with the sesame seeds and Rayu, if using, and serve immediately. The cucumbers will lose their crunch after a day in the refrigerator.

INGREDIENTS:

4 PERSIAN OR JAPANESE CUCUMBERS, CHOPPED INTO 3-INCH PIECES

1½ TABLESPOONS SOY SAUCE

1 TEASPOON SESAME OIL

1 TEASPOON UNSEASONED RICE WINE VINEGAR

½ TEASPOON CHILI FLAKES

KOSHER SALT, TO TASTE

1 TABLESPOON TOASTED SESAME SEEDS, FOR GARNISH

RAYU, TO TASTE, FOR GARNISH (SEE PAGE 234; OPTIONAL)

KOREAN-STYLE POTATO SALAD

YIELD: 6 SERVINGS / **ACTIVE TIME:** 30 MINUTES / **TOTAL TIME:** 1 HOUR

Korean potato (gamja) salad is an adaptation of the American-style potato salads served at barbeques with its use of mayonnaise, however, this version contains rice vinegar and apples, adding sweeter notes.

1. In a bowl, combine the onion and cucumber with a pinch of salt and mix well. Let sweat for 30 minutes. Squeeze out the excess liquid and set aside.

2. Meanwhile, bring a pot of water to a boil and blanch the carrot until slightly tender. Using a slotted spoon or kitchen spider, remove the carrot from the water, shock in an ice bath, and strain. Set aside.

3. In the same pot of boiling water, add 1 tablespoon of salt and the potatoes and boil for 15 to 20 minutes, or until fork tender. Strain the water and transfer the potatoes to a clean bowl.

4. While hot, using a masher or fork, mash the potatoes and eggs together. Add the sugar, vinegar, and most of the mayonnaise and incorporate well. Use the rest of the mayonnaise as needed for your desired consistency.

5. Fold in the apple, carrot, onion, and cucumber and adjust the seasoning with the salt and pepper.

6. Serve warm, at room temperature, or cold. It will keep for 3 to 4 days covered in the refrigerator.

INGREDIENTS:

¼ RED ONION, SMALL DICE

1 PERSIAN CUCUMBER, CUT INTO ¼-INCH CUBES

1 TABLESPOON SALT, PLUS MORE TO TASTE

1 MEDIUM CARROT, CUT INTO ¼-INCH CUBES

1½ LBS. RUSSET POTATOES, PEELED, MEDIUM DICE

2 HARD-BOILED EGGS, CHOPPED

1 TEASPOON SUGAR

1 TABLESPOON RICE VINEGAR

¾ CUP MAYONNAISE

1 APPLE, CUT INTO ¼-INCH CUBES

BLACK PEPPER, TO TASTE

YU XIANG EGGPLANT

YIELD: 6 SERVINGS / ACTIVE TIME: 30 MINUTES / TOTAL TIME: 45 MINUTES

Asian eggplants can be identified by their white-and-lavender coloring, and they are sweeter in taste, making them ideal for spicy Szechuan dishes.

1. In a bowl, combine all of the Meat Marinade ingredients, mix well, and set aside.

2. In a separate bowl, combine the Chicken Stock, chili paste, sugar, vinegar, soy sauce, oyster sauce, sweet bean sauce, and ground peppercorns, mix well, and set aside.

3. Quarter the eggplants lengthwise, then cut them into 2-inch lengths. Lightly salt the eggplant pieces and let rest for 15 minutes.

4. In a bowl, combine the pork with the prepared marinade and mix well.

5. Add the oil to a wok over high heat. Once the oil begins to shimmer, add the eggplants and stir-fry until the eggplants just start to get soft—make sure not to overcook. Remove them with a slotted spoon and drain on a paper towel–lined plate.

6. In the same wok with the same oil, stir-fry the pork with the garlic, ginger, and mushrooms for about 5 minutes. Add the jicama and the prepared marinade and cook for about 1 minute, and then add the eggplants and continue to simmer for several minutes, so the eggplants absorb all the flavors. Add the cornstarch slurry as needed to thicken.

7. Garnish with the jalapeños and scallions.

INGREDIENTS:

½	CUP CHICKEN STOCK (SEE PAGE 680)
2	TABLESPOONS CHILI PASTE
1½	TABLESPOONS SUGAR
1½	TABLESPOONS RICE VINEGAR
1	TABLESPOON SOY SAUCE
1	TABLESPOON OYSTER SAUCE
½	TABLESPOON SWEET BEAN SAUCE
½	TEASPOON GROUND SZECHUAN PEPPERCORNS
3-4	MEDIUM ASIAN EGGPLANTS
½	TABLESPOON SALT
½	CUP GROUND PORK
⅓	CUP VEGETABLE OIL
3	TABLESPOONS MINCED GARLIC
½	TABLESPOON MINCED GINGER
¼	CUP SLICED SHIITAKE MUSHROOMS
½	CUP JULIENNED JICAMA
	CORNSTARCH SLURRY (1:1 RATIO), AS NEEDED
1-2	RED JALAPEÑOS, DESEEDED AND JULIENNED, FOR GARNISH
1-2	SCALLIONS, SLICED THIN ON BIAS, FOR GARNISH

MEAT MARINADE

½	TEASPOON DARK SOY SAUCE
½	TEASPOON RICE WINE
½	TEASPOON CORNSTARCH
¼	TEASPOON SESAME OIL

SAVORY STEAMED EGG CUSTARD

YIELD: 6 SERVINGS / ACTIVE TIME: 20 MINUTES / TOTAL TIME: 1 HOUR

Hot egg custard is a common side dish to Korean barbeque, but it can also be served alongside any meal, or made into a stand-alone meal.

1. In a bowl, combine the eggs, Anchovy Stock, 1 teaspoon of soy sauce, and salt, mix well, and strain into another bowl.

2. Lightly oil your custard cups, and then fill each cup with the egg mixture. Sprinkle the scallion on top.

3. Using a bamboo steamer, bring water to a boil and steam on low heat until the custard is set, about 30 to 40 minutes.

4. To serve, pour the remaining soy sauce and the sesame oil on top of the custard.

INGREDIENTS:

6   EGGS, BEATEN, NO FOAM

        ANCHOVY STOCK (SEE PAGE 688), EQUAL AMOUNT TO EGG VOLUME

2   TEASPOONS SOY SAUCE, DIVIDED

1   TEASPOON SALT

1   TEASPOON CANOLA OIL

1   SCALLION, MINCED

1   TEASPOON SESAME OIL

GREEN PAPAYA SALAD

YIELD: 4 SERVINGS / **ACTIVE TIME:** 30 MINUTES / **TOTAL TIME:** 30 MINUTES

Popular in Laos, Thailand, Cambodia, and Vietnam, this fresh, tangy, and spicy salad brightens up any meal.

1. In a saucepan over low heat, combine the sugar and the fish sauce and cook until the sugar is dissolved and the liquid slightly thickens. Set aside.

2. Using a large mortar and pestle, pound the garlic until pulp and then, if using, add the chilies and the dried shrimp, and pound to release the oils.

3. Add the papaya, green beans, and carrot, and bruise gently with the pestle while using a spoon to mix everything together.

4. Add the lime juice, fish sauce syrup, and peanuts and mix well. Add the tomatoes at the end.

5. Adjust the seasoning with the salt, and garnish with the torn Thai basil, if using.

INGREDIENTS:

- ¼ CUP COCONUT OR PALM SUGAR
- ¼ CUP FISH SAUCE
- 3 GARLIC CLOVES
- 1-2 BIRD'S EYE CHILIES, SEEDED (OPTIONAL)
- 2 TABLESPOONS CHOPPED DRIED SHRIMP (OPTIONAL)
- 3 CUPS GRATED GREEN PAPAYA
- ⅓ CUP GREEN BEANS, CUT INTO 1½-INCH SLICES
- ⅓ CUP GRATED CARROT (OPTIONAL)
- 3 TABLESPOONS FRESH LIME JUICE
- ½ CUP FINELY CHOPPED ROASTED PEANUTS
- ⅓ CUP HALVED CHERRY TOMATOES
- SALT, TO TASTE
- THAI BASIL, FOR GARNISH (OPTIONAL)

DRY COOKED GREEN BEANS WITH GARLIC

YIELD: 4 SERVINGS / ACTIVE TIME: 30 MINUTES / TOTAL TIME: 30 MINUTES

This traditional Asian stir-fry dish can easily be prepared as either a vegetarian or meat dish to meet any craving. The crunch from the deep-fried green beans adds texture.

1. Add the oil to a wok or large pan over medium-high heat. Once the oil is hot, deep-fry the green beans until the skin blisters, 1 to 3 minutes; the beans should remain crispy. Work in batches to not overcrowd the pan. Drain the cooked beans on a paper towel–lined plate. Once finished, pour out all but 1 tablespoon of the oil.

2. Increase the heat to high and add the garlic and pork (if using). Cook through, being sure not to burn the garlic, and add the sugar, chili paste (if using), vinegar, salt, white pepper, and Szechuan peppercorns, and mix well.

3. Return the fried green beans to the pan, mix well, and adjust the seasoning.

4. Finish with the julienned chilies (if using) and serve immediately, with rice or as a side dish.

INGREDIENTS:

- 2 CUPS CANOLA OIL
- 1 LB. FRENCH GREEN BEANS, TRIMMED
- 2 TABLESPOONS MINCED GARLIC
- ¼ LB. GROUND PORK (OPTIONAL)
- 1 TEASPOON SUGAR
- 1 TABLESPOON CHILI PASTE (OPTIONAL)
- 1 TEASPOON CHINKIANG VINEGAR
- SALT, TO TASTE
- ¼ TEASPOON WHITE PEPPER
- ½ TEASPOON GROUND SZECHUAN PEPPERCORNS
- 1-2 RED CHILIES, SEEDED AND FINELY JULIENNED (OPTIONAL)

MACARONI SALAD

YIELD: 4 SERVINGS / **ACTIVE TIME:** 30 MINUTES / **TOTAL TIME:** 30 MINUTES

Like the American-style macaroni salad, the Korean version also uses mayonnaise and similar ingredients. Macaroni salad is a common side dish that's served with Korean barbeque because of its creamy texture and slight sweetness.

1. Bring a pot of water to a boil, salt generously, and cook the macaroni until very tender. Al dente will be undercooked for this dish. Drain well and transfer to a large bowl. Let cool slightly for 10 minutes.

2. Add the onion, ½ cup of mayonnaise, pickle juice, relish, and pepper to the macaroni and toss until well mixed. Adjust the seasoning with the salt and pepper if needed. Refrigerate for 1 hour.

3. When ready to serve, add an additional ½ cup of mayonnaise and the grated carrot, mixing well. If the salad looks dry, add more mayonnaise. Taste and adjust the seasoning before serving.

INGREDIENTS:

	KOSHER SALT, TO TASTE
8	OZ. DRY ELBOW MACARONI
¼	SWEET ONION, GRATED
1-1½	CUPS MAYONNAISE, DIVIDED
2	TABLESPOONS SWEET PICKLE JUICE
3	TABLESPOONS SWEET PICKLE RELISH
½	TABLESPOON BLACK PEPPER
¼	CUP GRATED CARROT

SPICY MANGO SALAD

YIELD: 2 SERVINGS / ACTIVE TIME: 30 MINUTES / TOTAL TIME: 1 HOUR

The sweetness of ripe mango marries with the funk of fish sauce and the heat of the chilies, making for a salad that works well as a side dish or condiment. If you don't want to fry up garlic and shallots, which are very common garnishes in Southeast Asia, both are readily available at Asian markets.

1. In a small bowl, soak the onion in water for 2 minutes, strain, and set aside.

2. In a separate bowl, combine the lemon juice, lime juice, fish sauce, sugar, and oil and whisk well.

3. In a large bowl, combine the mangoes, chilies, and onion, toss with the prepared dressing, and let stand for 1 hour, turning the ingredients several times. Adjust the seasoning if needed.

4. Before serving, fold in the fresh herbs and then transfer to a serving plate. Garnish with the Fried Shallots & Garlic, to taste.

FRIED SHALLOTS & GARLIC

1. Add the oil and shallots to a saucepan over high heat, stirring frequently. When the oil begins to bubble, turn down the heat and simmer for 5 minutes.

2. Add the garlic and continue to cook for 20 minutes, stirring frequently, or until the shallots and garlic have turned golden.

3. Strain, reserving the oil, and drain on a paper towel–lined plate. Season with the salt and let cool.

4. Store in an airtight container for 3 days; the oil will keep in the refrigerator for 6 weeks.

INGREDIENTS:

⅓   CUP JULIENNED RED ONION

2   TABLESPOONS FRESH LEMON JUICE

1   TABLESPOON FRESH LIME JUICE

1   TABLESPOON FISH SAUCE

2   TEASPOONS SUGAR

1   TABLESPOON GARLIC AND SHALLOT OIL (RESERVED FROM FRYING)

2   RIPE YET FIRM MANGOES, JULIENNED

2   RED JALAPEÑO OR FRESNO CHILIES, DESEEDED AND FINELY JULIENNED

2   TABLESPOONS TORN THAI BASIL

1   TABLESPOON TORN MINT LEAF

    SALT, TO TASTE

    FRIED SHALLOTS & GARLIC, TO TASTE (SEE RECIPE)

FRIED SHALLOTS & GARLIC

2   CUPS CANOLA OIL

8   SHALLOTS, SLICED ⅛-INCH THICK

12   GARLIC CLOVES, SLICED ⅛ INCH THICK

    SALT, TO TASTE

VIETNAMESE PICKLED CARROTS & DAIKONS

YIELD: 12 SERVINGS / **ACTIVE TIME:** 30 MINUTES / **TOTAL TIME:** 24 HOURS

This side dish is used for crunch and acid. These are also often found on delicious banh mi (see page 442).

1. Place the vegetables in a mixing bowl and add 1 tablespoon of sugar and the salt. Using your hands, massage the mixture for 2 to 3 minutes. Set aside for 30 minutes, until the vegetables have become more pliable.

2. Meanwhile, in a small saucepan, dissolve the remainder of the sugar with the water and vinegar, bring to a gentle simmer, and then turn off the heat.

3. Rinse the vegetables with water and strain well. Transfer to a container with a lid and pour the warm pickling liquid over the vegetables to cover.

4. Refrigerate overnight before using.

INGREDIENTS:

- 1   LB. DAIKON, CUT INTO 3-INCH STICKS, ¾ INCH THICK
- ½   LB. CARROTS, CUT INTO THIN STICKS
- ½   CUP GRANULATED SUGAR, PLUS 1 TABLESPOON, DIVIDED
- ½   TABLESPOON SALT
- 1   CUP WATER
- 1¼   CUPS DISTILLED WHITE VINEGAR

NUOC CHAM

YIELD: 1 CUP / **ACTIVE TIME**: 10 MINUTES / **TOTAL TIME**: 10 MINUTES

This dipping sauce is a staple condiment on any Vietnamese table.

1. In a mixing bowl, combine all of the ingredients and mix well, until the sugar dissolves completely.

2. Adjust the seasoning; add more fish sauce for boldness or chilies for spice.

3. Refrigerate for up to one week.

INGREDIENTS:

¼   CUP FISH SAUCE

⅓   CUP WATER

2   TABLESPOONS GRANULATED SUGAR

¼   CUP LIME JUICE

1   GARLIC CLOVE, MINCED

1-2   BIRD'S EYE CHILIES, THINLY SLICED (OPTIONAL)

1   TABLESPOON CHILI GARLIC SAUCE (SEE PAGE 180)

CHILI GARLIC SAUCE

YIELD: 1 CUP / **ACTIVE TIME:** 15 MINUTES / **TOTAL TIME:** 30 MINUTES

This is a staple condiment throughout Southeast Asia. If you like the bottled stuff, you'll love this homemade version.

1. Combine the chilies, garlic, and vinegar in a small saucepan over medium heat and simmer for 10 minutes.

2. Transfer to a blender and blend until smooth.

3. Pass the mixture through a fine strainer into a small saucepan, add the sugar and salt, and bring to a simmer. Adjust the seasoning with the salt and pepper.

4. Cool and refrigerate in an airtight container.

INGREDIENTS:

- 1 CUP STEMMED AND CHOPPED (WITH SEEDS) FRESNO CHILIES
- 6-8 GARLIC CLOVES, CHOPPED
- ¼ CUP DISTILLED WHITE VINEGAR
- 2 TABLESPOONS GRANULATED SUGAR
- 1 TEASPOON SALT, PLUS MORE TO TASTE

  BLACK PEPPER, TO TASTE (OPTIONAL)

CHINESE BROCCOLI W/ OYSTER SAUCE

YIELD: 4 SERVINGS / ACTIVE TIME: 30 MINUTES / TOTAL TIME: 30 MINUTES

Sweet and salty, oyster sauce not only adds a deep umami quality to any dish in which it is used, but it also imparts a rich color.

1. In a bowl, combine the soy sauce, oyster sauce, and vinegar, whisk well, and set aside.

2. Bring a pot of salted water to a boil and blanch the broccoli for 2 to 3 minutes, or until bright green and tender. Strain and shock in ice water. Set aside.

3. Add the oil to a sauté pan over medium-high heat. Once the oil begins to shimmer, add the garlic, then the broccoli, and stir-fry for 2 minutes. Add 2 to 3 tablespoons of water to the pan, turn down the heat to medium-low, and immediately cover and cook for another 2 to 3 minutes. Cook until the broccoli has heated through.

4. Transfer the broccoli to a serving platter, drizzle the prepared sauce over the greens, and garnish with the Crispy Onions.

INGREDIENTS:

- 1½ TABLESPOONS SOY SAUCE
- ¼ CUP OYSTER SAUCE
- 2 TABLESPOONS UNSEASONED RICE VINEGAR
- 6-8 CHINESE BROCCOLI, CLEANED AND ENDS TRIMMED
- 1 TABLESPOON CANOLA OIL
- 1 TABLESPOON MINCED GARLIC
- CRISPY ONIONS (SEE PAGE 196)

CALAMARI SALAD

YIELD: 4 SERVINGS / **ACTIVE TIME:** 30 MINUTES / **TOTAL TIM:E** 1 HOUR

This is a fragrant, tangy Thai-style salad that makes the most out of fresh squid.

1. In a large bowl, combine the chilies, garlic, fish sauce, lime juice, sugar, and chili powder and mix well. Set aside.

2. In a pot, bring the water, vinegar, and a pinch of salt to a boil. Once the water comes to a boil, blanch the squid for no more than 20 seconds,immediately shock in ice-cold water, and strain.

3. Mix the blanched squid with the prepared dressing and marinate for at least 30 minutes, or until needed.

4. Before serving, toss with the remainder of the ingredients, except the garnish, and adjust the seasoning.

5. Transfer to a serving platter and, if using, garnish with the Fried Shallots & Garlic.

INGREDIENTS:

4   RED THAI CHILIES, FINELY MINCED

4   GARLIC CLOVES, FINELY MINCED

3   TABLESPOONS FISH SAUCE

3   TABLESPOONS FRESH LIME JUICE

2   TEASPOONS SUGAR

½   TEASPOON CHILI POWDER

1   QUART WATER

¼   CUP WHITE WINE VINEGAR

SALT, AS NEEDED

1   LB. SQUID, CLEANED, SCORED ON INSIDE, AND QUARTERED

½   CUP JULIENNED CARROTS

¼   CUP TORN MINT LEAVES

½   CUP CHOPPED CILANTRO, LEAVES AND STEMS

1½   TABLESPOONS MINCED LEMONGRASS

2   CUPS COARSELY SHREDDED ICEBERG LETTUCE

FRIED SHALLOTS & GARLIC, FOR GARNISH (OPTIONAL; SEE PAGE 173)

GARLIC NOODLES

YIELD: 4 SERVINGS / **ACTIVE TIME:** 15 MINUTES / **TOTAL TIME:** 30 MINUTES

The dish was born in San Francisco, out of both Vietnamese and American influences. The combination of the ingredients adds levels of complexity not found in plain buttered noodles. Most any noodle will work in this recipe, but egg noodles are best.

1. Bring a pot of water to a boil, cook the noodles until al dente, and strain.

2. While the strained noodles are hot, toss with the oil and season with the salt.

3. Fold in the scallions and cilantro, transfer the noodles to a serving platter, and top with the Fried Shallots & Garlic.

INGREDIENTS:

1   LB. FAVORITE NOODLES

¼   CUP FRIED SHALLOTS & GARLIC OIL (SEE PAGE 173)

2   TEASPOONS SALT

2   SCALLIONS, MINCED

2   TABLESPOONS CHOPPED CILANTRO

FRIED SHALLOTS & GARLIC (SEE PAGE 173), TO TASTE

TAMAGOYAKI

YIELD: 2 SERVINGS / **ACTIVE TIME:** 15 MINUTES / **TOTAL TIME:** 15 MINUTES

This is a sweet-and-savory Japanese omelette that is traditionally made in a small rectangular pan. It takes a bit of practice to get just right, but once you master it, you'll find yourself making it all the time. It's equally good warm, cold, or in a sushi roll.

1. Place the eggs, salt, soy sauce, and mirin in a bowl and whisk to combine.

2. Place the vegetable oil in a rectangular cast-iron pan and warm over medium-high heat.

3. Pour a thin layer of the egg mixture into the pan, tilting and swirling to make sure the egg completely coats the bottom. When the bottom of the egg is just set and there is still liquid on top, use a chopstick to gently roll the egg up into a log. If you allow the egg to cook too much, it won't stick as you roll it.

4. When the first roll is at one end of the pan, pour another thin layer of egg mixture into the pan. When the bottom of this layer is set, roll the log back onto it. Roll the layer up to the other end of the pan. Repeat until all of the egg mixture has been used up.

5. Remove the omelette from the pan and let it set for a few minutes before trimming the ends and slicing into even pieces.

INGREDIENTS:

4	LARGE EGGS
¼	TEASPOON KOSHER SALT
1	TEASPOON SOY SAUCE
1	TABLESPOON MIRIN
1	TABLESPOON VEGETABLE OIL

SOMEN SALAD

YIELD: 4 SERVINGS / ACTIVE TIME: 30 MINUTES / TOTAL TIME: 1 HOUR

This chilled noodle salad is a take on the Hawaiian somen salad. In this recipe, Chef Brian uses char siu and Japanese fish cake (kamaboko), but any finely sliced protein, including tofu, makes a great alternative. As you prep the salad ingredients, keep in mind that great knife cuts will make the salad prettier.

1. In a bowl, make the dressing by combining the Chicken Stock, sugar, mirin, soy sauce, sesame oil, and salt and whisking well. Make sure all the sugar dissolves. Refrigerate covered until needed, for up to 2 weeks.

2. When ready to serve, evenly distribute the cabbage and watercress on a serving platter and then cover with the noodles.

3. Top the noodles with the pork, fish cake, cucumbers, carrots, snow peas, Tamagoyaki, and scallions, arranging each ingredient separately over the noodles.

4. Pour the dressing over the salad and mix well before eating.

INGREDIENTS:

- 1 CUP CHICKEN STOCK (SEE PAGE 680)
- ¼ CUP SUGAR
- ¼ CUP MIRIN
- ¼ CUP SOY SAUCE
- 2 TABLESPOONS SESAME OIL
- SALT, TO TASTE
- ½ HEAD NAPA CABBAGE, SHREDDED
- 1 BUNCH WATERCRESS, COARSELY CHOPPED
- 12 OZ. SOMEN NOODLES, COOKED, RINSED, AND STRAINED
- ⅔ CUP JULIENNED CHAR SIU PORK (SEE PAGE 336)
- ¼ CUP JULIENNED KAMABOKO
- 2 JAPANESE CUCUMBERS, JULIENNED
- 2 CARROTS, JULIENNED
- ½ CUP JULIENNED SNOW PEAS
- TAMAGOYAKI, THINLY SLICED (SEE PAGE 185)
- 3 SCALLIONS, GREEN PARTS THINLY SLICED

BABY BOK CHOY WITH DRIED SHRIMP

YIELD: 2 SERVINGS / **ACTIVE TIME:** 30 MINUTES / **TOTAL TIME:** 30 MINUTES

Baby bok choy is a Chinese green that is featured in countless dishes from the region. At times it is served simply steamed and lightly salted. Here we have a variation where the vegetable is cooked in a wok with rehydrated shrimp.

1. Add the oil to a wok or skillet over high heat. Once the oil begins to shimmer, add the shrimp and stir-fry for 30 to 45 seconds, until fragrant. Add the garlic and ginger, stir-fry for 30 seconds, and then add the bok choy and mix well for 30 seconds.

2. Deglaze with the rice wine. Once the alcohol burns off, add the soy sauce and a splash of water, if needed. Lower the heat to medium-high and cook the bok choy until wilted and most of the liquid has reduced.

3. Season with the white pepper and salt and serve immediately.

INGREDIENTS:

1   TABLESPOON CANOLA OIL

2½   TABLESPOONS DRIED SHRIMP, REHYDRATED IN BOILING WATER, DRAINED, AND PATTED DRY

½   TABLESPOON MINCED GARLIC CLOVE

1   TEASPOON MINCED GINGER

8   BABY BOK CHOY, QUARTERED

2   TABLESPOONS SHAOXING RICE WINE

2   TABLESPOONS SOY SAUCE

     WHITE PEPPER, TO TASTE

     SALT, TO TASTE

MISO BUTTER CORN ON THE COB

YIELD: 6 SERVINGS / **ACTIVE TIME:** 30 MINUTES / **TOTAL TIME:** 30 MINUTES

Do you like elote, the grilled Mexican corn on the cob, slathered with mayonnaise and Cotija cheese? Then you'll love this version, layered with the nutty and creamy flavors of Asia.

1. In a bowl, combine the butter, miso, and lime zest and mix well. Set aside.

2. In a dry skillet over medium heat, toast the panko and sesame seeds until golden. Add the Shichimi Togarashi and transfer the panko mixture to a plate to roll the grilled corn in.

3. On a hot grill or under a broiler, char the corn while frequently basting with miso butter throughout the cooking process.

4. Once the corn is cooked, roll each ear in the panko mixture.

5. Finish with a squeeze of lime and the cilantro, if using, and serve immediately.

INGREDIENTS:

½ CUP UNSALTED BUTTER, AT ROOM TEMPERATURE

¼ CUP SHIRO MISO PASTE

1 LIME, ZEST AND JUICE

½ CUP PANKO

1 TABLESPOON SESAME SEEDS

1 TABLESPOON SHICHIMI TOGARASHI (SEE PAGE 146)

6 EARS CORN, SHUCKED AND CLEANED

CILANTRO, CHOPPED, FOR GARNISH (OPTIONAL)

ROASTED BROCCOLINI WITH GOCHUJANG GINGER SCALLION SAUCE

YIELD: 4 SERVINGS / **ACTIVE TIME:** 30 MINUTES / **TOTAL TIME:** 30 MINUTES

This dish is inspired by gochujang sesame broccoli, a popular Korean dish. It pairs well with grilled chicken, pork, or fish.

1. Add the oil to a skillet over medium-high heat. Once the oil begins to shimmer, carefully place the broccolini in one even layer and season with the salt. Do not move the broccolini, in order to let it lightly char. After about 2 minutes, flip the broccolini and cook for another 2 minutes.

2. Add the Vegetable Stock and lower the heat to medium to steam the broccolini. Cook until all of the liquid has evaporated and the broccolini is tender. Remove from heat.

3. Add the Gochujang Ginger Scallion Sauce and toss in the same pan, that so residual heat helps to evenly coat the broccolini with sauce.

4. Transfer to a platter and serve immediately.

GOCHUJANG GINGER SCALLION SAUCE

1. Add 1 inch of the oil to a pot over medium heat. Once the oil is hot, fry the garlic until golden brown. Strain, reserving the oil for future use, and drain the garlic on a paper towel–lined plate.

2. Repeat the fry process with the ginger and drain on the same paper towel–lined plate.

3. Add 1 tablespoon of the oil to a separate pot over medium-low heat. Once the oil begins to shimmer, sweat the scallions' white parts until very tender.

4. Add the brown sugar, mix well, and cook until the sugar is about to caramelize. Add the gochujang paste and stir well to incorporate.

5. Add the soy sauce and ginger juice, mix well, and bring to a low simmer for 5 minutes, stirring frequently. Once all of the ingredients are cooked together, remove from heat.

INGREDIENTS:

CANOLA OIL

1 LB. BROCCOLINI, SLICED IN HALF LENGTHWISE

SALT, TO TASTE

3 TABLESPOONS VEGETABLE STOCK (SEE PAGE 684) OR WATER

2 TABLESPOONS GOCHUJANG GINGER SCALLION SAUCE (SEE RECIPE)

CRISPY ONIONS, FOR GARNISH (SEE RECIPE; OPTIONAL)

GOCHUJANG GINGER SCALLION SAUCE

CANOLA OIL, ENOUGH TO FRY

1 CUP MINCED GARLIC CLOVE

1 CUP MINCED GINGER

5 SCALLIONS, WHITE AND GREEN PARTS SEPARATED AND MINCED

½ CUP BROWN SUGAR

3 TABLESPOONS GOCHUJANG PASTE

1 CUP SOY SAUCE

1 TABLESPOON GINGER JUICE

Continued . . .

6. Add crispy garlic, crispy ginger, and the scallions' green parts and mix well.

7. Cool at room temperature, and refrigerate in an airtight container for up to a month.

CRISPY ONIONS

1. In a bowl, combine the onion slices and buttermilk and let soak for 20 minutes.

2. In a Deep fryer or Dutch oven, preheat the oil to 350°F.

3. Add the flour to a bowl and season it with the salt and pepper.

4. Remove the excess buttermilk from the soaked onions and dredge in the flour until well coated.

5. Shake off the excess flour dredge and fry in batches so as not to overcrowd the fryer.

6. Once golden brown and crispy, use a slotted spoon or kitchen spider to remove the onions, and drain on a paper towel–lined plate. Season with the salt while still hot.

7. Once cooled completely, store in an airtight container.

INGREDIENTS:

CRISPY ONIONS

1	ONION, THINLY SLICED
1-2	CUPS BUTTERMILK
4	CUPS CANOLA OIL, TO FRY
3	CUPS ALL-PURPOSE FLOUR
	SALT, TO TASTE
	BLACK PEPPER, TO TASTE

BABY KALE SALAD WITH SESAME TOFU DRESSING & PICKLED FRESNO

YIELD: 2 SERVINGS / **ACTIVE TIME**: 15 MINUTES / **TOTAL TIME**: 15 MINUTES

If you think you have an aversion to tofu, try this creamy dressing. You'll want to pour it over everything, though it works particularly well with this salad, which is perfect for fall.

1. In a salad bowl, combine the kale, tomatoes, and croutons, add the Sesame Tofu Dressing, and toss to coat.

2. Fold in the almonds, garnish with the Pickled Fresno Chilies, and serve.

SESAME TOFU DRESSING

1. In a blender, combine the tofu, lemon juice, vinegar, garlic, mustard, and sesame paste and blend until smooth.

2. Slowly blend in the oil to emulsify the dressing.

3. Adjust the seasoning with the salt and pepper.

INGREDIENTS:

4	CUPS BABY KALE
1	CUP HALVED CHERRY TOMATOES
	CROUTONS, TO TASTE
½	CUP SESAME TOFU DRESSING (SEE RECIPE)
¼	CUP SALTED ALMONDS
3	TABLESPOONS PICKLED FRESNO CHILIES, (SEE PAGE 36), FOR GARNISH

SESAME TOFU DRESSING

½	BLOCK FIRM TOFU
¼	CUP FRESH LEMON JUICE
2	TABLESPOONS WHITE WINE VINEGAR
1	GARLIC CLOVE, MINCED
¼	TEASPOON DIJON MUSTARD
1	TABLESPOON SESAME PASTE
¾	CUP CANOLA OIL
¼	TEASPOON SALT
	BLACK PEPPER, TO TASTE

POTATO JORIM

YIELD: 6 SERVINGS / **ACTIVE TIME:** 20 MINUTES / **TOTAL TIME:** 1 HOUR

These Korean sweet soy-braised potatoes make a great side and can be eaten at room temperature or warm.

1. Add the potatoes, garlic, soy sauce, mirin, sugar, corn syrup, kombu, jalapeño, and water to a pot over medium-high heat, stir well, and bring to a boil.

2. Reduce the heat to medium and simmer the potatoes, uncovered, until fork tender, stirring occasionally to coat the potatoes with the braising liquid. Make sure to reduce the braising liquid to create a syrupy consistency by the time the potatoes are cooked.

3. Remove from heat, let cool, and refrigerate in an airtight container until needed.

4. When ready to serve, garnish with the sesame seeds and chives.

INGREDIENTS:

2   LBS. BABY GOLD POTATOES, PEELED

4   GARLIC CLOVES, CRUSHED

2   CUPS SOY SAUCE

1   CUP MIRIN

1   CUP SUGAR

1   TABLESPOON CORN SYRUP

    2 X 2–INCH PIECE KOMBU

½   JALAPEÑO

2   CUPS WATER

1   TABLESPOON TOASTED SESAME SEEDS, FOR GARNISH

1   TABLESPOON MINCED CHIVES, FOR GARNISH

YU CHOY WITH BLACK BEAN GARLIC SAUCE & EXTRA GARLIC

YIELD: 4 SERVINGS / **ACTIVE TIME:** 15 MINUTES / **TOTAL TIME:** 20 MINUTES

Black bean garlic sauce is perfect with steamed yu choy because a spoonful makes for an intense, instant sauce.

1. Place the yu choy in a sauté pan large enough to fit all the greens, add the water, cover the pan, and cook over high heat.

2. After about 5 minutes, remove the lid and cook until most of the water cooks off.

3. Add the oil and garlic and stir-fry until the garlic is fragrant, about 2 minutes.

4. Add the black bean garlic sauce, stir to coat, and cook until heated through. Serve immediately.

INGREDIENTS:

1½   LBS. YU CHOY, CHOPPED
      INTO 3-INCH PIECES

¼   CUP WATER

½   TABLESPOON OLIVE OIL

1   GARLIC CLOVE, MINCED

1   TABLESPOON BLACK BEAN
      GARLIC SAUCE

YU CHOY WITH GARLIC & SOY

YIELD: 4 SERVINGS / **ACTIVE TIME:** 10 MINUTES / **TOTAL TIME:** 15 MINUTES

Steaming yu choy keeps it tender and light. If the stalks are large, leave them to cook a little longer.

1. Place the yu choy in a sauté pan large enough to fit all of the stalks, cover with the water, cover the pan, and cook over high heat.

2. After about 5 minutes, check the thickest stalk to see if it is tender. If not, cook until it is. Once tender, add the oil and garlic. Sauté until the garlic is fully cooked but not browned, about 2 minutes.

3. Add the vinegar and soy sauce, toss to combine, and serve.

INGREDIENTS:

- 1½   LBS. YU CHOY (IF ESPECIALLY LONG, CUT THEM IN HALF)
- ¼   CUP WATER
- 1   TABLESPOON OLIVE OIL
- 2   GARLIC CLOVES, CHOPPED
- ½   TABLESPOON RICE VINEGAR
- 1   TABLESPOON SOY SAUCE

STEAMED JAPANESE EGGPLANT
WITH BLACK BEAN GARLIC SAUCE & BASIL

YIELD: 4 SERVINGS / **ACTIVE TIME:** 30 MINUTES / **TOTAL TIME:** 45 MINUTES

This recipe is a great way to showcase the lovely, delicate flavor of steamed Japanese eggplant. The sauce is made from fermented black beans and garlic and is intense and salty. Thai basil is the best accompaniment for this dish, but if you can't find any, Italian basil will work fine.

1. Place 1 inch of water in a saucepan, set a steaming tray above it, and bring the water to a boil.

2. Place the eggplant in the steaming tray and steam until tender, 5 to 8 minutes. Remove from heat and place on a serving plate.

3. Place the garlic and shallot in a small saucepan with enough oil to coat the bottom. Sauté over medium heat until the vegetables start to brown, about 5 minutes.

4. Add the black bean garlic sauce, soy sauce, and vinegar and stir until the sauce starts to thicken. If the sauce thickens so much that it becomes clumpy, add the water 1 teaspoon at a time.

5. Taste, adjust the seasoning as needed, remove from heat, and pour over the eggplant. Garnish with the basil and serve.

INGREDIENTS:

1½ LBS. JAPANESE EGGPLANT, SLICED LENGTHWISE AND HALVED

1 GARLIC CLOVE, SLICED

1 TABLESPOON MINCED SHALLOT

OLIVE OIL, AS NEEDED

2 TABLESPOONS BLACK BEAN GARLIC SAUCE

2 TEASPOONS SOY SAUCE

2 TEASPOONS RICE VINEGAR

WATER, AS NEEDED

8 FRESH BASIL LEAVES, CHIFFONADE, FOR GARNISH

LARB GAI

YIELD: 4 SERVINGS / *ACTIVE TIME:* 20 MINUTES / *TOTAL TIME:* 35 MINUTES

This zippy chicken salad originated in Laos but is commonly found in Thailand, and it's a good example of ingredients common to the region's cuisine. The rice powder gives a subtle, toasty flavor to the whole dish.

1. Warm a skillet over medium heat and add the chicken and a little water. Cook, using a wooden spoon to break the chicken up, until the chicken starts to brown, about 5 minutes. Add the shallot and cook until the chicken is cooked through. Transfer the mixture to a bowl and let cool.

2. Once the mixture has cooled, add the lemongrass, lime leaves, chili peppers (if using), lime juice, fish sauce, soy sauce, Toasted Rice Powder, cilantro, and mint. Stir to combine, taste, and season with the salt and pepper.

3. Serve with the lettuce leaves, using them to scoop the mixture.

TIP: Lemongrass and lime leaves can be very fibrous, so make sure they are both minced very fine. Use an electric herb chopper, if one is available.

TOASTED RICE POWDER

1. Warm a cast-iron skillet over medium-high heat. Add the rice and toast until it starts to brown.

2. Remove and grind into a fine powder with a mortar and pestle.

INGREDIENTS:

1	LB. GROUND CHICKEN
1	SHALLOT, DICED
1	LEMONGRASS STALK, MINCED
2	MAKRUT LIME LEAVES, MINCED
3	RED CHILI PEPPERS, SEEDED AND CHOPPED (OPTIONAL)
¼	CUP FRESH LIME JUICE
1	TABLESPOON FISH SAUCE
1	TABLESPOON SOY SAUCE
1	TABLESPOON TOASTED RICE POWDER (SEE RECIPE)
¼	CUP CHOPPED FRESH CILANTRO
12	FRESH MINT LEAVES, CHOPPED
	SALT AND PEPPER, TO TASTE
	BIBB LETTUCE LEAVES, FOR SERVING

TOASTED RICE POWDER

½	CUP JASMINE RICE

SIMPLE STIR-FRIED BOK CHOY

YIELD: 2 SERVINGS / **ACTIVE TIME:** 10 MINUTES / **TOTAL TIME:** 10 MINUTES

Bok choy is sweet and delicate; the perfect accompaniment to any main dish. Adding a splash of mirin at the end of cooking brings out the sweetness of the vegetable without overwhelming it.

1. Place the oil in a small pan and warm over medium-high heat. When it starts to shimmer, add the bok choy and sauté until the green part of the cabbage has wilted, about 5 minutes.

2. Add the garlic and cook for 2 minutes, then add the mirin and soy sauce, stir to combine, and cook for 1 more minute.

3. Season with the salt and serve.

INGREDIENTS:

1	TABLESPOON OLIVE OIL
½	LB. BOK CHOY, SLICED
2	GARLIC CLOVES, MINCED
1	TABLESPOON MIRIN
1	TEASPOON SOY SAUCE
	SALT, TO TASTE

THAI BEEF & CUCUMBER SALAD

YIELD: 2 SERVINGS / **ACTIVE TIME**: 20 MINUTES / **TOTAL TIME**: 45 MINUTES

When the weather is hot, even the grill seems too much to bear. This is a light but filling salad, and it is a perfect use for leftover roast beef or steak, or deli-sliced roast beef. The whole recipe requires no cooking, save for boiling water for the noodles.

1. Bring 6 cups of water to a boil in a medium saucepan and place the noodles in a baking pan. Pour the water over the noodles and let sit until tender, about 20 minutes. Drain well and place them in a bowl.

2. Add the remaining ingredients, except for the sesame seeds, and toss to combine. Chill in the refrigerator for 1 hour, garnish with the sesame seeds, and serve.

INGREDIENTS:

- 2 OZ.-PACKAGE MUNG BEAN OR THIN RICE NOODLES
- 1 CARROT, PEELED AND GRATED
- 1 SMALL CUCUMBER, SEEDED AND DICED

  ZEST AND JUICE OF 1 LIME
- 10 FRESH MINT LEAVES, CHOPPED
- 1–2 TABLESPOONS SOY SAUCE
- 1 TEASPOON PALM SUGAR OR MAPLE SYRUP
- ½ TEASPOON KOSHER SALT
- 1 TABLESPOON THAI FISH SAUCE
- 2–4 OZ. THINLY SLICED ROAST BEEF OR LEFTOVER STEAK, TORN INTO BITE-SIZE PIECES

  RICE VINEGAR, TO TASTE

  HOT SAUCE, TO TASTE

  SESAME SEEDS, FOR GARNISH

CUCUMBER NOODLES
WITH COCONUT, LIME & CUMIN DRESSING

YIELD: 4 SERVINGS / **ACTIVE TIME:** 30 MINUTES / **TOTAL TIME:** 2 HOURS

The combination of warming, pungent cumin, sweet and soothing coconut, and crispy cucumber is endlessly satisfying. This salad is fairly easy to assemble as well, though it does require opening up a young Thai coconut. Thai coconuts are as large as melons, resemble a whitish yurt, and have a moist, aromatic pulp that is very different from the solid flesh of mature coconuts. .

1. Quarter each cucumber half and then cut the quarters into "noodles" that are ⅛ inch wide. Place the strands on paper towels to drain.

2. Place the coconut on a work surface and steady it by holding the bottom with one hand. Using a mallet and a very large, sharp knife, place the bottom corner of the knife blade about 1½ inches below the tip of the coconut. Gently strike the knife with the mallet to create a small indentation on the surface. Place the bottom corner of the blade in the indentation, and strike down harder on the mallet to crack the outer shell and break through to the inner shell of the coconut.

3. Make your second cut, using the same technique, so that the two combined incisions create a 90-degree angle. Continue this process with the third cut, which will create a "U" shape, and then the fourth cut, which will create a square shape at the top of the coconut.

4. Using the bottom corner of your knife blade, pry open the square at the top of the coconut. If the square doesn't release easily, go over the cuts made again, this time using more force.

5. Once pried open, invert the coconut and pour the coconut water into a glass or cup and set aside.

6. Open the coconut by turning it over so that its opening is now on the side. Place the bottom corner of the knife blade halfway along the length of the coconut. Gently strike the knife with a mallet to create a small indentation on the surface. Making sure the bottom corner of the blade is placed in the previous indentation, strike down harder on the mallet to split the coconut open. Using a spoon, scrape out the coconut flesh inside and transfer it to a small bowl.

INGREDIENTS:

5	LARGE CUCUMBERS, PEELED, HALVED LENGTHWISE, AND SEEDED
1	YOUNG THAI COCONUT
	ZEST AND JUICE FROM 2 LIMES
¼	CUP COCONUT WATER (RESERVED FROM THE YOUNG THAI COCONUT)
1	TEASPOON CHILI GARLIC SAUCE (SEE PAGE 180), PLUS MORE AS NEEDED
1	TEASPOON GRATED GINGER
1	TEASPOON SUGAR
1	TEASPOON CUMIN
1	TEASPOON KOSHER SALT
½	CUP SALTED, ROASTED PEANUTS, CHOPPED, FOR GARNISH
5-6	SCALLIONS, TRIMMED AND SLICED THIN, FOR GARNISH

Continued . . .

7. Put the coconut flesh, lime juice, coconut water, Chili Garlic Sauce, ginger, sugar, cumin, and salt in a small food processor or blender and puree until smooth.

8. Transfer the cucumber noodles to a large serving bowl. Top with the coconut mixture and toss to coat. Chill for at least 15 minutes and up to 2 hours in the refrigerator.

9. Sprinkle the lime zest, peanuts, and scallions on top of the dressed noodles and serve.

RICE SALAD BOWL WITH ADZUKI BEANS, AVOCADO, SNAP PEAS, JICAMA & BENIHANA'S GINGER DRESSING

YIELD: 2 SERVINGS / **ACTIVE TIME:** 15 MINUTES / **TOTAL TIME:** 20 MINUTES

If you've had the good fortune to go to a Benihana-style hibachi restaurant, you know that the theater of cooking on the open stovetop is always great. Know what else is great? The iceberg lettuce salad that is coated in an orange-colored ginger dressing. The dressing is so good, you don't even notice the bland lettuce or wan cherry tomatoes. Well, now you can make that salad at home, but with better ingredients.

1. Drain the adzuki beans and rinse under cool water. Drain again and set aside.

2. Divide the rice between two bowls. In this order, artfully arrange the beans, carrot, jicama, snap peas, and avocado on top of each portion.

3. Top each portion with a pinch of salt and some of the Benihana's Ginger Dressing, garnish with the sesame seeds, and serve.

BENIHANA'S GINGER DRESSING

1. Place all of the ingredients in a blender or food processor and puree until smooth.

INGREDIENTS:

- ½ CUP CANNED ADZUKI BEANS
- ½ CUP COOKED WHITE RICE, AT ROOM TEMPERATURE
- 1 CARROT, PEELED AND GRATED
- ½ JICAMA, PEELED AND JULIENNED
- 4-6 SUGAR SNAP PEAS, SLICED
- FLESH FROM 1 AVOCADO, SLICED THIN
- SALT, TO TASTE
- BENIHANA'S GINGER DRESSING (SEE RECIPE)
- WHITE SESAME SEEDS, FOR GARNISH

BENIHANA'S GINGER DRESSING

- ¼ CUP CHOPPED WHITE ONION
- ¼ CUP PEANUT OIL
- 1 TABLESPOON RICE VINEGAR
- 1 TABLESPOON MINCED FRESH GINGER
- 1 TABLESPOON MINCED CELERY
- 1 TABLESPOON SOY SAUCE
- 1 TEASPOON TOMATO PASTE
- 1½ TEASPOONS SUGAR
- 1 TEASPOON FRESH LEMON JUICE
- ½ TEASPOON KOSHER SALT
- BLACK PEPPER, TO TASTE

KOHLRABI SLAW WITH MISO DRESSING

YIELD: 4 SERVINGS / **ACTIVE TIME**: 30 MINUTES / **TOTAL TIME**: 30 MINUTES

The Asian flavors of this coleslaw are just perfect alongside grilled meat, especially pork and chicken. If you have a mandoline, it will make quick work of the vegetables. A hand grater will also work.

1. Place the white miso paste, vinegar, sesame oil, ginger, soy sauce, peanut oil, sesame seeds, and maple syrup in a mixing bowl and stir to combine. Set aside.

2. Place the kohlrabies, carrots, and cilantro in a separate bowl and stir to combine.

3. Drizzle a few spoonfuls of the dressing into the coleslaw and stir until evenly coated. Taste, add more dressing if desired, top with the pistachios, and serve.

INGREDIENTS:

1	TABLESPOON WHITE MISO PASTE
1	TABLESPOON RICE VINEGAR
1	TEASPOON SESAME OIL
1	TEASPOON MINCED GINGER
1	TEASPOON SOY SAUCE
3	TABLESPOONS PEANUT OIL
1	TABLESPOON SESAME SEEDS
1	TEASPOON REAL MAPLE SYRUP
3	KOHLRABIES, PEELED AND JULIENNED OR GRATED
2	CARROTS, PEELED AND JULIENNED OR GRATED
¼	CUP CHOPPED FRESH CILANTRO
¼	CUP SHELLED PISTACHIOS, CRUSHED

MISO-MAPLE TURNIPS

YIELD: 2 TO 4 SERVINGS / **ACTIVE TIME:** 30 MINUTES / **TOTAL TIME:** 30 MINUTES

Combining miso and maple syrup makes for magic. Get the two working together, and you have a savory-sweet topper that seems to bring out the best of whatever you have chosen to adorn with it, from scallops to cauliflower.. Here, the tang of the caramelized turnip is a perfect foil for this brilliant pair.

1. Place the bok choy in a 12-inch sauté pan and add the water. Raise the heat to high, cover the pan, and steam the bok choy for a few minutes. Remove the lid and continue to cook until all of the water has boiled off, about 1 minute more.

2. Remove the pan from heat and season with the salt and pepper. Transfer the bok choy to a plate and set aside.

3. Add the oil to the pan and warm over high heat. Add the turnips and reduce the heat to medium. Cook the turnips until the cut sides have browned, about 5 minutes per side.

4. While the turnips are cooking, combine the miso, maple syrup, and soy sauce.

5. When the turnips are fully browned and tender, pour the miso-maple mixture over them and toss to coat. Cook for another minute and then remove from heat.

6. Place the turnips on top of the bok choy and serve.

INGREDIENTS:

½	LB. BOK CHOY, QUARTERED
3	TABLESPOONS WATER
	SALT AND PEPPER, TO TASTE
1	TABLESPOON OLIVE OIL
¾	LB. SMALL PURPLE-TOP TURNIPS, QUARTERED
1	TABLESPOON WHITE MISO
1	TABLESPOON REAL MAPLE SYRUP
1	TEASPOON SOY SAUCE

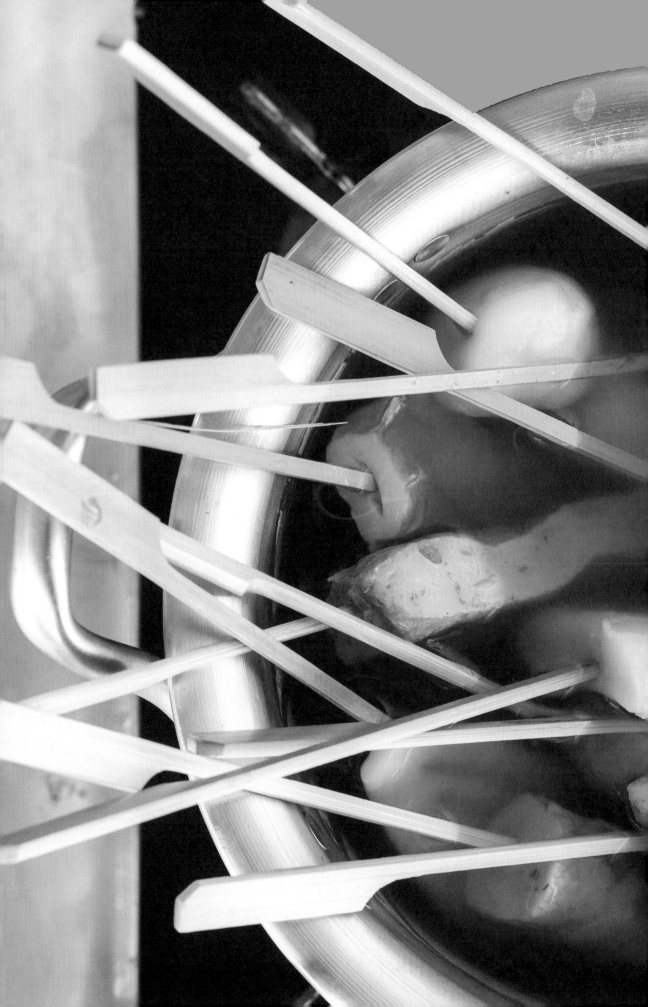

SOUPS & STEWS

N̶o matter where you are, soups and stews are the epitome of comfort food, imparting both warmth and satisfaction. The range of soups and stews featured in this chapter reflects both the similarities and differences found in various Asian cuisines, from light seaweed-based dashis to rich broths thick with coconut milk to fiery bowls of pork belly and kimchi. And, of course, ramen.

CLASSIC TONKOTSU RAMEN
WITH CHASHU PORK & SOY EGG

YIELD: 4 SERVINGS / **ACTIVE TIME:** 1 HOUR / **TOTAL TIME:** 10 HOURS

If part of the description of a ramen dish includes "tonkotsu," you know that it will feature a creamy and rich pork broth (kotteri). For this preparation, feel free to add any vegetables you desire.

1. Add the Tonkotsu (broth) to a large pot over high heat. Right when bubbles appear before boiling, stir in the soy sauce and salt.

2. Meanwhile, spoon 2 tablespoons of Shio Tare into 4 serving bowls.

3. Add the oil to a skillet over medium heat and warm up the pork slices, 2 minutes per side.

4. Cook the noodles and drain well.

5. Ladle roughly 2 cups of hot broth over the tare in each serving bowl.

6. Divide the cooked noodles into 4 servings and place in a bowl with the seasoned broth. Using chopsticks, gently stir the noodles to distribute the tare into the noodles and broth.

7. Garnish each bowl with the sliced pork, ½ Soy Sauce Egg, scallions, sesame seeds, and, if using, Black Garlic Oil and Red Pickled Ginger. Serve immediately.

BLACK GARLIC OIL

1. Add the garlic and canola oil to a skillet over medium heat. Stirring frequently, carefully cook the garlic until very dark brown but not burnt, about 20 to 30 minutes. Remove from heat and let the garlic cool in the oil to room temperature; the garlic will continue to darken, looking black.

2. Transfer the oil-garlic mixture to a blender, add the sesame oil, and blend until smooth.

3. Store in an airtight container for a week.

INGREDIENTS:

8	CUPS TONKOTSU (SEE RECIPE)
1	TEASPOON SOY SAUCE
1	PINCH KOSHER SALT
½	CUP SHIO TARE (SEE RECIPE)
1	TABLESPOON CANOLA OIL
8–12	SLICES CHASHU PORK BELLY (SEE PAGE 419), FOR GARNISH
18	OZ. FRESH RAMEN NOODLES (SEE PAGE 223) OR 12 OZ. DRY STORE BOUGHT
2-4	SOY SAUCE EGGS (SEE PAGE 92)
¼	CUP SLICED SCALLIONS
	TOASTED SESAME SEEDS, FOR GARNISH
2	TABLESPOONS BLACK GARLIC OIL (SEE RECIPE; OPTIONAL)
¼	CUP RED PICKLED GINGER (SEE RECIPE; OPTIONAL)

BLACK GARLIC OIL

½	CUP GARLIC CLOVES
½	CUP CANOLA OIL
⅓	CUP SESAME OIL

Continued . . .

RED PICKLED GINGER

1. In a bowl, combine all of the ingredients, except the ginger, and mix well, making sure to dissolve the sugar.

2. Add the ginger to the pickling liquid, mix well, and transfer to an airtight jar or container. Refrigerate for 2 weeks before using.

TONKOTSU

1. Place the pork bones and feet in a large stockpot, cover with tap water, and bring to a boil. Once boiling, remove from heat, drain, and wash the pork parts under cold water to remove any impurities.

2. Place the blanched pork parts and onion in a clean, large pot and cover with the purified water; the bones should be covered by 2 inches of water. Bring to a boil, lower the heat to medium, and gently boil for 8 hours. Continuously skim off and discard any brown foam and impurities that rise to the top. Add water as needed to keep the bones covered.

3. After 8 hours, increase the heat to high and bring to a rapid boil, stirring the bones around. Continue to cook for another hour, so there is no more cartilage or soft tissue left around the bones.

4. Strain the stock and discard the bones. Let cool completely at room temperature. Refrigerate covered until needed; it will keep for up to 1 week, and frozen for a month.

SHIO TARE

1. In a pot, bring the water to a boil. Add the mirin and sake and simmer for 1 to 2 minutes.

2. Reduce the heat to medium-low, add the kombu and mushroom, cover the pot, and simmer for 1 hour.

3. Remove from heat, add the salt, and stir to dissolve. Let cool to room temperature.

4. Strain through cheesecloth or a very fine strainer. Refrigerate for 3 to 4 weeks, or freeze for 3 months.

INGREDIENTS:

RED PICKLED GINGER

1	CUP UMEZU OR UMEBOSHI VINEGAR
¼	CUP MIRIN
1½	TABLESPOONS SUGAR
1½	TABLESPOONS KOSHER SALT
½	LB. GINGER, PEELED AND CUT INTO 2-INCH-LONG MATCHSTICKS

TONKOTSU

3	LBS. PORK BONES, CUT INTO 2-INCH PIECES
2	LBS. PORK FEET, HALVED (PORK SHANK WORKS IF FEET AREN'T AVAILABLE)
1	ONION, PEELED AND HALVED
16	CUPS PURIFIED WATER

SHIO TARE

1	CUP WATER
¼	CUP MIRIN
1	CUP SAKE
	4-INCH PIECE KOMBU
1	DRIED SHIITAKE MUSHROOM
½	CUP SEA SALT

RAMEN NOODLES

YIELD: 6 SERVINGS / **ACTIVE TIME:** 1 HOUR / **TOTAL TIME:** 2 HOURS

Ramen noodles can be stored by wrapping each noodle pile in plastic wrap or by placing it in a resealable bag. They should be covered and refrigerated for 4 to 5 days or frozen for 3 months. The noodles can be cooked frozen to make a bowl of comforting ramen soup when needed.

1. In a small bowl, combine the water and kansui powder and mix until the powder is dissolved. Add the salt and stir to dissolve.

2. In the bowl of a stand mixer fitted with the dough hook, combine the flours.

3. On low speed, slowly add the liquid. Continue to mix until a stiff dough forms, about 10 to 12 minutes. If the dough is too dry, add up to 2 tablespoons of cold water, a little at a time until the dough comes together. If you don't have a stand mixer, make by hand, mixing the wet ingredients into the dry; knead on a flour-dusted surface until the dough forms and is very stiff, about 20 to 30 minutes.

4. Remove the dough from the mixer, transfer to a lightly floured surface, and knead by hand for 5 minutes, until the dough becomes very stiff.

5. Place the dough in a clean bowl and cover with plastic wrap. Set aside and let rest for 1 hour at room temperature.

6. Line a sheet pan with parchment paper and dust with the cornstarch.

7. Split the dough into 8 equal balls. Sprinkle the balls with a little cornstarch and flatten into patties. Make sure to keep the dough covered when not working with it.

8. Using a rolling pin, roll out each dough patty as thin as you can.

9. Run the rolled-out sheets of dough through a pasta machine for the desired noodle width of the noodle. Use cornstarch if the dough sticks. If you don't have a pasta machine, use a dusted rolling pin to roll the dough out into very thin squares, and then dust the rolled-out dough with cornstarch and layer; using a knife, trim and discard the edges and cut the layered, sheeted dough into thin strips.

10. Once the noodles are made, toss them with a little cornstarch and set them in individual piles on the parchment-lined sheet pan.

11. When ready, cook the noodles in a pot of salted boiling water for 45 to 60 seconds. Drain immediately and serve in a ramen bowl.

12. To store the prepared noodles, wrap each noodle pile in plastic wrap or place in a resealable bag. Refrigerate covered for 4 to 5 days, or frozen for 3 months; noodles can be cooked straight from the freezer.

INGREDIENTS:

1	CUP COLD WATER
1¼	TEASPOONS KANSUI POWDER
1½	TEASPOONS KOSHER SALT
2	CUPS 00 FLOUR
2	CUPS BREAD FLOUR
	CORNSTARCH, FOR DUSTING

SHOYU RAMEN WITH CHASHU CHICKEN, SPINACH, SOY EGG & CHILI OIL

YIELD: 4 SERVINGS / **ACTIVE TIME:** 1 HOUR / **TOTAL TIME:** 24 HOURS

This soy-based broth variety of ramen is from Yokohama in the Kanto region of central Japan. If you finish all of your noodles, but have leftover broth, you can ask for kaedama, which is an additional helping of noodles.

1. Add the broth to a large pot over high heat. Right when it begins to boil, add the spinach, blanch for 30 seconds until just wilted, and use a slotted spoon or kitchen spider to remove the spinach and set aside. Keep the chicken broth hot.

2. Spoon 2 tablespoons of the Shoyu Tare into 4 serving bowls.

3. Cook the noodles and drain well.

4. Ladle roughly 2 cups of hot broth over the tare in each serving bowl.

5. Divide the cooked noodles into 4 servings and place in a bowl with the seasoned broth. Using chopsticks, gently stir the noodles to distribute the tare into the noodles and broth.

6. Top each bowl with the chicken, spinach, Soy Sauce Eggs, Rayu, and scallions. Serve immediately.

RAMEN CHICKEN BROTH

1. Place the chicken bones and feet in a large pot, cover with the water, and bring to a boil. Once boiling, strain and discard the water.

2. Place the parts in a clean pot, cover with the water, and bring to a simmer over medium heat. Cover and simmer for roughly 6 hours.

3. Strain the broth, let cool at room temperature, and refrigerate overnight.

4. Skim the fat that has hardened on top of the broth; the fat can be saved for seasoning.

5. Store the broth covered until needed.

SHOYU TARE

1. Add all of the ingredients to a saucepan over medium heat, bring to a simmer, and continue to simmer for 12 minutes.

2. Strain with a fine strainer and let cool at room temperature. Refrigerate covered for up to 1 month.

INGREDIENTS:

1	QT. RAMEN CHICKEN BROTH (SEE RECIPE)
4	CUPS SPINACH
	SHOYU TARE (SEE RECIPE)
18	OZ. FRESH RAMEN NOODLES (SEE PAGE 223) OR 12 OZ. DRY STORE BOUGHT
4-8	SLICES CHASHU CHICKEN (SEE PAGE 420)
2-4	SOY SAUCE EGGS (SEE PAGE 92)
4	TEASPOONS RAYU (SEE PAGE 234)
¼	CUP SLICED SCALLIONS

RAMEN CHICKEN BROTH

4	LBS. CHICKEN BONES
1	LB. CHICKEN FEET
¾	GALLON WATER, DIVIDED

SHOYU TARE

1¼	CUPS SOY SAUCE
½	CUP SAKE
½	CUP MIRIN
3	GARLIC CLOVES, CRUSHED
	2-INCH PIECE GINGER, PEELED AND CUT
1	TABLESPOON BROWN SUGAR

MISO RAMEN WITH GINGER CHICKEN, WOOD EAR MUSHROOMS, BEAN SPROUTS & SOY EGG

YIELD: 4 SERVINGS / ACTIVE TIME: 1 HOUR / TOTAL TIME: 9 HOURS

Chili oil can be added to help cut through the unctuous goodness of this deeply layered miso-broth ramen. The addition of soy sauce–flavored eggs provides another dynamic of texture and taste.

1. Add the Creamy Chicken Ramen Broth to a large pot over high heat, and right as it is about to boil, blanch the bean sprouts for 20 seconds. Using a slotted spoon or kitchen spider, remove the bean sprouts and set aside. Keep the broth hot to serve.

2. Spoon 2 tablespoons of the Miso Tare or Spicy Miso Tare into 4 serving bowls.

3. Bring another pot of water to a boil, cook the noodles, and drain well.

4. Ladle roughly 2 cups of hot broth over the tare in each serving bowl.

5. Divide the cooked noodles into 4 servings and place in a bowl with the seasoned broth. Using chopsticks, gently stir the noodles to distribute the tare into the noodles and broth.

6. Garnish each bowl with the Ginger Chicken, bean sprouts, mushrooms, scallions, and sesame seeds. If desired, add the spice element or the Soy Sauce Eggs.

CREAMY CHICKEN RAMEN BROTH

1. Add the chicken bones and feet to a large pot, add enough water to cover by 2 inches, and bring to a boil. Once boiling, strain and discard the water.

2. Place the blanched chicken parts in a clean, large pot, add enough water to cover by 2 inches, and bring to a boil. Once boiling, lower the heat to medium, cover, and boil for 6 to 8 hours, until the broth is creamy white.

3. Add the carrot, onion, scallions, garlic, and ginger and continue to gently boil for 1 hour. If the broth looks overreduced, add water as needed.

INGREDIENTS:

8	CUPS CREAMY CHICKEN RAMEN BROTH (SEE RECIPE)
2	CUPS BEAN SPROUTS
⅓	CUP MISO TARE OR SPICY MIRO TARE (SEE RECIPES)
18	OZ. FRESH RAMEN NOODLES (SEE PAGE 223) OR DRY STORE BOUGHT
	GINGER CHICKEN (SEE PAGE 421), TO TASTE
⅓	CUP WOOD EAR MUSHROOMS, SOAKED, DRAINED, AND JULIENNED
¼	CUP SLICED SCALLIONS
1	TABLESPOON TOASTED SESAME SEEDS
	RAYU (SEE PAGE 234, OPTIONAL)
2-4	SOY SAUCE EGGS (SEE PAGE 92, OPTIONAL)

CREAMY CHICKEN RAMEN BROTH

4	LBS. CHICKEN BONES
1	LB. CHICKEN FEET
½	CARROT, SLICED
½	ONION, SLICED
8	SCALLIONS, WHITE PARTS ONLY
12	GARLIC CLOVES, PEELED
	2-INCH PIECE GINGER, SLICED

4. Strain the broth, let cool, and then refrigerate until fully chilled. Once chilled, skim the hardened fat off the top.

5. Store the broth covered until needed.

MISO TARE

1. In a bowl, combine all of the ingredients and whisk well.

2. Refrigerate in an airtight container for up to 3 months.

SPICY MISO TARE

1. In a bowl, combine all of the ingredients and whisk well.

2. Refrigerate in an airtight container for up to 3 months.

MISO TARE

¼	CUP RED MISO
¼	CUP WHITE MISO
¼	CUP SALT
¼	CUP WATER
3	TABLESPOONS JAPANESE SESAME PASTE
2	TABLESPOONS SESAME OIL
1	TABLESPOON UNSEASONED RICE VINEGAR

SPICY MISO TARE

⅓	CUP GOCHUJANG OR CHILI PASTE
¼	CUP RED MISO
¼	CUP WHITE MISO
1	TABLESPOON GRATED GINGER
¼	CUP SALT
¼	CUP WATER
3	TABLESPOONS JAPANESE SESAME PASTE
2	TABLESPOONS SESAME OIL
1	TABLESPOON UNSEASONED RICE VINEGAR

SHIO RAMEN WITH GINGER CHICKEN, BAMBOO, BOK CHOY & SOY EGG

YIELD: 4 SERVINGS / ACTIVE TIME: 1 HOUR / TOTAL TIME: 3 HOURS

Originating in Hakodate, Japan, shio ramen is the oldest ramen variety. The broth is usually chicken or seafood-based and is lighter and saltier than the pork-enriched tonkotsu. Menma, seasoned bamboo, is a common ramen condiment.

1. Add the Creamy Chicken Ramen Broth to a large pot over high heat, and right as it is about to boil, blanch the bok choy for 20 seconds. Using a slotted spoon or kitchen spider, remove the bok choy and set aside. Keep the broth hot to serve.

2. Spoon 2 tablespoons of the Shio Tare into 4 serving bowls.

3. Bring another pot of water to a boil, cook the noodles, and drain well.

4. Ladle roughly 2 cups of hot broth over the tare in each serving bowl.

5. Divide the cooked noodles into 4 servings and place in a bowl with the seasoned broth. Using chopsticks, gently stir the noodles to distribute the tare into the noodles and broth.

6. Garnish each bowl with the Ginger Chicken, bok choy, Menma, Soy Sauce Eggs, and scallions. If desired, drizzle yuzu juice and sprinkle togarashi.

SHIO TARE

1. In a pot, bring water to a boil. Add sake and mirin and simmer for 2 minutes. Reduce heat to low, add kombu and mushrooms, cover, and gently simmer for 1 hour.

2. Add salt to the pot and stir to dissolve. Remove broth from heat and let cool at room temperature.

3. Strain through cheesecloth and refrigerate in an airtight container for up to 3 weeks.

INGREDIENTS:

8	CUPS CREAMY CHICKEN RAMEN BROTH (SEE PAGE 228)
4	BABY BOK CHOY, QUARTERED
⅓	CUP SHIO TARE (SEE RECIPE)
18	OZ. FRESH RAMEN NOODLES (SEE PAGE 223) OR DRY STORE BOUGHT
	GINGER CHICKEN (SEE PAGE 421)
⅓	CUP MENMA (SEE RECIPE)
2-4	SOY SAUCE EGGS (SEE PAGE 92)
¼	CUP SLICED SCALLIONS
2	TABLESPOONS YUZU JUICE (OPTIONAL)
1	TEASPOON SHICHIMI TOGARASHI (SEE PAGE 146; OPTIONAL)

SHIO TARE

1	CUP WATER
1	CUP SAKE
¼	CUP MIRIN
	4-INCH PIECE KOMBU
1½	OZ. DRIED SHIITAKE MUSHROOMS
½	CUP KOSHER SALT

AWASE RAMEN DASHI

1. Using a knife, make slits in the kombu. Place in a pot of water and bring to a simmer over medium heat. Lower the heat and gently simmer, covered, for 15 minutes. Remove from the heat and let the kombu steep for another 15 minutes.

2. Remove the kombu, add the bonito flakes, bring back to a boil, and then reduce the heat to low, simmer for 30 seconds, and remove from the heat. Let steep for 12 to 15 minutes, until the bonito flakes sink to the bottom.

3. Strain through cheesecloth and refrigerate in an airtight container for up to 1 week.

MENMA

1. In a pot, combine the Awase Ramen Dashi, soy sauce, sesame oil, sake, sugar, and salt and mix well. Add the bamboo shoots and bring to a boil. Lower the heat to medium and cook for roughly 20 minutes, until most of the liquid has been absorbed and reduced.

2. Serve immediately, or let cool and refrigerate covered for up to 1 week.

AWASE RAMEN DASHI

	5-INCH PIECE KOMBU
8	CUPS WATER
4	CUPS DRIED BONITO FLAKES

MENMA

2	CUPS AWASE RAMEN DASHI (SEE RECIPE)
1	TABLESPOON SOY SAUCE
1	TABLESPOON SESAME OIL
1	TABLESPOON SAKE
1	TABLESPOON SUGAR
1	TEASPOON SALT
1	LB. FRESH BAMBOO SHOOTS, HALVED LENGTHWISE AND CUT INTO STRIPS

RAYU

This is a spicy and smoky Japanese condiment that is customarily added to soups, like ramen, or vegetable dishes, thought it works on anything you deem fit.

1. In a small saucepan over medium heat, combine ¼ cup of sesame oil, and the garlic, ginger, and scallions and cook, stirring frequently, until the oil starts to shimmer. Lower the heat and gently simmer for another 3 minutes. Remove the pan from heat and transfer the mixture to a heat-safe bowl.

2. Add the Shichimi Togarashi and cayenne, stir to combine well, and let cool at room temperature.

3. Add the remaining sesame oil, mix well, and strain into an airtight container. Store in the refrigerator for up to 3 months.

INGREDIENTS:

½ CUP SESAME OIL, DIVIDED

1 TABLESPOON MINCED GARLIC

1 TABLESPOON MINCED GINGER

1 TABLESPOON MINCED SCALLION WHITES

1 TABLESPOON SHICHIMI TOGARASHI (SEE PAGE 146)

½ TABLESPOON CAYENNE

SPICY PEANUT RAMEN

YIELD: 4 SERVINGS / ACTIVE TIME: 30 MINUTES / TOTAL TIME: 24 HOURS

Spicy ramen with peanut butter is a unique combination that works because the nutty creaminess balances the heat. Consider using natural versus heavily processed peanut butter, since it carries a more concentrated peanut flavor. The mushroom dashi can be used as a rich umami base for any vegetarian ramen.

1. Add the oil to a sauté pan over medium-high heat. Once the oil begins to shimmer, add the garlic and ginger, stirring frequently so as not to burn, roughly 1 minute. Add the Chili Paste and mix well. Add the Shiitake Dashi and coconut milk and bring to a rapid simmer.

2. Reduce h the eat to low, and add the peanut butter and brown sugar, whisking to incorporate. Gently simmer for 12 to 14 minutes.

3. Bring a pot of water to a boil, cook the noodles, and drain well.

4. Remove the broth from heat, add the soy sauce and lime juice, and adjust the seasoning with the salt as needed.

5. Ladle roughly 2 cups of hot broth into 4 serving bowls.

6. Divide the cooked noodles into 4 servings and place in a bowl with the broth. Using chopsticks, gently stir the noodles.

7. Garnish with the tofu, cilantro, peanuts, and scallions, and anything else you desire.

SHIITAKE DASHI

1. Gently heat the water. As you wait, place the mushrooms in a large container with a lid.

2. Once the water is warm, pour it over the mushrooms and refrigerate covered overnight.

3. Strain through cheesecloth; press on the mushrooms to extract as much umami liquid as possible.

4. Refrigerate covered for up to 1 week.

INGREDIENTS:

1	TABLESPOON CANOLA OIL
4	GARLIC CLOVES, MINCED
1	TABLESPOON MINCED GINGER
1	TABLESPOON CHILI GARLIC SAUCE (SEE PAGE 180)
5¼	CUPS SHIITAKE DASHI (SEE RECIPE)
14	OZ. COCONUT MILK
½	CUP SUGAR-FREE PEANUT BUTTER
2	TABLESPOONS BROWN SUGAR
18	OZ. FRESH RAMEN NOODLES (SEE PAGE 223) OR 12 OZ. DRY STORE BOUGHT NOODLES
2	TABLESPOONS SOY SAUCE
	JUICE OF 3 LIMES
	SALT, AS NEEDED
1	CUP DICED SILKEN TOFU, FOR GARNISH
¼	CUP CHOPPED CILANTRO, FOR GARNISH
¼	CUP CHOPPED DRY-ROASTED PEANUTS FOR GARNISH
¼	CUP SLICED SCALLIONS, FOR GARNISH

SHIITAKE DASHI

9	CUPS WATER
3	OZ. DRIED SHIITAKE MUSHROOMS

VEGETARIAN CURRY RAMEN WITH PEAS, CARROTS & SIX-MINUTE EGG

YIELD: 4 SERVINGS / **ACTIVE TIME:** 45 MINUTES / **TOTAL TIME:** 45 MINUTES

There are few vegetarian ramen options. Chef Brian provides a comforting and tasty version that goes head-to-head with traditional ramen preparations.

1. In a food processor or blender, combine the garlic, ginger, shallot, brown sugar, curry powder, coriander, turmeric, Chili Garlic Sauce, and salt and blend until smooth.

2. Add 1 tablespoon of oil to a pot over medium-high heat. Once the oil begins to shimmer, add the curry mixture and cook for 1 minute, stirring well. Add the Shiitake Dashi, stir well, and right before it comes to a boil, add the soy sauce. Keep the broth warm for serving.

3. Add the remaining tablespoon of oil to a sauté pan over medium-high heat. Once the oil begins to shimmer, add the carrots and cook, stirring frequently, until they have softened, about 3 minutes. Add the peas and cook until heated through. Remove the pan from the heat and set aside.

4. Bring a pot of water to a boil, cook the noodles, and drain well.

5. Ladle roughly 2 cups of hot broth into 4 serving bowls.

6. Divide the cooked noodles into 4 servings and place in a bowl with the broth. Using chopsticks, gently stir the noodles.

7. Top each bowl with the carrots, peas, Six-Minute Eggs, nori strips, scallions, and daikon sprouts or shaved radish.

INGREDIENTS:

3	GARLIC CLOVES
	2-INCH PIECE GINGER, PEELED
1	SHALLOT
1	TABLESPOON BROWN SUGAR
1½	TABLESPOONS CURRY POWDER
1	TEASPOON CORIANDER, GROUND
½	TEASPOON TURMERIC, GROUND
1	TABLESPOON CHILI GARLIC SAUCE (SEE PAGE 180)
½	TEASPOON SALT
2	TABLESPOONS CANOLA OIL, DIVDED
8	CUPS SHIITAKE DASHI (PAGE 235)
1	TABLESPOON SOY SAUCE
2	CARROTS, DICED
1	CUP PEAS, FRESH OR FROZEN
18	OZ. FRESH RAMEN NOODLES (SEE PAGE 223) OR DRY STORE BOUGHT
2-4	SIX-MINUTE EGGS (SEE RECIPE)
1	NORI SHEET, CUT INTO 3-INCH STRIPS
¼	SLICED SCALLIONS
	DAIKON SPROUTS OR SHAVED RADISH, FOR GARNISH

SIX-MINUTE EGG

1. Bring a pot of water to a boil. Gently add the eggs into the boiling water, stirring the eggs for 2 minutes in the water as it boils.

2. Continue to gently boil the eggs for another 4 minutes. After 6 minutes of total cooking time, use a slotted spoon or kitchen spider to remove the eggs from the boiling water, and shock them in an ice bath.

3. Let the soft-boiled eggs rest in the ice bath for 8 to 10 minutes until completely chilled. Remove the eggs from the ice bath and refrigerate until needed.

4. When needed, carefully peel each egg and cut it in half.

SIX-MINUTE EGG

6-12 EGGS

YUKGAEJANG

YIELD: 6 SERVINGS / ACTIVE TIME: 30 MINUTES / TOTAL TIME: 1 HOUR AND 30 MINUTES

This spicy beef and green onion soup is a Korean favorite because of its believed health benefits and intense heat.

1. Combine the beef, onions, 4 garlic cloves, mushrooms, and water in a large pot over high heat and bring to a boil. Lower the heat, cover, and simmer for 1 hour. It is important to skim the top of the liquid as needed. If the stock boils off, add water to maintain 3 quarts of stock in the pot at all times.

2. Check the meat for doneness by seeing if it splits when probed with a fork or knife.

3. Strain the stock and discard the onions, garlic, and mushrooms. Cool the beef in the strained stock. Once cooled, remove the beef and shred into chunks.

4. Add the canola and sesame oils to a pot over medium heat.

5. Mince 10 cloves of garlic and add them to the pot, gently frying and making sure not to let the garlic turn golden. Add the gochugaru and stir, cooking to release the oils but making sure not to burn.

6. Remove from heat and add the shredded beef, scallions, soy sauce and salt and stir. Add the stock, fernbrake, and bean sprouts, bring to a boil, and then cook over medium heat for 10 minutes, until the vegetables are cooked through, but not overcooked.

7. Add the black pepper and adjust the seasoning with the salt, as needed.

8. About 2 minutes before serving, add the eggs, and let set.

9. If using the glass noodles, place them at the bottom of the serving bowls and then ladle the soup on top.

INGREDIENTS:

1½	LBS. FLANK STEAK
1½	YELLOW ONIONS, HALVED
14	GARLIC CLOVES, DIVIDED
4-6	DRIED SHIITAKE MUSHROOMS
4	QTS. WATER
1	TABLESPOON CANOLA OIL
2	TABLESPOONS SESAME OIL
⅓	CUP GOCHUGARU
10	SCALLIONS, CUT INTO 2-INCH PIECES
⅓	CUP SOY SAUCE
1	TABLESPOON KOSHER SALT, PLUS MORE TO TASTE
2	CUPS FERNBRAKE
2	CUPS BEAN SPROUTS
1	TEASPOON BLACK PEPPER
4	EGGS, BEATEN
	GLASS NOODLES (OPTIONAL)

KIMCHI JJIGAE

YIELD: 4 SERVINGS / **ACTIVE TIME:** 30 MINUTES / **TOTAL TIME:** 1 HOUR

The longer the kimchi is fermented, the better for this spicy, warming comfort food. Although the final touch of dashida or hondashi powder, or fish sauce, is small in amount, it is essential—think of it as the secret ingredient.

1. Add the canola oil to a large pot over medium-high heat. Once the oil begins to shimmer, add the pork, sear one side of the pieces, and season with a pinch of salt. Turn down the heat to render fat from the pork belly, about 2 minutes.

2. Add the kimchi and stir, cooking for 3 to 5 minutes to caramelize.

3. Add the sesame oil, garlic, and gochugaru and cook over medium heat for 2 minutes, stirring frequently so as not to burn the garlic and chili flakes.

4. Add the stock and brine, cover, and simmer for 45 minutes.

5. Add the tofu and scallions and simmer uncovered for 10 minutes.

6. Add the sugar, if using, and adjust the seasoning with the salt and one of the flavoring agents.

INGREDIENTS:

½   TABLESPOON CANOLA OIL

1   LB. PORK BELLY, SLICED INTO ¼-INCH PIECES

     SALT, TO TASTE

1¼   LBS. KIMCHI, CUT INTO 1-INCH PIECES (SEE PAGE 148)

1   TEASPOON SESAME OIL

1   LB. GARLIC, MINCED

1   TABLESPOON GOCHUGARU

1   QT. DASHI OR ANCHOVY STOCK (SEE PAGE 293 OR 688)

1   LB. FIRM TOFU, CUT TO YOUR PREFERENCE

¼   CUP KIMCHI BRINE

2   SCALLIONS, CUT INTO 1-INCH PIECES

½   TEASPOON SUGAR (OPTIONAL)

     DASH OF DASHIDA OR HONDASHI POWDER, OR FISH SAUCE

TOM YUM GOONG

YIELD: 4 SERVINGS / ACTIVE TIME: 30 MINUTES / TOTAL TIME: 30 MINUTES

This spicy and sour Thai soup is typically prepared with shrimp and rice noodles can be added to make it a more filling meal.

1. Trim the leafy part of the lemongrass and remove the outer toughest part. Cut off the bulb end and cut in quarters. Smash/-bruise with the back of a knife or with a heavy object.

2. In a small pot, bring the Chicken Stock, bouillon cube, lemongrass, galangal, lime leaves, and shallot to a boil, and simmer for 15 minutes.

3. Add the mushrooms, tomato, Thai Chili Jam, fish sauce, dried chilies, and shrimp (if using) and simmer for 2 to 3 minutes, until the shrimp is cooked through.

4. Right before serving add the bird's eye chilies, lime juice, cilantro, and scallions and adjust the seasoning with the salt, if needed.

5. Serve immediately. Traditionally the herbs and leaves are left in; however, you can remove them before serving.

THAI CHILI JAM

1. In a dry wok or sauté pan over medium heat, add the chilies and toast for 5 to 8 minutes, making sure not to burn them. Reserve on a paper towel–lined plate.

2. Add 1 cup of oil to the hot pan and fry the garlic over medium-high heat until light brown and crispy, 6 to 8 minutes. Once crispy, use a slotted spoon to transfer them to the same paper towel–lined plate.

3. Using the same oil, fry the shallots and shrimp until light golden. Once crispy, use a slotted spoon to transfer them to the same paper towel–lined plate. Save the fry oil in the pan.

4. Transfer all of the ingredients on the paper towel–lined plate to a food processor, add the shrimp paste, and blend until it forms a thick paste.

Continued . . .

INGREDIENTS:

1	STALK LEMONGRASS, BRUISED
1½	QUARTS CHICKEN STOCK (SEE PAGE 680)
½	CHICKEN BOUILLON CUBE
	3-INCH PIECE GALANGAL, CUT INTO COINS
5	KAFFIR LIME LEAVES, TORN AND BRUISED
1	SHALLOT, SLICED
1	CUP SLICED MUSHROOMS (BUTTON, STRAW, OR OYSTER)
1	ROMA TOMATO, QUARTERED AND SEEDED
3	TABLESPOONS THAI CHILI JAM (SEE RECIPE)
¼	CUP FISH SAUCE
2	SMALL DRIED CHILIES, TORN AND SEEDED
12-14	SHRIMP (OPTIONAL)
2	BIRD'S EYE CHILIES, STEMMED AND BRUISED
¼	CUP LIME JUICE
¼	CUP CILANTRO LEAVES
1	CUP SLICED SCALLIONS
	SALT

THAI CHILI JAM

8-10	DRIED THAI LONG CHILIES, SEEDED
1½	CUPS VEGETABLE OIL, DIVIDED, PLUS MORE AS NEEDED
1	CUP THINLY SLICED GARLIC CLOVES
4	SHALLOTS, THINLY SLICED
¼	CUP DRIED SHRIMP

5. Using the same pan with the oil in it, stir in the prepared paste, sugar, Tamarind Water, and fish sauce, and salt and cook over medium heat, stirring occasionally so all of the ingredients are cooked together and blended, 15 to 20 minutes, or until a loose jam consistency is achieved.

6. Refrigerate in an airtight container for up to a month.

TAMARIND WATER

1. In a bowl, break the tamarind paste into chunks, cover with the boiling water, cover, and let steep for 30 minutes.

2. Using your hands or a masher, break down the pulp further, and let stand for another 15 minutes.

3. Strain the mixture through a fine mesh sieve and scrape the "good stuff" from the underside of the sieve. Discard the stringy material. Mix the juice and pulp to incorporate.

4. Refrigerate in an airtight container for up to a month, or freeze for up to 6 months.

PRIK NAM PLA

1. In a bowl, combine all of the ingredients and whisk well. Adjust the seasoning to taste.

2. Refrigerate in an airtight container.

INGREDIENTS:

1	TABLESPOON SHRIMP PASTE
⅓	CUP COCONUT OR PALM SUGAR
⅓	CUP TAMARIND WATER (SEE RECIPE)
2	TABLESPOONS FISH SAUCE
1	TEASPOON SALT

TAMARIND WATER

3	TABLESPOONS SEEDLESS TAMARIND PASTE
3	CUPS BOILING WATER

PRIK NAM PLA

2	TABLESPOONS MINCED BIRD'S EYE CHILIES
2	TABLESPOONS MINCED GARLIC
1	CUP FISH SAUCE
⅓	CUP LIME JUICE

WONTON SOUP

YIELD: 6 SERVINGS / **ACTIVE TIME:** 45 MINUTES / **TOTAL TIME:** 45 MINUTES

Every region in Asia has its own variation of a dumpling soup, but they are commonly prepared with chicken broth. Noodles and vegetables can be added to make it a more filling meal.

1. In a bowl, make the wonton filling by combining the shrimp, pork, scallions, salt, pepper, egg, cornstarch, soy sauce, rice wine, and oil. Mix well and set aside.

2. In a pot, combine the Chicken Stock, garlic, and reserved shrimp shells, bring to a boil, and then simmer for 30 minutes. Strain and season with the salt, to taste.

3. To make the wontons, place 2 teaspoons of filler in the middle of a wrapper and fold in half, sealing with a bit of water on the edges. Bring the nearest corners together and seal the edges together, creating a "tortellini" shape. Repeat until all of the wontons are assembled.

4. Bring a pot of water to a boil and cook the wontons for 3 minutes. Remove with a slotted spoon and combine with the broth. Add the sesame oil and garnish with the scallions before serving.

INGREDIENTS:

30	SHRIMP, SHELLED, DEVEINED, AND COARSELY DICED; RESERVE THE SHELLS
⅓	LB. GROUND PORK
2	SCALLIONS, MINCED, PLUS MORE FOR GARNISH
2	TEASPOONS SALT, PLUS MORE AS NEEDED
¼	TEASPOON BLACK PEPPER
1	EGG, BEATEN
1	TEASPOON CORNSTARCH
1	TABLESPOON LIGHT SOY SAUCE
1	TABLESPOON RICE WINE
½	TEASPOON SESAME OIL
2½	QUARTS CHICKEN STOCK (SEE PAGE 680)
2	GARLIC CLOVES, CRUSHED
	SALT
	WONTON WRAPPERS (SEE PAGE 699)
2	TEASPOONS SESAME OIL

HOT & SOUR SOUP

YIELD: 6 SERVINGS / **ACTIVE TIME:** 30 MINUTES / **TOTAL TIME:** 1 HOUR AND 30 MINUTES

A staple soup that can found in most Chinese restaurants though it is easy to prepare at home. The diversity of the ingredients is what gives it its unique flavors.

1. Soak both mushrooms in separate bowls of water for 1 hour. Discard the water from the wood ears, but save the water from the shiitakes. Remove the stems of the shiitakes and finely julienne. Remove the hard cluster ends of the wood ears and finely julienne.

2. Snip off the hard end (if there is one) of each lily bud, and tie a knot in the middle.

3. In a bowl, combine the pork with 1 teaspoon of dark soy sauce, rice wine, cornstarch, and ¼ teaspoon of sesame oil, mix well, and marinate for 15 minutes or longer.

4. In a large soup pot, combine the saved shiitake soaking liquid, mushrooms, lily buds, jicama, and tofu and bring to a boil.

5. Add the vinegar, ¼ cup of dark soy sauce, chili paste, white pepper, and sugar and bring back to a boil.

6. Add the pork and stir to separate the meat while bringing the soup back to a boil. Add the pickled mustard greens and cornstarch slurry, and continue stirring to mix in the slurry.

7. Turn off the heat and drizzle in the beaten eggs. Let them set up without stirring; strands will form in the hot broth.

8. Adjust seasoning to taste before ladling into bowls, and garnish with the chili oil, sesame oil, and scallions.

INGREDIENTS:

6	DRY SHIITAKE MUSHROOMS
3	DRY WOOD EAR MUSHROOMS
20	DRY LILY BUDS
¼	LB. PORK, THINLY JULIENNED
¼	CUP, DARK SOY SAUCE, PLUS 1 TEASPOON, DIVIDED
1	TEASPOON RICE WINE
1	TEASPOON CORNSTARCH
2¼	TEASPOONS SESAME OIL, DIVIDED
2	QUARTS CHICKEN STOCK (SEE PAGE 680)
1	CUP THINLY JULIENNED JICAMA
1	CUP JULIENNED FIRM TOFU
¾	CUP RED WINE VINEGAR
2-3	TABLESPOONS CHILI PASTE
1	TABLESPOON WHITE PEPPER, PLUS MORE TO TASTE
1	TABLESPOON SUGAR
½	CUP THINLY JULIENNED SZECHUAN PICKLED MUSTARD GREENS
	CORNSTARCH SLURRY (⅓ CUP MIXED WITH EQUAL PART WATER)
3	EGGS, LIGHTLY BEATEN
1	TABLESPOON CHILI OI , FOR GARNISH
2	TEASPOONS SESAME OIL, FOR GARNISH
2	SCALLIONS, MINCED, FOR GARNISH

EGG DROP SOUP

YIELD: 6 SERVINGS / **ACTIVE TIME**: 30 MINUTES / **TOTAL TIME**: 30 MINUTES

This Chinese-soup is traditionally served at the beginning of meals and is sometimes called Egg Flower Soup for how the eggs set while swirled into the broth.

1. In a large pot, bring the Chicken Stock to a boil. Add the carrots and simmer for 4 to 5 minutes before adding the water chestnuts and tofu.

2. Return the soup to a boil, and then stir in enough of the cornstarch mixture that the soup thickens to a velvety consistency.

3. Turn off the heat and gently swirl the beaten eggs into the soup. Do not stir for several minutes; the eggs will cook in the hot soup and form into strands.

4. Adjust the seasoning to taste with the salt and white pepper, and finish with the sesame oil and scallion.

INGREDIENTS:

2   QUARTS CHICKEN STOCK, PLUS ⅓ CUP (SEE PAGE 680)

1   CUP THINLY SLICED AND MINCED CARROTS

6-8   WATER CHESTNUTS, THINLY SLICED

1   PACKAGE SILKEN TOFU, CUT INTO ½-INCH CUBES

¼   CUP CORNSTARCH SLURRY, WITH ⅓ CUP CHICKEN STOCK

3   EGGS, LIGHTLY BEATEN

     SALT, TO TASTE

     WHITE PEPPER, TO TASTE

½   TEASPOON SESAME OIL

1   SCALLION, FINELY CHOPPED

BEEF PHO

YIELD: 4 SERVINGS / ACTIVE TIME: 30 MINUTES / TOTAL TIME: 2 HOURS AND 30 MINUTES

This soup originated from Northern Vietnam and is now synonymous with Vietnamese cuisine. Along with all of the fresh herbs, chili paste and hoisin sauce are great condiments for pho.

1. Clean the bones in cold running water, and then soak for 30 minutes in cold water.

2. Place the bones and brisket in a large pot, add enough water to cover the bones by 1 inch, and bring to a boil. After 10 minutes, strain, discard the water, and rinse the bones and beef; these steps result in a cleaner stock.

3. Add the bones and beef to a clean pot, fill with 3 quarts of water (or more, if possible), bring to a boil, and then reduce the heat and simmer, constantly skimming.

4. Meanwhile, using a broiler, stove top, or skillet, char the onions, shallot, and ginger.

5. In a cheesecloth, combine the charred ingredients with the cloves, cinnamon stick, and star anise. Bundle up the cheesecloth and add it to the simmering stock, along with the parsnips.

6. Simmer broth for another 1½ hours, adding more water or beef broth as the stock evaporates.

7. Strain and reserve the brisket. Let the meat cool, and slice for serving.

8. Add the broth to a clean pot and keep hot; adjust the seasoning with the sugar and salt, as needed.

9. Bring another pot of water to a boil, and the cook noodles until al dente; do not overcook.

10. Place the cooked noodles in bowls and top with a few slices of brisket and the cilantro and scallions. Ladle a generous portion of aromatic broth over the noodles, covering them, and top with the tenderloin slices.

11. Serve immediately with a side plate of bean sprouts, jalapeños, Thai basil, cilantro sprigs, and lime wedges, to be added as desired.

INGREDIENTS:

10	LBS. BEEF BONES
2	LBS. BEEF BRISKET
2	LARGE ONIONS, HALVED
4	SHALLOTS
2	LARGE PIECES GINGER, SKIN ON AND CUT IN HALF
6	CLOVES
1	CINNAMON STICK
8	STAR ANISE
2-3	PARSNIPS, CUT INTO 2-INCH CHUNKS
½	TABLESPOON SUGAR, TO TASTE
	SALT, TO TASTE
½-1	PACKAGE MEDIUM DRY RICE STICK NOODLES, ¼-INCH THICK
1	CUP CILANTRO SPRIGS, AS NEEDED
1	CUP SCALLIONS, BIAS CUT ½- INCH, AS NEEDED
1	LB. BEEF FILLET TENDERLOIN, SLICED AS THIN AS POSSIBLE
1	CUP BEAN SPROUTS, AS NEEDED
½	CUP SLICED JALAPEÑOS, AS NEEDED
1	CUP THAI BASIL, AS NEEDED
1	CUP LIME WEDGES, AS NEEDED

PHO GA

YIELD: 4 SERVINGS / **ACTIVE TIME:** 30 MINUTES / **TOTAL TIME:** 2 HOURS AND 30 MINUTES

A Northern Vietnamese soup that originated in Hanoi, this is made with boiled and shredded chicken.

1. Using a broiler, stove top, or skillet, char the onions and ginger.

2. In a dry pan over medium heat, gently toast the coriander seeds, cinnamon stick, cloves, star anise, and fennel seeds until aromatic.

3. In a large pot, combine the charred ginger and onion, toasted spices, chicken, sugar, and water, bring to a boil, and lower the heat to a gentle simmer. Simmer for 2 hours, being sure to skim any impurities that float to the surface.

4. Using tongs, remove the chicken from the broth and let cool. Once cooled, shred the chicken off the bones and set aside.

5. Strain the broth into a clean pot. After simmering and reducing during cooking, the yield should be 1½ to 2 quarts; adjust with water if needed, or reduce more.

6. Add the salt and fish sauce to the strained broth, and then adjust the seasoning more, if needed; slightly salty, well-seasoned broth is recommended, since adding noodles will dilute the flavor. Keep the broth hot.

7. Bring another pot of water to a boil, and cook the noodles until al dente; do not overcook.

8. Place the cooked noodles in bowls. Arrange the shredded chicken on top of the noodles, and top with the onion and cilantro.

9. Ladle the broth over the top of the noodles and chicken, and garnish with the bean sprouts, jalapeños, Thai basil, and black pepper.

INGREDIENTS:

2	YELLOW ONIONS, HALVED
	3-INCH PIECE GINGER, SLICED THICK
2	TABLESPOONS CORIANDER SEEDS
1	CINNAMON STICK
4	CLOVES
4	STAR ANISE
1	TABLESPOON FENNEL SEEDS
1	WHOLE CHICKEN, HALVED
2	TABLESPOONS SUGAR
	WATER
3	TABLESPOONS SALT, PLUS MORE TO TASTE
1	TEASPOON FISH SAUCE
1	LB. THINK RICE NOODLES
½	CUP THINLY SHAVED ONION, AS NEEDED
1	CUP CILANTRO SPRIGS, AS NEEDED
1	CUP BEAN SPROUTS, FOR GARNISH, AS NEEDED
½	CUP SLICED JALAPEÑOS, FOR GARNISH, AS NEEDED
1	CUP THAI BASIL, FOR GARNISH, AS NEEDED
	FRESHLY CRACKED BLACK PEPPER, FOR GARNISH, TO TASTE
	HOISIN SAUCE, AS NEEDED
	SRIRACHA, AS NEEDED

MIYEOK GUK

YIELD: 6 SERVINGS / **ACTIVE TIME**: 10 MINUTES / **TOTAL TIME**: 1 HOUR AND 30 MINUTES

Rich in calcium and iodine, this Korean seaweed soup is traditionally given to new mothers to help with nursing and overall health. It is also consumed on birthdays as a way to celebrate mothers. The dried seaweed being used in this recipe is also known as "wakame."

1. Rinse and soak the miyeok in cold water for 30 minutes. Drain the seaweed, transfer to a cutting board, and cut into bite-size pieces.

2. In a pot, combine the chopped seaweed and water, cover, and bring to a boil. Add the sliced beef, cover, and simmer for 30 minutes.

3. Add the garlic and fish sauce, reduce the heat to low, and cook for another 20 minutes, until the broth is savory with umami and the beef is tender.

4. Adjust the seasoning with the salt and stir in the sesame oil to finish.

5. Ladle into bowls and serve with rice.

INGREDIENTS:

1	CUP DRIED MIYEOK
8	CUPS WATER
1	LB. BRISKET, CUT INTO THIN 1-INCH STRIPS
4	GARLIC CLOVES, MINCED
1	TABLESPOON FISH SAUCE
	SALT, TO TASTE
1	TEASPOON SESAME OIL

SOONDUBU JJIGAE

YIELD: 6 SERVINGS / **ACTIVE TIME:** 30 MINUTES / **TOTAL TIME:** 1 HOUR

This spicy Korean tofu-and-pork stew is traditionally served in a ceramic pot.

1. In a large pot, combine the Beef Stock, water, daikon, and kelp and bring to a boil. Reduce the heat to low and simmer for another 20 minutes. Strain and reserve.

2. Add the canola oil to a pot over medium-high heat. Once the oil begins to shimmer, lightly sauté the pork belly, garlic, and onion. When the pork fat is translucent, add the gochugaru and stir well to incorporate, about 30 seconds.

3. Add the stock, bring to a boil, reduce the heat, and simmer for 20 to 30 minutes, until the pork belly is tender. Skim off the excess fat that floats to the surface.

4. Add the tofu, scallion, sesame oil, and sugar and simmer for 1 minute. Add the salt and pepper to adjust the seasoning, if necessary.

5. When ready to serve, bring the tofu stew to a boil and drop in the raw egg; it will cook in the hot stew. Serve with rice.

INGREDIENTS:

1½ QUARTS BEEF STOCK (SEE PAGE 679)

1½ QUARTS WATER

1 CUP DAIKON, PEELED AND CUBED

4-INCH PIECE DRIED KELP

2 TABLESPOONS CANOLA OIL

1 LB. PORK BELLY, CUT INTO ¾-INCH X 3-INCH X ¼-INCH PIECES

6 GARLIC CLOVES, MINCED

¼ CUP DICED ONION

3-4 TABLESPOONS GOCHUGARU

2 CUPS CUBED SILKEN TOFU

1 SCALLION, CHOPPED

2 TEASPOONS SESAME OIL

½ TEASPOON SUGAR

SALT, TO TASTE

BLACK PEPPER, TO TASTE

1 EGG

DOENJANG JJIGAE

YIELD: 6 SERVINGS / **ACTIVE TIME:** 15 MINUTES / **TOTAL TIME:** 30 MINUTES

A hearty, earthy stew, doenjang jjigae is arguably Korea's national dish. It has vegetables, garlic, and doenjang (fermented soybean paste), the ingredient that gives the dish its unique flavor. It is best served with a side of white rice.

1. Add the oil to a heavy 2-quart pot or earthenware bowl over medium-high heat. Once the oil begins to shimmer, add the beef and garlic and stir for 2 minutes, until the beef is no longer pink.

2. Add 2 cups of water, cover, and cook for 10 to 12 minutes over medium-low heat, making sure not to let it come to a boil.

3. Add the potato, onion, doenjang, and gochujang, if using them, cover and simmer for 5 minutes. Add the mushrooms and zucchini, cover, and simmer for another 5 to 6 minutes.

4. Add the tofu, green chili, and scallion and simmer uncovered for 3 to 5 minutes, until the stew bubbles and the tofu softens. Check to make sure the potato is cooked.

5. Adjust the seasoning and serve with a bowl of rice.

INGREDIENTS:

- 1 TABLESPOON CANOLA OIL, PLUS MORE AS NEEDED
- 6 OZ. BRISKET, SLICED THIN
- 3 GARLIC CLOVES, MINCED
- ⅔ CUP PEELED AND DICED POTATO
- 1 CUP DICED ONION
- ⅓ CUP DOENJANG
- 1 TEASPOON GOCHUJANG (OPTIONAL)
- ½ CUP SLICED BUTTON MUSHROOMS
- 1 CUP DICED ZUCCHINI
- 1 CUP CUBED MEDIUM-FIRM TOFU
- 1 GREEN CHILI PEPPER, SLICED
- 1 SCALLION, CHOPPED

  SALT, TO TASTE

MISO SOUP

YIELD: 6 SERVINGS / **ACTIVE TIME:** 5 MINUTES / **TOTAL TIME:** 30 MINUTES

This Japanese fermented soybean soup is light but deeply satisfying.

1. Add the water to a pot, bring to a boil, and add the dashi powder.

2. Reduce the heat to low, add the miso, and stir well to incorporate. Adjust the seasoning, if necessary.

3. Add the tofu and scallions when ready to serve.

INGREDIENTS:

2	QUARTS WATER
1	TABLESPOON DASHI POWDER
1	CUP MISO
1	BLOCK SOFT TOFU, CUT INTO SMALL CUBES
¼	CUP MINCED SCALLIONS

ODEN

YIELD: 6 SERVINGS / **ACTIVE TIME:** 45 MINUTES / **TOTAL TIME:** 1 HOUR AND 30 MINUTES

This is a Japanese-style, fish cake hot-pot stew that is a popular dish to order when out drinking.

1. Place the fish cake and fish in a food processor and pulse until finely minced. Bind the fish mousse with the egg and flour. Add the grated carrot and season the mixture with the salt and a little white pepper. Shape the fish mousse into small quenelles, using two teaspoons.

2. Preheat the oil to 350°F. Deep-fry the fish quenelles until golden brown. Drain on a paper towel.

3. Deep-fry the cubed tofu until lightly golden and the outside is firm. Drain on a paper towel.

4. Meanwhile, heat dashi, soy sauce, sake, mirin, and sugar. Bring to a boil and simmer for 30 minutes. Stir well.

5. Add the daikon to the Dashi broth and bring to a boil, and then lower heat and simmer for roughly 10 minutes. Add the carrot, quail eggs, and fish quenelles and simmer for another 8 to 10 minutes. Add the scallions and simmer for another 1 to 2 minutes.

6. Serve hot with hot mustard or your favorite dipping sauce.

INGREDIENTS:

½	LB. FISH CAKE
1	WHITE FISH FILLET
1	EGG
1	TABLESPOON ALL-PURPOSE FLOUR
2	TABLESPOONS GRATED CARROT
	SALT, TO TASTE
	WHITE PEPPER, TO TASTE
2	CUPS CANOLA OIL, FOR DEEP-FRYING
1	CUP CUBED FIRM TOFU
6	CUPS DASHI (SEE PAGE 293)
¼	CUP SOY SAUCE
2	TABLESPOONS SAKE
1	TABLESPOON MIRIN
1	TABLESPOON SUGAR
1½	CUPS DAIKON, CUT INTO THIN SQUARES
¼	CUP SLICED CARROT
6-8	SOFT-BOILED QUAIL EGGS, SHELLED
1	MEDIUM RUSSET POTATO, PEELED AND TURNED
2	SCALLIONS, CHOPPED

GAMJATANG SPICY PORK NECK & POTATO STEW

YIELD: 6 SERVINGS / ACTIVE TIME: 45 MINUTES / TOTAL TIME: 3 HOURS

While "gamja" means "potato" in Korean, it also refers to the type of bones used in this hearty soup, which are also called "gamja."

1. Rinse and soak the pork bones for 30 minutes to 1 hour in cold water.

2. In a large pot of boiling water, blanch the cabbage for 1 minute, remove, run under cold water, strain, and set aside for later.

3. Using the same pot of boiling water, add the pork bones, cover with water, and bring to a boil. Cook for 8 to 10 minutes over medium-high heat. Impurities and dark foam will come up.

4. Strain the bones and rinse under cold water to wash off the foamy, dark substance. Put the cleaned, blanched bones into a clean, large pot. Add the ginger, doenjang, dried shiitake, onion, chili pepper, and water. Bring to a boil, cover, and cook at medium heat for roughly 1½ hours.

5. While the pork bones are cooking, mix all of the sauce mixture ingredients well in a bowl and set aside. After 90 minutes of cooking, take out the onion and discard.

6. Take the shiitake mushrooms out, slice them in half, and return them to the pot. Add the potatoes, seasoning mixture, cabbage, soybean sprouts, and scallions and cook over medium heat for another 30 to 40 minutes. The potatoes should be fully cooked through. If needed, add water if the stew becomes overreduced. Taste and adjust the seasoning.

7. Ladle the stew into a serving bowl or an earthenware bowl to serve bubbling hot. Garnish with more chopped scallions, some perilla leaves, and a sprinkle of perilla seeds, if using.

INGREDIENTS:

4	LBS. PORK NECK BONES
1	LB. NAPA CABBAGE, WHOLE LEAVES, CORED
1	TABLESPOON SLICED GINGER
2½	TABLESPOONS DOENJANG
4	DRIED SHIITAKE MUSHROOMS
1	ONION, HALVED
1	CHILI PEPPER
3	QUARTS WATER, FOR BASE STOCK
4	POTATOES
1	CUP SOYBEAN SPROUTS, CLEANED
3	SCALLIONS, CHOPPED, PLUS MORE FOR GARNISH
12	PERILLA LEAVES, SLICED
	PERILLA SEEDS, FOR GARNISH (OPTIONAL)

SAUCE MIXTURE

3	TABLESPOONS GOCHUGARU
2	TABLESPOONS GOCHUJANG
8	GARLIC CLOVES, MINCED
3	TABLESPOONS FISH SAUCE
½	TEASPOON BLACK PEPPER
⅔	CUP WATER

THAI FISH BROTH

YIELD: 4 SERVINGS / ACTIVE TIME: 20 MINUTES / TOTAL TIME: 45 MINUTES

This is a very fragrant broth, thanks to the lemongrass, chilies, galangal root, lime juice, and lime leaf. It's meant to be very sour, which makes it perfect as a palate cleanser.

1. In a medium saucepan, add the fish stock, lemongrass, lime zest, galangal root, cilantro stalks, and lime leaf and bring to a boil. Reduce the heat so that the broth simmers, and cook for 5 minutes.

2. Turn off the heat and let stand for 15 minutes.

3. Strain the broth through a fine sieve. Return to a cleaned pan and bring to a boil.

4. Reduce the heat so that the broth simmers. Add the lime juice, monkfish, shrimp, Thai chilies, vinegar, and fish sauce. Simmer for 3 to 4 minutes, or until the fish is cooked.

5. Ladle into warmed bowls and garnish with the cilantro leaves, bean sprouts, toasted sesame seeds, and sesame oil.

INGREDIENTS:

- 4 CUPS FISH STOCK
- 2 STALKS LEMONGRASS, BRUISED WITH THE BACK OF A KNIFE
- ZEST AND JUICE OF 2 LIMES
- 1-INCH PIECE GALANGAL ROOT, PEELED AND THINLY SLICED
- 6 STALKS CILANTRO
- 1 KAFFIR LIME LEAF
- 2 MONKFISH FILLETS, SKINNED AND CUT INTO 1-INCH PIECES
- 12 SMALL SHRIMP
- 2 THAI CHILIES, SEEDED AND THINLY SLICED
- 1 TABLESPOON RICE WINE VINEGAR
- 4 TABLESPOONS FISH SAUCE
- CILANTRO LEAVES, CHOPPED, FOR GARNISH
- BEAN SPROUTS, FOR GARNISH
- TOASTED SESAME SEEDS, FOR GARNISH
- SESAME OIL, FOR GARNISH

MISO BROTH WITH FRIED TOFU

YIELD: 4 SERVINGS / ACTIVE TIME: 30 MINUTES / TOTAL TIME: 1 HOUR

I used Azuki Bean Miso from South River Miso, in Conway, Massachusetts, for this recipe. If you have yet to try their miso, you certainly should. They are a family-run company and their products are outstanding.,

1. In a stockpot, add the scallion greens, cilantro stalks, ginger, star anise, cinnamon stick, cardamom seeds, bay leaf, red pepper flakes, and Dashi stock. Cook over medium heat until boiling, reduce the heat, and simmer for 10 minutes.

2. Strain the broth through a fine sieve. Return to the stockpot and bring to a simmer.

3. Add the bok choy and cook for 5 minutes. Add the scallion whites and cook for an additional 2 minutes.

4. Place the miso in a small bowl, add a bit of the hot stock, and then place in the soup.

5. Add the soy sauce. Ladle into warm bowls, garnish with the cilantro leaves and Thai chili, and serve with the Fried Tofu and Crispy Wonton Skins.

INGREDIENTS:

- 4   SCALLIONS, WHITES SLICED THIN, GREENS RESERVED FOR BROTH
- 4   CILANTRO SPRIGS, LEAVES RESERVED FOR GARNISH, STALKS RESERVED FOR BROTH
-     1-INCH PIECE GINGER, SLICED
- 1   STAR ANISE
- 1   CINNAMON STICK
- 4   CARDAMOM PODS, SEEDS REMOVED FROM SHELL AND CRUSHED
- 1   BAY LEAF
- ½   TEASPOON RED PEPPER FLAKES
- 4   CUPS DASHI (SEE PAGE 293)
- 3   BOK CHOY, CUT LENGTHWISE INTO EIGHTHS
- ¼   CUP RED MISO
- 2   TABLESPOONS SOY SAUCE
-     THAI CHILIES, SEEDS REMOVED, THINLY SLICED, FOR GARNISH
-     FRIED TOFU (SEE RECIPE), TO SERVE
-     CRISPY WONTON SKINS (SEE RECIPE), TO SERVE

FRIED TOFU

For all the people who think they don't like tofu, this recipe is a good introduction—crispy and hot.

1. Place the oil in a medium saucepan and heat to 350°F.

2. Place the eggs, flour, and panko bread crumbs in 3 separate bowls.

3. Dredge the tofu in the flour, remove, and shake to remove any excess flour. Place the coated tofu in the egg wash. Remove from the egg wash, shake to release any excess egg, and gently coat with bread crumbs.

4. If there is any tofu exposed, return to the egg wash and repeat with the bread crumbs.

5. Once all the tofu is coated, place in oil and fry in batches until golden brown. Remove with a slotted spoon, place on a paper towel, and season with the salt.

Continued . . .

6. Reduce the heat of the oil to 300°F and reserve for the Crispy Wonton Skins.

CRISPY WONTON SKINS

1. Place the wonton wrappers in the reserved oil and turn frequently, until they are crisp and golden brown.

2. Use a slotted spoon to remove the fried wonton wrappers from the oil and set on paper towels to drain.

3. Season with the salt, and serve.

INGREDIENTS:

RIED TOFU

2	CUPS VEGETABLE OIL
2	EGGS, WHISKED TOGETHER
¼	CUP ALL-PURPOSE FLOUR
1½	CUPS PANKO BREAD CRUMBS, GROUND TO A FINE POWDER IN A FOOD PROCESSOR
5	OZ. TOFU, CUT INTO ¾-INCH CUBES, DRIED ON A PAPER TOWEL
	SALT, TO TASTE

CRISPY WONTON SKINS

4	WONTON WRAPPERS, CUT INTO TRIANGLES
	SALT, TO TASTE

INDO-CHINESE VEGETABLE HOT & SOUR SOUP

YIELD: 4 SERVINGS / ACTIVE TIME: 30 MINUTES / TOTAL TIME: 45 MINUTES

The secret to this fast-cooking dish is to have all your ingredients prepped and cut in advance.

1. Place the cornstarch and the water in a bowl. Stir until the cornstarch dissolves, and set aside.

2. In a medium saucepan, add the oil and warm over medium heat. Add the onion, ginger, garlic, and celery and cook for 5 minutes, or until soft.

3. Add the green beans, carrot, mushrooms, cabbage, and bell pepper. Sauté for 1 minute, add the Vegetable Stock, and bring to a boil.

4. Reduce to a simmer, and add the soy sauce and vinegar.

5. Slowly add the dissolved cornstarch to the soup, whisking constantly until combined. Simmer for 5 minutes, or until thickened, stirring often.

6. Season with the salt and pepper, ladle into warm bowls, and garnish with the bean sprouts and scallions.

INGREDIENTS:

3	TABLESPOONS CORNSTARCH
1	CUP WATER
1	TABLESPOON SESAME OIL
½	CUP ONION, FINELY CHOPPED
2	TEASPOONS GINGER, MINCED
2	TEASPOONS GARLIC, MINCED
2	TABLESPOONS CELERY, FINELY CHOPPED
¼	CUP GREEN BEANS, FINELY SLICED
¼	CUP CARROT, PEELED AND FINELY CHOPPED
¼	CUP MUSHROOMS, FINELY CHOPPED
½	CUP GREEN CABBAGE, FINELY SLICED
¼	CUP GREEN BELL PEPPER, FINELY CHOPPED
4	CUPS VEGETABLE STOCK (SEE PAGE 684)
3	TABLESPOONS SOY SAUCE
1	TEASPOON WHITE DISTILLED VINEGAR
	SALT AND PEPPER, TO TASTE
	BEAN SPROUTS, FOR GARNISH
2	SCALLIONS, FINELY SLICED, FOR GARNISH

THAI COCONUT BROTH
WITH LOBSTER WONTONS

YIELD: 4 SERVINGS / ACTIVE TIME: 30 MINUTES / TOTAL TIME: 1 HOUR

This is a wonderful fusion of Thailand and the great state of Maine!

THAI CURRY PASTE

1. Place all of the ingredients in a food processor and puree until smooth. Refrigerate until ready to use.

LOBSTER WONTONS

1. Place the lobster meat, scallion, salt, and pepper in a mixing bowl, and stir to combine.

2. Place 1 tablespoon of the lobster filling in the center of a wonton wrapper. Dip a finger into the egg and then rub it around the edge of the wrapper. Bring each corner of the wrapper together, and seal (see page 748).

3. Repeat Step 2 with the remaining wonton wrappers. When all of the wontons have been made, refrigerate until ready to use.

SOUP

1. In a medium saucepan, add the sesame oil and warm over low heat. Add the curry paste and cook, while stirring constantly, for 5 minutes.

2. Meanwhile, bring 8 cups of water to boil in a large saucepan. Add the wontons and cook for 3 minutes.

3. Remove the wontons from the water with a slotted spoon and place in warm bowls.

4. Add the sugar, fish sauce, and coconut milk to the medium saucepan. Cook on low heat for 4 minutes, while stirring constantly. Season with the lime juice, salt, and pepper, while taking care not to bring to a boil.

5. Pour the soup over the wontons. Garnish with the cilantro and Thai chilies, and serve.

INGREDIENTS:

THAI CURRY PASTE

2	SHALLOTS, FINELY CHOPPED
	2-INCH PIECE LEMONGRASS, FINELY CHOPPED
	1-INCH GALANGAL ROOT, GRATED
3	GARLIC CLOVES, MINCED

LOBSTER WONTONS

1½	CUPS LOBSTER MEAT, COOKED, FINELY CHOPPED
1	SCALLION, FINELY SLICED
	SALT AND PEPPER, TO TASTE
24	WONTON WRAPPERS
1	EGG, BEATEN

SOUP

1	TABLESPOON SESAME OIL
1	TABLESPOON RED THAI CURRY PASTE (SEE RECIPE)
2	TEASPOONS SUGAR
3	TABLESPOONS FISH SAUCE
1	14-OZ. CAN COCONUT MILK
	JUICE OF 1 LIME
	SALT AND PEPPER, TO TASTE
	CILANTRO, CHOPPED, FOR GARNISH
	THAI CHILIES, SLICED, FOR GARNISH

TANUKI JIRU

YIELD: 4 SERVINGS / **ACTIVE TIME:** 20 MINUTES / **TOTAL TIME:** 40 MINUTES

This soup was traditionally made with raccoon in Japan, but nowadays pork is the go-to protein.

1. Trim the pork loin into thin slices. Cut those slices into 1-inch pieces.

2. Place the sesame oil in a medium saucepan and cook over medium heat until it starts to smoke.

3. Add the pork, burdock root/parsnips, daikon, and mushrooms. Cook for 5 minutes.

4. Once the pork is cooked through, add the fish stock and tofu.

5. Bring to a boil. Reduce the heat so that the soup simmers, and cook for 10 minutes.

6. Place the miso in a bowl. Add 4 tablespoons of the broth and stir to make a smooth paste.

7. Stir ⅓ of the miso mixture into the soup. Taste and add more if desired.

8. Ladle into bowls, garnish with the scallions, and serve with the Daikon Salad.

DAIKON SALAD

1. Place all of the ingredients in a mixing bowl and stir until combined.

2. Place in the refrigerator for at least 10 minutes before serving.

INGREDIENTS:

8	OZ. BONELESS PORK LOIN
2	TABLESPOONS SESAME OIL
	6-INCH PIECE BURDOCK ROOT; IF UNAVAILABLE, USE PARSNIPS, PEELED AND SLICED
½	CUP CHOPPED DAIKON
4	SHIITAKE MUSHROOMS, STALKS REMOVED AND SLICED
2½	CUPS FISH STOCK
¾	CUP CHOPPED TOFU
4	TABLESPOONS MISO
	SCALLIONS, CHOPPED, FOR GARNISH
	DAIKON SALAD (SEE RECIPE), TO SERVE

DAIKON SALAD

	3-INCH PIECE DAIKON
1	TABLESPOON SESAME SEEDS, TOASTED
2	TABLESPOONS CHOPPED SCALLION GREENS
1	TEASPOON SESAME OIL
1	TEASPOON SOY SAUCE

LEMONGRASS-SCENTED CHICKEN & RICE SOUP

YIELD: 4 SERVINGS / ACTIVE TIME: 30 MINUTES / TOTAL TIME: 2 HOURS AND 30 MINUTES

Also known as Chnor Chrook, this soup is Cambodia's version of chicken noodle soup. It is light and refreshing. This soup awakens the senses with the chili and the citrus aroma.

1. In a large saucepan, add the chicken thighs, Chicken Stock, ginger, lemongrass, Thai chili, and fish sauce.

2. Bring to a boil and simmer for 2 hours, or until the chicken thighs are tender.

3. Skim off any fat.

4. Remove the chicken thighs and pick apart the meat. Discard the skin and bones.

5. Strain the stock through a fine sieve.

6. Reboil the stock, stir in the rice, and simmer for 30 minutes, or until the rice is cooked.

7. Remove the Thai chili, add the chicken thigh meat until hot, and serve.

8. Garnish with the chili strips, cilantro, and lime wedges and serve with the Naan.

NAAN

1. Combine the yeast and warm water in a bowl and let stand for 10 minutes.

2. In a separate bowl, combine the yeast mixture, sugar, milk, egg, salt, and flour and mix by hand until it is formed into a ball of dough.

3. On a lightly floured surface, knead the dough for 5 minutes. Place the dough in a bowl, cover it with a towel, and let stand for 30 to 45 minutes in a warm place, until it doubles in size.

4. Cut into 4 pieces and roll on a lightly floured work surface. Each piece should be ¼ inch thick.

5. Brush both sides with the melted butter and cook on a grill until golden brown. Remove from the grill and brush the tops with the melted butter before serving.

INGREDIENTS:

2	CHICKEN THIGHS
8	CUPS CHICKEN STOCK (SEE PAGE 680)
	1-INCH PIECE GINGER, SLICED
3	LEMONGRASS STALKS, CUT IN HALF AND BRUISED WITH THE BACK OF A KNIFE
1	THAI CHILI WITH SEEDS
3	TABLESPOONS FISH SAUCE
½	CUP LONG-GRAIN RICE, RINSED
	CHILI, CUT INTO THIN STRIPS, FOR GARNISH
	CHOPPED CILANTRO, FOR GARNISH
	LIME WEDGES, FOR GARNISH
	NAAN (SEE RECIPE), TO SERVE

NAAN

½	TEASPOON YEAST
1	CUP WARM WATER
2	TABLESPOONS SUGAR
1	TABLESPOON MILK
1	EGG
1	TEASPOON SALT
2.	CUPS BREAD FLOUR, PLUS MORE AS NEEDED
½	CUP BUTTER, MELTED

TOM KHA KAI

YIELD: 4 TO 6 SERVINGS / ACTIVE TIME: 20 MINUTES / TOTAL TIME: 45 MINUTES

This is one of the most popular soups in Thai cuisine. The combination of the spices in this soup makes it sour, sweet, hot, and salty all at the same time.

1. Rinse, dry, and remove the stems from the mushrooms.

2. In a medium saucepan, add the coconut milk and bring to a simmer over medium heat.

3. Add the mushrooms, scallions, lemongrass, galangal root, red chili pepper, lime leaf, and ginger. Cook, while lightly stirring, for about 5 minutes, until the contents of the pan are fragrant.

4. Add the fish sauce, lime juice, chicken breasts, and sugar. Raise the heat to medium-high and cook for 10 minutes, or until the chicken is cooked through.

5. Remove the lemongrass and galangal, ladle into warm bowls, and garnish with the bean sprouts.

INGREDIENTS:

- 2 CUPS SHIITAKE MUSHROOMS, SLICED
- 2 14-OZ. CANS COCONUT MILK
- 4 SCALLIONS, WHITE PART ONLY, SLICED

  4-INCH LEMONGRASS STALK, BRUISED WITH THE BACK OF A KNIFE

  1-INCH PIECE GALANGAL ROOT
- 1 SMALL RED CHILI PEPPER, SEEDS REMOVED, FINELY DICED
- 1 LIME LEAF
- 2 TEASPOONS GINGER, FINELY GRATED
- ½ CUP FISH SAUCE, OR TO TASTE

  JUICE OF 2 LIMES
- 1 LB. OF CHICKEN BREASTS, CUT INTO 1-INCH CUBES
- 1 TEASPOON SUGAR

  BEAN SPROUTS, FOR GARNISH

SEAFOOD WONTON SOUP

YIELD: 4 SERVINGS / **ACTIVE TIME:** 40 MINUTES / **TOTAL TIME:** 1 HOUR

Wonton soup is probably one of the most popular Chinese soups. The mere mention of it sets my mouth watering.

1. In a medium saucepan, add the sesame oil and cook over medium heat until warm.

2. Add the onion and carrots and cook for 5 minutes, or until soft. Add the garlic, cook for 2 minutes, and then add the sake, fish stock, lemongrass, soy sauce, and fish sauce.

3. Simmer for 10 minutes, then remove the lemongrass and season with the salt and pepper.

4. Bring the soup to a boil and add the Seafood Wontons. Reduce the heat so that the soup simmers, and cook for 5 minutes, or until the wontons float to the top.

5. Place 3 wontons in each bowl. Ladle the broth over the wontons, and garnish with the romaine lettuce, toasted sesame seeds, cilantro, and shaved radish.

SEAFOOD WONTONS

1. Place all of the ingredients, except for the wonton wrappers, in a bowl and mix until combined.

2. Place 2 teaspoons of the mixture into the center of a wrapper.

3. Dip your finger into cold water and rub a small amount around the edge of the wrapper. Bring each corner together to make a purse and seal.

4. Repeat with the remaining wrappers, and refrigerate until ready to use.

INGREDIENTS:

1	TABLESPOON SESAME OIL
1	ONION, FINELY CHOPPED
2	CARROTS, FINELY CHOPPED
2	GARLIC CLOVES, FINELY CHOPPED
1	CUP SAKE
4	CUPS FISH STOCK
1	STALK LEMONGRASS, SMASHED WITH THE BACK OF A KNIFE
1	TABLESPOON SOY SAUCE
1	TABLESPOON FISH SAUCE
	SALT AND PEPPER, TO TASTE
12	SEAFOOD WONTONS (SEE RECIPE)
1	ROMAINE LETTUCE LEAF, SHREDDED, FOR GARNISH
	TOASTED SESAME SEEDS, FOR GARNISH
	CILANTRO, CHOPPED, FOR GARNISH
	RADISH, SHAVED, FOR GARNISH

SEAFOOD WONTONS

4	OZ. RAW SHRIMP, PEELED, DEVEINED, AND FINELY CHOPPED
4	OZ. COOKED CRAB, CLEANED AND FINELY CHOPPED
1	TABLESPOON MINCED SHALLOTS
1	TABLESPOON CHOPPED CHIVES
1	TABLESPOON FISH SAUCE
2	TABLESPOONS MISO
1	TABLESPOON SHRIMP PASTE
2	TABLESPOONS CHOPPED RADISH
1	TABLESPOON SESAME SEEDS, TOASTED
1	TEASPOON SESAME OIL
1	TEASPOON SHERRY
12	WONTON WRAPPERS

SPICY & SOUR FISH SOUP

YIELD: 4 SERVINGS / **ACTIVE TIME:** 40 MINUTES / **TOTAL TIME:** 1 HOUR AND 30 MINUTES

This is based on Canh Chua Cá, a very popular soup in Southeast Asia. It is tart, sweet, and spicy—a real roller coaster for your taste buds.

1. Place the swordfish, 2 tablespoons of fish sauce, and the garlic in a bowl. Toss until the swordfish is coated and set aside.

2. Drain and rinse the squid.

3. In a medium saucepan, add the oil and warm over medium heat. Add the squid, scallions, shallots, ginger, and lemongrass and cook for 2 minutes. Add the fish stock, bring to a boil, and then reduce the heat so that the soup simmers. Cook for 10 minutes, and then strain through a fine sieve.

4. Return the stock to a clean pan and bring to a boil. Stir in the remaining fish sauce, tamarind concentrate, and chilies and simmer for 3 minutes.

5. Add the pineapple, tomatoes, bamboo shoots, and calamari and cook for 3 minutes. Stir in the marinated swordfish and cilantro and cook for 3 minutes, or until the swordfish is cooked through.

6. Place the rice noodles in a bowl and cover with boiling water. Leave to soak for 4 minutes, or follow the manufacturer's instructions.

7. Season the soup with the salt and pepper to taste and place the noodles in a warm bowl or hollowed pineapple shell. Ladle the soup over the noodles and garnish with the bean sprouts, alfalfa sprouts, lime wedges, and cilantro.

INGREDIENTS:

12	OZ. SWORDFISH, CUT INTO ½-INCH CUBES
8	TABLESPOONS FISH SAUCE, DIVIDED
2	GARLIC CLOVES, MINCED
1	OZ. DRIED SQUID, SOAKED FOR 30 MINUTES
1	TABLESPOON VEGETABLE OIL
4	SCALLIONS, SLICED
2	SHALLOTS, FINELY CHOPPED
2	TABLESPOONS GINGER ROOT, PEELED AND MINCED
2	STALKS LEMONGRASS, BRUISED WITH THE BACK OF A KNIFE
4	CUPS FISH STOCK
2	TABLESPOONS TAMARIND CONCENTRATE
2	THAI CHILIES, SEEDED AND SLICED
12	OZ. PINEAPPLE, DICED
4	PLUM TOMATOES, CONCASSE (SEE PAGE 749) AND CUT INTO ¼-INCH PIECES
3	OZ. CANNED SLICED BAMBOO SHOOTS, DRAINED
8	OZ. CALAMARI, BODIES SLICED INTO ¼-INCH-THICK PIECES, TENTACLES LEFT WHOLE
2	TABLESPOONS CILANTRO, LEAVES REMOVED AND FINELY CHOPPED, PLUS MORE FOR GARNISH
3	OZ. RICE NOODLES
	SALT AND PEPPER, TO TASTE
	BEAN SPROUTS, FOR GARNISH
	ALFALFA SPROUTS, FOR GARNISH
	LIME WEDGES, FOR GARNISH

JOGAETANG

YIELD: 4 SERVINGS / ACTIVE TIME: 30 MINUTES / TOTAL TIME: 1 HOUR AND 30 MINUTES

A Korean home remedy for a hangover, this simple, clear broth clam soup is fortifying, whether or not you were out late the night before.

1. In a large bowl of ice water, soak the clams for between 45 minutes and 1 hour to purge them of sand. Strain and set aside.

2. Add the kombu, radish, water, and soju to a pot over high heat, bring to a boil, and then immediately reduce the heat to low and simmer for 3 to 4 minutes. Using tongs, remove the kombu.

3. Bring the stock to a boil, add the cleaned clams, garlic, and jalapeños, and boil covered for 3 to 4 minutes, until the clams open.

4. Once the clams are open, use the tongs or a slotted spoon to remove them from the broth and set aside so they don't overcook. Continue to cook the unopened clams; if they don't open after a few more minutes, discard.

5. Adjust the seasoning with the salt.

6. Divide the cooked clams into bowls and ladle the broth over the clams.

7. Garnish with the scallions and sliced chilies.

INGREDIENTS:

3	LBS. LITTLENECK CLAMS
	4 X 4–INCH PIECE KOMBU
⅓	CUP THINLY SLICED SQUARES KOREAN RADISH
3½	CUPS WATER
½	CUP SOJU
2-3	GARLIC CLOVES, SLICED
1-2	JALAPEÑOS, SLICED
	KOSHER SALT, TO TASTE
2	SCALLIONS, CHOPPED INTO 2-INCH PIECES
½	RED CHILI, THINLY SLICED

UDON POT

YIELD: 4 SERVINGS / **ACTIVE TIME**: 15 MINUTES / **TOTAL TIME**: 45 MINUTES

Japanese udon are chewy wheat-flour noodles that are typically served in a light and clean dashi broth, like in this recipe, which also happens to be a great one-pot dish.

1. In a pot or earthenware donabe, combine the Dashi, soy sauce, mirin, and shiitake stems, bring to a boil, and then simmer for 4 to 5 minutes. Using a slotted spoon or kitchen spider, remove the shiitake stems.

2. Poach the shrimp in the same broth until 90 percent done. Using a slotted spoon or kitchen spider, remove from the broth and set aside.

3. Put the uncooked noodles in the bottom of the pot of broth, and arrange the raw vegetables on top of the noodles. Cover, bring to a boil, reduce the heat, and simmer until the noodles are done, about 5 minutes.

4. Return the shrimp to the pot and add the scallions.

5. Ladle into serving bowls and garnish with the grated radish, if using, and the Shichimi Togarashi.

DASHI

1. In a pot, put the kombu and purified cold water. Over medium heat, bring to a boil, making sure the process takes roughly 15 minutes. Press your thumbnail into the thickest part of the kelp; if it dents easily, all the umami/flavor has been extracted. Remove the kelp.

2. Add the bonito flakes and bring to a boil, and once the bonito flakes sink to the bottom, strain.

3. Cool and store until needed.

INGREDIENTS:

1	QUART DASHI (SEE RECIPE)
⅓	CUP SOY SAUCE
1	TABLESPOON MIRIN
6	DRIED SHIITAKE MUSHROOMS, CAPS AND STEMS SOAKED IN WATER
8-12	SHRIMP, CLEANED AND DEVEINED
18	OZ. UDON
4	NAPA CABBAGE LEAVES, CUT INTO LARGE PIECES
1	BUNCH SPINACH, STEMS REMOVED
8-12	SNOW PEAS, TRIMMED
½	CUP THINLY SLICED CARROTS
3	SCALLIONS, CHOPPED
2	TABLESPOONS FINELY GRATED RADISH, FOR GARNISH (OPTIONAL)
	SHICHIMI TOGARASHI (SEE PAGE 146), FOR GARNISH

DASHI

	8-INCH PIECE KOMBU (DRY SEA KELP)
2	QUARTS PURIFIED COLD WATER
3	CUPS DRIED BONITO FLAKES

CONGEE

YIELD: 2 SERVINGS / **ACTIVE TIME:** 15 MINUTES / **TOTAL TIME:** 2 HOURS

Making congee with uncooked rice takes a little time, but is well worth the wait. If you have leftover rice, however, this is a great way to use it up. Start with less liquid in the pot, as the cooked rice will absorb much less; add more to achieve the right consistency.

1. Rinse the rice, put it into a pot with your stock of choice, and bring it to a boil. Lower heat and simmer while stirring so the rice doesn't stick to the bottom of the pot and burn.

2. Add stock as needed to cook the rice until achieving a loose porridge consistency and the rice kernels have burst, about 1 ½ hours.

3. At the end of the cooking process fold in the ginger and season to taste with the salt or soy sauce.

4. To serve, ladle the congee into bowls, drizzle sesame oil, and garnish as you deem fit.

INGREDIENTS:

- 1 CUP RICE, JASMINE OR SHORT GRAIN
- 3 CUPS CHICKEN OR VEGETABLE STOCK (SEE PAGE 680 OR PAGE 684), OR WATER
- 1 TEASPOON FINELY MINCED GINGER

  KOSHER SALT OR SOY SAUCE, TO TASTE
- 3-4 TABLESPOONS SESAME OIL

  SHREDDED COOKED CHICKEN OR RENDERED CHINESE SAUSAGE (OPTIONAL), TO TASTE

  CHOPPED CILANTRO (OPTIONAL), FOR GARNISH

  SLICED SCALLIONS (OPTIONAL), FOR GARNISH

  FRIED SHALLOTS & GARLIC (SEE PAGE 173; OPTIONAL), FOR GARNISH

  CHOPPED ROASTED PEANUTS (OPTIONAL), FOR GARNISH

ENTREES

From spicy and light to decadent and hearty, the entrees collected here include plenty of favorites and some dishes that might be new to you. They will all improve the table around which you and yours gather, whether for a quick weeknight meal or a sumptuous banquet.

YELLOW CHICKEN CURRY

YIELD: 4 SERVINGS / **ACTIVE TIME:** 30 MINUTES / **TOTAL TIME:** 1 HOUR

The use of curry to prepare dishes that are now quintessential to Thai cuisine began after its introduction by the British colonizers.

1. Season the chicken with the salt and pepper.

2. Add 1 tablespoon of oil to a saucepan over medium-high heat. Once the oil begins to shimmer, sear the chicken pieces on both sides and remove from the pan.

3. Add 1 tablespoon of oil to the same pan over medium-high heat, and then combine the curry paste, onions, and carrots and cook until fragrant. Add the potatoes and coconut cream and stir to incorporate all of the ingredients. Add the seared chicken, coconut milk, fish sauce, and Chicken Stock and simmer covered for 15 to 20 minutes, or until the potatoes are tender.

4. Remove the lid and simmer for another 10 minutes, reducing to the desired consistency.

5. Adjust the seasoning with the salt, fish sauce, lime, and sugar and serve.

YELLOW CURRY PASTE

1. Reserve ½ cup of chili soaking water.

2. In a food processor or blender, combine all of the ingredients and blend until smooth; add the reserved chili water as needed to aid with blending.

3. Refrigerate in an airtight container, or freeze for up to 6 months.

INGREDIENTS:

1½	LBS. CHICKEN THIGHS OR BREASTS, CUT INTO 2-INCH CUBES
	SALT, TO TASTE
	BLACK PEPPER, TO TASTE
2	TABLESPOONS CANOLA OIL OR COCONUT OIL, DIVIDED
⅓	CUP YELLOW CURRY PASTE (SEE RECIPE)
1	LB. YELLOW ONIONS, CUT INTO MEDIUM DICE
1	LB. CARROTS, CUT INTO MEDIUM DICE
1	LB. YUKON GOLD POTATOES, CUT INTO 2-INCH DICE
½	CUP COCONUT CREAM
1¼	CUPS COCONUT MILK
2	TABLESPOONS FISH SAUCE, PLUS MORE TO TASTE
1½	CUPS CHICKEN STOCK (SEE PAGE 680)
	LIME JUICE, TO TASTE
	SUGAR, TO TASTE

YELLOW CURRY PASTE

10	DRIED CHILIES, SEEDED AND SOAKED IN HOT WATER FOR 30 MINUTES
2	SHALLOTS, CHOPPED
2	TABLESPOONS CILANTRO STEMS
3	TABLESPOONS SLICED LEMONGRASS, WHITE PART
8	GARLIC CLOVES
2	TABLESPOONS GRATED GALANGAL
1	TEASPOON CUMIN
1	TEASPOON CORIANDER
1	TEASPOON GROUND FENNEL SEED
2	TABLESPOONS FRESH CHOPPED TURMERIC
2	TABLESPOONS CURRY POWDER
1	TEASPOON SALT
½	TEASPOON WHITE PEPPER
1½	TABLESPOONS SHRIMP PASTE
1	KAFFIR LIME LEAF, MINCED

VEGETABLE GREEN CURRY

YIELD: 4 SERVINGS / **ACTIVE TIME:** 30 MINUTES / **TOTAL TIME:** 30 MINUTES

This is a signature Thai dish that incorporates green chilies and fragrant herbs, and is usually milder than red or yellow curry.

1. Add the coconut cream to a saucepan over medium-high heat and cook until it bubbles.

2. Add the curry paste, reduce the heat to low, and stir for 3 to 4 minutes, until fragrant.

3. Add the vegetables, stir to combine, and cook for 2 to 3 minutes.

4. Stir in the coconut milk, Vegetable Stock or water, sugar, and fish sauce, bring to a boil, and then simmer uncovered until the vegetables are tender.

5. Adjust the seasoning and remove from heat. Garnish with the basil and lime wedge, and serve along with rice.

GREEN CURRY PASTE

1. In a food processor or blender, combine all of the ingredients and blend until smooth.

2. Refrigerate in an airtight container, or freeze for up to 6 months.

INGREDIENTS:

⅓	CUP COCONUT CREAM
2	TABLESPOONS GREEN CURRY PASTE
1	CUP DICED THAI EGGPLANT
1	YELLOW ONION, DICED
⅔	CUP DICED RED BELL PEPPER
⅔	CUP DICED ZUCCHINI
⅔	CUP BAMBOO SHOOTS, RINSED
⅔	CUP CHOPPED GREEN BEANS
1⅓	CUPS COCONUT MILK
1½	CUPS VEGETABLE STOCK (SEE PAGE 684) OR WATER
½	TABLESPOON PALM OR COCONUT SUGAR
2	TABLESPOONS FISH SAUCE
	THAI BASIL, FOR GARNISH
	LIME WEDGE, FOR GARNISH

GREEN CURRY PASTE

12	GREEN THAI LONG CHILIES, SEEDED AND CHOPPED
12	GREEN BIRD'S EYE CHILIES
1	TEASPOON CUMIN SEEDS, GROUND
1	TEASPOON CORIANDER SEEDS
½	TEASPOON WHITE PEPPERCORN
1	TEASPOON SALT
2	TABLESPOONS FINELY CHOPPED GALANGAL
3	TABLESPOONS FINELY SLICED LEMONGRASS, WHITE PART
8	GARLIC CLOVES, PEELED
2	SHALLOTS, SLICED
1	KAFFIR LIME LEAF, SLICED
1½	TABLESPOONS SHRIMP PASTE
2	TABLESPOONS FINELY CHOPPED CILANTRO ROOT

SEAFOOD CRISPY EGG NOODLE

YIELD: 4 SERVINGS / **ACTIVE TIME:** 30 MINUTES / **TOTAL TIME:** 45 MINUTES

There are different varieties of crispy noodles. This Hong Kong–style chow mein is a layer of fried egg noodles with gravy and seafood stir-fry spooned on top. The contrasting textures make it a playful and surprising meal with every bite. The larger the wok or skillet, the thinner the crispy noodles.

1. If using dry noodles, soak the noodles in cold water for 15 minutes, until pliable, and strain.

2. Bring a pot of water to a boil, and then pour over the noodles and let stand for 1 to 2 minutes, using tongs or chopsticks to gently separate the noodles. Pour the noodles into an ice bath, cool, and strain well. Pat dry if needed.

3. Add the oil to a wok or skillet over medium-high heat. Once it is hot, but not yet smoking, carefully slide the noodles into the wok and spread out. Lower the heat to medium-low. Depending on the thickness, fry until golden brown, 2 to 5 minutes.

4. Carefully flip the noodles to fry the other side until golden brown.

5. Remove from the oil and transfer to a paper towel–lined plate.

SEAFOOD SEASONING

1. In a bowl, break up the bouillon and mix all of the ingredients well.

2. Dredge the seafood.

SAUCE

1. In a bowl, combine all of the ingredients, mix well, and set aside.

INGREDIENTS:

6–8 OZ. EGG NOODLES, FRESH OR DRY

¾ CUP VEGETABLE OIL

SEAFOOD SEASONING

1 TABLESPOON CHICKEN BOUILLON

½ TEASPOON SALT

2 TEASPOONS WHITE PEPPER

1 CUP CORNSTARCH

SAUCE

1 TABLESPOON LIGHT SOY SAUCE

2 TABLESPOON OYSTER SAUCE

2 TEASPOONS SUGAR

1 CUP CHICKEN STOCK (SEE PAGE 680)

1½ TABLESPOONS SHAOXING RICE WINE

2 TABLESPOONS CORNSTARCH SLURRY (1:1 RATIO)

Continued . . .

STIR FRY

1. Blanch the carrot, snow peas, and bok choy and transfer to an ice bath. Chill and strain.

2. Add the oil to a wok or sauté pan over medium-high heat. When the oil begins to shimmer, sauté the garlic, ginger, and scallion whites for 30 seconds.

3. Add the marinated seafood, cook for 3 minutes, and then add the blanched vegetables and mushrooms. Add the prepared sauce and cook until the sauce thickens, stirring frequently.

4. Remove from heat, add the scallion greens, and the adjust seasoning.

5. To serve, place the crispy noodles on a plate and pour the seafood mixture over the noodles.

INGREDIENTS:

STIR FRY

- ¼ CUP THINLY SLICED CARROT
- ¼ CUP SNOW PEAS
- ¼ CUP SLICED BABY BOK CHOY
- 3 TABLESPOONS VEGETABLE OIL
- 1 TABLESPOON MINCED GARLIC
- 2 TEASPOONS THINLY SLICED GINGER
- 2 TABLESPOONS SLICED SCALLIONS, WHITE PART
- ¼ CUP BUTTON OR STRAW MUSHROOMS
- 5-6 SHRIMP, PEELED AND DEVEINED
- ¼ LB. COD, SLICED (OR ANY OTHER SIMILAR FISH)
- ¼ CUP CLEANED AND SLICED SQUID
- 3-6 SCALLOPS (DEPENDING ON SIZE)
- 2 TABLESPOONS SLICED SCALLIONS, GREEN PART

BEEF RED CURRY

YIELD: 4 SERVINGS / **ACTIVE TIME:** 30 MINUTES / **TOTAL TIME:** 1 HOUR AND 30 MINUTES

This dish uses red curry that has its roots in Central Thailand.

1. Season the beef with the salt and pepper.

2. Add the oil to a saucepan over medium-high heat. Once the oil begins to shimmer, sear the beef on all sides.

3. Add the coconut milk and heat until bubbling, stirring frequently.

4. Add the curry paste, fish sauce, sugar, and Beef Stock or water, bring to a simmer, and cook covered until the meat is tender, about 1 hour. Add more water if the curry becomes too thick; it should be a gravy consistency.

5. Add the beans and cook for another 2 minutes.

6. Once done, remove from heat and stir in the peanut butter. Adjust the seasoning with the salt if necessary.

7. Garnish with the Kaffir lime leaves and chilies and serve with rice.

THAI RED CURRY PASTE

1. Reserve ½ cup of chili soaking water.

2. In a food processor or blender, combine all of the ingredients and blend until smooth; add the reserved chili water as needed to aid with blending.

3. Refrigerate in an airtight container, or freeze for up to 6 months.

INGREDIENTS:

1	LB. CHUCK STEAK, ¼ INCH THICK
	SALT, TO TASTE
	PEPPER, TO TASTE
1	TABLESPOON CANOLA OIL
1⅔	CUPS COCONUT MILK
2	TABLESPOONS THAI RED CURRY PASTE (SEE RECIPE)
1	TABLESPOON FISH SAUCE
½	TABLESPOON PALM OR COCONUT SUGAR
1½	CUPS BEEF STOCK (SEE PAGE 679) OR WATER
½	CUP CHOPPED STRING BEANS
1	TABLESPOON CHUNKY PEANUT BUTTER
	KAFFIR LIME LEAVES, DEVEINED AND SLICED THIN, FOR GARNISH
1	FRESNO CHILI, SLICED, FOR GARNISH

THAI RED CURRY PASTE

20	DRIED CHILIES, SEEDED AND SOAKED IN HOT WATER FOR 30 MINUTES
2	SHALLOTS, CHOPPED
2	TABLESPOONS CILANTRO STEMS
3	TABLESPOONS SLICED LEMONGRASS, WHITE PART
8	GARLIC CLOVES
2	TABLESPOONS GRATED GALANGAL
1	TEASPOON CUMIN
1	TEASPOON CORIANDER
1	TEASPOON SALT
½	TEASPOON WHITE PEPPER
1½	TABLESPOONS SHRIMP PASTE
1	KAFFIR LIME LEAF, SLICED

PAD THAI

YIELD: 4 SERVINGS / **ACTIVE TIME:** 30 MINUTES / **TOTAL TIME:** 1 HOUR

This noodle dish is easily the most popular Thai dish worldwide. In Thailand, it is found in restaurants and street food stands.

1. Soak the noodles in warm water for 30 to 40 minutes until pliable enough to bend. Drain and refrigerate covered until needed.

2. In a small bowl, whisk together the sugar, Tamarind Water, ketchup, vinegar, and fish sauce until the sugar dissolves. Set aside.

3. In a wok or nonstick sauté pan, add half the oil over medium-high heat. Once it's smoking, add the chicken and tofu and fry until the meat is opaque but not fully cooked.

4. Add the noodles and stir until they are coated with oil, approximately 1 minute.

5. Increase the heat to high, add the prepared sauce, and cook for 1 minute, until everything is coated with sauce. Move the noodles to the side of the pan. Add the rest of the oil and fry the shrimp (if using) and garlic for 1 minute, and then mix all of the ingredients that are in the pan.

6. Make a well at the center of the pan and add the eggs. Scramble with a spatula for 1 minute, and then that are in the pan mix all of the ingredients that are in the pan.

7. Check the noodles for doneness, and make sure most of the liquid has evaporated while cooking.

8. Fold in the bean sprouts and scallions or Chinese chives.

9. Garnish with the peanuts, lime wedge and Roasted Chili Powder. Serve.

ROASTED CHILI POWDER

1. In a dry wok or nonstick pan, toast the chilies, making sure not to burn. Remove from heat and let cool.

2. Place the chilies in a food processor, spice grinder, or blender and grind until the mixture is fine.

3. Store at room temperature in an airtight container.

INGREDIENTS:

6	OZ. DRIED RICE STICK NOODLES (⅛ TO ⅓-INCH THICK)
3	TABLESPOONS PALM OR DARK BROWN SUGAR
2	TABLESPOONS TAMARIND WATER (SEE PAGE 244)
1	TABLESPOON KETCHUP
3	TABLESPOONS DISTILLED WHITE VINEGAR
2	TABLESPOONS FISH SAUCE
3	TABLESPOONS VEGETABLE OIL, DIVIDED
¼	LB. CHICKEN BREAST, SLICED
⅓	CUP CUBED EXTRA-FIRM TOFU
1	TABLESPOON DRIED SMALL SHRIMP, CHOPPED (OPTIONAL)
2	GARLIC CLOVES, MINCED
2	EGGS, LIGHTLY BEATEN
1½	CUPS BEAN SPROUTS
¼	CUP CHOPPED SCALLIONS OR CHINESE CHIVES
2	TABLESPOONS CRUSHED ROASTED PEANUTS
	LIME WEDGE, FOR GARNISH
1	TEASPOON ROASTED CHILI POWDER (SEE RECIPE), TO TASTE

ROASTED CHILI POWDER

2	CUPS DRIED THAI BIRD'S EYE OR ARBOL CHILIES, STEMMED

CHICKEN PAD SEE EW

YIELD: 4 SERVINGS / **ACTIVE TIME:** 15 MINUTES / **TOTAL TIME:** 30 MINUTES

The dark soy, fish, and oyster sauces used in this traditional Thai rice noodle dish pack it with umami. Be sure not to overcrowd the pan when cooking the noodles; work in batches if necessary.

1. If using dry noodles, steep them in warm water until pliable.

2. Cut the broccoli stalks on a bias lengthwise; keep the leafy part and sliced stalks separate.

3. Add the oil to a wok or nonstick pan over high heat. Once it is smoking, add the chicken and sauté for 1 minute. Add the broccoli stalks and garlic and stir-fry for 1 minute. Add the egg and scramble, mixing all of the ingredients well.

4. Once the chicken is cooked through, add the noodles, sweet soy, oyster sauce, soy sauce, vinegar, and sugar and cook for 1 minute, until the mixture is well coated with sauce.

5. Turn down the heat to medium-high and do not the disturb noodles; let the underside of the noodles start to brown and caramelize, about 1 minute. Flip the noodles and cook for another minute undisturbed to get a char flavor.

6. Fold in the broccoli leaves at the end, and finish with the white pepper and fish sauce.

7. Garnish with the lime wedge and serve with Chili Garlic Sauce and Roasted Chili Powder.

INGREDIENTS:

1   LB. FRESH THICK RICE NOODLES OR 8 OZ. DRY THICK RICE NOODLES

¾   LB. CHINESE BROCCOLI OR BROCCOLI FLORETS

2   TABLESPOONS VEGETABLE OIL

½   LB. CHICKEN, SKINLESS AND BONELESS, BITE-SIZE PIECES

2-3   GARLIC CLOVES, MINCED

1   EGG

2   TABLESPOONS DARK SWEET SOY SAUCE

2   TABLESPOONS OYSTER SAUCE

2   TABLESPOONS SOY SAUCE

2   TEASPOONS DISTILLED VINEGAR

1   TEASPOON SUGAR

WHITE PEPPER, TO TASTE

FISH SAUCE, TO TASTE

LIME WEDGE, FOR GARNISH

CHILI GARLIC SAUCE (SEE PAGE 180), TO SERVE

ROASTED CHILI POWDER (SEE PAGE 309), TO SERVE

VIETNAMESE CREPE

YIELD: 4 SERVINGS / **ACTIVE TIME:** 30 MINUTES / **TOTAL TIME:** 30 MINUTES

French culinary influence is woven into many elements of Vietnamese cuisine, this dish is one prominent example of a French technique being fused with ingredients like coconut milk and perilla leaves.

1. In a large bowl, combine all of the batter ingredients, except the scallions, and incorporate well, but don't overmix, and make sure the batter isn't too thick. Fold in the scallions when ready to use the crepe batter.

2. Add the oil to a nonstick pan over medium-high heat, and once the oil is shimmering, add some of the sliced onion and some of the shrimp and sauté for 2 minutes.

3. Turn down the heat to low-medium and pour in ⅓ cup of batter, being sure to tilt and rotate the pan so the batter spreads evenly. Add more batter if needed to cover the nonstick pan. Cook for 2 to 3 minutes.

4. Add some of the bean sprouts, torn mint, perilla leaf, and chicharrón to the pan and cover with the lid for 1 to 2 minutes.

5. Remove the lid and continue to cook to crisp up the crepe, approximately 3 to 4 minutes. Brush the oil on the edges if needed.

6. Once ready, fold the crepe in half and serve immediately. Garnish with more of the herbs, bean sprouts, and Nuoc Cham.

INGREDIENTS:

BATTER

2	CUPS RICE FLOUR
⅔	CUP ALL-PURPOSE FLOUR
½	TABLESPOON TURMERIC
3	CUPS SODA WATER, AS NEEDED
¾	CUP COCONUT MILK
2	TABLESPOONS SALT
	VEGETABLE OIL, AS NEEDED
3	TABLESPOONS CHOPPED SCALLIONS

FILLING

2	TEASPOONS VEGETABLE OIL, PLUS MORE AS NEEDED
1	YELLOW ONION, THINLY SLICED
1	LB. SHRIMP, CLEANED AND DEVEINED
1	LB. BEAN SPROUTS
1	BUNCH MINT
1	BUNCH PERILLA LEAF
¼	CUP PORK CHICHARRÓN, CHOPPED
1	BUNCH CILANTRO, FOR GARNISH

SAUCE

	NUOC CHAM (SEE PAGE 179), TO TASTE

SPICY SHRIMP WITH SNAP PEAS

YIELD: 4 SERVINGS / **ACTIVE TIME:** 30 MINUTES / **TOTAL TIME:** 30 MINUTES

This is a Classic Chinese stir-fry dish that can be quickly prepared and served over rice for a well-balanced and flavorful meal.

1. Combine the sugar, soy sauce, water, vinegar, garlic, ginger, wine, sesame oil, and chili flakes in a bowl and mix well. Set aside.

2. Combine the shrimp with the salt in a bowl, mix well, and let stand for 5 minutes. Rinse and pat dry.

3. Add the canola oil to a wok over medium-high heat, and once hot, carefully blanch the shrimp until they just turn pink; the shrimp should not be fully cooked. Use a slotted spoon or kitchen spider to remove and set aside.

4. Remove all but 1 or 2 tablespoons of the hot oil and heat the wok to high. Add the sauce mixture and cook until bubbly, then stir in enough cornstarch slurry to thicken the sauce.

5. Return the shrimp to the pan, along with the snap peas, and stir to coat, then cook the shrimp through, about 2 minutes.

6. Transfer to a plate and garnish with the scallions and sesame seeds.

INGREDIENTS:

⅓ CUP GRANULATED SUGAR

½ CUP SOY SAUCE

½ CUP WATER

2 TABLESPOONS RICE VINEGAR

3 TABLESPOONS MINCED GARLIC

3 TABLESPOONS MINCED GINGER

2 TABLESPOONS RICE WINE

2 TABLESPOONS SESAME OIL

1 TEASPOON DRIED CHILI FLAKES

2 LBS. SHRIMP, PEELED AND DEVEINED

3 TABLESPOONS COARSE SEA SALT

3 CUPS CANOLA OIL

1–2 TABLESPOONS CORNSTARCH SLURRY (2:1 RATIO), AS PREFERRED

1 CUP SNAP PEAS, BLANCHED

3 TABLESPOONS CHOPPED SCALLIONS, FOR GARNISH

1–2 TABLESPOONS TOASTED SESAME SEEDS, FOR GARNISH

BEEF WITH STRAW MUSHROOMS
& OYSTER SAUCE

YIELD: 4 SERVINGS / ACTIVE TIME: 30 MINUTES / TOTAL TIME: 1 HOUR

This is a humble Chinese steak and mushroom dish. Straw mushrooms are native to the East and Southeast Asian regions; they can be found fresh, canned, or in dried format.

1. Cut the flank steak into 3 large strips, then slice against the grain into ⅛-inch-thick slices. Mix the beef slices with 3 tablespoons of the cornstarch and the salt and, white pepper, then add the egg white and let rest for 30 minutes.

2. Combine of the cornstarch and the salt and, oyster sauce, hoisin sauce, wine, soy sauce, ketchup, sugar, and sesame oil in a bowl, mix well, and set aside. Using the remaining cornstarch, make a slurry (1:1 ratio) in a separate bowl and set aside.

3. Add the canola oil to a wok or sauté pan over medium heat. Once the oil is hot, add the beef slices and quickly fry until mostly done. Remove with a slotted spoon or kitchen spider and set aside.

4. Remove all but 2 tablespoons of the hot oil, increase the heat to mediumthehigh, and cook the carrots, mushrooms, garlic, and ginger for 1 minute.

5. Add the prepared sauce mixture and bring to a boil, stirring regularly, and add enough slurry to thicken to a medium gravy consistency.

6. Return the beef to the pan, cook in the sauce for 1 minute, and finish with the scallions.

INGREDIENTS:

½–⅔	LB. FLANK STEAK
5	TEASPOONS CORNSTARCH, DIVIDED
½	TEASPOON SALT
¼	TEASPOON WHITE PEPPER
1	EGG WHITE, BEATEN
½	CUP CHICKEN STOCK (SEE PAGE 680)
3	TABLESPOONS OYSTER SAUCE
1	TABLESPOON HOISIN SAUCE
¼	CUP RICE WINE
1	TABLESPOON DARK SOY SAUCE
1	TABLESPOON KETCHUP
1	TEASPOON SUGAR
1	TEASPOON SESAME OIL
2	CUPS CANOLA OIL
½	CUP THINLY SLICED CARROTS
10–12	STRAW MUSHROOMS
2	TABLESPOONS MINCED GARLIC
3	TABLESPOONS FINE JULIENNED GINGER
½	YELLOW MEDIUM ONION, JULIENNED
2	SCALLIONS, CUT ON A BIAS INTO 2-INCH PIECES

KUNG PAO CHICKEN

YIELD: 4 SERVINGS / **ACTIVE TIME**: 30 MINUTES / **TOTAL TIME**: 30 MINUTES

The most popular Szechuan Chinese dish is kung pao chicken due to the combination of dry red chilies and toasted peanuts. This dish is easily found in Chinese restaurants outside of China.

1. Combine the chicken and the Meat Marinade, being sure to massage the marinade into the meat.

2. In a bowl, combine the soy sauce, sugar, vinegar, bean sauce, garlic sauce, chili flakes, and Szechuan peppercorns, mix well, and set aside.

3. Add the oil to a wok over medium heat, and when the oil is hot, fry the peanuts until golden brown. Remove the peanuts with a slotted spoon, drain the excess oil, and set aside.

4. Remove all but 2 tablespoons of the hot oil from the wok and increase the heat to medium-high. Add the dried chilies and sauté for 10 to 20 seconds, being sure not to burn, and then add the garlic and ginger, and cook for 1 minute.

5. Add the chicken and cook until two-thirds done. Add the vegetables and stir-fry for 1 minute, and then add the prepared sauce. When the liquid starts to bubble, add enough slurry to thicken the sauce.

6. Adjust the seasoning and serve immediately with rice and your favorite condiments.

INGREDIENTS:

1	LB. SKINLESS AND BONELESS CHICKEN, BREASTS OR THIGHS, CUT INTO ¾-INCH PIECES
1	TABLESPOON MEAT MARINADE (SEE PAGE 353)
3	TABLESPOONS SOY SAUCE
2	TABLESPOONS SUGAR
3	TABLESPOONS RICE VINEGAR
2	TABLESPOONS SWEET BEAN SAUCE
3	TABLESPOONS CHILI GARLIC SAUCE (SEE PAGE 180)
1-2	TEASPOONS CHILI FLAKES
1	TEASPOON GROUND SZECHUAN PEPPERCORNS
1	CUP VEGETABLE OIL
½	CUP RAW AND SHELLED PEANUTS
6-8	DRIED RED CHILI PEPPERS
1	TABLESPOON MINCED GARLIC
1	TABLESPOON MINCED GINGER
1	CUP BABY CORN, CUT IN ¾-INCH PIECES (OPTIONAL)
1	RED BELL PEPPER, CUT INTO ¾-INCH PIECES
1	GREEN BELL PEPPER, CUT INTO ¾-INCH PIECES
2	SCALLIONS, WHITE PARTS CHOPPED INTO ½-INCH PIECES
1-2	TABLESPOONS CORNSTARCH SLURRY (1:2 RATIO), AS NEEDED

MAPO TOFU

YIELD: 4 SERVINGS / **ACTIVE TIME:** 30 MINUTES / **TOTAL TIME:** 30 MINUTES

A popular Szechuan dish, it features soft tofu and ground pork in a spicy chili sauce. Szechuan peppers and peppercorns pack a lot of heat, but the level of spice can be adjusted, based on preference, by adding less than the suggested amount.

1. Drain the tofu, pat dry, and cut into 1-inch cubes.

2. In a bowl, combine the water, chili sauce, soy sauce, brown sugar, Szechuan peppercorns, and sesame oil, mix well, and set aside.

3. Add the vegetable oil to a wok over medium heat, and when the oil begins to shimmer, add the pork. Cook until browned, adding the garlic, ginger, and bean sauce at the midway point of browning.

4. Once the pork is browned, add the prepared sauce and bring to a boil. Add the tofu, mushrooms, water chestnuts, and oyster sauce and bring to a simmer. Do not stir too much; you don't want to break up the tofu.

5. Stir in the slurry to thicken the mapo tofu.

6. Adjust the seasoning, finish with the scallions, and serve with rice and chili oil.

INGREDIENTS:

1	PACKAGE SILKEN TOFU
¼	CUP WATER
2	TABLESPOONS CHILI SAUCE
1	TABLESPOON SOY SAUCE
½	TABLESPOON BROWN SUGAR
¼	TEASPOON GROUND SZECHUAN PEPPERCORNS
1	TEASPOON SESAME OIL
2	TABLESPOONS VEGETABLE OIL
½	LB. GROUND PORK
1	TABLESPOON MINCED GARLIC
½	TABLESPOON MINCED GINGER
2	TEASPOONS GROUND BEAN SAUCE OR FERMENTED BLACK BEANS
5-6	SHIITAKE MUSHROOMS, SLICED
2	TABLESPOONS DICED WATER CHESTNUTS
2	TABLESPOONS OYSTER SAUCE
1-2	TABLESPOONS CORNSTARCH SLURRY (1:1 RATIO), AS NEEDED
¼	CUP MINCED SCALLIONS

MONGOLIAN BEEF

YIELD: 4 SERVINGS / **ACTIVE TIME**: 30 MINUTES / **TOTAL TIME**: 1 HOUR

This popular stir-fry dish has become a staple in Chinese–American restaurants. It is cooked with a lot of scallions and is not spicy, but that can be adjusted to taste.

1. In a bowl, combine the steak with the cornstarch, white pepper, and salt. Add the egg whites, mix, and let the beef marinate for 30 minutes.

2. In a separate bowl, make the sauce by combining the soy sauce, sambal, sugar, hoisin sauce, wine, garlic, vinegar, and chili flakes and mixing well. Set aside.

3. If using the bean thread noodles, add the oil to a wok over medium-high heat, and once the oil is hot, deep-fry the bean thread noodles according to the package directions. Drain the cooked noodles on a paper towel–lined plate and set aside on a serving platter.

4. Using the same oil, and adding more oil if needed, blanch the steak until two-thirds cooked. Drain on a paper towel–lined plate and set aside.

5. In a clean pan over medium heat, combine the prepared sauce, peppers, and scallions and bring to a simmer. Once bubbling, add the slurry to thicken the sauce.

6. Add the beef to the simmering sauce to finish cooking, about 5 minutes.

7. Adjust the seasoning as needed and serve.

8. If using the bean thread noodles, pour the contents of the pan over the prepared noodles. Otherwise, serve with rice and your favorite condiments.

INGREDIENTS:

1	LB. FLANK STEAK, THINLY SLICED ACROSS THE GRAIN INTO ⅛-INCH PIECES
1	TABLESPOON CORNSTARCH
¼	TEASPOON WHITE PEPPER
½	TEASPOON SALT
3	EGG WHITES, BEATEN
¼	CUP SOY SAUCE
2	TABLESPOONS SAMBAL
1½	TABLESPOONS GRANULATED SUGAR
1	TABLESPOON HOISIN SAUCE
1	TABLESPOON RICE WINE
2	TABLESPOONS MINCED GARLIC
1	TEASPOON WHITE DISTILLED VINEGAR
1	TEASPOON DRIED CHILI FLAKES
1	CUP CANOLA OIL, PLUS MORE AS NEEDED
½	OZ. BEAN THREAD NOODLES (OPTIONAL)
2	BELL PEPPERS, DIAGONALLY CUT INTO 2-INCH PIECES
3-4	SCALLIONS, CUT ON A BIAS INTO 2-INCH-LONG PIECES
3	RED CHILIES, SEEDED AND SLICED
1-2	TABLESPOONS CORNSTARCH SLURRY (1:1 RATIO), AS NEEDED

MU SHU PORK WITH CHINESE PANCAKES

YIELD: 4 SERVINGS / **ACTIVE TIME:** 30 MINUTES / **TOTAL TIME:** 1 HOUR AND 30 MINUTES

This staple of Chinese-American restaurants originated in Northern China. It's a fun DIY dish, creating "tacos" with the pancakes and stir-fry.

1. In a bowl, combine the pork, cornstarch, dark soy sauce, wine, and 1 teaspoon of sesame oil, mix well, and set aside.

2. Add a little vegetable oil to a wok or pan over medium-high heat. Once the oil begins to shimmer, stir-fry the mushrooms, lily buds, and mustard greens for 2 to 3 minutes. Remove from the wok and set aside.

3. Add a little more oil to the pan, along with the jicama, and cook for 10 to 20 seconds. Add the bean sprouts and spinach and cook until the vegetables start to wilt without becoming soggy. Remove and set aside.

4. In the same wok, add a little more oil, along with the pork, ginger, and garlic, and cook until the meat starts to brown.

5. Add the light soy sauce, oyster sauce, Chicken Stock or water, and 2 teaspoons of sesame oil, bring the mixture to a boil, and then add enough slurry to thicken. As the mixture simmers, return the cooked vegetables to the pan, along with the scallions. Mix well and transfer to a serving plate.

6. Serve with the Mandarin Pancakes and hoisin sauce. Use the scallion "brush" to sauce the pancakes, and place the mu shu pork filling on the pancakes and roll up like a burrito.

INGREDIENTS:

½	LB. PORK, CUT INTO THIN STRIPS
2	TEASPOONS CORNSTARCH
2	TEASPOONS DARK SOY SAUCE
2	TEASPOONS RICE WINE
3	TEASPOONS SESAME OIL, DIVIDED
	VEGETABLE OIL, AS NEEDED
4	WOOD EAR MUSHROOMS, SOAKED AND CUT INTO THIN STRIPS
16	DRIED LILY BUDS, SOAKED AND HARD ENDS CUT OFF
¼	CUP SZECHUAN PICKLED MUSTARD GREENS, CUT INTO STRIPS
1	CUP THINLY SLICED JICAMA
2	CUPS BEAN SPROUTS
2	CUPS SPINACH, WITH STEMS
3	TABLESPOONS THINLY SLICED GINGER
2	TABLESPOONS MINCED GARLIC
1	TABLESPOON LIGHT SOY SAUCE
1½	TABLESPOONS OYSTER SAUCE
¼	CUP CHICKEN STOCK (SEE PAGE 680) OR WATER
2-3	TABLESPOONS CORNSTARCH SLURRY (1:1 RATIO), AS NEEDED
2	SCALLIONS, SLICED IN THIN, DIAGONAL STRIPS
	MANDARIN PANCAKES (SEE RECIPE)
	HOISIN SAUCE
	SCALLION "BRUSH," FOR GARNISH

Continued . . .

MANDARIN PANCAKES

1. Add the flour to a bowl, stir well, and make a well in the center of the flour.

2. Carefully pour the boiling water into the well and mix in the flour with chopsticks or a spoon. Then pour in the cold water, continuing to stir until the mixture turns into a shaggy ball.

3. Place the shaggy dough on a clean, flour-dusted, work surface and knead the dough by hand until it forms a smooth ball. Cover the dough and let rest for 30 minutes at room temperature.

4. After resting, on a clean, flour-dusted work surface, separate the dough into two parts. Roll each into a rope, and cut into 12 to 14 pieces. Roll each piece of dough into a smaller ball and let rest, covered, for 15 minutes at room temperature.

5. Flatten each ball with the palm of your hand, brush the tips with the sesame oil, and dust with a little flour. Make stacks of 2 pieces of dough, making sure the oiled sides are pressed together.

6. Roll each dough stack with a rolling pin into a thin round. Dust the pin and work surface with flour as needed.

7. Preheat a nonstick skillet over medium heat, and when hot, place the rolled dough in the pan. Cook until lightly brown on one side, and then flip the pancake and lightly brown the other side. Once done, remove from the skillet, and at the seam of the 2 pressed doughs, separate them.

8. Serve immediately, or fold in half and place in a bamboo steamer or wrapped in a clean kitchen towel to keep warm until serving time, or reheat gently in a microwave.

INGREDIENTS:

MANDARIN PANCAKES

- 3   CUPS ALL-PURPOSE FLOUR, PLUS MORE AS NEEDED
- ½   CUP BOILING WATER
- ½   CUP COLD WATER, PLUS MORE AS NEEDED
- 2   TABLESPOONS SESAME OIL

SPICY CHICKEN SALAD

YIELD: 4 SERVINGS / **ACTIVE TIME:** 30 MINUTES / **TOTAL TIME:** 1 HOUR

Adding Chinese flavors and ingredients gives new life to this popular American dish. To prepare this recipe faster, use leftover chicken.

1. In a bowl, make a marinade by combining 2 tablespoons of soy sauce, 2 tablespoons of hoisin sauce, 3 garlic cloves, and 1 teaspoon of sugar and mixing well.

2. Lightly score the chicken breasts on both sides and marinate them for at least 30 minutes.

3. Grill, broil, or panfry the chicken, cool, and slice thinly or cut into a small dice.

4. Add the vegetable oil to a wok over medium-high heat. When the oil is hot, deep-fry the peanuts until golden brown. Drain on a paper towel–lined plate, and once cool, chop and set aside.

5. In same oil, deep-fry the bean thread noodles, drain on a paper towel–lined plate, and set aside.

6. In a bowl, prepare the salad dressing by combining the vinegar, sugar, soy sauce, 1 tablespoon of hoisin sauce, the remainder of the garlic, chili flakes, and chili paste and mixing well. Slowly whisk in the canola and sesame oils.

7. In a large bowl, toss the cut chicken, cabbages, carrots, scallions, cilantro, and half of the peanuts. Add the dressing and mix well.

8. Transfer to a platter and garnish with the remaining peanuts, fried bean thread noodles, and orange segments.

INGREDIENTS:

4	TABLESPOONS SOY SAUCE, DIVIDED
3	TABLESPOONS HOISIN SAUCE, DIVIDED
5	GARLIC CLOVES, MINCED, DIVIDED
2	TABLESPOONS SUGAR, PLUS 1 TEASPOON, DIVIDED
2	SKINLESS AND BONELESS CHICKEN BREASTS
2	CUPS VEGETABLE OIL, FOR DEEP-FRYING
⅔	CUP PEANUTS, DIVIDED
⅔	OZ. BEAN THREAD NOODLES, FOR GARNISH
2	TABLESPOONS WHITE WINE VINEGAR
2	TABLESPOONS SUGAR
2	TABLESPOONS SOY SAUCE
½	TEASPOON DRY CHILI FLAKES
1	TABLESPOON CHILI PASTE
2	TABLESPOONS CANOLA OIL
1	TABLESPOON SESAME OIL
4	CUPS JULIENNED NAPA CABBAGE
1	CUP JULIENNED RED CABBAGE
1	CUP JULIENNED CARROTS
3	SCALLIONS, CHOPPED
¼	CUP COARSELY CHOPPED CILANTRO
⅔	CUP MANDARIN ORANGE SEGMENTS, FOR GARNISH

JAJANGMYEON

YIELD: 4 SERVINGS / **ACTIVE TIME:** 30 MINUTES / **TOTAL TIME:** 30 MINUTES

This black bean and pork gravy noodle dish is a very popular Korean–Chinese comfort food.

1. Prepare the sauce by combining the water, 1 teaspoon of sesame oil, bean sauce, chili paste, vinegar, sugar, and soy sauce in a bowl and mixing well. Set aside.

2. While bringing a pot of water to boil, add the oil to a wok or pan over medium-high heat. Once the oil begins to shimmer, add the pork and onion and stir-fry until the onion is translucent.

3. Add the prepared sauce to the pork and stir, cooking until bubbly. Thicken with the slurry until the gravy is consistent. Adjust the seasoning and remove from heat.

4. Cook the noodles until done, strain, toss with 1 tablespoon of sesame oil, and place in a serving bowl. Spoon the pork sauce over the noodles and garnish with the cucumber.

INGREDIENTS:

- ½ CUP WATER, PLUS MORE TO COOK NOODLES
- 1 TABLESPOON SESAME OIL, PLUS 1 TEASPOON, DIVIDED
- 2 TABLESPOONS GROUND BEAN SAUCE
- 3 TABLESPOONS CHILI PASTE
- 2 TEASPOONS CHINKIANG VINEGAR
- 1 TEASPOON SUGAR
- 2 TABLESPOONS DARK SOY SAUCE
- 1 TABLESPOON CANOLA OIL
- ½ LB. GROUND PORK
- 1 CUP SMALL DICED YELLOW ONION
- CORNSTARCH SLURRY (1:1 RATIO), AS NEEDED
- ½ LB. FRESH NOODLES
- ½ CUP THINLY JULIENNED ENGLISH CUCUMBER, FOR GARNISH

TEA-SMOKED CHICKEN

YIELD: 4 SERVINGS / **ACTIVE TIME:** 1 HOUR / **TOTAL TIME:** 24 HOURS

Smoking meat, vegetables, or tofu with tea leaves is a traditional Chinese cooking method. Black, green, or jasmine tea leaves can be used, and aromatics like ginger and star anise can be added to the mix to experiment with flavors and aromas. The ginger punch from the sauce goes perfectly with this chicken, but it is, in fact, a universal dipping sauce.

1. In a small bowl, combine the salt, Szechuan peppercorns, and five-spice powder and rub it all over the chicken—inside and outside. Refrigerate uncovered for at least 8 hours and for as many as 24 hours.

2. When ready to steam the chicken, prepare a steamer and steam the chicken breast side up for 45 minutes to 1 hour, or until an internal temperature of 170°F is achieved. Set aside.

3. Combine the rice, brown sugar, and tea leaves in a bowl and mix well.

4. Line a roasting pan with double foil and spread out the black tea leaf mixture. Place the chicken breast side up on a roasting rack and place the rack in the roasting pan; the chicken should not be touching the tea leaf mixture. Tent the entire chicken with heavy-duty foil, making sure the chicken is well sealed.

5. Set the roasting pan over medium-high heat for 2 to 3 minutes, and then lower the heat to medium-low and cook until you detect smoke. Once smoke is detected, smoke for 30 minutes. Turn off the heat let stand, still tented, for 30 more minutes.

6. Place the chicken on a cutting board, brush lightly with sesame oil, and let cool before chopping and serving.

7. Serve with the Scallion Ginger Sauce and shrimp chips.

SCALLION GINGER SAUCE

1. In a bowl, combine all of the ingredients, mix well, and let stand for 1 hour before using. Adjust the seasoning with salt, to taste.

INGREDIENTS:

1	TABLESPOON SALT
1	TEASPOON GROUND SZECHUAN PEPPERCORNS
½	TEASPOON FIVE-SPICE POWDER
3½	LBS. WHOLE CHICKEN
⅔	CUP RICE
⅔	CUP BROWN SUGAR
½	CUP BLACK TEA LEAVES
	SCALLION GINGER SAUCE (SEE RECIPE)
	FRIED SHRIMP CHIPS, FOR GARNISH (OPTIONAL)

SCALLION GINGER SAUCE

4-6	SCALLIONS, WHITE AND LIGHT GREEN PARTS ONLY, MINCED
3	TABLESPOONS FINELY GRATED GINGER
¼	CUP VEGETABLE OIL
	SALT, TO TASTE

DAN DAN NOODLES

This Szechuan street food has gone international, thanks to these spicy noodles with preserved vegetables.

1. Add 1 tablespoon of vegetable oil to a wok or sauté pan over medium-high heat. Once the oil begins to shimmer, stir-fry the pork and pickled mustard greens for about 5 minutes.

2. Add the sugar, soy sauces, vinegar, chili paste, peanut butter, sesame oil, and sriracha and cook for about 2 minutes, stirring well. Add the slurry to thicken, and let simmer.

3. Bring a pot of water to a boil and cook the noodles until al dente. Drain and portion the noodles into bowls. Pour the sauce over the noodles and garnish with the peanuts, chili flakes, and scallions.

INGREDIENTS:

- 2 TABLESPOONS VEGETABLE OIL, DIVIDED
- 1 CUP GROUND PORK
- 2 TABLESPOONS MINCED PICKLED SZECHUAN MUSTARD GREENS
- 1 TABLESPOON SUGAR
- 1 TABLESPOON DARK SOY SAUCE
- 2 TEASPOONS LIGHT SOY SAUCE
- 2 TEASPOONS CHINKIANG VINEGAR
- 1 TABLESPOON CHILI PASTE
- 1 TABLESPOON PEANUT BUTTER
- 3 TEASPOONS SESAME OIL
- 2 TEASPOONS SRIRACHA
- CORNSTARCH SLURRY (1:1 RATION), AS NEEDED
- 1 LB. FRESH EGG NOODLES
- ¼ CUP FINELY CHOPPED ROASTED PEANUTS, FOR GARNISH
- DRY CHILI FLAKES, FOR GARNISH
- 1 SCALLION, MINCED, FOR GARNISH

CHAR SIU PORK

YIELD: 8 SERVINGS / **ACTIVE TIME**: 30 MINUTES / **TOTAL TIME**: 49 HOURS

This Cantonese-style barbeque dates to the third century; it can be accompanied with any vegetable dish, fried rice, or white rice.

1. In a large bowl, combine all of the ingredients, except the pork and honey, and mix well. Add the pork, massaging the marinade into the meat. Cover the bowl and refrigerate for 48 hours.

2. When ready to cook the pork, let stand at room temperature for 1 hour.

3. Preheat the oven to 375°F, with a pan of water at the bottom of the oven.

4. Place the pork on a sheet pan, reserving the marinade, and roast for 25 to 30 minutes. In a bowl, combine the reserved marinade with the honey and mix well.

5. Using tongs, turn over the pork, brush with the reserved marinade, and continue to roast. After 20 minutes, turn the pork over again, brush with the marinade, and roast for another 10 to 20 minutes, until the pork is cooked.

6. Let the pork rest before slicing against the grain to serve.

INGREDIENTS:

¼ CUP HOISIN SAUCE

1 TABLESPOON DARK SOY SAUCE

2 TABLESPOONS COOKING WINE

2 TABLESPOONS KETCHUP

1 TABLESPOON OYSTER SAUCE

¼ CUP SUGAR

2 TEASPOONS SALT

3 PINCHES CURING SALT

1 TEASPOON CHINESE FIVE-SPICE POWDER

1 TEASPOON RED FOOD COLORING (OPTIONAL)

4 LBS. PORK SHOULDER, CUT WITH THE GRAIN INTO 3 OR 4 LONG STRIPS 2 TO 3 INCHES THICK

¼ CUP HONEY

PORK FRIED RICE

YIELD: 4 SERVINGS / ACTIVE TIME: 30 MINUTES / TOTAL TIME: 30 MINUTES

This is a favorite Chinese Cantonese-style fried rice. If you like runny eggs, skip cooking the eggs in the rice and top each serving with an egg cooked the way you like it.

1. Add 1 tablespoon of vegetable oil to a wok over medium-high heat. Once the oil begins to shimmer, add the onion, carrot, and celery and stir-fry for 1 minute. Set aside.

2. Using the same pan, heat the remaining oil and add the Char Siu Pork or sausage and stir-fry for 30 seconds. Add the rice and cook until heated through, stirring frequently.

3. Return the vegetables to the pan, along with the eggs, peas, scallions, both soy sauces, and sesame oil and stir-fry for another minute.

4. Adjust the seasoning and serve immediately.

INGREDIENTS:

3	TABLESPOONS VEGETABLE OIL, DIVIDED
½	CUP FINELY DICED ONION
½	CUP FINELY DICED CARROT
½	CUP FINELY DICED CELERY
½	CUP SMALL DICED CHAR SIU PORK (SEE PAGE 336) OR LAP CHEONG
4	CUPS COOKED RICE, COOLED AND LUMPS SEPARATED
3	EGGS, BEATEN
1	CUP FROZEN PEAS
½	CUP FINELY CHOPPED SCALLIONS
2	TABLESPOONS DARK SOY SAUCE
1	TABLESPOON LIGHT SOY SAUCE
½	TEASPOON SESAME OIL

SWEET & SOUR PORK

YIELD: 4 SERVINGS / **ACTIVE TIME:** 30 MINUTES / **TOTAL TIME:** 1 HOUR

Chinese cuisine is built around flavors that complement one another through contrast, with sweet and sour being the most emblematic. This stir-fry is one of the most well-known Asian dishes outside of China.

1. In a bowl, combine the pork, wine, and soy sauce, mix well, and let stand for 15 minutes.

2. Toss the marinated pork with the cornstarch until the pieces of pork are not sticking together.

3. In a large pan or Dutch oven, heat the vegetable oil to 375°F, and then deep-fry the pork pieces until golden brown. Remove with a slotted spoon or kitchen spider, drain on a paper towel–lined plate, and set aside.

4. Add 1 tablespoon of oil to a wok over high heat. Once the oil begins to shimmer, stir-fry the onion and pepper for 1 minute and set aside.

5. In same wok, add the brown sugar, pineapple juice, vinegars, ketchup, and salt and mix well. When the sauce comes to a boil, add the slurry to thicken, and let simmer. Return the onion and pepper to the pan, add the carrot and pineapple, and cook for 1 minute.

6. Add the pork to the sauce, stir to combine, and serve immediately.

INGREDIENTS:

1½	LBS. PORK SHOULDER, CUT INTO ½-INCH CUBES
1	TABLESPOON RICE WINE
1	TABLESPOON SOY SAUCE
1	CUP CORNSTARCH
	VEGETABLE OIL, FOR DEEP-FRYING AND AS NEEDED
½	ONION, CUT INTO 1-INCH CUBES
½	GREEN BELL PEPPER, CUT INTO 1-INCH CUBES
½	CUP BROWN SUGAR
⅓	CUP PINEAPPLE JUICE
¼	CUP RED VINEGAR
3	TABLESPOONS WHITE WINE VINEGAR
1	TABLESPOON KETCHUP
1	TEASPOON SALT
	CORNSTARCH SLURRY (1:1 RATIO), AS NEEDED
½	CARROT, CUT INTO ¼-INCH CUBES AND PARBOILED
1	CUP CUBED PINEAPPLE

YANG CHOW FRIED RICE

YIELD: 4 SERVINGS / **ACTIVE TIME:** 15 MINUTES / **TOTAL TIME:** 15 MINUTES

When you order "house-fried rice" at a Chinese restaurant, you will be served yang chow. What makes this style of fried rice distinct is the combination of protein—meat, seafood, and pork —that is added.

1. Add the oil to a wok over medium-high heat. Once the oil begins to shimmer, add the shrimp and Char Siu Pork and stir-fry until the shrimp turns pink.

2. Add the garlic, carrots, and peas and stir-fry well. Season with the salt, white pepper, and sesame oil, and then add the rice and mix well.

3. When the rice is heated through, add the eggs and scallions and mix well.

4. Adjust the seasoning as needed and serve.

INGREDIENTS:

2-3	TABLESPOONS CANOLA OIL
10-12	SHRIMP, PEELED, DEVEINED, AND CUT INTO ½-INCH PIECES
¼	CUP CHAR SIU PORK (SEE PAGE 336) OR LAP CHEONG, CUT INTO SMALL DICE
3	GARLIC CLOVES, MINCED
⅓	CUP SMALL DICED CARROTS, BLANCHED
⅔	CUP FROZEN PEAS
	SALT, TO TASTE
	WHITE PEPPER, TO TASTE
1	TEASPOON SESAME OIL
4	CUPS DAY-OLD COOKED RICE
3	EGGS, BEATEN
4	SCALLIONS, FINELY CHOPPED

STEAMED FISH WITH FRESH GINGER & SCALLIONS

YIELD: 4 SERVINGS / **ACTIVE TIME:** 30 MINUTES / **TOTAL TIME:** 30 MINUTES

This Cantonese-influenced dish is light and subtle, with aromatics from the ginger and fresh herbs. It is a great element to a big family-style meal.

1. Make 2 to 3 diagonal scores on both sides of the fish. Season both sides with the salt and place one-third of the ginger in the cavity of the fish.

2. If you do not have a bamboo steamer ,make a steamer by placing a metal rack in a wok or large pan with a lid. Add water to the pan and steam the fish for 15 minutes, or until just done.

3. Place the steamed fish on a serving plate, and scatter the rest of the ginger, and the scallions and cilantro over the fish.

4. Heat the oil in a small pan until hot. As it heats, pour the soy sauce over the fish.

5. As soon as the oil is hot, pour it over the entire fish; the oil should sizzle, and the fish should smell aromatic from the hot oil over the ginger, cilantro, and scallions.

6. Serve immediately with the rice.

INGREDIENTS:

1	WHOLE STRIPED BASS, CLEANED, SCALED, AND GUTTED
	SALT, TO TASTE
¼	CUP THINLY SLICED GINGER SLIVERS, DIVIDED
¼	CUP THINLY SLICED SCALLION SLIVERS
8-10	CILANTRO SPRIGS
¼	CUP CANOLA OIL
½	CUP LIGHT SOY SAUCE
	RICE, FOR SERVING

CRYSTAL PRAWNS WITH GINGER & VEGETABLES

YIELD: 4 SERVINGS / ACTIVE TIME: 30 MINUTES / TOTAL TIME: 1 HOUR

This Shanghai dish gets its name from the texture and look of the shrimp once it is salted and cooked. While it is a meal that is easy to prepare, note that one must allot time for letting the shrimp sit in the rice wine. It's best enjoyed over white rice.

1. Rub the cleaned prawns with rock salt, let the shrimp rest for 5 minutes, and then rinse off the salted prawns and pat dry.

2. In a bowl, combine the prawns with 1 tablespoon of wine, and let stand for at least 30 minutes.

3. Add the canola oil to a wok over medium heat, and once warm, blanch canola prawns until they just turn pink; do not cook through. Remove with a slotted spoon or kitchen spider and drain on a paper towel–lined plate.

4. Drain off all but 1 tablespoon of oil, add the ginger and garlic, and increase the heat to medium-high. Add the snap peas or snow peas and stir-fry for 1 minute, then add the onions and stir-fry for another 2 minutes, until the onion is just cooked. Remove the vegetables from the pan and set aside.

5. In the same wok, add a little more canola oil, and over medium heat, stir-fry the bell peppers, baby corn, and mushrooms, and season lightly with the salt and a pinch of sugar. When heated through, return the peas, onions, garlic, and ginger to the pan.

6. Stir in the Chicken stock, vinegar, 1 teaspoon of wine, and the sugar and sesame oil until the sauce is bubbly. Add the slurry to thicken, and stir.

7. Return the prawns to the pan and mix well, cooking for 1 minute.

8. Finish with the scallions and serve.

INGREDIENTS:

- 1 LB. PRAWNS, SHELLED AND DEVEINED
- 1 TABLESPOON ROCK SALT
- 1 TABLESPOON MICHIU RICE WINE, PLUS 1 TEASPOON, DIVIDED
- 2 CUPS CANOLA OIL, PLUS MORE AS NEEDED
- 1 TABLESPOON MINCED GINGER
- 1 TABLESPOON MINCED GARLIC
- 12 SNAP PEAS OR SNOW PEAS, ENDS TRIMMED
- ½ CUP ONION WEDGES, CUT INTO ½-INCH PIECES
- ½ CUP CHOPPED RED BELL PEPPERS
- 1 CUP BABY CORN, DIAGONALLY CUT INTO HALVES OR THIRDS
- 1 CUP STRAW MUSHROOMS
  SALT, TO TASTE
- ½ TEASPOON SUGAR, PLUS MORE TO TASTE
- ½ CUP CHICKEN STOCK (SEE PAGE 680)
- 1 TEASPOON RICE VINEGAR
- ¼ TEASPOON SESAME OIL
  CORNSTARCH SLURRY (1:1 RATIO)
- 2 SCALLIONS, DIAGONALLY CUT INTO 2-INCH-LONG PIECES

CHICKEN IN MASTER SAUCE

YIELD: 4 SERVINGS / **ACTIVE TIME:** 30 MINUTES / **TOTAL TIME:** 2 HOURS

"Master sauce" is a Cantonese-style sauce that is believed to have been passed down, generation after generation, for centuries, changing names as it evolved and traveled through China. The chicken in this dish can be served either warm or cool, but the sauce should be served warm.

1. Set a deep pot (that the chicken just fits in) over medium heat. Add the oil and gently sauté the scallion whites, garlic, and ginger for 2 minutes, making sure not to let the aromatics color. Add the sugar and cook, stirring frequently, until lightly caramelized.

2. Add the wine, soy sauces, star anise, orange peel, and water, and add the chicken, breast side down. Bring to a boil, reduce the heat, and simmer covered for 20 to 30 minutes.

3. Turn the chicken over and continue to simmer covered for another 20 to 30 minutes.

4. Turn off the heat and let the chicken rest in the poaching liquid for 15 minutes.

5. Remove the chicken from the pot and let it rest, breast side up, for 30 minutes before cutting.

6. Arrange the cut chicken on a serving platter, garnish with the cilantro, and spoon a small amount of the cooking sauce over the chicken before serving with the rice.

INGREDIENTS:

1	TABLESPOON CANOLA OIL
¼	CUP MINCED SCALLIONS, WHITE PART ONLY
4	GARLIC CLOVES, SMASHED
	2-INCH PIECE GINGER, CUT INTO THIN COINS AND SMASHED
1¾	CUPS SUGAR
½	CUP RICE WINE
1½	CUPS DARK SOY SAUCE
½	CUP LIGHT SOY SAUCE
2	STAR ANISE
½	ORANGE, PEEL ONLY
½	CUP WATER
1	(3½ LB.) WHOLE CHICKEN
	CILANTRO, FOR GARNISH
	RICE, FOR SERVING

BEEF CHOW FUN

YIELD: 4 SERVINGS / ACTIVE TIME: 30 MINUTES / TOTAL TIME: 30 MINUTES

This is a staple Chinese stir-fry made with rice noodles. It can be found in restaurants in Hong Kong, Southern China, and any other country with a love for Chinese cuisine.

1. In a bowl, combine all of the sauce ingredients, mix well, and set aside.

2. In a bowl, combine the meat with the cornstarch, dark soy sauce, wine, sesame oil, and baking soda and coat well.

3. Add 1 tablespoon of canola oil to a wok over high heat. Once the oil begins to shimmer, stir-fry the green beans, bell pepper, and onion for about 2 minutes. Add ½ tablespoon of canola oil to quickly steam the vegetables, and cook for another 2 minutes. Season with the salt, to taste, and then remove the vegetables from the wok and set aside.

4. Add 1 tablespoon of canola oil to the hot wok over high heat, and stir-fry the ginger and garlic for 2 minutes. Then, using a slotted spoon, remove the ginger and garlic and discard.

5. Add the beef into the hot, flavored oil and stir-fry until barely done. Remove and set aside.

6. Add 2 tablespoons of canola oil to the hot wok over medium-high heat, and stir-fry the rice noodles until they start to stick to each other and soften. Set aside.

7. Reduce the heat to medium, add the prepared sauce to the wok, and bring to a boil. Add the slurry to thicken slightly, and then return all of the ingredients to the pan and coat well.

8. Fold in the scallions right before serving.

INGREDIENTS:

½   LB. FLANK STEAK, CUT INTO 2-INCH-WIDE STRIPS, THEN SLICED ACROSS THE GRAIN INTO ⅛-INCH PIECES

2   TEASPOONS CORNSTARCH

2   TEASPOONS DARK SOY SAUCE

2   TEASPOONS RICE WINE

½   TEASPOON SESAME OIL

¼   TEASPOON BAKING SODA

¼   CUP CANOLA OIL, DIVIDED

1   CUP GREEN BEANS, ENDS TRIMMED AND HALVED

1   RED BELL PEPPER, CUT INTO ½-INCH-WIDE AND 1½-INCH-LONG PIECES

1   ONION, CUT INTO ½-INCH WEDGES

  SALT, TO TASTE

  1-INCH PIECE GINGER, CRUSHED

2   GARLIC CLOVES, CRUSHED

1   LB. FRESH, PRECUT RICE NOODLES, SEPARATED BY HAND, OR ¾ LB. DRY RICE STICKS, ¼ INCH TO ⅝ INCH WIDE

  CORNSTARCH SLURRY (1:1 RATIO), AS NEEDED

2   SCALLION STALKS, CUT INTO 1-INCH PIECES

SAUCE

1   CUP CHICKEN STOCK (SEE PAGE 680)

1   TABLESPOON LIGHT SOY SAUCE

1   TEASPOON SESAME OIL

2   TABLESPOONS OYSTER SAUCE

2   TEASPOONS SUGAR

CHICKEN CHOW MEIN

YIELD: 2 SERVINGS / **ACTIVE TIME:** 30 MINUTES / **TOTAL TIME:** 1 HOUR

"Chow Mein" translates to "stir-fried noodles," and it has become, like many other Chinese noodle dishes, a prominent dish around the world. Its origins are rooted in Northern China, where cooking vegetables in a wok and mixing them with boiled noodles was the typical cooking method.

1. In a bowl, combine the chicken with the Meat Marinade and set aside.

2. Bring a pot of water to a boil, cook the noodles until al dente, strain, rinse with cold water, and drain well. Toss with 1 tablespoon of oil.

3. Preheat the oven to 400°F. Line a sheet pan with foil and lightly brush the surface with oil.

4. Spread out the cooked noodles evenly on the foiled sheet pan, and bake for 25 to 35 minutes, or until lightly browned and slightly crispy. Remove, and when cool enough to handle, break the noodles into smaller pieces.

5. Meanwhile, in a bowl, combine all of the sauce ingredients, except the slurry, and mix well.

6. Add 1 tablespoon of oil to a wok or skillet over high heat. Once the oil begins to shimmer, add the onions and cook until translucent, then add the celery, carrots, and bean sprouts and stir-fry for 2 to 3 minutes. Season with a little salt and sugar, to taste, and transfer the vegetables to a plate.

7. Add 2 tablespoons of oil to the wok over medium-high heat, and stir-fry the chicken until almost done, then add the garlic. Cook until the chicken is done, and transfer the chicken to the same plate as the vegetables.

8. Add the prepared sauce to the hot wok over medium heat, bring to a boil, and then add the slurry to thicken the sauce.

9. Add the noodles to the sauce, coat well, and then return the chicken and vegetables to the pan, along with the scallions. Toss well and serve immediately.

INGREDIENTS:

1	SKINLESS AND BONELESS CHICKEN BREAST, THINLY SLICED
2	TABLESPOONS MEAT MARINADE (SEE PAGE 353)
½	LB. FRESH EGG NOODLES
¼	CUP CANOLA OIL, DIVIDED
1	CUP JULIENNED ONIONS
1	CELERY STALK, SLICED THIN ON A BIAS
½	CUP FINELY JULIENNED CARROTS
1	CUP BEAN SPROUTS
	SALT, TO TASTE
	SUGAR, TO TASTE
1-2	GARLIC CLOVES, MINCED
2	SCALLIONS, CUT INTO 2-INCH-LONG PIECES

SAUCE

⅔	CUP CHICKEN STOCK (SEE PAGE 680)
1	TABLESPOON OYSTER SAUCE
1	TABLESPOON DARK SOY SAUCE
1	TEASPOON LIGHT SOY SAUCE
1½	TEASPOONS CORNSTARCH SLURRY (1:1 RATIO)

BEEF & BROCCOLI

YIELD: 4 SERVINGS / **ACTIVE TIME:** 30 MINUTES / **TOTAL TIME:** 1 HOUR

This dish is thought to be inspired by another Chinese dish, gai lan chao niu rou. One noticeable adaptation is the use of everyday broccoli versus the Chinese variety, which is known as gai lan.

1. Cut the beef into 2-inch strips with the grain; then slice against the grain into thin slices. Pat dry any excess blood.

2. In a bowl, combine all of the Meat Marinade ingredients, mix well, and then add the sliced beef, massaging to incorporate the marinade well. Marinate for 20 to 30 minutes. Right before cooking, mix 1 tablespoon of oil into beef.

3. Meanwhile, in a bowl, combine all of the sauce ingredients, mix well, and set aside.

4. Bring a pot of salted water to a boil, blanch the broccoli, strain, and shock in ice water. Set aside.

5. Add 1 tablespoon of oil to a wok or skillet over medium-high heat. Once the oil begins to shimmer, add the beef and caramelize both sides, cooking until almost done. Transfer the beef to a plate.

6. Add 1 tablespoon of oil to the hot pan over medium heat and add the garlic, ginger, carrot, and scallion and cook for 20 to 30 seconds. Add the prepared sauce and simmer for 1 minute to incorporate the flavors.

7. Return the beef to the pan and coat well before adding the broccoli, stirring to coat well. Add a little more water if the pan is dry.

8. Adjust the seasoning and finish with the sesame oil.

INGREDIENTS:

1	LB. BEEF (FLANK, TRI TIP, OR SIRLOIN)
	CANOLA OIL, AS NEEDED
	SALT, TO TASTE
4	CUPS BITE-SIZE BROCCOLI FLORETS
2-3	GARLIC CLOVES, MINCED
2	TEASPOONS MINCED GINGER
½	CARROT, CUT INTO THIN SLIVERS
1	SCALLION, CUT ON A BIAS
	SESAME OIL, FOR GARNISH

MEAT MARINADE

2	TEASPOONS BAKING SODA
1	TABLESPOON CORNSTARCH
2	TABLESPOONS LIGHT SOY SAUCE
2	TABLESPOONS OYSTER SAUCE
2	TABLESPOONS RICE WINE
2	TABLESPOONS WATER
½	TEASPOON GROUND WHITE PEPPER
1	TEASPOON SUGAR

SAUCE

2	TEASPOONS LIGHT SOY SAUCE
2	TEASPOONS DARK SOY SAUCE
2	TABLESPOONS OYSTER SAUCE
3	TABLESPOONS WATER, PLUS MORE AS NEEDED
1	TABLESPOON RICE WINE

HONEY WALNUT SHRIMP

YIELD: 4 SERVINGS / ACTIVE TIME: 1 HOUR / TOTAL TIME: 1 HOUR

Creamy and sweet, with a crunch from the fried shrimp and walnuts, this dish originated in Hong Kong and is believed to have been introduced to the United States in the late 1980s.

1. In a bowl, combine the shrimp and salt, mix well, and set aside.

2. In a separate bowl, combine all of the sauce ingredients, mix well, and set aside.

3. In another separate bowl, make the batter by combining the flour, cornstarch, and baking powder and whisking well. Fold in ½ of the beaten egg and add the water and oil, whisking to achieve a smooth consistency. Add a little more water if needed. Refrigerate until needed.

4. Add oil to a pot and bring to 300°F. Fry the walnuts for 3 to 4 minutes, making sure not to burn. Using a slotted spoon or kitchen spider, remove the walnuts from the oil, drain well, and toss with the honey to coat.

5. Fry the honey-coated walnuts a second time at 300°F for roughly 2 minutes. Remove from the oil and set aside on a paper towel–lined plate.

6. Strain the walnut fry oil to remove any debris, and then heat the oil to 350°F in a wok.

7. Once the oil is ready, coat the shrimp with the prepared batter and carefully set the shrimp aren't the wok, one at a time, so they don't stick together. Make sure the shrimp isn't covered with excess batter. Fry for 2 to 3 minutes, until the batter turns golden brown. Using a slotted spoon or kitchen spider, remove the cooked shrimp and drain on a paper towel–lined plate.

8. Once all of the shrimp have been fried, bring the oil to 400°F and fry the shrimp a second time for 1 minute to get extra crispy.

9. Once all of the shrimp have been fried a second time, transfer to a bowl and coat with the prepared sauce. Add the candied walnuts.

10. Serve on a plate and garnish with the toasted sesame seeds.

INGREDIENTS:

24	SHRIMP, SHELLED AND DEVEINED
½	TEASPOON SALT
	CANOLA OIL, FOR FRYING
½	CUP WALNUTS
2	TABLESPOONS HONEY
	TOASTED SESAME SEEDS, FOR GARNISH

BATTER

¼	CUP ALL-PURPOSE FLOUR
3	TABLESPOONS CORNSTARCH
2	TEASPOONS BAKING POWDER
1	EGG, BEATEN
½	CUP WATER
2	TEASPOONS CANOLA OIL

SAUCE

⅔	CUP MAYONNAISE
¼	CUP SWEETENED CONDENSED MILK
1	TABLESPOON FRESH LEMON JUICE

SINGAPORE CURRY NOODLES

YIELD: 4 SERVINGS / ACTIVE TIME: 45 MINUTES / TOTAL TIME: 45 MINUTES

Emblematic of the rich cultural fusion that defines Singapore, this popular dish marries Indian curry powder with Chinese flavors and cooking techniques. The thinner the noodle, the better in here.

1. Bring a pot of water to a boil and cook the noodles until barely done; do not overcook. Drain, rinse with cold water, and transfer to a bowl.

2. In a separate bowl, combine the shrimp, Michiu rice wine, ginger, and garlic, mix well, and set aside.

3. In another separate bowl, combine the chicken, 1 teaspoon of soy sauce, rice wine, cornstarch, and sesame oil, mix well, and set aside.

4. Add 1 tablespoon of canola oil to a nonstick skillet over medium heat, and cook the beaten eggs to form a crepe. Slide out of the pan, cool, cut into thin strips, and set aside.

5. Add 1 tablespoon of canola oil to a wok over medium heat. Once the oil begins to shimmer, stir-fry the shrimp until just pink. Transfer to a plate.

6. Add 1 tablespoon of canola oil to the hot wok and stir-fry the chicken until opaque. Transfer to the same plate as the shrimp.

7. Turn up the heat to medium-high and add 2 tablespoons of canola oil to the hot wok, along with the garlic, and cook until fragrant. Discard the garlic before it burns.

8. Add the bell pepper, carrots, bean sprouts, and mushrooms to the flavored oil and stir-fry for 2 to 3 minutes, until the vegetables are cooked but still crispy. Transfer to the same plate as the shrimp and chicken.

9. Add 2 tablespoons of canola oil to the hot wok, along with the noodles and toss to reheat.

10. Add 1 tablespoon of light soy sauce and mix well into the noodles, before adding the curry powder. Season with the salt and a little sugar, to taste.

11. Return the shrimp and chicken to the pan and mix well.

12. Return the vegetables to the pan, making sure not to add any of the vegetable juices, and mix well.

13. Transfer to a serving platter and finish with the scallions, egg strips, and fresh herbs.

INGREDIENTS:

- 8 OZ. THIN RICE STICK NOODLES, THINNEST SIZE
- 12 SHRIMP, SHELLED AND DEVEINED
- 2 TEASPOONS MICHIU RICE WINE
- 1 TEASPOON FINELY MINCED GINGER
- 1 TEASPOON FINELY MINCED GARLIC
- ½ CHICKEN BREAST, SLICED THIN
- 1 TABLESPOON LIGHT SOY SAUCE, PLUS 1 TEASPOON
- 1 TEASPOON RICE WINE
- 1 TEASPOON CORNSTARCH
- ½ TEASPOON SESAME OIL
- ½ CUP CANOLA OIL, DIVIDED
- 1 EGG, BEATEN
- 2 EGG YOLKS, BEATEN
- 3 GARLIC CLOVES, CRUSHED
- ½ GREEN BELL PEPPER, FINELY JULIENNED
- ½ CUP FINELY JULIENNED CARROTS
- 1 CUP BEAN SPROUTS
- ¼ CUP WOOD EAR MUSHROOMS, SOAKED AND JULIENNED
- 1½ TABLESPOONS CURRY POWDER
- SALT, TO TASTE
- ¼ TEASPOON SUGAR
- 2-3 SCALLIONS, , FINELY JULIENNED ON A BIAS, FOR GARNISH
- FRESH HERBS, FOR GARNISH

VEGETARIAN JAPCHAE

YIELD: 4 SERVINGS / ACTIVE TIME: 30 MINUTES / TOTAL TIME: 30 MINUTES

This is a Korean staple of savory and sweet stir-fried sweet potato starch noodles, also known as glass noodles, that was initially reserved for royal families. It became a widely enjoyed meal beginning in the twentieth century.

1. Add a little canola oil to a nonstick pan over medium heat. Cook the 2 yolks in a thin layers, and then cook the 2 whites in a thin layer. Roll up each one into a tube, thinly slice, and set aside to use as garnish.

2. Add a little more canola oil to the pan, turn up the heat to medium-high, and stir-fry the shiitake mushrooms, cabbage, and onion. After 2 minutes, add the carrots, wood ear mushrooms, and bell pepper and season with the salt and pepper, to taste. When all of the vegetables are cooked but still firm and crispy, remove the pan from heat and set aside.

3. In a bowl, combine the stock, soy sauce, mirin, sesame oil, sugar, and garlic, and mix well.

4. Add the mixture to a wok or skillet and bring to a boil. Add the noodles and lower the heat to a simmer, until the noodles absorb all of the liquid; if more liquid is needed in cooking the noodles, add extra stock or water.

5. Add the cooked vegetables to the wok, along with the scallions and spinach, and mix well into the noodles.

6. Remove from heat, toss with the sesame seeds, and garnish with the egg strips.

INGREDIENTS:

CANOLA OIL, AS NEEDED

2 LARGE EGGS, YOLKS AND WHITES SEPARATED

6 DRIED SHIITAKE MUSHROOMS, SOAKED, STEMS DISCARDED, AND CAPS JULIENNED

1 CUP THINLY SLICED CABBAGE

1 ONION, SLICED THIN

½ CUP JULIENNED CARROTS

4-6 WOOD EAR MUSHROOMS, SOAKED AND TOUGH CLUSTER END CUT OFF

½ RED BELL PEPPER, JULIENNED

SALT, TO TASTE

BLACK PEPPER, TO TASTE

½ CUP VEGETABLE STOCK OR CHICKEN STOCK (SEE PAGE 684 OR PAGE 680), OR WATER

¼ CUP SOY SAUCE

2 TABLESPOONS MIRIN

2 TABLESPOONS SESAME OIL, PLUS MORE AS NEEDED

1 TABLESPOON SUGAR

3-4 GARLIC CLOVES, MINCED

4 OZ. SWEET POTATO STARCH NOODLES, SOAKED AT ROOM TEMPERATURE UNTIL PLIABLE OR SOFT

2-3 SCALLIONS, CUT ON A BIAS LENGTHWISE IN 1½-INCH PIECES

¼ CUP SPINACH, BLANCHED AND STRAINED WELL

1 TABLESPOON TOASTED SESAME SEEDS

ORANGE CHICKEN

YIELD: 4 SERVINGS / **ACTIVE TIME:** 1 HOUR / **TOTAL TIME:** 1 HOUR

Originally from the Hunan province of China, orange chicken can easily be dubbed the most famous and popular Chinese-American dish. Crispy chicken glazed in a sweet citrus chili sauce makes each bite memorable—and leaves you wanting more.

1. Make the marinade in a bowl by combining the egg white, soy sauce, wine, and soda water and whisking well. Set aside half of the marinade for later use. With the other half of the marinade, add the baking soda and cornstarch and whisk well. Add the chicken to the baking-soda-and-cornstarch marinade, cover, and set aside.

2. For the dredge mixture, combine all of the dry ingredients and mix well. With the reserved marinade, whisk in only enough to the dry ingredients to create a mixture that is course and mealy. Set aside.

3. For the sauce, combine the soy sauce, wine, vinegar, Chicken Stock, sugar, sesame oil, orange juice and zest, cornstarch, and orange peels and mix well, making sure the cornstarch is well incorporated,

4. Add 2 teaspoons of canola oil to a sauté pan over medium-low heat, and cook garlic, ginger, and scallions until they are soft, 2 to 3 minutes; make sure they don't brown.

5. Stir the prepared sauce mixture, add it to the sauté pan, stirring well, and bring to a boil so sauce the thickens, about 2 minutes. Remove from heat and set aside.

6. Bring a pot of frying oil to 350°F.

7. Working with a couple of marinated chicken pieces at a time, transfer to the dredge mixture and toss to coat well. Set on a rack until all of the pieces are coated.

8. Increase the frying oil temperature to 375°F.

9. Shake off any excess dredge mixture and fry the chicken pieces in batches, making sure not to overcrowd the pot. Cook until the chicken is cooked through and very crispy. Remove with a slotted spoon or kitchen spider, and transfer to paper towel–lined bowl.

INGREDIENTS:

MARINADE

1	EGG WHITE, BEATEN WELL UNTIL FOAMY
2	TABLESPOONS DARK SOY SAUCE
2	TABLESPOONS SHAOXING RICE WINE OR DRY SHERRY
2	TABLESPOONS SODA WATER
½	TEASPOON BAKING SODA
3	TABLESPOONS CORNSTARCH

CHICKEN

1	LB. CHICKEN BREASTS OR THIGHS, CUT INTO ½-INCH TO ¾-INCH PIECES
2	QUARTS CANOLA OIL, FOR FRYING, PLUS 2 TEASPOONS
1	TABLESPOON MINCED GARLIC
½	TABLESPOON MINCED GINGER
1-2	SCALLIONS, THINLY SLICED
	TOASTED SESAME SEEDS, FOR GARNISH (OPTIONAL)

DREDGE MIXTURE

1	CUP ALL-PURPOSE FLOUR
1	CUP CORNSTARCH
1	TEASPOON BAKING POWDER
½	TABLESPOON SALT

Continued . . .

10. Once all of the chicken is cooked, carefully toss it into the prepared sauce.

11. Serve garnished with the sesame seeds.

SAUCE

1   TABLESPOON DARK SOY
     SAUCE

2   TABLESPOONS SHAOXING
     RICE WINE OR DRY
     SHERRY

2   TABLESPOONS
     UNSEASONED RICE
     VINEGAR

3   TABLESPOONS CHICKEN
     STOCK (SEE PAGE 680)

¼   CUP SUGAR

1   TEASPOON SESAME OIL

¼   CUP ORANGE JUICE

     ZEST OF 2 ORANGES

4   DRIED ORANGE PEELS, CUT
     INTO 1-INCH STRIPS

SALT & PEPPER SHRIMP

YIELD: 4 SERVINGS / ACTIVE TIME: 30 MINUTES / TOTAL TIME: 30 MINUTES

Cantonese cooking showcases the freshness of the region's local seafood, as is the case with this garlic-heavy dish. Don't be shy about using the salt-and-pepper seasoning for fried squid or as a pork rub.

1. Add 2 tablespoons of oil to a wok or skillet over medium-high heat and fry the garlic until just golden brown; do not overcook and burn. Set aside on a paper towel–lined plate.

2. Rinse the shrimp, pat dry, and dredge in the potato starch.

3. Place enough oil for shallow frying in a cast-iron skillet and bring to 375°F.

4. Shallow fry the shrimp for roughly 30 seconds to 1 minute on each side, or until golden and crispy. Cook in batches, so as not to overcrowd. Using a slotted spoon or kitchen spider, transfer to a paper towel–lined plate.

5. In the wok, stir-fry the chilies for about 30 seconds with very little oil, then add the garlic and stir for 30 more seconds. Turn off the heat, add the scallions, and shrimp, and season with the Chinese-Style Salt & Pepper Mixture, to taste.

6. Toss all of the ingredients and transfer to a serving platter.

CHINESE-STYLE SALT & PEPPER MIXTURE

1. In a sauté pan over medium-low heat, dry roast the peppercorns for 5 to 10 minutes, or until very fragrant. Make sure not to burn. Cool completely and grind to a powder, using a spice grinder or mortar and pestle.

2. In the same pan, dry roast the salt until it turns slightly yellow in color. Let cool.

3. Combine the ground peppercorn and salt in an airtight container, mix well, and store.

INGREDIENTS:

- ½ CUP CANOLA OIL, FOR SHALLOW FRYING, DIVIDED
- 8-10 GARLIC CLOVES, FINELY CHOPPED
- 1-2 LBS. LARGE SHRIMP, SHELLS AND HEADS ON, DEVEINED
- ¼ CUP POTATO STARCH
- 1-2 JALAPEÑO PEPPERS OR FRESNO CHILIES, THINLY SLICED
- 1-2 SCALLIONS STALKS, THINLY SLICED

  CHINESE-STYLE SALT & PEPPER MIXTURE (SEE RECIPE), TO TASTE

CHINESE-STYLE SALT & PEPPER MIXTURE

- 2 PARTS WHOLE PEPPERCORNS (MIX OF BLACK, WHITE, AND SZECHUAN)
- 1 PART SEA SALT

SPICY THAI-STYLE FRIED RICE

YIELD: 4 SERVINGS / ACTIVE TIME: 30 MINUTES / TOTAL TIME: 30 MINUTES

Southeast Asian fried rice tends to incorporate fresh, fragrant herbs, like basil, making the classic dish special and very much different from Chinese versions. This is a great way to use leftover rice.

1. Add 2 tablespoons of oil to a pan over medium-high heat. Once the oil begins to shimmer, stir-fry the garlic, chilies, and onions for about 30 seconds.

2. Add the shrimp and cook until they turn pink.

3. Add the day-old rice and stir-fry to heat through, about 2 minutes. Add more oil if needed.

4. Add the soy sauce, fish sauce, and sugar and continue to stir-fry, making sure the rice doesn't stick to the pan.

5. Add the eggs, scallions, jalapeños, and basil, mix into the rice, and adjust the seasoning if needed.

6. Garnish with the Fried Shallots and Garlic and more fresh herbs.

INGREDIENTS:

¼ CUP CANOLA OIL, DIVIDED

2 TABLESPOONS MINCED GARLIC

2-3 RED THAI CHILIES, FINELY CUT INTO RINGS

½ CUP ONIONS, CUT INTO THIN WEDGES

12 SHRIMP, PEELED, DEVEINED, AND HALVED

4 CUPS COOKED JASMINE RICE

3 TABLESPOONS SWEET SOY SAUCE

2 TABLESPOONS FISH SAUCE

2 TEASPOONS SUGAR

2 SCRAMBLED EGGS

2 SCALLIONS, SLICED

2 RED JALAPEÑOS, SEEDED AND CUT INTO MATCHSTICKS

¼ CUP TORN THAI BASIL

FRIED SHALLOTS AND GARLIC (SEE PAGE 173), FOR GARNISH

FRESH HERBS, FOR GARNISH

SINGAPOREAN FRIED RICE

YIELD: 4 SERVINGS / **ACTIVE TIME:** 30 MINUTES / **TOTAL TIME:** 30 MINUTES

Making fried rice is the optimal way to eat leftover rice. It can be prepared as a vegetarian, beef, chicken, or seafood dish.

1. Add the ghee to a wok or skillet over medium heat, and the sauté almonds until golden.

2. Add the rice, turmeric, and salt and stir-fry for 1 minute. Add the peas, raisins, and chilies and mix well.

3. Adjust the seasoning, transfer to a plate, and garnish with the cilantro, scallions, and tomatoes.

INGREDIENTS:

3	TABLESPOONS GHEE
¼	CUP SLIVERED ALMONDS
3	CUPS COOKED RICE
½	TEASPOON TURMERIC
	SALT, TO TASTE
⅓	CUP FROZEN PEAS
⅓	CUP RAISINS, SOAKED IN WATER AND DRAINED
2	RED JALAPEÑO PEPPERS, DESEEDED AND CUT INTO SLIVERS
6-8	CILANTRO SPRIGS, CUT INTO 1-INCH PIECES, FOR GARNISH
2	TABLESPOONS MINCED SCALLIONS, FOR GARNISH
8	SMALL TOMATO WEDGES, FOR GARNISH

THAI CHICKEN WITH BASIL LEAVES

YIELD: 4 SERVINGS / **ACTIVE TIME:** 30 MINUTES / **TOTAL TIME:** 30 MINUTES

A classic Thai dish built around a strong garlic flavor balanced with the spicy licorice taste of Thai basil. It is commonly enjoyed with white rice and a fried egg.

1. In a bowl, combine the fish sauce, kecap manis, oyster sauce, Tamarind Juice, and sugar and mix well, until the sugar dissolves. Set aside.

2. Add the oil to a skillet over medium-high heat. Once the oil begins to shimmer, stir-fry the garlic and chilies for a few seconds, and then add the chicken and cook until the chicken is almost done. Add the bell pepper and mix well.

3. Add the prepared sauce and simmer until most of the liquid is absorbed by the chicken.

4. Add the basil, stir well, adjust the seasoning, and serve immediately with the rice.

INGREDIENTS:

3   TABLESPOONS FISH SAUCE

2   TABLESPOONS KECAP MANIS

1½   TABLESPOONS OYSTER SAUCE

1   TABLESPOON TAMARIND JUICE

1   TABLESPOON SUGAR

2   TABLESPOONS CANOLA OIL

3   TABLESPOONS MINCED GARLIC

2-4   RED THAI CHILIES, THINLY SLICED

1   LB. CHICKEN, DARK MEAT, COARSELY CHOPPED

1   BELL PEPPER, JULIENNED

1   CUP THAI BASIL LEAVES

    RICE, FOR SERVING

LEMONGRASS CHICKEN RICE POT CASSEROLE

YIELD: 4 SERVINGS / **ACTIVE TIME:** 30 MINUTES / **TOTAL TIME:** 1 HOUR

This dish is real home-style cooking. It is light, flavorful, and bursting with lemongrass aromas.

1. Add 2 tablespoons of oil to a wok or skillet over medium-high heat. Once the oil begins to shimmer, stir-fry the shallots, ginger, 3 tablespoons of garlic, and mushrooms until fragrant, about 10 to 20 seconds. Make sure not to burn the garlic.

2. Add the chicken and cook until it is almost done. Add the baby corn, fish sauce, soy sauce, and sugar and cook for a few minutes. Adjust the seasoning if needed. Remove from heat and set aside.

3. Add 2 tablespoons of oil to a pot or clay pot over high heat. Once the oil begins to shimmer, stir-fry the onion, 2 tablespoons of garlic, and lemongrass for 1 minute. Add the rice and cook until lightly golden.

4. Add the Chicken Stock, bring to a boil, and then turn down the heat to low and cover. Cook for 20 minutes, then turn off the heat and let stand covered for 10 minutes.

5. Quickly add the chicken mixture over the rice and let stand covered for 10 minutes longer.

6. Fluff the rice mixture and chicken together and remove the lemongrass.

7. Serve topped with the scallions and cilantro.

INGREDIENTS:

4	TABLESPOONS CANOLA OIL, DIVIDED
3-4	SHALLOTS, MINCED
1	TABLESPOON FINELY MINCED GINGER
5	TABLESPOONS MINCED GARLIC CLOVES, DIVIDED
8	DRIED SHIITAKE MUSHROOMS, SOAKED, STEMMED, AND QUARTERED
5-6	SKINLESS AND BONELESS CHICKEN THIGHS, CUT INTO 1-INCH PIECES
1	CUP CHOPPED BABY CORN, CUT INTO ½-INCH PIECES
2	TABLESPOONS FISH SAUCE
1	TABLESPOON DARK SOY SAUCE
1	TEASPOON SUGAR
1	SMALL ONION, DICED
2-3	LEMONGRASS STALKS, ENDS REMOVED, CUT INTO 4-INCH PIECES AND CRUSHED
2	CUPS JASMINE RICE
2⅔	CUPS CHICKEN STOCK (SEE PAGE 680)
2	SCALLIONS, ROUGHLY CHOPPED, FOR GARNISH
½	CUP CHOPPED CILANTRO SPRIGS, CUT INTO ½-INCH PIECES, FOR GARNISH

WHOLE ROAST PEKING-STYLE DUCK

YIELD: 12 SERVINGS / **ACTIVE TIME:** 1 HOUR / **TOTAL TIME:** 48 HOURS

This iconic Beijing dish has been gracing family meals for over 600 years. It is a meticulous, labor-intensive process to perfectly prepare the duck for cooking. This preparation, particularly separating the skin, is what allows cooks to create that craved crunchy skin and juicy meat.

1. Clean the duck, trim the excess fat, and use your fingers to carefully separate the skin from the breast meat; also separate the skin from the backbone through the neck, separating the skin all the way down to the thighs and legs. Air dry uncovered in the refrigerator overnight.

2. In a saucepan over low heat, combine the brown sugar, honey, soy sauce, wine, vinegar, 1 teaspoon of salt, and ½ tablespoon of five-spice powder and cook until the sugar is dissolved. Set aside.

3. Fill a large pot or wok with the water, ginger, and scallions, and bring to a boil. Place the duck in a strainer over an empty pot and carefully ladle the boiling water evenly over the duck. Turn the duck and continue to ladle hot water over it, making sure to get all sides. Repeat the ladle blanching process for 10 minutes, and reuse the water ladled over the duck by returning it to the boiling pot.

4. Drain the duck and pat dry. Hang if possible, or place the duck on a resting rack uncovered in the refrigerator for 6 hours, or overnight.

5. Remove the duck from the refrigerator.

6. In a bowl, combine ½ tablespoon of five-spice powder, 1 tablespoon of salt, white pepper, and 1 tablespoon of the prepared marinade and mix well. Rub the seasoning mixture all over the inside of the duck cavity.

7. Using a pastry brush, apply the rest of the marinade evenly on the entire duck. Refrigerate uncovered for 6 hours, or overnight.

8. Preheat the oven to 425°F and place an extra pan filled with 2 inches of water at the bottom of the oven below the duck. Wrap the wing tips and drumstick ends in foil to prevent burning (optional).

9. Roast the duck on a wire rack, breast side up, for 10 minutes.

INGREDIENTS:

1	(5-6 LB.) WHOLE DUCK
1	TABLESPOON BROWN SUGAR
3	TABLESPOONS HONEY
2	TABLESPOONS DARK SOY
1	TABLESPOON SHAOXING RICE WINE OR SHERRY
1	TABLESPOON WHITE VINEGAR
1	TABLESPOON SALT, PLUS 1 TEASPOON, DIVIDED
1	TABLESPOON FIVE-SPICE POWDER, DIVIDED
8	CUPS WATER, PLUS MORE AS NEEDED
	1-INCH PIECE GINGER, SLICED
	SCALLIONS FINELY JULIENNED, PLUS MORE FOR SERVING
½	TEASPOON WHITE PEPPER
	MANDARIN PANCAKES (SEE PAGE 326), FOR SERVING
	BAO BUNS, (SEE PAGE 463), FOR SERVING
	HOISIN SAUCE, FOR SERVING
	CUCUMBERS, CUT INTO MATCHSTICKS, FOR SERVING

Continued . . .

10. Turn down the oven to 350°F and flip over the duck, so it is breast side down; roast for 30 minutes.

11. Turn the duck breast side up again and roast for between 30 minutes and 1 hour, until a meat thermometer inserted in the thickest part of the thigh reads 165°F and the skin is mahogany in color. Add more water to the water pan if needed. If the skin is darkening too quickly before the duck is fully cooked, use foil to tent the duck.

12. Once cooked, let the duck rest for 30 minutes on a wire rack to keep the skin crispy.

13. Carefully carve off the crispy skin from the entire duck and slice into strips.

14. Carve off the breast and thinly slice.

15. Shred the dark meat from the thigh and serve the drumsticks and wings as is.

16. Place the carved duck on a serving platter and serve with Mandarin Pancakes, bao buns, hoisin sauce, scallions, and cucumbers.

CHILI CRAB

YIELD: 4 SERVINGS / *ACTIVE TIME:* 1 HOUR / *TOTAL TIME:* 1 HOUR

This Southeast Asian stir-fry dish with sweet and savory chili tomato sauce is originally from Singapore.

1. Kill the crab, remove the shell (carapace), and boil the shell in water for 1 to 2 minutes. Drain and rub a little oil on the shell. Set aside for later.

2. Clean the rest of the crab by removing the gills and any soft tissue. Remove the legs and claws from the body and crack the legs and claws with the back of a knife. Chop the body into 4 to 6 pieces, depending on the size.

3. In a bowl, toss the crab lightly with the cornstarch.

4. Add the oil to a wok over medium-high heat, and once it is very hot, stir-fry the crab pieces, claws, and legs with the ginger, garlic, and lemongrass for 1 to 2 minutes.

5. Add the wine, chili paste, ketchup, kecap manis, and turmeric powder and continue to stir-fry for 1 to 2 minutes.

6. Add the scallions, season with the salt, to taste, and stir-fry for another 1 to 2 minutes, or until the crab is cooked through.

7. Transfer to a plate lined with lettuce leaves. Garnish with the crab shell on top and fresh herbs before serving.

INGREDIENTS:

1	DUNGENESS CRAB
¼	CUP CANOLA OIL, PLUS MORE AS NEEDED
¼	CUP CORNSTARCH
3	TABLESPOONS MINCED GINGER
3	TABLESPOONS MINCED GARLIC
3	TABLESPOONS FINELY MINCED LEMONGRASS
3	TABLESPOONS MICHIU VINEGAR
2-3	TABLESPOONS CHILI PASTE
2	TABLESPOONS KETCHUP
2-3	TABLESPOONS KECAP MANIS
¼	TEASPOON TURMERIC POWDER
2	SCALLIONS, CUT INTO 2-INCH PIECES
	SALT, TO TASTE
	LETTUCE LEAVES, FOR GARNISH
	FRESH HERBS, FOR GARNISH

KIMCHI SPAM FRIED RICE

YIELD: 4 SERVINGS / **ACTIVE TIME:** 30 MINUTES / **TOTAL TIME:** 30 MINUTES

Do you have leftover rice and ripe kimchi on hand? If you do, this classic Korean fried rice is the meal to make. This was a favorite of Chef Brian's while growing up in Southern California.

1. Add ½ tablespoon of oil to a large nonstick pan over medium-high heat. Once the oil begins to shimmer, add the Spam and crisp it up, about 2 minutes. Add the mushrooms and cook for 1 minute.

2. Add 1 tablespoon of oil to the pan, along with the kimchi. Mix well and season with the salt and pepper. Transfer the contents of the pan to a plate.

3. Add 1 tablespoon of oil to the hot pan, along with the rice, breaking up any clumps with a spatula. Cook for 1 minute and add the soy sauce, kimchi juice, and gochujang and stir-fry for about 30 seconds.

4. Return the Spam mixture to the pan and stir-fry over high heat until all of the ingredients are well incorporated. Add the butter, mix well, and adjust the seasoning if needed.

5. Remove from heat and fold in the scallions.

6. Serve on a plate garnished with the fried eggs, sesame seeds, and a drizzle of sesame oil.

INGREDIENTS:

- 2½ TABLESPOONS CANOLA OIL, DIVIDED
- ⅓ CUP DICED SPAM OR PORK BELLY
- 3 SHIITAKE MUSHROOMS, SLICED
- ⅔ CUPS KIMCHI, CHOPPED
- ½ TABLESPOON SALT
- ½ TEASPOON BLACK PEPPER
- 2 CUPS COOKED WHITE RICE
- 1 TABLESPOON SOY SAUCE
- 2 TABLESPOONS KIMCHI JUICE
- 1 TABLESPOON GOCHUJANG
- 1 TABLESPOON UNSALTED BUTTER
- ¼ CUP FINELY CHOPPED SCALLIONS
- 2-4 FRIED EGGS, FOR GARNISH
- 1 TABLESPOON SESAME SEEDS, FOR GARNISH
- ½ TABLESPOON SESAME OIL, FOR GARNISH

KALBI

YIELD: 4 SERVINGS / ACTIVE TIME: 30 MINUTES / TOTAL TIME: 24 HOURS

This Southern California creation was popularized by Korean barbeque restaurants in Los Angeles. What differentiates Los Angeles–style galbi from the traditional Korean galbi is the cut. The Los Angeles–style short ribs are cut through the rib bone, leaving three small rib bones in each piece of meat, whereas the Korean style is cut perpendicularly along the bone, resulting in thicker pieces. Ideally, this is cooked on a grill, but if you don't have access to one, use the oven broiler. Extra marinade and extra marinated short ribs will keep in the freezer for up to 4 months.

1. Rinse the short ribs in cold water to remove any bone chips, and pat dry.

2. In a bowl, combine all of the marinade ingredients and mix well, until the sugar is dissolved; adjust the seasoning if necessary.

3. Layer the short ribs with marinade into a container and refrigerate covered for 6 to 24 hours; the longer they marinate, the deeper the flavor.

4. Heat the grill to 450°F. Remove any excess marinade from the short ribs.

5. Grill over medium to medium-high heat, caramelizing both sides.

6. Garnish with the sesame seeds and scallions before serving.

INGREDIENTS:

5   LBS. FLANKEN CUT SHORT RIBS

TOASTED SESAME SEEDS, FOR GARNISH

CHOPPED SCALLIONS, FOR GARNISH

KALBI MARINADE

1½   CUPS SOY SAUCE

1   CUP SUGAR

1   CUP 7-UP OR WATER

½   CUP MIRIN

½   CUP ONION, GRATED, PUREED, OR FINELY MINCED

2   TABLESPOONS MINCED GARLIC

½   TABLESPOON MINCED GINGER

1   TABLESPOON BLACK PEPPER

2   TABLESPOONS CORN SYRUP

2   TABLESPOONS SESAME OIL

¼   PEAR, GRATED, FOR TENDERIZER (OPTIONAL)

DWAEJI BULGOGI

YIELD: 6 SERVINGS / ACTIVE TIME: 1 HOUR / TOTAL TIME: 24 HOURS

In Korean, dwaeji means "pork," and bulgogi translates to "fire meat"; consequently, dwaeji bulgogi means "pork fire meat" or "pork on fire." This sweet and spicy dish can be ordered at Korean BBQ restaurants both in Korea and elsewhere. If using thicker cuts of meat, scoring is recommended. Ideally, this is cooked on a grill, but if you don't have access to one, use a nonstick pan.

1. In a bowl, combine all of the marinade ingredients and mix well.

2. Massage the pork with the marinade, cover, and refrigerate overnight.

3. Remove any excess marinade from the pork, and cook over medium heat on both sides until done. Make sure not to overcaramelize; lower the temperature if needed.

4. Using scissors, cut the pork belly into bite-size pieces and garnish with the sesame seeds and scallions. Serve with the rice and your favorite condiments and sides.

INGREDIENTS:

2	LBS. PORK BELLY OR PORK SHOULDER, SLICED ⅛ INCH THICK
	TOASTED SESAME SEEDS, FOR GARNISH
	CHOPPED SCALLIONS, FOR GARNISH
	RICE, FOR SERVING

MARINADE

½	CUP SOY SAUCE
1	TABLESPOON MIRIN
1	TABLESPOON SUGAR
1	TABLESPOON HONEY
6	GARLIC CLOVES, MINCED
1	TEASPOON MINCED GINGER
¼	CUP PUREED OR GRATED ONION
⅓	CUP GOCHUJANG
¼	CUP PUREED OR GRATED APPLE
1	TEASPOON BLACK PEPPER
1	TABLESPOON SESAME OIL

AHI TUNA POKE BOWL

YIELD: 2 SERVINGS / ACTIVE TIME: 30 MINUTES / TOTAL TIME: 30 MINUTES

Poke bowls have gained notoriety worldwide, especially in coastal cities that have access to fresh local catch. These can be prepared with any fish or seafood.

1. In a small mixing bowl, marinate the tuna with the Soy Sesame Dressing, using more if needed, and ½ tablespoon of scallions.

2. Place the rice at the bottom of the bowl and sprinkle furikake over the rice. Spoon the marinated tuna over the rice and top with the cucumber and onion.

3. Drizzle the Spicy Mayo Poke Sauce in a zigzag motion over all of the ingredients in the bowl, and then add an even layer of Crispy Onions.

4. Garnish with the chopped scallions and serve immediately.

SOY SESAME DRESSING

1. In a bowl, combine all of the ingredients and mix well.

2. Refrigerate in an airtight container until needed.

SPICY MAYO POKE SAUCE

1. In a bowl, combine all of the ingredients, except the masago, and mix well.

2. Gently fold in the masago until fully incorporated.

3. Refrigerate in an airtight container for up to a week.

INGREDIENTS:

1	CUP AHI TUNA, CUT INTO ½-INCH TO 1-INCH CUBES
2	TABLESPOONS SOY SESAME DRESSING (SEE RECIPE), PLUS MORE AS NEEDED
1	FINELY CHOPPED SCALLION, PLUS ½ TABLESPOON, DIVIDED
2	CUPS COOKED SUSHI RICE (SEE PAGE 140)
1	TABLESPOON FURIKAKE (SEE PAGE 146), PLUS MORE AS NEEDED
¼	CUP SLICED PERSIAN CUCUMBER, CUT INTO THIN HALF-MOONS
¼	CUP JULIENNED MAUI SWEET ONION, SOAKED IN ICE WATER AND DRAINED
3	TABLESPOONS SPICY MAYO POKE SAUCE (SEE RECIPE), PLUS MORE AS NEEDED
	CRISPY ONIONS (SEE PAGE 196), TO TASTE

SOY SESAME DRESSING

½	CUP SOY SAUCE
2	TABLESPOONS SESAME OIL
1	TEASPOON WASABI

SPICY MAYO POKE SAUCE

1	CUP MAYONNAISE
1	TABLESPOON RICE VINEGAR
1	TABLESPOON SUGAR
1	TABLESPOON SRIRACHA
1	TABLESPOON MASAGO OR FLYING FISH ROE

CHICKEN ADOBO

YIELD: 4 SERVINGS / **ACTIVE TIME:** 30 MINUTES / **TOTAL TIME:** 1 HOUR

This classic Filipino sweet and tangy dish with strong soy notes is traditionally served over a bed of rice.

1. Lightly season the chicken with the salt.

2. Add the oil to a skillet over medium-high heat. Once the oil begins to shimmer, sear the chicken on all sides, transfer to a plate, and set aside.

3. In the same skillet, add the onion and sauté until just starting to caramelize. Add a little more oil if needed, and add the garlic.

4. Return the seared chicken to the pan, along with the beer or water, soy sauce, vinegar, brown sugar, bay leaves, and peppercorns, bring to a boil, and then simmer uncovered for 10 minutes.

5. Add the potatoes and continue to simmer for another 30 to 40 minutes, depending on if you're using bone-in or boneless chicken (longer for bone-in pieces). Make sure the potatoes and chicken are cooked through.

6. Cook off most of the braising liquid while basting the chicken during the cooking process.

7. If desired, finish the adobo with the coconut milk and continue to cook until heated through.

8. Garnish with the scallion and chilies and serve with the Garlic Rice and Quick Pickled Cucumbers.

INGREDIENTS:

3	LBS. CHICKEN THIGHS OR LEGS
	SALT, TO TASTE
3	TABLESPOONS CANOLA OIL, PLUS MORE AS NEEDED
1	MEDIUM ONION, SLICED
6-8	GARLIC CLOVES, MINCED
¾	CUP BEER OR WATER
¾	CUP SOY SAUCE
¾	CUP APPLE CIDER VINEGAR
2	TABLESPOONS BROWN SUGAR
3-4	BAY LEAVES
½	TABLESPOON WHOLE BLACK PEPPERCORNS, TOASTED AND CRUSHED
4	RED POTATOES, CUT INTO 1-INCH PIECES
½	CUP COCONUT MILK (OPTIONAL)
1	SCALLION, SLICED THIN ON A BIAS, FOR GARNISH
1	RED JALAPEÑO PEPPER, SLICED THIN ON A BIAS, FOR GARNISH
	GARLIC RICE (SEE PAGE 143), FOR SERVING
	QUICK PICKLED CUCUMBERS (SEE RECIPE), FOR SERVING

Continued . . .

QUICK PICKLED CUCUMBERS

1. In a heat-resistant bowl, combine the cucumbers with the salt, mix well, and set aside.

2. Add the star anise to a pan over medium heat and toast until fragrant. Add the sesame oil, vinegar, sugar, water, and gochugaru and bring to a boil, stirring to dissolve the sugar.

3. Once boiling, pour the liquid over the cucumbers just to cover. Cover and refrigerate until cool.

4. Before serving, add the pepper and sesame seeds and toss.

INGREDIENTS:

QUICK PICKLED CUCUMBERS

6	PERSIAN CUCUMBERS, SLICED INTO RINGS
2	TEASPOONS SALT
1	STAR ANISE
2	TEASPOONS SESAME OIL
¼	CUP UNSEASONED RICE VINEGAR
2	TABLESPOONS SUGAR
2	TABLESPOONS WATER
¼	TEASPOON GOCHUGARU
	GROUND BLACK PEPPER, TO TASTE
1	TABLESPOON TOASTED SESAME SEEDS, FOR SERVING

GINGER LIME MISO BUTTERFISH

YIELD: 4 SERVINGS / **ACTIVE TIME:** 1 HOUR / **TOTAL TIME:** 72 HOURS

Popular in Japan and Hawaii, this preparation of butterfish is aromatic, sweet, and full of acidity and umami from the lime and the paste.

1. In a saucepan, whisk together the miso, brown sugar, sake, mirin, vinegar, soy sauce, and ginger and bring to a simmer over medium heat. Cook for 10 to 15 minutes, and then lower the heat and simmer until the mixture has reduced by a quarter, about 20 or 30 minutes. Let cool completely, then add the lime juice and lime zest. Set aside.

2. In a resealable bag or container, combine the prepared marinade with the fillets, being sure to completely cover the fish. Refrigerate for 1 to 3 days.

3. When ready to cook the fish, preheat the broiler.

4. Remove the fish from the container and shake off any excess marinade. Let sit at room temperature for 30 minutes before cooking.

5. Line a sheet pan with foil and grease the foil with pan spray or a little oil. Place the fish on sheet pan, skin side down.

6. Broil the fish for 6 to 10 minutes until opaque, and then broil for another minute, closer to the broiler, to caramelize the outer edges.

7. Serve immediately with the rice, some vegetables, and your favorite sides.

INGREDIENTS:

1   CUP WHITE MISO PASTE

1   CUP BROWN SUGAR

1   CUP SAKE

1   CUP MIRIN

½   CUP RICE VINEGAR, UNSEASONED

⅓   CUP SOY SAUCE

1   TABLESPOON FINELY GRATED GINGER

    JUICE AND ZEST OF 1 LIME

1   LB. BUTTERFISH OR BLACK COD, CLEANED AND DIVIDED INTO 4-OZ. FILLETS

    RICE, FOR SERVING

VEGETARIAN BIBIMBAP

YIELD: 4 SERVINGS / ACTIVE TIME: 1 HOUR / TOTAL TIME: 1 HOUR

Koreans have made bibimbap since the late 1500s, during the Joseon dynasty. It is believed that they made the dish to offer to their ancestors. Variations of the dish reflect regional ingredients and protein, but this version is a classic vegetarian one. This can also be served in a hot stone bowl to develop crispy rice.

1. Bring a pot of water to a boil, blanch the spinach for 30 seconds, drain, rinse in cold water, and squeeze out any excess water. Rough chop the spinach and toss with 1 teaspoon of sesame oil and ¼ teaspoon of salt. Set aside.

2. Add the soybean sprouts and 1 cup of water to a saucepan over medium-high heat. Cover and cook until the sprouts start to smell nutty, 8 to 10 minutes. Drain and transfer to a clean bowl. Let cool before seasoning with 1 tablespoon of sesame oil and 1 teaspoon of salt and mixing well. Set aside.

3. Toss the zucchini with ½ teaspoon of salt and let stand for 6 to 8 minutes.

4. Add a little canola oil to a pan over medium heat and cook the zucchini for about 4 minutes, being sure not to overcook. Remove from heat, cool, and season with the sesame oil and salt, to taste. Set aside.

5. Add 1 tablespoon of the canola oil, the daikon, and ½ teaspoon of salt to a sauté pan over medium heat. Cook and stir for 1 minute. Add 3 tablespoons of water, cover, cook for another 6 to 8 minutes, until the daikon is fully cooked. Season with the sesame oil and set aside.

6. Rinse the fernbrake, add to a pot with 5 quarts of water, and bring to a boil. Once boiling, cover and simmer for roughly 40 minutes. Remove from heat and let cool in the cooking water for another hour. Drain, rinse in cold water, and remove any excess water. Cut into 2-inch pieces.

7. Add 1 tablespoon of canola oil to a sauté pan over high heat. Once the oil begins to shimmer, sauté the fernbrake for 2 minutes, then add the soy sauce and sugar and stir to coat the fernbrake. Remove from heat and toss with the sesame oil. Adjust the seasoning if needed and set aside.

INGREDIENTS:

2   BUNCHES SPINACH, TRIMMED

1   TABLESPOON SESAME OIL, PLUS 1 TEASPOON, PLUS MORE TO TASTE

2¼ TEASPOONS SALT, DIVIDED, PLUS MORE TO TASTE

4   CUPS SOYBEAN SPROUTS

1   CUP WATER, PLUS MORE AS NEEDED

4   TABLESPOONS CANOLA OIL, DIVIDED

2   CUPS THINLY SLICED ZUCCHINI

3   CUPS DAIKON, CUT INTO MATCHSTICKS

1   CUP FERNBRAKE, SOAKED AND COOKED

2   TEASPOONS SOY SAUCE

¼   TEASPOON SUGAR

3-4 CUPS COOKED WHITE RICE, FOR SERVING

⅓   CUP CHOJANG SAUCE (SEE RECIPE), TO TASTE

1   FRIED EGG, FOR GARNISH

1   TABLESPOON TOASTED SESAME SEEDS, FOR GARNISH

8. Once all of the vegetables and rice are cooked, place the rice in bottom of a shallow bowl. Arrange each seasoned ,cooked vegetable around the top of the rice. Drizzle 1 to 2 tablespoons of Chojang Sauce over the top.

9. Garnish with the egg, sesame seeds, and a drizzle of sesame oil. Mix together all of the ingredients to eat.

CHOJANG SAUCE

1. In a bowl, combine all of the ingredients and whisk well.

2. Refrigerate in a squeeze bottle, so it's ready to drizzle on your favorite dish.

INGREDIENTS:

CHOJANG SAUCE

1	CUP GOCHUJANG
2	TABLESPOONS DISTILLED VINEGAR
1	TABLESPOON SOY SAUCE
1	TABLESPOON HONEY
¼	TEASPOON GARLIC POWDER

TTEOKBOKKI

YIELD: 4 SERVINGS / **ACTIVE TIME:** 30 MINUTES / **TOTAL TIME:** 1 HOUR

This is a very popular sweet-and-spicy dish that is enjoyed as a snack or a meal on its own. In Korea, you can easily find tteokbokki near universities, since it's a favorite amongst young bar hoppers.

1. In a shallow pot, make a stock by combining the water, anchovies, and kombu. Bring to a boil uncovered and simmer for 20 to 30 minutes. Strain; it should yield about 3 cups.

2. Add the stock to a saucepan, along with the rice cakes, gochujang, ketchup, gochugaru, and sugar, stir, and cook over medium-high heat for about 10 minutes, until the sauce starts to thicken and the rice cakes start to become soft.

3. Add the fish cakes and eggs to the sauce and cook for another 5 minutes, stirring to coat all of the ingredients with the sauce. Add more water if the sauce becomes too dry.

4. Transfer to a serving bowl and, if using, garnish with the sesame seeds and scallions. Serve immediately.

INGREDIENTS:

1   QUART WATE , PLUS MORE AS NEEDED

6   DRIED ANCHOVIES, CLEANED, WITH HEADS AND INNARDS REMOVED

1   6 X 6-INCH KOMBU SQUARE

1   LB. RICE CAKES

⅓   CUP GOCHUJANG

½   TABLESPOON KETCHUP

½   TABLESPOON GOCHUGARU

1   TABLESPOON SUGAR

½   LB. FISH CAKES, SLICED (OPTIONAL)

2-4   HARD-BOILED EGGS, PEELED

     TOASTED SESAME SEEDS, FOR GARNISH (OPTIONAL)

2-3   SCALLIONS, CUT INTO 3-INCH PIECES, FOR GARNISH (OPTIONAL)

BAKED SNAPPER
WITH GOCHUJANG RADISH SAUCE

YIELD: 4 SERVINGS / **ACTIVE TIME:** 30 MINUTES / **TOTAL TIME:** 1 HOUR

Korean cuisine has an abundance of recipes to make mouthwatering seafood dishes to enjoy with friends and family. This recipe calls for baking a whole fish, with the head on, giving it a bit of a wow factor. The fish can also be grilled or broiled, based on personal preference.

1. Preheat the oven to 350°F.

2. Score both sides of the fish with 3 diagonal slits.

3. In a bowl, combine all of the sauce ingredients and mix well.

4. Line a sheet pan or shallow casserole dish with heavy-duty foil and evenly spread out the daikon, onion, and carrot.

5. Rub the prepared sauce all over the fish and place it on top of the vegetables. Spoon any extra sauce on top of the fish. Add ¼ cup of water around the fish and vegetables to help steam.

6. Cook for 15 minutes, and then add the jalapeños and scallions, and baste the fish with the sauce that has formed. Continue to cook the fish for another 15 minutes.

7. Serve in the casserole dish (if you used one) or transfer to a serving platter.

INGREDIENTS:

1½ LBS. SNAPPER, SCALED, GUTTED, AND CLEANED

1 CUP CHOPPED DAIKON, CUT INTO 1½ X 1-INCH PIECES AND ¼ INCH THICK

½ ONION, SLICED

½ CARROT, SLICED

1-2 JALAPEÑOS, SLICED

2-3 SCALLIONS, SLICED INTO 1-INCH PIECES

RICE, FOR SERVING

SAUCE

⅓ CUP SOY SAUCE

1-2 TABLESPOONS GOCHUGARU

2 TABLESPOONS GOCHUJANG

1 TEASPOON SUGAR

8 GARLIC CLOVES, MINCED

1 TEASPOON MINCED GINGER

2 TABLESPOONS MIRIN

TERIYAKI CHICKEN

YIELD: 4 SERVINGS / **ACTIVE TIME**: 30 MINUTES / **TOTAL TIME**: 8 HOURS

Teriyaki is a Japanese cooking technique that calls for protein or vegetables to be glazed with a sauce made from soy sauce, mirin, and sugar, and then grilled over flame. While boiling the marinade makes it safe to use as a sauce, if you prefer to discard the marinade use the Teriyaki Sauce recipe.

1. Add the soy sauce, mirin, sugars, ginger, garlic, and pineapple juice to a pot over medium-high heat and bring to a boil, stirring to dissolve the sugars. Remove from heat and let cool.

2. Once the marinade has cooled, combine it with the chicken in a resealable bag or container ,and refrigerate for at least 1 hour, and as long as 8 hours.

3. Preheat the grill or broiler.

4. Remove the chicken from the marinade, pour the marinade into a saucepan, and bring to a boil. Add the slurry and simmer to thicken the sauce. Add water if the sauce is too thick; it should have the consistency of heavy cream.

5. Once the grill or broiler is ready, cook the chicken for about 4 minutes per side.

6. Slice before garnishing with the sesame seeds and scallions (if using) and serving with the rice and your favorite sides. Drizzle with the sauce, to taste, or serve with additional sauce on the side.

TERIYAKI SAUCE

1. Add the soy sauce, 1 cup of water, mirin, brown sugar, honey, garlic, and ginger powder to a pot over medium-high heat, bring to a boil, and then simmer for 2 minutes, dissolving the sugar.

2. In a bowl, combine the cornstarch with ¼ cup of water and mix well. Add to the sauce and simmer to thicken to the desired consistency.

3. Cool and refrigerate covered for up to 2 weeks.

INGREDIENTS:

1	CUP SOY SAUCE
1	TABLESPOON MIRIN
1	CUP SUGAR
2	TEASPOONS BROWN SUGAR
2	TABLESPOONS GRATED GINGER
6	GARLIC CLOVES, MINCED
2	TABLESPOONS PINEAPPLE JUICE
8-10	SKINLESS AND BONELESS CHICKEN THIGHS
	CORNSTARCH SLURRY (1:1 RATIO), AS NEEDED
	TOASTED SESAME SEEDS, FOR GARNISH (OPTIONAL)
2	TABLESPOONS CHOPPED SCALLIONS, FOR GARNISH (OPTIONAL)
	RICE, FOR SERVING

TERIYAKI SAUCE

½	CUP SOY SAUCE
1¼	CUPS WATER, DIVIDED
1	TABLESPOON MIRIN
¼	CUP BROWN SUGAR
2	TABLESPOONS HONEY
¼	TEASPOON GARLIC POWDER
½	TEASPOON GINGER POWDER
2	TABLESPOONS CORNSTARCH

HIBACHI STEAK

YIELD: 4 SERVINGS / **ACTIVE TIME:** 30 MINUTES / **TOTAL TIME:** 24 HOURS

It is customary to make this dish using a small, portable hibachi grill that's called a shichirin. It uses charcoal, but you can also find electric grills for indoor use. Be careful with the Kimchi Salt—it is addictive. It takes this steak to the next level, but the truth is that it will improve almost anything.

1. Combine all of the marinade ingredients in a blender or food processor and puree.

2. Combine the steak and the marinade in a resealable bag or container and refrigerate overnight. Reserve some marinade to deglaze the pan during cooking.

3. Remove the steak from the marinade and shake off any excess marinade.

4. Preheat a skillet over medium-high heat.

5. Add the oil to the hot skillet and sear the steak on both sides.

6. Add the onion and scallions and cook everything for an additional 2 to 3 minutes.

7. Deglaze the skillet with the reserved marinade and finish with the butter, shaking the pan to incorporate.

8. Remove from heat, garnish with the sesame seeds, and serve immediately with rice and your favorite sides.

KIMCHI SALT

1. Using a dehydrator or very low-temperature oven, dehydrate the Kimchi overnight.

2. Combine the dehydrated Kimchi and dried shrimp in a food processor and blend into a powder.

3. In a bowl, add the Kimchi powder, gochugaru, and salt and mix well.

4. Store in an airtight container until needed.

INGREDIENTS:

MARINADE

1	CUP SOY SAUCE
¼	CUP PEELED AND CHOPPED GINGER
½	CUP ROUGHLY CHOPPED SCALLIONS
½	CUP ROUGHLY CHOPPED YELLOW ONION
8	GARLIC CLOVES
1	JALAPEÑO PEPPER, DESEEDED
1	CUP WATER
½	CUP SUGAR
2	TABLESPOONS MIRIN
¼	CUP ORANGE JUICE
1	TABLESPOON RICE VINEGAR
1	TABLESPOON TOASTED SESAME SEEDS

STEAK

1½	LBS. SKIRT STEAK, TRIMMED, POUNDED, AND SLICED INTO ⅛-INCH PIECES
3	TABLESPOONS CANOLA OIL, PLUS MORE AS NEEDED
1	CUP THINLY SLICED ONION
¾	CUP THINLY SLICED SCALLIONS, CUT ON A BIAS
1-2	TABLESPOONS UNSALTED BUTTER
	TOASTED SESAME SEEDS, FOR GARNISH (OPTIONAL)

KIMCHI SALT

2	CUPS CHOPPED KIMCHI (SEE PAGE 148)
¼	CUP DRIED BABY SHRIMP
2	TABLESPOONS GOCHUGARU
1	CUP MALDON SALT OR SIMILAR HIGH-QUALITY FINISHING SEA SALT

GALBI JJIM

YIELD: 8 SERVINGS / **ACTIVE TIME**: 30 MINUTES / **TOTAL TIME**: 3 HOURS

This dish was initially reserved for the elite, but then it became customary to serve it to celebrate holidays like the Mid-Autumn Festival, or Daeboreum, which celebrates the first full moon of the Lunar New Year.

1. Rinse and soak the short ribs in cold water for between 30 minutes and 1 hour, to draw out excess blood and impurities. Drain well.

2. In a large pot, combine the water, short ribs, onion, ginger, garlic, and the white parts of the scallions and bring to a boil. Lower the heat and simmer uncovered for 30 minutes, skimming any foam and impurities that float to the surface.

3. Using tongs, remove the short ribs and set aside.

4. Strain the stock and refrigerate to help solidify the fat, which can then be skimmed off and discarded.

5. Meanwhile, in a bowl, combine all of the sauce ingredients, except the sesame oil, and mix well.

6. In a clean pot, combine the short ribs and the prepared sauce and mix well. Add 3 cups of the reserved stock, cover, bring to a boil, and then reduce the heat and simmer over medium-low heat for 20 to 30 minutes.

7. Add the daikon, mushrooms, jujubes, and carrot and stir well. Simmer covered for another 20 to 30 minutes.

8. Uncover and simmer until the sauce has thickened to the desired consistency and the meat is tender but not completely falling apart.

9. Add the sliced scallion greens and sesame oil right before removing from heat.

10. Transfer to a serving platter and garnish with the pine nuts, if using.

INGREDIENTS:

4	LBS. MEATY BEEF SHORT RIBS
6	CUPS WATER
1	ONION, HALVED
½	TABLESPOON SLICED GINGER
6	GARLIC CLOVES
2-3	SCALLIONS, CHOPPED AND WHITE AND GREEN PARTS SEPARATED
¾	LB. DAIKON, CUT INTO LARGE PIECES
4-6	SHIITAKE MUSHROOMS, QUARTERED
4-6	DRIED JUJUBES, PITTED
1	CARROT, CUT INTO LARGE PIECES
	TOASTED PINE NUTS, FOR GARNISH (OPTIONAL)

SAUCE

1	CUP SOY SAUCE
3	TABLESPOONS SUGAR
2	TABLESPOONS HONEY
¼	CUP MIRIN
¼	CUP GRATED ASIAN PEAR
¼	CUP GRATED ONION
1	TEASPOON FINELY MINCED GINGER
½	TEASPOON GROUND BLACK PEPPER
2	TABLESPOONS SESAME OIL

CHICKEN OR PORK KATSU

YIELD: 2 SERVINGS / **ACTIVE TIME:** 30 MINUTES / **TOTAL TIME:** 30 MINUTES

The panko batter creates a crispy and tender cutlet when panfried. It is best enjoyed with rice and a tangy sauce for dipping.

1. Season both sides of the meat with the salt, pepper, and garlic.

2. Put the flour, eggs, and panko in three separate shallow containers.

3. Dip the meat into the flour, shake off any excess flour, then dip into the eggs, and finally press the egg-covered meat in the panko, coating all sides well. Set on a plate until ready to fry.

4. Add ¼ inch of oil to a large skillet over medium-high heat. Once the oil is hot, panfry the breaded meat for 3 to 4 minutes per side, until golden brown and crispy. Work in batches. Set aside the cooked meat on a wire rack or paper towel–lined plate. Repeat until all of the meat is cooked.

5. Slice, if preferred, and serve immediately with the Katsu Sauce, rice, and your favorite side.

KATSU SAUCE

1. In a bowl, combine all of the ingredients, except the ketchup, and whisk to dissolve the sugar. Add the ketchup and whisk well.

2. Refrigerate in an airtight container until needed.

INGREDIENTS:

- 1   LB. SKINLESS AND BONELESS CHICKEN OR PORK LOIN, POUNDED ¼ INCH THICK
- 1   TEASPOON KOSHER SALT
- ½   TEASPOON GROUND BLACK PEPPER
- ¼   TEASPOON GRANULATED GARLIC
- ¼   CUP ALL-PURPOSE FLOUR
- 2   LARGE EGGS, BEATEN
- 2   CUPS PANKO BREAD CRUMBS
-     CANOLA OIL, FOR FRYING
- ¼   CUP KATSU SAUCE (SEE RECIPE), TO TASTE
-     RICE, FOR SERVING

KATSU SAUCE

- 2   TEASPOONS SUGAR
- ⅛   TEASPOON GARLIC POWDER
- 3½ TABLESPOONS WORCESTERSHIRE SAUCE
- 1   TABLESPOON MIRIN
- 1   TABLESPOON SOY SAUCE
- ½   CUP KETCHUP

CHICKEN KARAAGE

YIELD: 4 SERVINGS / **ACTIVE TIME:** 30 MINUTES / **TOTAL TIME:** 24 HOURS

This Japan's version of fried chicken, in which the chicken is marinated prior to deep-frying.

1. In a bowl, combine the soy sauce, sake, sesame oil, ginger, and sugar and whisk well, dissolving the sugar. Add the chicken and refrigerate covered for at least 30 minutes, but ideally overnight.

2. Fill a deep pot with 3 inches of canola oil, and over medium-high heat, bring to between 325°F and 350°F.

3. In a separate bowl, combine the potato starch, salt, and pepper and mix well.

4. Remove the chicken from the marinade and dredge in the seasoned potato starch, making sure all sides are thoroughly coated. Shake excess dredge from chicken before frying.

5. Working in batches so as not to overcrowd the pot, carefully place the dredged chicken into the oil and cook for about 3 minutes. Turn the pieces in order to brown all of the sides evenly. Using a slotted spoon or kitchen spider, remove the crispy chicken from the oil and drain on a paper towel–lined plate. Repeat until all of the chicken is cooked. Let cool.

6. When ready to eat, fry the chicken again for about 1 minute to make extra crispy. Drain on a paper towel–lined plate.

7. Serve hot with your favorite dipping sauce.

INGREDIENTS:

3	TABLESPOONS SOY SAUCE
1	TABLESPOON SAKE
1½	TEASPOONS SESAME OIL
1½	TEASPOONS GRATED GINGER
2	TEASPOONS SUGAR
1½	LBS. SKINLESS AND BONELESS CHICKEN THIGHS, CUT INTO 2-INCH PIECES
	CANOLA OIL, FOR DEEP-FRYING
1	CUP POTATO STARCH
½	TEASPOON KOSHER SALT
1	TEASPOON GROUND BLACK PEPPER

BOSSAM

YIELD: 8 SERVINGS / ACTIVE TIME: 1 HOUR / TOTAL TIME: 2 HOURS

Unctuous braised pork belly is perfectly complemented with crunchy, tangy, and spicy condiments, and bundled up in a salted cabbage wrap.

1. Cut the pork belly into 3 or 4 smaller rectangular pieces.

2. Add the canola oil to a pot over medium-high heat. Once the oil begins to shimmer, add the onions and cook for 3 minutes to develop caramelization. Add the garlic and ginger and cook for another minute, stirring.

3. While stirring, add the soy sauce, sake, beer or water, sugar, doenjang, and mushrooms.

4. Add the pork belly to the pot, making sure the braising liquid covers the pork completely. Lay parchment over the pork belly, if needed, to keep it submerged.

5. Bring the pot to a boil. Once boiling for 3 or 4 minutes, lower the heat to medium-low and simmer covered for 45 minutes to 1¼ hours, until the pork belly is tender.

6. Uncover and remove from heat, and let the pork belly cool in the braising liquid.

7. As the pork cools, begin to prepare the Salted Cabbage by slicing the cabbage into lengthwise quarters.

8. In a large bowl, combine the salt, sugar, and water and whisk to dissolve. Add the cabbage to the water and soak for 30 minutes to 1 hour.

9. Drain the cabbage, squeezing out any excess liquid, and set aside. When ready to serve, remove the core of the cabbage so individual leaves are separated.

10. In a bowl, combine all of the Salted Shrimp Dipping Sauce ingredients, mix well, and refrigerate covered until needed.

11. When ready to serve, slice the pork belly into thin slices; if desired, reheat the sliced pork in the oven.

12. Arrange the sliced pork, cabbage, dipping sauce and condiments on a platter and serve family style.

13. Dip the pork into the sauce and wrap in the cabbage, adding condiments of your choosing.

INGREDIENTS:

3	LBS. PORK BELLY
1	TABLESPOON CANOLA OIL
1	LARGE ONION, DICED
10	GARLIC CLOVES
	½-INCH PIECE GINGER, SLICED
2	CUPS SOY SAUCE
2	CUPS SAKE
2-3	CUPS BEER OR WATER
½	CUP SUGAR
1	TABLESPOON DOENJANG
4	DRIED SHIITAKE MUSHROOMS
	MUSAENG CHAE (SEE PAGE 414), AS NEEDED
	JALAPEÑOS, SLICED THIN (OPTIONAL)

SALTED CABBAGE

1	NAPA CABBAGE
½	CUP SALT
¼	CUP SUGAR
2-3	CUPS WATER

SALTED SHRIMP DIPPING SAUCE

2	TABLESPOONS SALTED SHRIMP
¼	CUP SESAME OIL
1	TEASPOON TOASTED SESAME SEEDS
1-2	TEASPOONS GOCHUGARU
1	TABLESPOON FINELY CHOPPED SCALLIONS

MUSAENG CHAE

YIELD: 8 SERVINGS / **ACTIVE TIME:** 30 MINUTES / **TOTAL TIME:** 1 HOUR

This spicy dehydrated Korean radish banchan is traditionally served with bossam, but can accompany any meal as a banchan. Similar to daikon, the Korean radish is typically shorter and more round, with a denser texture and sweeter flavor.

1. In a large container, salt the cut radishes with the salt, coating the radishes evenly. Set aside until the radishes have released their water content and have softened. Squeeze out and drain any excess liquid.

2. Add the onion, gochugaru, garlic, ginger, fish sauce, and sugar to the radish and, using your hands, combine all of the ingredients well. It should be a pasty consistency. Adjust the seasoning with the fish sauce, sugar, and/or gochugaru if needed.

3. Refrigerate in an airtight container until needed.

INGREDIENTS:

1½ LBS. KOREAN RADISHES, CUT INTO MATCHSTICKS

1 TABLESPOON KOSHER SALT

¼ ONION, SLICED THIN

2-3 TABLESPOONS GOCHUGARU

½ TABLESPOON MINCED GARLIC

1 TEASPOON MINCED GINGER

1½ TABLESPOONS FISH SAUCE

1½ TEASPOONS SUGAR

CHASHU PORK BELLY

YIELD: 6 SERVINGS / **ACTIVE TIME:** 30 MINUTES / **TOTAL TIME:** 4 HOURS

This is a popular Japanese-style braised pork that is added to tonkotsu ramen, but it can be used in many dishes or eaten as is with a side of rice. If it is difficult to find pork belly, pork shoulder is a great alternative.

1. Preheat the oven to 275°F.

2. Place the pork belly on a cutting board, fat side down, and roll the belly into a tight cylindrical log. Use kitchen twine to tie the log together and secure the shape, spacing each tie ½ inch apart.

3. Add the oil to an oven-safe skillet over medium-high heat. Once the oil begins to shimmer, sear the pork belly on all sides until well browned, about 8 to 10 minutes.

4. Remove from heat, remove the pork belly from the skillet, and discard any excess rendered oil from the skillet. Return the seared belly to the hot pan.

5. In a saucepan, combine the soy sauce, sake, mirin, sugar, water, ginger, and star anise and bring to a boil. Once boiling, pour over the pork belly in the skillet.

6. Tent the pork belly with foil and cook in the oven for 3 to 4 hours, occasionally rotating the pork belly in the cooking liquid. Cook until the pork belly is very knife tender.

7. Remove the skillet from the oven and transfer the cooked pork belly and cooking liquid to a heat-resistant container. Let cool at room temperature uncovered, then cover and refrigerate overnight.

8. To serve, remove the kitchen twine and slice thin with a sharp knife.

INGREDIENTS:

2-3	LBS. SKINLESS PORK BELLY
3	TABLESPOONS CANOLA OIL
1	CUP SOY SAUCE
1	CUP SAKE
1	CUP MIRIN
¼	CUP SUGAR
⅓	CUP WATER
	3-INCH PIECE GINGER, PEELED AND SLICED INTO ROUNDS
	1 STAR ANISE

CHASHU CHICKEN

YIELD: 6 SERVINGS / ACTIVE TIME: 30 MINUTES / TOTAL TIME: 6 HOURS

The preparation of chicken in this manner is inspired by how chashu pork belly is cooked. Slices of the savory and sweet chicken are added on top of ramen.

1. In a large bowl, combine the soy sauce, sake, sugar, and ginger, mix well, and add the chicken. Marinate in the refrigerator for 2 to 4 hours.

2. Remove the chicken from the marinade and shake off any excess marinade.

3. On a clean work surface, roll the chicken thighs into tight logs. Use kitchen twine to keep the chicken rolled up. Tightly foil wrap the tied chicken logs.

4. Set up a steamer in a pot with water. Once the water is boiling, place the foiled chicken in the steamer, cover, and lower the heat to medium-low and steam for about 1 hour, or until cooked. Add more water to the steamer as needed during the cooking time.

5. Remove the chicken from the steamer and let rest for 30 minutes; do not remove the foil. Refrigerate overnight before slicing and serving.

INGREDIENTS:

⅓ CUP SOY SAUCE

2 TABLESPOONS SAKE

1¼ TABLESPOONS SUGAR

2 TEASPOONS GRATED GINGER

2-3 LBS. SKIN-ON, BONELESS CHICKEN THIGHS

RAMEN OR RICE, FOR SERVING

GINGER CHICKEN

YIELD: 4 SERVINGS / **ACTIVE TIME:** 30 MINUTES / **TOTAL TIME:** 24 HOURS

Tender and aromatic ginger chicken is ideal for ramen or rice bowls.

1. In a bowl, combine the soy sauce, sake, honey, and ginger and whisk well. Add the chicken, mix well, and refrigerate covered for at least 1 hour, and ideally overnight.

2. Shake off any excess marinade from the chicken before cooking; reserve the marinade.

3. Add the oil to a large skillet over medium heat. When the oil begins to shimmer, add the chicken and sear all sides, about 4 to 6 minutes; make sure the pan doesn't get too hot and burn the marinade.

4. Reduce the heat to low and add the marinade to the skillet. Cook for 2 to 3 minutes, until the chicken has cooked through and is glazed.

5. Remove from the pan and set aside until needed.

INGREDIENTS:

2   TABLESPOONS SOY SAUCE

1½ TABLESPOONS SAKE

1   TABLESPOON HONEY

2   TABLESPOONS GRATED GINGER

1   LB. BONELESS CHICKEN THIGHS, CUT INTO BITE-SIZE PIECES

1   TABLESPOON CANOLA OIL, PLUS MORE AS NEEDED

    RAMEN OR RICE, FOR SERVING

SWEET CHILI PORK BOWL
WITH BELL PEPPERS & CANDIED PEANUTS

YIELD: 6 SERVINGS / ACTIVE TIME: 30 MINUTES / TOTAL TIME: 1 HOUR

The rice really soaks up all the wonderful flavors in this dish, and the sweet crunch of peanuts adds a great element of texture.

1. Add the rice and water to a small pot over medium-high heat. When it comes to a boil, cover the pot, lower the heat, and simmer for 20 minutes. After 20 minutes, turn off the heat and let stand covered for another 10 minutes. Remove the lid, add the lime zest, and fluff the rice with a fork. Set aside.

2. Add 1½ tablespoons of oil to a nonstick pan over high heat. When the oil begins to shimmer, add the bell peppers and onion and cook, without stirring, for 3 to 5 minutes to develop caramelization.

3. Season with a pinch of salt, add the garlic, stir the vegetables, and cook until tender and browned, 7 to 9 minutes. Remove from heat and set aside on a plate.

4. Add 1 tablespoon of oil to the same pan over high heat, add the pork, and season with the salt and pepper. Using a wooden spoon or spatula, press the pork to cover the pan evenly. Cook undisturbed for 3 to 5 minutes to brown. Break the meat into pieces with a spoon or spatula and cook the pork through, 2 to 4 minutes.

5. Reduce the heat to medium and add the soy sauce, sweet soy sauce, chili sauce, and butter. Mix well and cook for 1 minute. Add the cooked peppers and onion, mix well, cook for another minute, and remove from heat. Adjust the seasoning if needed.

6. Divide the rice into 4 serving bowls and top with the pork mixture, Candied Peanuts, cilantro, and lime wedges. Top with the fried egg, if using.

CANDIED PEANUTS

1. Add the peanuts, sugar, and water to a nonstick pan over medium heat and bring to a simmer, stirring often.

2. Once all of the water has evaporated and the peanuts are coated and sticky, turn off the heat.

3. Season with the Shichimi Togarashi or your spice mixture of choice, if desired.

4. Transfer to a parchment-lined sheet pan and let cool completely before storing in an airtight container.

INGREDIENTS:

1	CUP JASMINE RICE, RINSED AND STRAINED WELL
1½	CUPS WATER
1	LIME, ZESTED AND QUARTERED
	CANOLA OIL, AS NEEDED
2	BELL PEPPERS, CLEANED AND THINLY SLICED
1	MEDIUM ONIO , HALVED AND SLICED
	SALT, TO TASTE
1	GARLIC CLOVE, MINCED
1½	LBS. GROUND PORK
	PEPPER, TO TASTE
2	TABLESPOONS SOY SAUCE
4	TABLESPOONS SWEET SOY SAUCE
1½	TABLESPOONS SWEET CHILI DIPPING SAUCE (SEE PAGE 42)
1½	TABLESPOONS UNSALTED BUTTER
	CANDIED PEANUTS (SEE RECIPE), FOR GARNISH
2-3	TABLESPOONS CHOPPED CILANTRO, FOR GARNISH
	LIME WEDGES, FOR GARNISH
1	FRIED EGG, FOR GARNISH (OPTIONAL)

CANDIED PEANUTS

⅓	CUP ROASTED PEANUTS
1½	TEASPOONS SUGAR
2½	TABLESPOONS WATER
¼	TEASPOON SHICHIMI TOGARASHI (SEE PAGE 146) OR SPICE MIXTURE OF CHOICE (OPTIONAL)

GRILLED LEMONGRASS CHICKEN WINGS

YIELD: 4 SERVINGS / **ACTIVE TIME:** 30 MINUTES / **TOTAL TIME:** 12 HOURS

This sticky, sweet, and slightly funky marinade is a wonderful twist on standard wings.

1. In a bowl, combine all of the ingredients, except the chicken, and mix well. Reserve ¼ cup of the prepared marinade in a separate bowl.

2. Use the rest of the marinade to toss chicken wings and refrigerate for 3 to 6 hours, or up to 12 hours.

3. Heat a grill to medium high heat or preheat the oven to 400°F.

4. Grill the wings, basting with the reserved marinade, until wings are cooked. Or, in oven, place the marinated wings on a wire rack over a baking sheet and bake for 30 to 45 minutes, until done. Flip the wings halfway through cooking process and baste with the reserved marinade.

5. If using the oven, finish wings under the broiler until charred.

INGREDIENTS:

½	CUP SOY SAUCE
½	CUP FISH SAUCE
2	TABLESPOONS MINCED GARLIC
1	TABLESPOON MINCED GINGER
2	TABLESPOONS MINCED LEMONGRASS, MINCED
¼	CUP HONEY
3	LIMES, ZESTED AND JUICED
2	TABLESPOONS CANOLA OIL
3	LBS. CHICKEN WINGS

GIMBAP

YIELD: 8 SERVINGS / ACTIVE TIME: 1 HOUR / TOTAL TIME: 1 HOUR

"Gim" is the Korean word for dried seaweed sheets, which are what hold together these hearty rolls of rice and a variety of complementary fillings. While it isn't absolutely necessary, having a bamboo sushi rolling mat on hand is incredibly helpful when it comes time to assemble these.

1. Put the hot cooked rice into a shallow bowl and drizzle 2 teaspoons of sesame oil over the rice, followed by a pinch of salt. Using a wooden spoon or rubber spatula, fold in the seasonings and then let the rice cool until no longer steaming. Cover with plastic wrap and set aside.

2. In a bowl, combine the soy sauce, garlic, black pepper, sugar, and remaining sesame oil and mix well.

3. Add a little oil to a pan over medium-high heat and when the oil begins to shimmer add lightly sear the fishcake strips.

4. Turn heat to low and add enough marinade to the pan to coat and glaze the fishcake. Set aside

5. In a bowl, season the carrots with a generous pinch of salt and let stand for 10 minutes. Squeeze out excess water from carrots.

6. Add a little oil to a pan over medium-high heat and when the oil begins to shimmer add the carrots. Cook for 1 minute, remove from pan, and set aside.

7. Rough chop the spinach and season with a pinch of salt and sesame oil. Set aside.

8. In a bowl, whisk the eggs well.

9. Add some oil and the whisked eggs to a large nonstick pan over low heat, spreading the eggs into a thin layer. When the bottom of the eggs are cooked, flip with a spatula, turn off heat, and cook the flipped side with residual heat. Be sure not to let the eggs brown. Once cooked, remove the eggs from the heat and cut into ½ inch-wide strips. Set aside.

10. Place a sheet of gim on a bamboo mat with the shiny side down. Evenly spread roughly ¾ cup of the rice over the top of the sheet of seaweed. Make sure to leave 1 ½ inches uncovered on the top edge of the sheet.

INGREDIENTS:

4   CUPS COOKED SHORT-GRAIN RICE (SEE PAGE 140)

1   TABLESPOON SESAME OIL, DIVIDED, PLUS MORE TO TASTE

    SALT, TO TASTE

1   TABLESPOON SOY SAUCE

1   GARLIC CLOVE, MINCED

¼   TEASPOONS BLACK PEPPER

1   TABLESPOONS SUGAR

    CANOLA OIL, AS NEEDED

½   LB. FISH CAKE, CUT INTO MATCHSTICKS

1   LARGE CARROT, CUT INTO MATCHSTICKS

1-2   BUNCHES SPINACH, BLANCHED, RINSED, AND STRAINED WELL

3-4   EGGS

4-5   YELLOW PICKLED RADISH, CUT INTO 8-INCH STRIPS

4-5   SHEETS GIM

    SESAME SEEDS, FOR GARNISH

Continued . . .

11. Arrange the prepared fish cake, carrot, spinach, pickled radish strip, and egg strips in the center of the rice in a row lengthwise.

12. Using both hands, roll the mat over the fillings so the bottom edge of the rice and gim wrap and reach the opposite edge. With both hands grab the mat and press tightly as you continue rolling the gimbap. Push back the mat as you roll so it doesn't get wrapped into the gimbap. Roll as tight as possible to center the fillings in the roll so all the ingredients will be together when the roll is sliced.

13. Once enclosed and rolled, remove the gimbap from the mat and set aside, seam side down. Repeat steps until all of the rolls have been assembled.

14. Before slicing, brush each roll with a little sesame oil.

15. Using a sharp knife, slice each roll. Between every few slices clean the knife blade with a wet paper towel to remove starch residue and make the slicing easier.

16. Garnish with sesame seed. Serve immediately or pack to eat later.

SHAKEN BEEF

YIELD: 6 SERVINGS / **ACTIVE TIME:** 30 MINUTES / **TOTAL TIME:** 1 HOUR AND 30 MINUTES

Prior to the colonization of Vietnam by the French, beef was scarce and rare. Therefore, dishes like Shaken Beef were reserved for the elite and were considered delicacies. In Vietnamese, the dish is called bò lúc lắc. "Bò" means beef, and "lúc lắc" is the sound that is made when something is shaken.

1. In a bowl, make the marinade by combining the soy sauce, oyster sauce, garlic, sugar, fish sauce, and black pepper and whisking well. Add the beef and refrigerate covered for 30 minutes to 1 hour.

2. While the beef marinates, make the salad dressing. In a bowl, combine the rice vinegar, water, sugar, and fish sauce, whisk well, adjust the seasoning if needed, and set aside.

3. Add the cornstarch to a shallow bowl.

4. Remove any excess marinade from the beef, and dredge the beef in the cornstarch to coat.

5. Add 2 tablespoons of the oil to a wok or skillet over medium-high heat. Once the oil begins to shimmer, add an even layer of beef to the pan and cook for 3 to 5 minutes. Do not stir the beef; only shake the pan every 30 seconds, making sure to sear all sides while cooking to medium rare. Once caramelized and cooked, remove from heat.

6. In a bowl, combine the cucumber, tomatoes, onion, watercress or arugula, and mint and toss with the prepared dressing.

7. Transfer the salad to a serving platter and arrange the meat around and on top of the salad. Serve immediately with rice.

INGREDIENTS:

2	TABLESPOONS SOY SAUCE
2	TABLESPOONS OYSTER SAUCE
3	GARLIC CLOVES, MINCED
½	TEASPOON SUGAR
1	TEASPOON FISH SAUCE
1	TEASPOON GROUND BLACK PEPPER
1½	LBS. BEEF TENDERLOIN OR RIBEYE, CUT INTO 1-INCH CUBES
1-2	TABLESPOONS CORNSTARCH, PLUS MORE AS NEEDED
2	TABLESPOONS CANOLA OIL, PLUS MORE AS NEEDED
2	DASHES MAGGI SAUCE, FOR GARNISH
	SEA SALT, FOR GARNISH

SALAD

2	TABLESPOONS SEASONED RICE VINEGAR
1	TABLESPOON WATER
1	TEASPOON SUGAR
1	TEASPOON FISH SAUCE
⅔	ENGLISH CUCUMBER, SLICED ¼ INCH-THICK ON A BIAS
1-2	TOMATOES, SLICED INTO ¼-INCH THICK ROUNDS
¼	CUP THINLY SLICED RED ONION, RINSED IN COLD WATER
2-3	CUPS WATERCRESS OR ARUGULA
3	TABLESPOONS CHOPPED MINT
1	PINCH SALT, PLUS MORE AS NEEDED

MUL-NAENGMYEON

YIELD: 4 SERVINGS / ACTIVE TIME: 1 HOUR / TOTAL TIME: 2 HOURS AND 30 MINUTES

These spicy Korean cold buckwheat noodles in chilled bone broth are perfect for hot days.

1. Prep the radishes first by cleaning them and then cutting them into large rectangles. Use a mandoline to slice each large rectangle into thin slices.

2. In a bowl, combine the vinegar, sugar, and salt, and whisk well until dissolved. Add the vinegar mixture to the sliced radishes and mix well by hand. Adjust the seasoning, cover, and set aside.

3. In a large pot, make the broth by combining the beef brisket, radish, onion, scallions, garlic, ginger, peppercorns, and 1 gallon of water and bringing to a boil. Skim the top to remove any impurities that rise to the surface. Lower the heat to medium-low and simmer for 20 minutes, continuing to skim. Cover and simmer on low for 1 hour, until the brisket is tender.

4. Right before removing the broth from heat, stir in the soy sauce and then remove from heat. Let the brisket cool completely in the broth.

5. Once cooled to room temperature, remove the brisket and strain the broth, discarding the vegetables. Refrigerate the brisket until needed.

6. Pour 10 to 12 cups of strained broth into a pot. Add 1 to 2 cups of Dongchimi. Mix well and bring to a simmer over medium heat, and reduce until there are about 10 to 12 cups of broth in the pot. Stir in the sugar if needed and season with the salt, to taste. Store the broth in the freezer until it becomes slightly slushy.

7. Bring a pot of water to a boil, cook the noodles until they are chewy, and then shock in an ice bath to stop cooking. Before straining, make sure the noodles are chilled from the ice bath.

8. In 4 large bowls, place an equal portion of chilled cooked noodles in the bottom of each bowl.

9. Slice the brisket against the grain and arrange on top of the noodles, along with the cucumber, pear, and prepared radish.

INGREDIENTS:

SWEET & SOUR RADISH

1½	LBS. KOREAN RADISHES
½	CUP WHITE VINEGAR
¼	CUP GRANULATED SUGAR
1½	TEASPOONS SALT

BROTH

1	LB. BEEF BRISKET
1	KOREAN RADISH
1	ONION
4	SCALLIONS, WHITE PARTS ONLY
10-12	GARLIC CLOVES
	1-INCH PIECE GINGER, SLICED
1	TEASPOON PEPPERCORN
4	TABLESPOONS SOY SAUCE
	DONGCHIMI (SEE RECIPE), AS NEEDED
2	TEASPOONS SUGAR
	KOSHER SALT, AS NEEDED

MUL-NAENGMYEON

1	PACKAGE DRY NAENGMYEON BUCKWHEAT NOODLES
1	CUCUMBER, SLICED THIN
1	ASIAN PEAR, SLICED THIN
2	SOY SAUCE EGGS (SEE PAGE 192) OR HARD-BOILED EGGS, HALVED
	WHITE VINEGAR, AS NEEDED
	CHINESE HOT MUSTARD, AS NEEDED

Continued . . .

10. Pour roughly 3 cups of slushy broth around the noodles, and garnish with the egg halves.

11. Serve with the white vinegar and hot mustard on the side.

DONGCHIMI

1. In a bowl, toss the the radishes with the salt and sugar to evenly coat and let stand for 45 minutes, until radishes release their water content and soften. Save the radish liquid to use for the brine. Do not rinse the radishes. Set aside.

2. Cut each cleaned napa cabbage leaf into 1-inch pieces and place in a bowl.

3. Dissolve 1 tablespoon of salt into 1½ cups of water, pour over cabbage, and let soak for 30 minutes. Drain and save the cabbage water. Do not rinse the cabbage. Set aside.

4. In a saucepan, make a rice slurry by mixing together the glutinous rice powder with 1 cup of water, and bring to a simmer. Make sure to stir frequently to not burn the bottom. Cook until the mixture thickens into a light paste. Cool and set aside.

5. Add the Asian pear, garlic, ginger, and ½ cup of water to a blender and blend into a puree.

6. In a large pot, combine the puree with the saved radish water, saved napa cabbage water, and glutinous rice paste. Add the salt 1 tablespoon at a time, stirring to dissolve; continue adding salt until it tastes a bit too salty to eat.

7. Place the radishes and cabbage in a nonreactive, airtight container. Add the scallions and chilies, and then pour the brine over to cover and mix well. Adjust the salt by adding more water if too salty or more salt if not enough—it should taste a little salty.

8. Leave covered at a cool room temperature for 1 to 2 days, until bubbles are noticeable. Move to the refrigerator and, for optimal acidic, sweet, tangy flavor, store for 1 to 2 weeks before eating.

9. Serve as a side dish to any meal.

INGREDIENTS:

DONGCHIMI

2	LBS. KOREAN RADISHES, CLEANED AND CUT INTO LARGE RECTANGLES
¼	CUP KOSHER SALT, PLUS MORE AS NEEDED
	WATER, AS NEEDED
1	TEASPOON SUGAR
1	NAPA CABBAGE HEART, THE MOST INNER PART
1	TABLESPOON GLUTINOUS RICE POWDER
½	ASIAN PEAR
4-6	GARLIC CLOVES, MINCED
	1-INCH PIECE GINGER
2	SCALLIONS, CHOPPED INTO 1-INCH PIECES
2	GREEN CHILI PEPPERS, SLICED
2	RED CHILI PEPPERS, SLICED

COLD SESAME NOODLES

YIELD: 6 SERVINGS / ACTIVE TIME: 30 MINUTES / TOTAL TIME: 30 MINUTES

Cold noodle dishes are most popular, and often needed, when the weather is unbearably hot and humid. This Japanese variety uses ramen noodles, but soba noodles can be substituted. It is filling as is, but adding tofu or Ginger Chicken (see page 421) makes these noodles even more of a full meal.

1. In a bowl, combine all of the sauce ingredients and mix well. Incorporate the hot water as needed to achieve a consistency that just coats the back of a spoon. Refrigerate in an airtight container until needed.

2. In a pot, boil the noodles until al dente, strain, and rinse with cold water until the noodles are completely chilled. Toss the noodles with the sesame oil and set aside.

3. When ready to serve, mix the noodles with the sauce in a bowl and adjust the seasoning if needed.

4. Mix in the scallions, cucumber, bean sprouts, and anything else you like. Garnish with the sesame seeds and, if using, the Rayu and cilantro.

INGREDIENTS:

SAUCE

2	TABLESPOONS JAPANESE SESAME PASTE OR TAHINI
1½	TABLESPOONS PEANUT BUTTER
3	TABLESPOONS SOY SAUCE
2	TABLESPOONS CHINKIANG VINEGAR
1½	TEASPOONS LIGHT BROWN SUGAR
⅓	CUP HOT WATER, PLUS MORE AS NEEDED

NOODLES

14	OZ. FRESH RAMEN NOODLES (SEE PAGE 223) OR STORE BOUGHT
3	TEASPOONS SESAME OIL
2	SCALLIONS, SLICED
1	PERSIAN OR JAPANESE CUCUMBER, CUT INTO MATCHSTICKS
2	CUPS BEAN SPROUTS, BLANCHED
1	TABLESPOON TOASTED SESAME SEEDS, FOR GARNISH
	RAYU (SEE PAGE 234), FOR GARNISH (OPTIONAL)
2	TABLESPOONS ROUGHLY CHOPPED CILANTRO, FOR GARNISH (OPTIONAL)

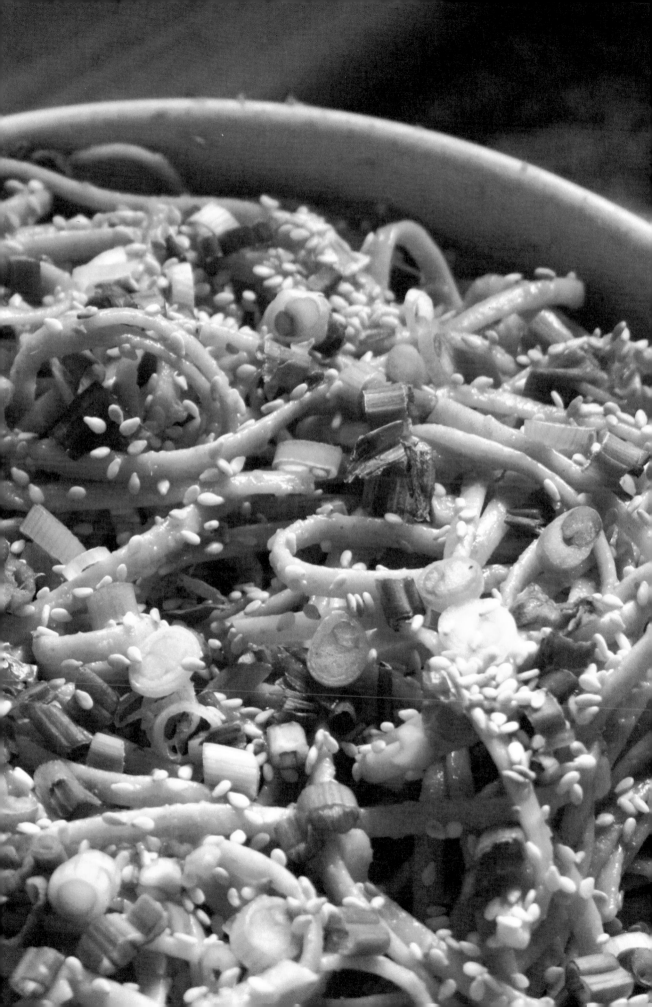

KOREAN FRIED CHICKEN

YIELD: 2 SERVINGS / ACTIVE TIME: 30 MINUTES / TOTAL TIME: 30 MINUTES

The crunchiness of Korean fried chicken is the result of the double-frying method. Make sure to place the chicken in the fryer *only* until the oil has reached the desired heat, to ensure that the protein will be fully cooked with crunchy skin, and that it is not burnt or too oily.

1. In a large Dutch oven or stock pot, add 6 to 8 inches of oil and heat to 375°F.

2. In a shallow bowl, combine the potato starch with the salt and mix well. Lightly dredge the chicken with the seasoned potato starch and shake off any excess.

3. Working in batches so as not to overcrowd, fry the chicken for 7 to 9 minutes, until crispy. Using a slotted spoon or kitchen spider, remove from the oil and drain on a paper towel–lined plate.

4. Meanwhile, heat the Roasted Garlic Soy Glaze in a wok or skillet over medium heat, making sure the glaze is hot.

5. With the frying oil still at 375°F, fry the chicken a second time for 3 to 5 minutes, to cook through and make extra crispy. Using a slotted spoon or kitchen spider, remove from the oil, add to the hot soy glaze, and coat well.

6. Shake off any excess glaze and transfer the chicken to a serving platter.

7. Garnish with the scallions and sesame seeds and serve with the Pickled Daikon.

ROASTED GARLIC SOY GLAZE

1. Add all of the ingredients to a saucepan over medium heat and whisk well to dissolve the brown sugar. Simmer for 20 to 30 minutes, until the sauce has reduced by one-third into a glaze consistency that coats the back of a spoon.

2. Remove from heat and use immediately, or cool at room temperature and refrigerate for up to a week in an airtight container.

INGREDIENTS:

CANOLA OIL, FOR FRYING

2-3 CUPS POTATO STARCH

SALT, TO TASTE

14 CHICKEN WINGS OR DRUMSTICKS

3-4 CUPS ROASTED GARLIC SOY GLAZE (SEE RECIPE)

1 TABLESPOON SLICED SCALLIONS, FOR GARNISH

1 TABLESPOON TOASTED SESAME SEEDS, FOR GARNISH

1 CUP PICKLED DAIKON (SEE PAGE 437)

ROASTED GARLIC SOY GLAZE

1 CUP CHICKEN STOCK (SEE PAGE 680)

1 CUP SOY SAUCE

1 CUP MIRIN

1 CUP BROWN SUGAR

2 CUPS ROASTED GARLIC PUREE

PICKLED DAIKON

YIELD: 4 SERVINGS / **ACTIVE TIME:** 30 MINUTES / **TOTAL TIME:** 96 HOURS

This banchan works with any number of dishes, but it pairs perfectly with Korean Fried Chicken. Use your favorite brand of lemon-lime soda; any one will do the trick.

1. Place the daikon in a colander, season with the salt, and set aside for 30 to 40 minutes to extract the liquid. Rinse well with cold water and drain. The daikon should be slightly soft.

2. In a bowl, combine the remainder of the ingredients and mix well.

3. Place the daikon in a container and cover with the pickling liquid. Cover and leave in a dark, cool place for 2 to 4 days. Check on the second day. The daikon is ready when it is slightly acidic and subtly sweet, and it has a pickled taste. Once ready, refrigerate in an airtight container for up to a month.

INGREDIENTS:

1	DAIKON, PEELED AND CUT INTO 1-INCH PIECES
¼	CUP KOSHER SALT
1½	QUARTS LEMON-LIME SODA
1	TABLESPOON RICE VINEGAR
1	JALAPEÑO PEPPER, SLICED INTO RINGS
2-3	GARLIC CLOVES
1	TABLESPOON MINCED GINGER
2	TABLESPOONS SUGAR

NAKJI BOKKEUM

YIELD: 4 SERVINGS / **ACTIVE TIME:** 30 MINUTES / **TOTAL TIME:** 30 MINUTES

Culinary creations of mouth-numbing spicy seafood are plenty. And using the entire baby octopus is common in Korean cuisine; there's even a dish, sannakji, in which the octopuses are moving! But the only things that will come alive while eating this dish are your taste buds.

1. Rub the octopuses with the salt, then remove the outer skins and rinse off the salt. Cut into 2-inch pieces.

2. Bring a pot of water to a boil and blanch the octopuses for 1 minute; remove, rinse in cold water, and set aside.

3. In a bowl, combine all of the sauce ingredients, mix well, and set aside.

4. Add oil to a wok or skillet over medium-high heat. Once the oil begins to shimmer, add the onion, carrot, zucchini, and bell pepper and stir-fry until al dente. Remove from heat and set aside on a plate.

5. Add oil to the same pan and stir-fry the octopuses for 30 to 40 seconds. Add the prepared sauce and stir-fry to combine, about 1 minute. Add the cooked vegetables and mix well.

6. Fold in the sesame leaves and scallions and remove from heat.

7. Meanwhile, bring a pot of water to a boil, cook the noodles until done, rinse, and drain. Toss the cooked noodles with the sesame oil and salt to season.

8. On a serving platter, plate the cooked noodles and arrange the octopus over the noodles.

INGREDIENTS:

8-12	BABY OCTOPUSES
	SALT, TO TASTE
1-2	TABLESPOONS SESAME OIL, PLUS MORE AS NEEDED
½	ONION, SLICED THIN
½	CUP THINLY SLICED CARROT
½	CUP THINLY SLICED ZUCCHINI
1	BELL PEPPER, SLICED THIN
4-6	SESAME LEAVES
2	SCALLIONS, CUT ON A BIAS
1	PACKAGE SOMYEON

SAUCE

¼	CUP GOCHUJANG
2	TABLESPOONS GOCHUGARU
3	TABLESPOONS SOY SAUCE
2	TABLESPOONS SUGAR
1½	TABLESPOONS RICE WINE
2	GARLIC CLOVES, MINCED
2	TEASPOONS FINELY MINCED GINGER
3	TABLESPOONS CHOPPED SCALLIONS
1	TABLESPOON SESAME OIL
	BLACK PEPPER, TO TASTE

PORK BELLY BANH MI

YIELD: 8 SERVINGS / ACTIVE TIME: 30 MINUTES / TOTAL TIME: 2 HOURS

Banh mi is a Vietnamese sandwich influenced by French culture; hence the use of the baguette. There are a lot of banh mi types, including some made with grilled shrimp, egg, and sardines; however, the pork variety is the most traditional and common.

1. Preheat the oven to 375°F. Season the pork belly with the salt.

2. Add the oil to a Dutch oven over medium-high heat and brown the pork belly, skin side down, rendering out the fat, for 3 to 4 minutes. Flip the pork belly and brown the other side for another 3 to 4 minutes. Transfer to a plate.

3. Lower the heat to medium and add the shallots, stirring to cook until softened, 2 to 3 minutes. Add the garlic and ginger and cook for 1 minute. Add the sugar and cook until the sugar starts to caramelize, and it looks almost like maple syrup. Add the soy sauce and fish sauce and stir well to incorporate all of the flavors.

4. Return the pork belly to the pot and add the coconut water until it is one-quarter from the top of the meat; make sure the skin isn't submerged.

5. Bake in the oven for 1 to 1½ hours, until the skin is super crispy and the meat is tender. Once cooked, transfer to a plate to cool.

6. When the pork is cool enough to handle, slice it into slabs of the desired thickness.

7. Slice the baguette lengthwise; toast if desired. Spread the Spicy Mayo on both pieces of bread, layer the pork belly, and preferred condiment, and add a couple of dashes of Maggi Seasoning before putting on the top piece of bread.

8. Serve immediately, or wrap and enjoy later.

SPICY MAYONNAISE

1. In a bowl, combine all of the ingredients and whisk well. Adjust the seasoning if desired.

2. Refrigerate in a squeeze bottle until needed.

INGREDIENTS:

1½-2	LBS. PORK BELLY, SKIN ON, SCORED, AND SLAB CUT IN HALF
	SALT, TO TASTE
1½	TABLESPOONS CANOLA OIL
2	SHALLOTS, SLICED
4	GARLIC CLOVES, MINCED
½	TABLESPOON FINELY MINCED GINGER
1½	TABLESPOONS SUGAR
3	TABLESPOONS SOY SAUCE
1	TABLESPOON FISH SAUCE
1-1½	CUPS COCONUT WATER, PLUS MORE AS NEEDED
1	FRENCH BAGUETTE
⅓	CUP SPICY MAYO (SEE RECIPE), PLUS MORE AS NEEDED
8	CILANTRO SPRIGS, PLUS MORE AS NEEDED
1-3	JALAPEÑO PEPPERS, SLICED THIN ON A BIAS
1-2	CUCUMBERS, CUT INTO MATCHSTICKS
½	CUP PICKLED DAIKON & CARROT (SEE PAGE 176), PLUS MORE AS NEEDED
	MAGGI SEASONING, TO TASTE

SPICY MAYONNAISE

1	CUP MAYONNAISE
½	TABLESPOON GOCHUJANG
½	TABLESPOON PUREED SAMBAL CHILI
	JUICE AND ZEST OF ½ LIME

ROAST BBQ PORK RIBS

YIELD: 6 SERVINGS / **ACTIVE TIME:** 30 MINUTES / **TOTAL TIME:** 24 HOURS

Sticky, savory, and sweet, these ribs hit all of the familiar notes while also being elevated by the decidedly Asian flavor profile.

1. Scorch the top of the spare ribs and cut slits between each bone one-quarter of the way through the thick side of the ribs. Pat prepped ribs dry with paper towel and place on a sheet pan.

2. In a bowl, combine all of the remaining ingredients, except the maltose, and mix well.

3. Rub ribs generously with marinade. Cover the ribs with foil and refrigerate for at least 4 hours, or overnight.

4. Preheat the oven to 400°F. Uncover the ribs, remove excess marinade, and mix the excess marinade with maltose.

5. Place ribs on a wire rack over a sheet pan and bake for 40 to 50 minutes.

6. Lower the oven temperature to 350°F, baste ribs with the marinade-maltose mixture, and continue to bake the ribs for another 20 to 35 minutes, cooking until desired doneness and charr is achieved.

7. Let the ribs rest for 10 to 15 minutes before cutting into portions. Serve with favorite condiments or side dishes

INGREDIENTS:

1	RACK PORK SPARE RIBS
1	TABLESPOON GARLIC POWDER
3	TABLESPOONS SOY SAUCE
½	TEASPOON CHINESE FIVE SPICE
½	TEASPOON WHITE PEPPER
3	TABLESPOONS SHAOXING WINE
1	TABLESPOON HOISIN SAUCE
3	TABLESPOONS KETCHUP
½	TEASPOON RED FOOD COLORING (OPTIONAL)
2	TABLESPOONS MALTOSE OR HONEY, PLUS MORE AS NEEDED

GRILLED LOBSTER WITH YUZU KOSHO BUTTER

YIELD: 2 SERVINGS / **ACTIVE TIME:** 30 MINUTES / **TOTAL TIME:** 30 MINUTES

Yuzu is a citrus fruit that has long been cultivated in Asia; it imparts a tang somewhere between a lemon and a grapefruit. Yuzu kosho is a Japanese seasoning mix made from chili peppers, yuzu peel, and salt. This flavored butter works on all seafood.

1. Using a sharp knife, split the lobster in half lengthwise. Start from the head and work down to the tail. Then turn the lobster around and split the remaining part of the head to separate the two halves.

2. Using the back end of the knife, crack the claws to ensure that butter gets into the claws; this also makes for easier eating.

3. Heat the grill or broiler to medium-high. Also make sure the butter is at room temperature, so it's easier to baste the lobster.

4. Smear the lobster with the Yuzu Kosho Butter.

5. If using a grill, place the lobster shell side down, and cook and baste until cooked through, 6 to 8 minutes. Watch out for flare-ups from the melting butter.

6. If using a broiler, place the lobster shell side down, so the meat is facing the broiler. Cook and baste until cooked through, 6 to 8 minutes.

7. Once done, place the lobster on a platter, drizzle with the oil, season with a pinch of salt, sprinkle with the chives, and arrange the chilies to garnish. Serve with lemon wedges.

INGREDIENTS:

1-2	LIVE LOBSTERS, CUT IN HALF LENGTHWISE
½	CUP YUZU KOSHO BUTTER (SEE RECIPE)
1	TABLESPOON EXTRA-VIRGIN OLIVE OIL
½	TEASPOONS MALDON OR FLAKE SEA SALT
2	TEASPOONS MINCED CHIVES
½	FRESNO CHILI, THINLY SLICED, FOR GARNISH
	LEMON WEDGES, FOR SERVING

YUZU KOSHO BUTTER

1	LB. UNSALTED BUTTER, AT ROOM TEMPERATURE
1½	TABLESPOONS YUZU KOSHO
2	TEASPOONS FINELY CHOPPED PARSLEY

YUZU KOSHO BUTTER

1. In a stand mixer, or using a whisk and bowl, mix all of the ingredients until well incorporated.

2. Once fully incorporated, use parchment paper or plastic wrap to roll the butter into a cylindrical shape, and refrigerate until needed.

CHINESE EGGPLANT WITH SAUSAGE

YIELD: 4 SERVINGS / **ACTIVE TIME:** 15 MINUTES / **TOTAL TIME:** 1 HOUR

The addition of sausage gives this flavor-packed dish a depth and flavor you will love.

1. Place the eggplant in a bowl, add the salt, cover with water, and let soak for 30 minutes. Drain the eggplant on a paper towel–lined plate.

2. In a small bowl, combine the soy sauces, Chili Garlic Sauce, wine, vinegar, sugar, and Chicken Stock and mix well. Set aside.

3. Add the oil to a wok over medium-high heat. When the oil begins to shimmer, add the pork sausage and cook for about 3 minutes, using a spatula to break up the meat into small pieces.

4. Add the eggplant and red pepper, turn down the heat to medium-low, cover, and simmer for about 10 minutes, or until the eggplant is tender.

5. Add the prepared sauce and mix it all together. Bring up the heat to medium-high and stir until the sauce coats everything.

6. Serve, garnishing with the scallion and cilantro, if using.

INGREDIENTS:

2	CHINESE EGGPLANTS, SLICED ON A BIAS, ¾ INCH THICK
1	TABLESPOON SALT
1½	TABLESPOONS DARK SOY SAUCE
1½	TABLESPOONS LIGHT SOY SAUCE
1	TABLESPOON CHILI GARLIC SAUCE (SEE PAGE 180)
1	TABLESPOON SHAOXING RICE WINE
1	TABLESPOON RICE VINEGAR
½	TEASPOON SUGAR
⅓	CUP CHICKEN STOCK (SEE PAGE 680)
1	TABLESPOON CANOLA OIL
½	LB. GROUND PORK SAUSAGE
1	RED PEPPER, CHOPPED
1	SCALLION, CHOPPED, FOR GARNISH (OPTIONAL)
	CILANTRO, TO TASTE, FOR GARNISH (OPTIONAL)

KOREAN CHICKEN THIGHS
WITH SWEET POTATO VERMICELLI

YIELD: 6 SERVINGS / ACTIVE TIME: 45 MINUTES / TOTAL TIME: 3 HOURS AND 30 MINUTES

This is a Korean take on lo mein, the Chinese classic. The umami flavor of the sweet potato noodles, shiitake mushrooms, and cabbage is the perfect complement to the sweetness of the marinated chicken.

1. To prepare the marinade, place all of the ingredients in a blender and blend until smooth. Pour over the chicken thighs and let them marinate in the refrigerator for at least 2 hours.

2. Fill a large cast-iron Dutch oven with water and bring to a boil. Add the vermicelli and cook for about 6 minutes. Drain, rinse with cold water to keep them from sticking, and set aside.

3. Preheat the oven to 375°F. Remove the chicken from the refrigerator and place the pot back on the stove. Add the vegetable oil and warm over medium-high heat. Remove the chicken thighs from the marinade and place them skin side down in the Dutch oven. Reserve the marinade. Sear the chicken until a crust forms on the skin, about 5 to 7 minutes. Turn the chicken thighs over, add the reserved marinade, place the pot in the oven, and cook for about 15 to 20 minutes, until the centers of the chicken thighs reach 165°F.

4. Remove from the oven and set the chicken aside. Drain the Dutch oven and wipe it clean. Return it to the stove, add the cabbage, mushrooms, shallot, onion, garlic, scallion whites, and ginger, and cook for 8 minutes or until the cabbage is wilted.

5. In a small bowl, add the brown sugar, sesame oil, fish sauce, soy sauce, and rice vinegar and stir until combined. Add this sauce and the vermicelli to the pot, stir until the noodles are coated, and then return the chicken thighs to the Dutch oven. Top with the scallion greens and sesame seeds, return to the oven for 5 minutes, and then serve.

INGREDIENTS:

MARINADE

1	LEMONGRASS STALK, TENDER PART ONLY (THE BOTTOM HALF)
2	GARLIC CLOVES
1	TABLESPOON MINCED GINGER
1	SCALLION
¼	CUP BROWN SUGAR
2	TABLESPOONS CHILI PASTE
1	TABLESPOON SESAME OIL
1	TABLESPOON RICE VINEGAR
2	TABLESPOONS FISH SAUCE
1	TABLESPOON BLACK PEPPER

CHICKEN THIGHS & VERMICELLI

4–6	CHICKEN THIGHS
10	OZ. SWEET POTATO VERMICELLI
2	TABLESPOONS VEGETABLE OIL
¼	HEAD NAPA CABBAGE, CHOPPED
4	OZ. SHIITAKE MUSHROOMS, SLICED THIN
1	SHALLOT, SLICED THIN
1	YELLOW ONION, SLICED THIN
2	GARLIC CLOVES, MINCED
2	SCALLIONS, CHOPPED AND GREENS RESERVED
2	TABLESPOONS MINCED GINGER
¼	CUP BROWN SUGAR
2	TABLESPOONS SESAME OIL
2	TABLESPOONS FISH SAUCE
¼	CUP SOY SAUCE
¼	CUP RICE VINEGAR
¼	CUP SESAME SEEDS

SWEET & STICKY CHICKEN WINGS

YIELD: 4 SERVINGS / **ACTIVE TIME:** 10 MINUTES / **TOTAL TIME:** 25 HOURS

Layered with sweet and savory Asian flavors, these wings don't last long.

1. Use paper towels to pat dry the chicken wings. Place the wings in a resealable plastic bag, add all of the remaining ingredients, except for the sesame seeds, and shake to evenly coat the wings. Refrigerate the chicken for 24 hours.

2. Preheat the oven to 375°F.

3. Spread out the chicken wings on a sheet pan and bake for 25 to 30 minutes.

4. When the wings are done, let rest for 5 minutes, season to taste, garnish with the sesame seeds, and serve.

INGREDIENTS:

4   LBS. CHICKEN WINGS, CUT
     INTO DRUMETTES AND
     FLATS

¼   CUP SOY SAUCE

2   TABLESPOONS MIRIN

3   TABLESPOONS OLIVE OIL

2   TABLESPOONS BROWN
     SUGAR

2   GARLIC CLOVES, MINCED

1   TABLESPOON MINCED
     GINGER

2   TABLESPOONS CHILI
     GARLIC SAUCE (SEE PAGE
     180)

2   TABLESPOONS HOISIN
     SAUCE

     SESAME SEEDS, FOR
     GARNISH

ROASTED DUCK BREAST
& FIVE-SPICE CONFIT DUCK LEGS

YIELD: 4 SERVINGS / ACTIVE TIME: 1 HOUR / TOTAL TIME: 24 HOURS

This dish really speaks to the versatility of cooking whole ducks. The breast is brined to allow the hoisin, soy, and spices to really penetrate throughout the breast and glaze the skin. The breast is then roasted on the bone, while the duck legs are cured overnight and braised in duck fat until they are meltingly tender.

1. Add all of the ingredients, except for the duck, to a saucepan over medium-high heat and bring to a boil. Cook until the salt and syrup have dissolved. Cool the brine in the refrigerator until it's at or below 40°F.

2. Place the breast in a container and pour the brine over it. Cover the container and refrigerate overnight.

3. Remove the breast from the brine, pat dry, and place the breast skin side up on a rack over a sheet pan. Salt the skin with a light dusting of salt, roughly 1 teaspoon. This will draw out any excess moisture.

4. Refrigerate, uncovered, for 12 to 24 hours to dry out the skin.

5. Preheat the oven to 380°F.

6. Roast the breast for about 30 minutes, or until the internal temperature of the breast is 115°F. If the skin has not become golden brown, toast under your broiler for 2 to 3 minutes. Keep a close eye on it; the skin can go from golden brown to burnt very quickly.

7. Rest for 10 to 15 minutes. To serve, carefully carve the breast off the bone. Slice along the middle ridge of the breastplate, allowing the bones to guide your knife to remove the meat. Slice thin at a slight bias.

FIVE-SPICE CURE FOR DUCK LEGS

1. Place the star anise, cinnamon stick, and bay leaves in a small plastic bag and crush them, using the bottom of a heavy pan.

2. Add the crushed aromatics, cloves, fennel seeds, and peppercorns to a dry sauté pan over medium-high heat and toast for 1 to 2 minutes.

Continued . . .

INGREDIENTS:

4	CUPS WATER
¼	CUP SALT, PLUS MORE AS NEEDED
¼	CUP MAPLE SYRUP
2	TABLESPOONS HOISIN SAUCE
2	TABLESPOONS SOY SAUCE
1	CINNAMON STICK
3	STAR ANISE PODS
1	TABLESPOON FENNEL SEED
2	BAY LEAVES
1	TEASPOON SZECHUAN PEPPERCORNS
1	TEASPOON MINCED GINGER
1	TEASPOON WHOLE CLOVE
1	(5-6 LB.) WHOLE DUCK, BROKEN DOWN (SEE PAGE 458)

FIVE-SPICE CURE FOR DUCK LEGS

2	STAR ANISE PODS
1	CINNAMON STICK
2	BAY LEAVES
½	TEASPOON CLOVES
1	TEASPOON FENNEL SEEDS
½	TEASPOON SZECHUAN PEPPERCORNS
¼	CUP SALT
¼	CUP BROWN SUGAR
1	CUP DUCK FAT

BREAKING DOWN A DUCK

1. Remove the backbone from the duck by standing it with the cavity and legs sitting on the cutting board in a stable position. Trace along each side of the backbone with a sharp knife, cutting through the back ribs until you reach the joints of the legs.

2. Use the tip of your knife to sever the connection between the leg joints; you should feel and hear a slight pop. Repeat with the opposite leg.

3. Cut through the rest of the backbone, keeping your knife tight to the spine, releasing each side.

4. To remove the legs, set the duck down, breast side up. Pinch the fat between the leg and the breast. Pinch closer to the leg to make sure you leave ample skin coverage for the breast. Carefully cut through the skin just above your pinched fingers, and follow the contours of the leg to remove.

5. Find the joint between the drumette and flat of the wing and cut down to the cutting board, using the heel of your knife. The joint should have a slight ball shape, and your knife should be able to gently cleave through the cartilage.

3. Once the spices are cooled, thoroughly mix with the salt and brown sugar in a bowl.

4. Coat the legs generously with the mixture and refrigerate in a covered container overnight.

5. Remove the legs from the cure, rinse, and pat dry. Preheat the oven to 300°F.

6. Place the duck legs skin side down in a high-sided baking dish or ovenproof saucepan with the duck fat. Cover tightly with a lid or foil and place in the oven for 2½ hours, or until a fork can slide in and out of the leg with little resistance.*

7. To finish, add 1 tablespoon of duck fat to a medium sauté pan over medium-high heat, and sear the confit legs until crispy on both sides, about 1 to 2 minutes per side.

* This can be done a day in advance and sit submerged in the fat in the refrigerator until ready to use.

GENERAL TSO'S PORK BELLY STEAM BUNS WITH SESAME BOK CHOY, RADISH & SPICY MAYONNAISE

YIELD: 6 SERVINGS / ACTIVE TIME: 30 MINUTES / TOTAL TIME: 24 HOURS

Pork belly bao are a pub grub standard today, thanks to David Chang. But Chang will be the first to admit that he didn't invent the idea. These fluffy buns have long been popular in Asia.

1. In a small bowl, combine the Chinese five-spice powder, garlic, soy sauce, hoisin sauce, and vinegar and mix until it becomes smooth. Rub the mixture all over the pork belly, and let marinate for 12 to 24 hours in the refrigerator.

2. After marinating the pork belly, remove it from the refrigerator. Preheat the oven to 325°F.

3. Put the carrot, onion, celery, salt, and stock in a baking dish and place the pork belly on top. Cover the baking dish with plastic wrap and then aluminum foil. Bake for 2 hours.

4. Take the baking dish out of the oven, remove the plastic and foil, and return the dish to the oven for 45 more minutes, or until the pork belly is slightly caramelized.

5. As the pork cooks, sauté the bok choy with the oil in a frying pan over low heat until tender, about 3 minutes. Season with the prepared salt and pepper and set aside.

6. When the pork belly is done, let rest on a sheet pan. Once the pork is cooled, slice it into 2-inch pieces that each weigh approximately 2 oz.

7. Preheat the oven to 350°F. To serve, place the sliced pork belly on a sheet pan and warm in the oven for 5 minutes, or until hot throughout. Once hot, rub the pork belly slices with the General Tso's Sauce. Place the Steam Buns in a steamer basket with a lid and steam for 4 minutes. Remove the buns from the steamer and place ½ tablespoon of yuzu mayo in the middle of the buns, then add the warmed glazed pork. Top the pork with the sesame bok choy and garnish with the radishes, jalapeños, and cilantro, if using.

INGREDIENTS:

2	TEASPOONS CHINESE FIVE-SPICE POWDER
2	GARLIC CLOVES, MINCED
¼	CUP SOY SAUCE
¼	CUP HOISIN SAUCE
2	TABLESPOONS RICE WINE VINEGAR
2	LBS. PORK BELLY
1	CARROT, CHOPPED
1	ONION, CHOPPED
2	CELERY STALKS, CHOPPED
1	TABLESPOON SALT, PLUS MORE TO TASTE
1½	CUP CHICKEN STOCK (SEE PAGE 680)
1	CUP BOK CHOY, THINLY SLICED
2	TEASPOONS SESAME OIL
	PEPPER
1	CUP GENERAL TSO'S SAUCE (SEE RECIPE)
6	BAO BUNS (SEE RECIPE)
½	CUP SPICY MAYONNAISE (SEE PAGE 442)
	THINLY SLICED RADISHES, FOR GARNISH (OPTIONAL)
	JALAPEÑOS, FOR GARNISH (OPTIONAL)
	CILANTRO, FOR GARNISH (OPTIONAL)

Continued . . .

GENERAL TSO'S SAUCE

1. In a pot over medium heat, combine the oil, red pepper flakes, garlic, ginger, scallions, and jalapeño and sauté for 3 to 5 minutes, until fragrant.

2. Add the soy sauce, hoisin sauce, vinegar, honey, and Chicken Stock and simmer for 15 to 20 minutes.

3. In a bowl, combine the cornstarch with the water to make a slurry. Add the slurry to the simmering sauce and cook for 1 minute, or until slightly thickened. Remove from heat. The sauce can be blended to be very smooth or can be used as is.

BAO BUNS

1. Place the yeast and water in the mixing bowl of a stand mixer fitted with a dough hook and let sit until the mixture becomes foamy, about 10 minutes.

2. Add the remaining ingredients and mix on low for 10 minutes. Cover the bowl with a kitchen towel and place it in a naturally warm spot until the mixture doubles in size, about 45 minutes.

3. Place the risen dough on a flour-dusted work surface and cut into 12 pieces. Roll them into balls, cover with plastic wrap, and let them rise for 30 minutes.

4. Cut a dozen 4" squares of parchment paper. Roll each ball into a 4" oval. Grease a chopstick with the shortening, gently press the chopstick down in the middle of each oval, and fold the dough over to create a bun. Place each bun on a square of parchment paper and let stand for 30 minutes.

5. To cook the buns, place 1" of water in a saucepan and bring to a boil. Place a steaming tray in the pan, and, working in batches if necessary, place the buns in the steamer tray, making sure to leave them on the parchment. Steam for 10 minutes.

INGREDIENTS:

GENERAL TSO'S SAUCE

2	TABLESPOONS CANOLA OIL
1	TEASPOON RED PEPPER FLAKES
3	GARLIC CLOVES, MINCED
2	TABLESPOONS FRESH GINGER, MINCED
4	TABLESPOONS SLICED SCALLIONS
1	JALAPEÑO PEPPER, SEEDED AND MINCED
½	CUP SOY SAUCE
½	CUP HOISIN SAUCE
¼	CUP RICE WINE VINEGAR
3	TABLESPOONS HONEY
1	CUP CHICKEN STOCK (SEE PAGE 680)
2	TABLESPOONS CORNSTARC
4	TABLESPOONS WATER

BAO BUNS

1	TEASPOON ACTIVE DRY YEAST
3	TABLESPOONS WATER, AT ROOM TEMPERATURE
1	CUP BREAD FLOUR, PLUS MORE FOR DUSTING
4	TEASPOONS SUGAR
2	TEASPOONS NONFAT DRY MILK POWDER
1	TEASPOON KOSHER SALT
⅛	TEASPOON BAKING POWDER
⅛	TEASPOON BAKING SODA
4	TEASPOONS VEGETABLE SHORTENING, PLUS MORE AS NEEDED

EARTH'S HARVEST KITCHEN PORK BELLY

YIELD: 8 SERVINGS / **ACTIVE TIME:** 15 MINUTES / **TOTAL TIME:** 15 HOURS

This preparation of pork belly is so perfect that it can be used in any dish that requires pork belly. In terms of using skin-on or skinless pork belly, it is a matter of preference; both are equally delicious. As with most recipes, ingredients are essential for the best final product. If you can find local pork belly, that is ideal, but any pork belly will do the trick.

1. If using skin-on pork belly, score the skin with a few slices across the surface, trying not to pierce the flesh beneath.

2. In a small bowl, mix together the remainder of the ingredients except for the oil and water.

3. Coat the pork belly with the seasoning mixture. Really massage the pork belly with the mixture. Place the prepared belly in a large bowl, cover with plastic wrap, and refrigerate for 12 hours.

4. Once the pork belly has cured, preheat the oven to 425°F and prepare a pan that has higher sides than the height of the pork belly. Rub some oil inside the bottom and sides of the pan until evenly coated.

5. Remove the pork belly from the refrigerator, rinse off the seasoning mixture with cold water, and pat dry with paper towels. Place the pork belly skin side up in the prepared pan, put it in the oven uncovered, and cook for 30 to 45 minutes, or until the skin becomes golden brown but not burnt.

6. Remove p the mixture ork belly from the oven and lower the oven temperature to 300°F. Pour about 1 cup of water into the hot pan, or just enough to cover the bottom of the pan. Make sure not to pour water directly onto the belly—keep that skin crispy! Cover the pan with foil and return it to the oven. Cook for 2 hours, or until the belly is fork-tender but not falling apart.

7. Using a flat metal spatula, lift the pork belly onto a cooling rack or sheet pan and let rest until it is cool enough to be safely sliced, eaten, or stored in the refrigerator or freezer.

TIP: When the cooked pork belly is cool enough to handle, place another sheet pan on top of the belly and use something heavy, like a few cans of beans, to weigh it down, and then refrigerate it overnight. Doing this will result in uniform slices that crisp up perfectly in the pan when you are ready to cook.

INGREDIENTS:

3–4	LBS. SKIN-ON OR SKINLESS PORK BELLY
½	CUP SALT
¼	CUP SUGAR
2	TABLESPOONS FRESHLY GROUND BLACK PEPPER
	CANOLA OIL, AS NEEDED
1	CUP WATER

ULTIMATE XO SAUCE

YIELD: 1 QUART / **ACTIVE TIME:** 15 MINUTES / **TOTAL TIME:** 30 MINUTES

This is a take on the XO sauce from Ivan Ramen in New York City. The umami-rich condiment can be put on just about anything, like pork belly.

1. In separate bowls, soak the dried shrimp and mushrooms in very hot water until soft but still slightly firm, about 15 to 20 minutes. Drain and set aside.

2. Using a food processor, keeping the ingredients separate, chop the shrimp, mushrooms, bacon, and Chinese sausage. Set aside.

3. Add 1½ cups of oil to a wok or large sauté pan over medium-high heat. Once the oil is shimmering, add the shallots and cook until soft, about 1 minute, continuously moving the shallots around with a wooden spoon to prevent scorching around the edges. Next, add the garlic and ginger, cook for another minute, and then add the chili flakes, star anise, and cinnamon stick and fry for another minute, stirring constantly.

4. Add the remaining oil and mushrooms, and cook for 1 minute, stirring and keeping the oil simmering the whole time. Repeat this process with the sausage, shrimp, bacon, and pork.

5. Cautiously add the wine all at once; please be careful, as there may be some flames when adding the alcohol. Simmer for about 30 seconds, then add the soy sauce, fish sauce, and sugar and simmer for another 30 seconds. Now add the fried garlic and fried shallot, mix everything together, and turn off the heat.

6. Don't let cool for more than 5 minutes, in order to prevent further cooking. Pour the sauce into a nonreactive container and store in the refrigerator for up to 1 month.

INGREDIENTS:

- ½ CUP DRIED SHRIMP
- 6 DRIED SHIITAKE MUSHROOM CAPS
- ½ CUP COOKED BACON
- ½ CUP CHINESE SAUSAGE OR SOPRESSATA
- 2 CUPS CANOLA OIL, DIVIDED
- 2 SHALLOTS, MINCED
- ¼ CUP THINLY SLICED GARLIC
- ¼ CUP MINCED GINGER
- ¼ CUP CHILI FLAKES
- 3–4 STAR ANISE
- 1 CINNAMON STICK
- ½ CUP DRIED PORK
- ½ CUP CHINESE SHAOXING RICE WINE OR DRY SHERRY
- ½ CUP SOY SAUCE
- 1 TABLESPOON FISH SAUCE
- ½ CUP SUGAR
- ½ CUP FRIED GARLIC
- ½ CUP FRIED SHALLOT

YUZU SESAME LAMB RIBS

YIELD: 4 SERVINGS / ACTIVE TIME: 1 HOUR / TOTAL TIME: 4 HOURS

Yuzu is a fragrant and tart citrus fruit that is the base of this Japanese-style yakiniku sauce.

1. To begin preparations for the ribs, stir together the salt, sugar, pepper, and five-spice powder in a small bowl. Rub the mixture into the ribs and let sit at room temperature for 1 hour.

2. To begin preparations for the sauce, in a saucepan, combine everything for the sauce, except for the cornstarch slurry and sesame seeds. Bring to a boil over medium heat, and then reduce to a simmer until slightly thickened, about 5 minutes.

3. Strain the sauce into a small saucepan and return to a simmer. Whisk in the cornstarch slurry and sesame seeds, and return to a simmer until the sauce has thickened. Remove from heat and cover until ready to use.

4. Preheat a gas or charcoal grill to 325°F. Make sure to bank the mixture coals to one side, if using a charcoal grill. Place the ribs on the grill and cook, turning once, until browned, about 10 minutes total.

5. Reduce the temperature to 250°F, or move the ribs away from the coals on a charcoal grill, and cook until tender, about 1 hour and 45 minutes, turning and basting with the prepared sauce every 10 to 15 minutes.

6. Remove the ribs and let rest under aluminum foil for 10 minutes. Cut the rack into double ribs and serve.

INGREDIENTS:

RIBS

1	TABLESPOON SALT
1	TABLESPOON GRANULATED SUGAR
1	TEASPOON FRESHLY GROUND BLACK PEPPER
1	TEASPOON CHINESE FIVE-SPICE POWDER
1	(4-LB.) RACK LAMB RIBS, TRIMMED

YAKINIKU SAUCE

1	GARLIC CLOVE, CHOPPED
½	CUP YUZU JUICE
⅓	CUP SOY SAUCE
3	TABLESPOONS MIRIN
3	TABLESPOONS GRANULATED SUGAR
2	TEASPOONS HONEY
2	TEASPOONS SESAME OIL
1	TABLESPOON CORNSTARCH, MIXED TO A SLURRY WITH 1 TABLESPOON WATER
2	TEASPOONS SESAME SEEDS, TOASTED AND GROUND

CHILI CHICKEN

YIELD: 4 SERVINGS / **ACTIVE TIME:** 15 MINUTES / **TOTAL TIME:** 2 HOURS AND 50 MINUTES

This is an Indo-Chinese dish is inspired by the city of Mumbai and it serves as a great reminder of the amazing flavors fushion cuisine can deliver..

1. In a bowl, combine ½ tablespoon of chili sauce, ½ tablespoon of soy sauce, pepper, and vinegar and mix well. Add the chicken and marinate for at least 45 minutes, though 2 hours is ideal.

2. Sprinkle the cornstarch on the chicken, along with the salt, and mix well. Add ¼ teaspoon of chili powder. If you wish to use the egg, you can add it now. Mix well.

3. In a bowl, combine ¾ tablespoon of soy sauce, ¼ tablespoon of chili sauce, ½ teaspoon of chili powder, and the sugar and mix well.

4. Add the oil to a cast-iron skillet over high heat. When the oil reaches 350°F, fry the chicken until it turns golden brown. Drain the fried chicken on a paper towel–lined plate. If you prefer, the chicken can be baked in a 450°F oven for 20 to 25 minutes.

5. Remove any excess oil, leaving 1 tablespoon. Add the garlic and fry for about a minute. Add the onion, scallion (if using), bell pepper, and green chilies and fry until they turn slightly soft, about 1 minute. Add the prepared sauce and bring to a simmer.

6. Add the cooked chicken and heat the mixture for 2 to 3 minutes.

7. Serve with the fried rice or noodles.

INGREDIENTS:

¾	TABLESPOON CHILI SAUCE, DIVIDED
1¼	TABLESPOONS SOY SAUCE, DIVIDED
¼	TEASPOON BLACK PEPPER
¾	TEASPOON DISTILLED VINEGAR
1	LB. BONELESS CHICKEN
2	TABLESPOONS CORNSTARCH
	SALT, TO TASTE
2	TABLESPOONS ALL-PURPOSE FLOUR
¾	TEASPOON RED CHILI POWDER, DIVIDED
1	SMALL EGG (OPTIONAL)
½	TEASPOON SUGAR
1	ONION, THINLY SLICED
¾	TABLESPOON MINCED GARLIC
2	CUPS CANOLA OIL
1	SCALLION, CHOPPED (OPTIONAL)
¼	CUP CHOPPED BELL PEPPER
1–2	GREEN CHILIES, HALVED DESEEDED
	FRIED RICE OR NOODLES, TO SERVE

CHINESE POTTED CHICKEN

YIELD: 6 SERVINGS / *ACTIVE TIME:* 20 MINUTES / *TOTAL TIME:* 24 HOURS

This recipe was handed down by the Chinese father of some dear friends. I am honored to share it now.

1. In a large bowl, whisk together all of the marinade ingredients. Add the chicken pieces, cover the bowl, and refrigerate for at least 2 hours, but ideally for 24 hours.

2. When the chicken is done marinating, remove it from the bowl and pat dry. Reserve the marinade.

3. Grill the chicken on medium-high heat to char, about 4 minutes per side. Do not cook completely. Remove from the grill.

4. In a Dutch oven, place 3 strips of bacon, add the chicken, and then place the rest of the bacon on top of the chicken. Pour the marinade over the chicken, and add the ginger and garlic.

5. Cover the pot, bring to a boil, and then lower the heat and simmer for 1½ hours.

6. Test the chicken; if it pulls apart with a fork, remove it from the pot, along with the bacon. Continue to simmer the sauce. If the chicken isn't fork-tender, cook for another 20 minutes before testing again. Tent the chicken and bacon with aluminum foil to keep warm.

7. In a small bowl, combine the cornstarch and water, stir into the sauce, and cook until the sauce thickens.

8. Serve the chicken over the rice and garnish with the sesame seeds.

INGREDIENTS:

MARINADE

2	TABLESPOONS SOY SAUCE
2	TABLESPOONS WHITE WINE
½	TABLESPOON SESAME OIL
1	TABLESPOON HOISIN SAUCE
1½	TEASPOONS HOT SAUCE
1½	TEASPOONS SUGAR
4	GARLIC CLOVES, MINCED
2	TABLESPOONS MINCED GINGER
1	TEASPOON BLACK PEPPER

CHICKEN

4–6	LBS. SKIN-ON, BONE-IN CHICKEN PARTS (THIGHS WORK PARTICULARLY WELL); IF USING BREASTS, CUT IN HALF OR THIRDS
6	STRIPS BACON
1	CUP CHICKEN STOCK (SEE PAGE 680)
¼	CUP CHOPPED GINGER
¼	CUP CHOPPED GARLIC
2	TABLESPOONS CORNSTARCH
1	TABLESPOON WATER
	SESAME SEEDS, FOR GARNISH
	COOKED RICE, TO SERVE

THAI DUCK STIR-FRY

YIELD: 5 SERVINGS / **ACTIVE TIME**: 15 MINUTES / **TOTAL TIME**: 40 MINUTES

S tart this Thai-inspired dish by searing the duck breast, and then add a bunch of fresh vegetables and sauce to make a great stir-fry.

1. Pat the duck dry with paper towels.

2. With a sharp knife, score the skin of the duck breasts diagonally, making sure not to cut into the meat. Aim for a ⅛-inch-deep cut. Season with the salt.

3. Place the breasts skin side down on a cold cast-iron pan and turn on the heat to medium-low. After 5 minutes, the breasts should begin to bubble a bit as the fat renders. Keep rendering the fat until the skin is golden and a meat thermometer inserted in the breasts registers about 125°F.

4. Increase the heat to medium and brown the skin for another 2 minutes, then flip until the duck registers a temperature of 130°F.

5. Transfer the duck to a cutting board and tent with aluminum foil until ready to serve.

6. In a bowl, combine the fish sauce, oyster sauce, sugar, and pepper and mix well.

7. Place the pan you used to sear the duck over medium-high heat. Pour off all but 1 tablespoon of duck fat from the pan (and reserve the rest of the fat). Add the garlic and ginger, stirring constantly until softened, about a minute. Add the chilies, bell peppers, onion, and peppercorns and cook for about 3 minutes.

8. Add the fish sauce mixture, stir to combine, and add half of the basil. Simmer for 2 minutes, and then remove from heat. Scatter the remaining basil leaves on top of the sauce.

9. Serve with slices of duck over the rice, generously topped with the sauce.

INGREDIENTS:

2	SKIN-ON DUCK BREASTS
	SALT, TO TASTE
2	TABLESPOONS FISH SAUCE
2	TABLESPOONS OYSTER SAUCE
1	TABLESPOON SUGAR
1	PINCH WHITE PEPPER
2	GARLIC CLOVES, MINCED
1	TABLESPOON MINCED GINGER
2	LARGE RED CHILIES, THINLY SLICED
1	RED BELL PEPPER, CHOPPED
1	GREEN BELL PEPPER, CHOPPED
1	ONION, THINLY SLICED
2	STRANDS GREEN PEPPERCORNS IN BRINE, DRAINED
½	BUNCH FRESH THAI BASIL LEAVES, DIVIDED
	STEAMED JASMINE RICE, TO SERVE

GENERAL TSO'S CHICKEN

YIELD: 6 SERVINGS / *ACTIVE TIME*: 25 MINUTES / *TOTAL TIME*: 50 MINUTES

Say good-bye to take-out with this recipe.

1. Prepare the chicken. In a large bowl, beat the egg white until broken down and lightly foamy. Add the soy sauce, wine, and vodka and whisk to combine. Set aside half of the marinade in a small bowl. Add the baking soda and cornstarch to the large bowl and whisk to combine. Add the chicken to a large bowl and turn until coated thoroughly. Cover with plastic wrap and set aside.

2. Prepare the dry coating. In a large bowl, combine the flour, cornstarch, baking powder, and salt and mix well. Add the reserved marinade and whisk until the mixture has coarse, mealy clumps. Set aside.

3. Prepare the sauce. In a small bowl, combine the soy sauce, wine, vinegar, Chicken Stock, sugar, sesame seed oil, and cornstarch and stir with a fork until the cornstarch is dissolved and no lumps remain. Set aside.

4. Add canola oil to a Dutch oven over medium-high heat and bring to 350°F. As the oil heats up, dredge the marinated chicken in the dry coating. When the oil is ready, fry the chicken, being sure not to overcrowd the pan, and cook until golden all over, about 10 minutes. Set aside.

5. Add the sauce and peanut oil to a wok or large frying pan over medium-high heat. Add the garlic, ginger, scallions, and chilies and cook, stirring constantly, for about 3 minutes. Add the chicken to the pan and toss to coat.

6. Serve with the rice.

INGREDIENTS:

CHICKEN

1	EGG WHITE
2	TABLESPOONS DARK SOY SAUCE
3	TABLESPOONS SHAOXING RICE WINE
2	TABLESPOONS VODKA
¼	TEASPOON BAKING SODA
3	TABLESPOONS CORNSTARCH
1	LB. SKINLESS AND BONELESS CHICKEN THIGHS, CUT INTO CHUNKS
4	CUPS CANOLA OIL, FOR FRYING

DRY COATING

½	CUP ALL-PURPOSE FLOUR
½	CUP CORNSTARCH
½	TEASPOON BAKING POWDER
½	TEASPOON SALT

SAUCE

3	TABLESPOONS DARK SOY SAUCE
2½	TABLESPOONS SHAOXING RICE WINE
2	TABLESPOONS CHINESE RICE VINEGAR OR DISTILLED WHITE VINEGAR
3	TABLESPOONS CHICKEN STOCK (SEE PAGE 680)
4	TABLESPOONS SUGAR
1	TEASPOON ROASTED SESAME SEED OIL
1	TABLESPOON CORNSTARCH
2	TEASPOONS PEANUT OIL
2	TEASPOONS MINCED GARLIC
2	TEASPOONS MINCED FRESH GINGER
2	TEASPOONS MINCED SCALLION WHITES
8	SMALL DRIED RED ARBOL CHILIES
	RICE, TO SERVE

DRY-FRIED BEANS

YIELD: 4 SERVINGS / ACTIVE TIME: 30 MINUTES / TOTAL TIME: 45 MINUTES

Despite its name, the beans in this recipe are not fried but seared over high heat until almost charred. They are then removed, and a sauce is made with pork, Chinese pickled veggies, fermented black beans, garlic, and soy sauce. No need to add extra salt—you will get plenty from the soy and black beans.

1. Place the oil in a large sauté pan, warm over high heat, and add the green beans. Let the beans sear on one side, stir, and sear on the other side. Continue until they are well browned all over. Transfer to a bowl and set aside.

2. Add the pork to the pan and brown over medium-high heat, while breaking it up with a wooden spoon, for about 6 minutes. Add the pickled vegetables, sauerkraut, or kimchi, and the garlic. Cook, stirring continuously, until the contents of the pan are fragrant. Add more oil if the pan starts to look dry.

3. Add the sherry and cook until it is nearly evaporated. Add the soy sauce, garlic sauce, and sugar and stir to incorporate.

4. Return the beans to the pan, heat through, and serve with white rice.

INGREDIENTS:

- 1   TABLESPOON OLIVE OIL, PLUS MORE AS NEEDED
- 1   LB. GREEN BEANS, TRIMMED
- 4   OZ. GROUND PORK
- 2   TABLESPOONS CHINESE PICKLED VEGETABLES, SAUERKRAUT, OR KIMCHI (SEE PAGE 150), CHOPPED
- 1   GARLIC CLOVE, CHOPPED
- 2   TABLESPOONS SHERRY
- 2   TABLESPOONS SOY SAUCE
- 1   TABLESPOON FERMENTED BLACK BEAN GARLIC SAUCE
- 1   TEASPOON SUGAR
-    WHITE RICE, TO SERVE

SNOW PEA & CHICKEN STIR-FRY
WITH GINGER SAUCE

YIELD: 4 SERVINGS / ACTIVE TIME: 40 MINUTES / TOTAL TIME: 40 MINUTES

This is an easy weeknight meal that hits all the right notes: salty, sweet, and tangy. Snow peas hardly require any cooking, so add them at the very last minute. Using cornstarch to coat the chicken not only gives it a nice crust, it also helps to thicken the finished sauce. If you'd like to make this vegetarian, substituting firm tofu for the chicken is delicious.

1. Place a wide sauté pan over high heat and add the oil and onion. Cook the onion is browned, about 7 minutes, transfer to a bowl, and add the mushrooms to the pan. Cook, stirring occasionally, until browned all over, about 7 minutes. Transfer to a separate bowl.

2. Place the cornstarch in a separate bowl, add the chicken, and toss to coat. Shake to remove any excess cornstarch, and add the chicken to the pan. Sauté until browned all over and cooked through, about 8 minutes. Add more oil if the pan starts to look dry while the chicken is cooking. Transfer the cooked chicken to the bowl containing the mushrooms.

3. Place the ginger in the pan and cook until fragrant, about 1 minute. Deglaze the pan with the sherry, scraping up any browned bits from the bottom of the pan, and then add the soy sauce and maple syrup. Cook for a few minutes, until the sauce has thickened.

4. Return the onion, mushrooms, and chicken to the pan and add the water chestnuts, peas, sesame oil, and sesame seeds. Stir to incorporate, reduce the heat to medium, and cook until the peas have turned bright green. Serve with white rice.

INGREDIENTS:

- 2 TABLESPOONS OLIVE OIL, PLUS MORE AS NEEDED
- 1 SMALL ONION, DICED
- ½ LB. WHITE MUSHROOMS, SLICED
- ¼ CUP CORNSTARCH
- ½ LB. SKINLESS AND BONELESS CHICKEN BREASTS, CHOPPED
- 1 TABLESPOON PEELED AND MINCED GINGER
- ¼ CUP DRY SHERRY
- 2 TABLESPOONS SOY SAUCE
- 1 TEASPOON MAPLE SYRUP
- 1 CAN SLICED WATER CHESTNUTS, DRAINED AND RINSED
- ½ LB. SNOW PEAS
- 1 TEASPOON TOASTED SESAME OIL
- 2 TEASPOONS SESAME SEEDS

  WHITE RICE, TO SERVE

RAMEN NOODLES & TOFU SAN BEI

YIELD: 4 SERVINGS / ACTIVE TIME: 30 MINUTES / TOTAL TIME: 1 HOUR AND 45 MINUTES

San bei, which means "3 cups" in Mandarin, is a reference to the quantities of soy sauce, sesame oil, and rice wine used in the sauce. Altering the formula a tad results in this scrumptious ramen dish.

1. Drain the tofu and cut it into ½-inch slices. Arrange them in a single layer on a paper towel–lined tray. Cover with paper towels and pat dry. Let sit for 30 minutes, changing the paper towels after 15 minutes.

2. Warm the largest skillet you have over medium heat for 2 to 3 minutes. Add the peanut or grapeseed oil and warm until it starts to shimmer. Dredge the tofu slices in a shallow bowl filled with the cornstarch and tap to remove any excess. Working in batches, add the tofu in a single layer to the skillet. Raise the heat to medium-high and cook until the tofu has browned all over, 3 to 4 minutes per side. Transfer to a paper towel–lined plate to drain.

3. Wipe out the skillet and add the sesame oil to the pan. Reduce the heat to medium and add the garlic, ginger, scallions, and 2 pinches of salt once the oil starts to shimmer. Cook, stirring frequently, until fragrant, about 2 minutes. Add the sugar and stir until it has melted. Add ¾ cup of water, wine or sherry, and soy sauce and stir. Raise the heat to medium-high and bring to a boil. Reduce the heat to low, cover, and simmer, stirring occasionally, for 10 minutes.

4. Place 1½ teaspoons of cornstarch and 1 tablespoon of water in a small bowl and stir until the mixture is smooth. Add the mixture to the sauce and stir until thoroughly incorporated. Continue to cook, stirring occasionally, until the sauce slightly thickens, about 5 minutes. Add the tofu slices and cook until warmed through.

5. As the sauce simmers, bring a large pot of water to a boil. Add the ramen noodles and stir for the first minute to prevent any sticking. Cook until tender and chewy, drain, and divide the noodles between four warmed, shallow bowls. Top with the tofu slices, ladle the sauce over the top, garnish with the basil, and serve.

INGREDIENTS:

1	LB. EXTRA-FIRM TOFU
3	TABLESPOONS PEANUT OR GRAPESEED OIL
1½	TEASPOONS CORNSTARCH, PLUS MORE AS NEEDED
3	TABLESPOONS TOASTED SESAME OIL
8	GARLIC CLOVES, SMASHED
	2-INCH PIECE GINGER, PEELED AND SLICED INTO 8 PIECES
10	SCALLIONS, TRIMMED AND CUT INTO ½-INCH PIECES
	SALT, TO TASTE
3	TABLESPOONS SUGAR
¾	CUP WATER, PLUS 1 TABLESPOON
¾	CUP SHAOXING RICE WINE OR DRY SHERRY
⅓	CUP SOY SAUCE
⅓	LB. RAMEN NOODLES
2	HANDFULS FRESH BASIL LEAVES (THAI BASIL PREFERRED), SLICED THIN, FOR GARNISH

THAI FRIED RICE WITH SEITAN

YIELD: 4 SERVINGS / **ACTIVE TIME:** 35 MINUTES / **TOTAL TIME:** 1 HOUR

Thai fried rice is similar to Chinese fried rice, except it includes pineapple and substitues fish sauce for soy sauce. The seitan takes on the, role of both salty and chewy.

1. Place the rice and water in a saucepan and simmer for 20 minutes. Remove from heat, fluff with a fork, and let cool, uncovered, so that it dries out a little. Set aside.

2. Place 1 tablespoon of oil in a wide skillet and warm over high heat. When the oil is shimmering, add the seitan and sauté for a few minutes, until it starts to brown.

3. In a small bowl, combine the soy sauce, 1 tablespoon of vinegar, and sugar. Pour this mixture over the seitan and cook until the liquid has reduced to a glaze. Transfer the seitan to a bowl and set aside.

4. Place 1 tablespoon of oil in a larger skillet and warm over high heat. When the oil is shimmering, add the shallot and kohlrabi. Sauté until browned, about 8 minutes, and then transfer to the bowl containing the seitan.

5. Add the ginger to the skillet, and more oil if the pan looks dry. Sauté for a few minutes, and then add the rice. It is very likely that the rice will stick to the bottom of the pan. Do your best to scrape it off with a spatula, and add more oil if needed. Cook the rice until it starts to brown, about 5 to 10 minutes, taking care not to let it become too mushy. Add the fish sauce and the remaining vinegar and stir to incorporate.

6. Add the pineapple, kohlrabi, shallots, peas, and seitan to the pan. Gently fold to incorporate, and cook for another minute to heat everything through. Season to taste, garnish with the cilantro, and serve with the lime wedges.

INGREDIENTS:

1	CUP JASMINE RICE
2	CUPS WATER
2	TABLESPOONS OLIVE OIL, DIVIDED, PLUS MORE AS NEEDED
6	OZ. SEITAN (SEE PAGE 743), RINSED AND DICED
2	TABLESPOONS SOY SAUCE
2	TABLESPOONS RICE VINEGAR, DIVIDED
1	TABLESPOON SUGAR
1	SHALLOT, DICED
1	KOHLRABI, PEELED AND DICED
1	TABLESPOON PEELED AND MINCED GINGER
1	TABLESPOON FISH SAUCE
½	CUP PINEAPPLE, DICED
½	CUP FROZEN PEAS
¼	CUP CHOPPED FRESH CILANTRO, FOR GARNISH
	LIME WEDGES, TO SERVE

BUDDHA SEITAN

YIELD: 6 SERVINGS / **ACTIVE TIME:** 35 MINUTES / **TOTAL TIME:** 1 HOUR

This recipe is adapted from the Buddha Sesame "Beef" at A Single Pebble, a Chinese restaurant in Burlington, Vermont.

1. To prepare the sauce, place all of the ingredients in a bowl and whisk to combine. Set the sauce aside.

2. Assuming you are using premade seitan, rinse to remove any broth and tear it into large bite-size pieces. Pat the seitan dry with paper towels. Place the oil in a small bowl and gradually add the cornstarch, stirring constantly. You want to add the cornstarch slowly to prevent lumps from forming.

3. Add oil to a Dutch oven until it is about 3 inches deep. Heat to 350°F or until a pea-sized bit of seitan dropped in the oil sizzles on contact. Dredge the pieces of seitan in the cornstarch mixture until completely coated. Working in batches, gently drop the seitan in the oil and fry for about 3 to 5 minutes, turning the pieces so they cook evenly. Transfer the cooked seitan to a paper towel–lined plate. Do not discard the cornstarch mixture, because you will use it to thicken the sauce later on.

4. Place a small amount of oil in a large skillet and warm over medium heat. Add the mushrooms, making sure they are in one layer, and cook until they are browned all over, about 10 minutes. Transfer the mushrooms to a bowl, add the shallot to the pan, and sauté until it is fragrant, about 1 minute. Add the asparagus and cook until slightly browned, about 4 minutes. Transfer the shallot and asparagus to the bowl containing the mushrooms.

5. Pour the sauce into the pan and scrape up any browned bits from the bottom of the pan. Bring to a boil, add a teaspoon of the cornstarch mixture, and stir until the sauce has thickened. If it does not thicken enough, add another teaspoon. If it is too thick, add a little water. When the sauce has reached the desired consistency, return the seitan and vegetables to the pan and toss to coat. Sprinkle with the sesame seeds and serve over the rice.

INGREDIENTS:

SAUCE

- ½ CUP WATER, PLUS MORE AS NEEDED
- ⅓ CUP SUGAR
- ¼ CUP MUSHROOM SOY SAUCE
- ½ CUP SOY SAUCE
- ¼ CUP WHITE WINE VINEGAR
- 2 GARLIC CLOVES, MINCED
- 1 TABLESPOON PEELED AND MINCED GINGER

BUDDHA SEITAN

- 1 LB. SEITAN (SEE PAGE 743)
- ⅓ CUP VEGETABLE OIL, PLUS MORE AS NEEDED
- ⅓ CUP CORNSTARCH
- ½ LB. MUSHROOMS, TRIMMED AND QUARTERED
- 1 SHALLOT, DICED
- 1 LB. ASPARAGUS, TRIMMED AND CUT INTO 3-INCH PIECES
- SESAME SEEDS, FOR GARNISH
- RICE, TO SERVE

DESSERTS

For many people, dessert is a buttery, chocolate-filled end to a meal. And there's nothing wrong with that! But tropical fruit, creamy custard, and sticky rice treats add a new dimension to how dessert can taste, and look. And, for good measure, some ice cream recipes have been included, because all desserts taste better with ice cream on the side.

MATCHA WAFFLES

YIELD: 4 SERVINGS / ACTIVE TIME: 30 MINUTES / TOTAL TIME: 45 MINUTES

Call it breakfast for dinner, or breakfast for dessert—no matter what you call it, or when you eat it, these waffles get a kick of flavor and color from the green tea leaf powder known as matcha. If making ahead of time, you can toast these to crisp back up; they also freeze well.

1. Preheat the waffle maker.

2. In a bowl, combine the flour, sugar, cornstarch, baking powder, matcha, and salt and whisk well.

3. In a separate bowl, combine the eggs, coconut milk and cream, oil, and vanilla and mix well.

4. Pour the wet ingredients into the dry ingredients and whisk until a smooth, slightly thick batter forms. Cover and let stand for 5 to 10 minutes.

5. Use the waffle maker to make the waffles.

6. Serve immediately with the Macerated Berries, maple syrup, and, if desired, a sprinkle of powdered sugar.

MACERATED BERRIES

1. In a bowl, combine the berries, mix well, and then toss with the sugar, vanilla, and orange zest.

2. Before serving, mix the mint or Thai basil into the berries.

INGREDIENTS:

2	CUPS ALL-PURPOSE FLOUR
½	CUP SUGAR
3	TABLESPOONS CORNSTARCH
½	TABLESPOON BAKING POWDER
1½	TABLESPOONS MATCHA POWDER
½	TEASPOON SEA SALT
2	EGGS
1½	CUPS COCONUT MILK AND COCONUT CREAM (TOP PART OF CANNED COCONUT MILK)
¼	CUP COCONUT OIL
1½	TEASPOONS VANILLA EXTRACT
1	CUP MACERATED BERRIES (SEE RECIPE), PLUS MORE AS NEEDED
	MAPLE SYRUP, TO TASTE
	POWDERED SUGAR (OPTIONAL)

MACERATED BERRIES

1	CUP BLUEBERRIES
1	CUP BLACKBERRIES
1	CUP STRAWBERRIES, STEMMED AND QUARTERED OR HALVED
¼	CUP SUGAR
¼	TEASPOON VANILLA EXTRACT
¼	CUP ORANGE ZEST
½	TABLESPOON TORN MINT OR THAI BASIL

PEKING-STYLE CANDIED APPLES

YIELD: 4 SERVINGS / **ACTIVE TIME**: 30 MINUTES / **TOTAL TIME**: 45 MINUTES

Small, bright-red candied apples are common street food snacks in China and Hong Kong during festive days like Lunar New Year, because red symbolizes good luck. This iteration of the candied apple is battered, deep-fried, and sprinkled with sesame seeds. It's not red, but equally satisfying. Bananas can also be used for this recipe.

1. Peel and core the apples and cut into quarters. Cut each piece again into halves or thirds, depending on their size.

2. In a bowl, combine the eggs and soda water and then add the flour, mixing until smooth without overworking the batter.

3. Add the sugar and water to a saucepan over medium-high heat, and, without stirring, bring to a bubbling point and let turn a little golden around the edges, so it is fairly thick and almost to the caramelized stage. To test, drop a small dollop of syrup into some ice-cold water; the syrup should immediately form into a hard ball. Reduce the heat to low.

4. Bring a fryer or pot with oil to 375°F.

5. Coat the apple pieces in the batter, then deep-fry, working in batches so as not to overcrowd. When the batter is golden, remove immediately, using a slotted spoon or kitchen spider, and put the apples into the syrup mixture. When the apples are coated, drop them immediately into a bowl of ice water. Once the syrup hardens, immediately remove with a slotted spoon, removing any excess water.

6. Rest the apples on a very lightly oiled plate and sprinkle with the sesame seeds.

INGREDIENTS:

3-4	MEDIUM GREEN APPLES
3	EGGS, BEATEN
2½	CUPS COLD SODA WATER
2⅔	CUPS ALL-PURPOSE FLOUR
3	CUPS SUGAR
1	CUP WATER
	CANOLA OIL, FOR DEEP-FRYING, PLUS MORE AS NEEDED
¼	CUP TOASTED SESAME SEEDS, FOR GARNISH

FRIED COCONUT MOCHI BALLS

YIELD: 4 SERVINGS / **ACTIVE TIME:** 30 MINUTES / **TOTAL TIME:** 45 MINUTES

This glutinous snack from the Philippines is called carioca. Its crunchy exterior and chewy inside makes it memorable, especially for coconut lovers.

1. In a bowl, combine the flour, ½ cup of brown sugar, and coconut and mix well. Pour in the coconut milk and stir until there are no more clumps in the batter.

2. Form the batter into small balls.

3. Bring the fryer or pot with oil to 325°F.

4. Fry the balls in batches so as not to overcrowd. Once golden and cooked through, use a slotted spoon or kitchen spider to transfer to a paper towel–lined plate.

5. Thread 3 to 4 balls onto a bamboo skewer and set on a wire rack over a sheet pan lined with parchment paper.

6. Add 1 cup of brown sugar and the water and bring to a boil over medium-high heat, stirring well. Cook the until sugar is completely dissolved and starts to slightly caramelize.

7. Pour the sugar mixture over the fried mochi balls, turning the skewers to get all sides.

8. Let cool slightly and serve warm.

INGREDIENTS:

- 1 LB. MOCHIKO FLOUR
- 1½ CUPS BROWN SUGAR, DIVIDED
- 2 CUPS UNSWEETENED SHREDDED COCONUT
- 2 CUPS COCONUT MILK
- CANOLA OIL, FOR DEEP-FRYING
- ⅓ CUP WATER

SWEET BANANA & WATER CHESTNUTS
WITH COCONUT MILK TAPIOCA

YIELD: 4 SERVINGS / ACTIVE TIME: 30 MINUTES / TOTAL TIME: 1 HOUR

One of the beauties of Asian food is the abundant levels of texture found in dishes, including desserts. This variation of tapioca pudding has the creaminess from the coconut milk and ripe bananas, the crunch from the diced water chestnuts, and the playfulness from the tapioca pearls.

1. In a pot, soak the tapioca pearls in the water for 30 minutes.

2. Add the coconut milk and sugar to the soaked tapioca pearls, bring to a boil, and then reduce the heat to low and simmer until the tapioca pearls are translucent, about 30 minutes.

3. When the tapioca pearls are ready, and the consistency is like thick soup, add the water chestnuts and bananas, stir well, and cook to warm the bananas. Adjust the seasoning if needed. If the consistency is too thick, add more coconut milk.

4. Serve hot or warm.

INGREDIENTS:

1	CUP TAPIOCA PEARLS
4	CUPS WATER
4	CUPS COCONUT MILK
1½	CUPS SUGAR
6-8	FRESH WATER CHESTNUTS, FINELY DICED
4	BANANAS, CUT INTO ¼-INCH PIECES

BUTTER MOCHI BARS

YIELD: 16 BARS / **ACTIVE TIME**: 30 MINUTES / **TOTAL TIME**: 1 HOUR AND 30 MINUTES

Mochiko rice flour gives this Hawaiian dessert its fluffy yet sticky texture that is like marshmallows. The shredded coconut topping is optional, depending on one's personal preference.

1. Preheat the oven to 350°F. Using butter or oil, grease a 9 x 13–inch baking pan.

2. In a bowl, combine the eggs, vanilla, and skim milk and whisk well.

3. In a separate bowl, combine the flour, sugar, baking powder, and salt and mix well.

4. Pour the wet ingredients into the dry ingredients and mix with a spatula until all of the ingredients are combined. Add the butter and coconut milk and mix well.

5. Pour the mixture into the greased baking pan, and tap the pan on the counter to remove any air bubbles.

6. Sprinkle the coconut evenly on top of the batter, if using, being careful to make sure the coconut stays on top. Sprinkle the salt, if using.

7. Bake for 45 minutes to 1 hour, until the mochi has set and the top is golden brown.

8. Let cool completely before slicing.

9. Serve, or store in an airtight container at room temperature for 2 to 3 days.

INGREDIENTS:

4	LARGE EGGS
1	TEASPOON VANILLA EXTRACT
2	CUPS SKIM MILK
1	LB. MOCHIKO FLOUR
2	CUPS SUGAR
2	TEASPOONS BAKING POWDER
½	TEASPOON KOSHER SALT
½	CUP UNSALTED BUTTER, MELTED
1	CAN COCONUT MILK
½	CUP UNSWEETENED SHREDDED COCONUT, FOR TOPPING (OPTIONAL)
	MALDON SALT, FOR TOPPING (OPTIONAL)

STICKY RICE WITH TROPICAL FRUIT

YIELD: 4 SERVINGS / ACTIVE TIME: 30 MINUTES / TOTAL TIME: 1 HOUR AND 30 MINUTES

One cannot visit Thailand without trying this tropical dessert that is emblematic of the country. The contrast of the tangy fruit with the creamy, sugary rice makes this simple dish a play on flavors and texture. It is a spoonful of comfort. Using mango is traditionally how it's prepared, but you can use any fruit of choice.

1. Drain the soaked rice.

2. Line a bamboo steamer with parchment paper all the way up the sides.

3. Evenly spread out the rice on the parchment and sprinkle 1 to 2 tablespoons of water on top. Steam over boiling water for 40 minutes.

4. While the rice is steaming, combine the coconut cream, sugar, and salt in a saucepan over low heat and cook until the sugar is dissolved. Set aside.

5. In a bowl, 30 minutes before serving, combine the cooked rice with the cooled coconut mixture and mix well.

6. Transfer to a mold lined with plastic, and let the coconut–sticky rice mixture become firm at room temperature.

7. Invert onto a serving plate and remove the plastic. Garnish with the kiwis or your favorite tropical fruit. Brush with the Simple Syrup and serve.

INGREDIENTS:

1½ CUPS SWEET RICE OR GLUTINOUS RICE, SOAKED FOR 2 HOURS OR MORE

1½ CUPS COCONUT CREAM (TOP PART OF CANNED COCONUT MILK)

½ CUP SUGAR

¼ TEASPOON SALT

2 KIWIS OR FAVORITE TROPICAL FRUIT, SLICED

SIMPLE SYRUP (SEE RECIPE)

SIMPLE SYRUP

1 PART SUGAR

1 PART WATER

SIMPLE SYRUP

1. Add the sugar and water to a pot over medium heat and cook, stirring often, until all of the sugar dissolves and the syrup thickens slightly.

2. Remove from heat, cool, and store in an airtight container until needed.

BANANA & JACKFRUIT TURON

YIELD: 4 SERVINGS / **ACTIVE TIME:** 1 HOUR / **TOTAL TIME:** 1 HOUR AND 30 MINUTES

Turon is a sweet snack found on the streets of the Philippines, which is filled typically with ripe saba bananas. This version includes jackfruit, a tropical fruit that has quickly become a popular meatless alternative.

1. Drain the jackfruit from the can liquid and cut into 1 x 2-inch strips.

2. Peel the bananas and slice lengthwise, then cut into half width-wise; each piece should be 2 to 3 inches long.

3. Roll the banana pieces liberally in the brown sugar.

4. Place a wrapper with the top and bottom corners lined up at the top and bottom of the work surface. Place a sugar-coated banana in the center of the wrapper, one-third of the way up from the bottom corner. Place the jackfruit strips on top of the banana to cover.

5. Roll the bottom corner of the wrapper over the banana and jackfruit. Fold the side corners over and seal tightly. Continue to wrap the banana spring roll until fully enclosed. Seal with the flour paste. Repeat until all of the bananas and jackfruit are rolled up.

6. Bring a fryer or pot with oil to 325°F.

7. Deep-fry the turons, working in batches so as not to overcrowd, until golden brown.

8. Using a slotted spoon or kitchen spider, transfer to a paper towel–lined plate to drain.

9. Sprinkle with the powdered sugar and serve.

INGREDIENTS:

1	CAN JACKFRUIT
6	BANANAS
1½-2	CUPS BROWN SUGAR
1	PACKAGE SPRING ROLL WRAPPERS
	FLOUR PASTE (¼ CUP FLOUR MIXED WITH WATER TO MAKE THICK PASTE)
4	CUPS CANOLA OIL, FOR DEEP-FRYING
½	CUP POWDERED SUGAR
	ICE CREAM, FOR SERVING (OPTIONAL)

SWEET RED BEANS

YIELD: 4 SERVINGS / ACTIVE TIME: 30 MINUTES / TOTAL TIME: 24 HOURS

Desserts with red bean paste can be found almost anywhere in Asia. They're found in sweet breads and small cakes. Fish-shaped pastries stuffed with sweet beans, known as taiyaki in Japan and bungeoppang in Korea, are popular and fun to eat! Adzuki beans are also known as red mung beans.

1. Rinse the soaked beans, add to a pot, cover with water, and bring to a boil. Simmer for 1 hour, until the beans are soft and tender. Remove from heat and strain, reserving 1 cup of cooking liquid in case needed.

2. Return the cooked beans to the pot while still hot and add the sugar, vanilla, and salt and stir well. Slightly mash the beans, using a wooden spoon. Let the beans cool and marinate in the sugar mixture. Add the bean cooking liquid if needed, so the mixture isn't dry.

3. Let cool and refrigerate in an airtight container until needed.

INGREDIENTS:

1 CUP DRIED ADZUKI BEANS, SOAKED IN WATER OVERNIGHT

4-6 CUPS WATER

1 CUP SUGAR

½ TEASPOON VANILLA EXTRACT

1 TEASPOON SALT

JIAN DUI

YIELD: 4 SERVINGS / **ACTIVE TIME:** 1 HOUR / **TOTAL TIME:** 1 HOUR

This is one of the most beloved Asian sweet dumplings. Red bean paste is another popular filling for these crispy and chewy balls.

1. Place the peanuts, sugar, and salt in a food processor and pulse until ground. Be careful not to process the mixture too much and make peanut butter. Place the mixture in a small bowl and set aside. Place the rice flour in a separate bowl and make a well in the center. Place the water in a small pot and bring to a boil. Add the brown sugar to the pot, stir until dissolved, and then pour the mixture into the well. Stir until a ball of dough forms. Transfer the dough to a flour-dusted work surface and knead until smooth. The dough needs to be hot, so be careful.

2. Cut the dough into 2 pieces and roll each one into a log. The dough tends to dry out quickly, so keep a bowl of water near the work surface and dip your hands into it as necessary. Cut each log into eight pieces, and roll each piece into a ball. Cover the pieces with plastic wrap to keep them from drying out.

3. Place a ball in the palm of one hand, and use the thumb of your free hand to make a hole in the center of the ball. Fill with 1 teaspoon of the peanut mixture, and smooth the dough over the filling. Pinch the seam and twist to remove any excess dough. Roll into a smooth ball, place on a parchment paper–lined baking sheet, and cover with plastic wrap. Repeat with the remaining balls and filling.

4. Add the peanut oil to a Dutch oven until it is 2" deep, and bring to 350°F over medium heat. Place the sesame seeds in a small bowl. Dip each ball into the bowl of water, shake to remove any excess, and roll it in the sesame seeds until coated. Working in batches of four, drop the dumplings into the hot oil and cook, while gently stirring initially, until they float to the surface, about 3 minutes. Push the dumplings to the edge of the Dutch oven and baste them with the hot oil as they cook. Cook for another 3 to 4 minutes, and then transfer to a paper towel–lined plate. Serving the dumplings warm is preferred, but they are also delicious at room temperature.

INGREDIENTS:

- ¼   CUP ROASTED PEANUTS, CHOPPED
- 2½   TABLESPOONS SUGAR
- ⅛   TEASPOON KOSHER SALT
- 2   CUPS SWEET RICE FLOUR (GLUTINOUS RICE FLOUR), PLUS MORE FOR DUSTING
- ¾   CUP WATER, PLUS MORE AS NEEDED
- ⅔   CUP PACKED LIGHT BROWN SUGAR
-      PEANUT OIL, FOR FRYING
- ⅓   CUP SESAME SEEDS

CHINESE EGG CUSTARD TART

YIELD: 6 SERVINGS / **ACTIVE TIME:** 1 HOUR / **TOTAL TIME:** 2 HOURS

This version of a tart is inspired by the pastel de nata from Portugal and the custard tart from England. Most dim sum restaurants serve these egg tarts.

1. Make the dough by sifting the flour and powdered sugar into a large bowl. Add the lard and butter, and use your hands to incorporate into the dry ingredients until you get a bread-crumb consistency.

2. Add the egg and vanilla and bring the ingredients together to form a ball. Cover with plastic wrap and refrigerate for 40 minutes to 1 hour.

3. Preheat the oven to 400°F.

4. Make the filling by whisking the caster sugar into the water until it dissolves.

5. In a separate bowl, whisk together the eggs and milk. Slowly add the hot sugar water into the egg mixture and whisk to combine. Add the vanilla.

6. Strain to remove any foam, and set aside.

7. Working quickly, roll out the rested dough on a flour-dusted work surface to a ¼-inch thickness. It is important not to over-handle the dough, and not to do this process in a hot area.

8. Using a cookie cutter, cut out 10 to 12 discs that are slightly wider than your small tart shell molds or the wells in your muffin tray.

9. Using your thumbs, slightly press the pastry discs into each hole. Work from the bottom and up the sides to make an even tart shell.

10. Carefully pour the custard mixture into each tart shell, making sure not to overfill.

11. Bake for 10 to 15 minutes, until the edges are lightly colored.

12. Lower the oven temperature to 300°F and bake for another 10 to 15 minutes, until the custard is cooked through.

13. Serve warm. After baking, you can refrigerate covered for 2 to 3 days, and reheat in the oven or eat chilled.

INGREDIENTS:

TART DOUGH
- 1¾ CUPS ALL-PURPOSE FLOUR, PLUS MORE FOR DUSTING
- 3 TABLESPOONS POWDERED SUGAR
- 2¼ OZ. LARD, CHILLED AND GRATED
- 2 OZ. SALTED BUTTER, CHILLED AND GRATED
- 1 EGG, BEATEN
- ¼ TEASPOON VANILLA EXTRACT

CUSTARD FILLING
- ¼ CUP CASTER SUGAR
- ⅔ CUP HOT WATER
- 2 EGGS
- 5 TABLESPOONS EVAPORATED MILK
- ¼ TEASPOON VANILLA EXTRACT

TANG YUAN DANGO

YIELD: 4 TO 6 SERVINGS / **ACTIVE TIME:** 30 MINUTES / **TOTAL TIME:** 2 HOURS

Topping these sweet rice dumplings with freeze-dried berries adds a burst of color and flavor.

1. Place the strawberries and sugar in a glass mixing bowl and stir to combine. Place 1" of water in a small saucepan and bring it to a boil. Cover the bowl with plastic wrap, place it over the saucepan, and let cook for 1 hour. Check the water level every 15 minutes, and add more if it has evaporated. After 1 hour, turn off the heat and let the mixture cool. When cool, strain and discard the solids.

2. Bring water to a boil in a large pot. Place the flour, ⅓ cup of water, and ¾ cup of the strawberry syrup in a large mixing bowl, and use a fork to work the mixture until combined and very dry. Remove 2-tablespoon portions of the mixture and roll each into a ball. Place the balls in the boiling water, and cook until they float to the surface and double in size, about 5 minutes. Return the balls to the mixture, add the oil, and use a fork to incorporate.

3. Bring the water back to a boil, and prepare an ice-water bath. Place the mixture on a work surface, and knead until it is a smooth and slightly tacky dough. If the dough is too dry or too sticky, incorporate the water or flour as needed. Divide the dough into 18 pieces, roll them into balls, and use a slotted spoon to gently lower them into the pot. Gently stir to keep them from sticking to the bottom, and then cook until they float to the surface and double in size, about 8 minutes. Remove with a slotted spoon, refresh in the ice-water bath, drain, and place 2 balls on each of the skewers. Garnish with the freeze-dried strawberries and drizzle some of the remaining syrup over the top.

INGREDIENTS:

4	CUPS FRESH STRAWBERRIES, HULLED AND CHOPPED
1¼	CUPS SUGAR
1½	CUPS SWEET RICE FLOUR (GLUTINOUS RICE FLOUR), PLUS MORE AS NEEDED
⅓	CUP WATER, PLUS MORE AS NEEDED
2	TABLESPOONS CANOLA OIL
	FREEZE-DRIED STRAWBERRIES, FOR GARNISH

COCONUT PUDDING PANCAKES

YIELD: 30 PANCAKES / **ACTIVE TIME**: 20 MINUTES / **TOTAL TIME**: 50 MINUTES

This is a take on a very popular street food in Thailand that is known as kanom krok, or "candy bowl," because of its traditional shape and sweetness. To make the perfectly spherical cakes found on the streets of Bangkok, you will need to purchase a kanom krok pan, which is similar to the aebleskiver pan used here.

1. Preheat the oven to 350°F and coat an aebleskiver pan with non-stick cooking spray.

2. Place the coconut milk, 1 cup of flour, coconut, 1 tablespoon of sugar, and salt in a bowl and whisk vigorously until the sugar has dissolved. Set the mixture aside.

3. Place the coconut cream, remaining flour, remaining sugar, and tapioca starch or cornstarch in another bowl and whisk until the starch has dissolved. Add this mixture to the coconut milk mixture and stir until combined.

4. Fill the wells of the aebleskiver pan with the batter, and top with some of the corn, if using.

5. Place the pan in the oven and bake until the pancakes are firm, 15 to 20 minutes. Remove from the oven, transfer the to a platter, and tent it with aluminum foil to keep warm. Repeat Steps 4 and 5 with any remaining batter.

INGREDIENTS:

- 1½ CUPS COCONUT MILK
- 1½ CUPS RICE FLOUR, DIVIDED
- ½ CUP SWEETENED SHREDDED COCONUT
- 5 TABLESPOONS CASTER SUGAR, DIVIDED
- ½ TEASPOON FINE SEA SALT
- 1 CUP COCONUT CREAM (TOP PART OF CANNED COCONUT MILK)
- ½ TABLESPOON TAPIOCA STARCH OR CORNSTARCH
- ¼ CUP CORN KERNELS , FOR TOPPING (OPTIONAL)

PASSION FRUIT CURD

YIELD: 3 CUPS / **ACTIVE TIME:** 25 MINUTES / **TOTAL TIME:** 2 HOURS

At once, tangy, floral, and sweet, passion fruit is one of the world's most underappreciated fruits. Serving this curd to loved ones will help change that.

1. Fill a small saucepan halfway with water and bring it to a gentle simmer.

2. Place the passion fruit juice in another small saucepan and warm it over low heat.

3. Combine the eggs, sugar, salt, and vanilla in a metal mixing bowl. Place the bowl over the simmering water and whisk the mixture continually until it is 135°F on an instant-read thermometer.

4. When the passion fruit juice comes to a simmer, gradually add it to the egg mixture, while whisking constantly.

5. When all of the passion fruit juice has been incorporated, whisk the curd until it has thickened and is 155°F. Remove the bowl from heat, add the butter, and stir until thoroughly incorporated.

6. Transfer the curd to a mason jar and let cool. Once cool, store the curd in the refrigerator, where it will keep for up to 2 weeks.

INGREDIENTS:

- ¾   CUP PASSION FRUIT JUICE
- 4   EGGS
- ½   CUP SUGAR
- ⅛   TEASPOON KOSHER SALT
- ¼   TEASPOON PURE VANILLA EXTRACT
- 4   OZ. UNSALTED BUTTER, SOFTENED

COCONUT FLAN

YIELD: 6 SERVINGS / **ACTIVE TIME:** 30 MINUTES / **TOTAL TIME:** 6 HOURS AND 30 MINUTES

Feel free to top this flan with some fresh tropical fruit, such as mango, passion fruit, or lychee.

1. Preheat the oven to 350°F. In a pot, bring 8 cups of water to a boil and keep at a steady boil.

2. Place the sugar and water in a small saucepan and bring to a boil over high heat, swirling the pan instead of stirring. Cook until the caramel is a deep golden brown, taking care not to burn. Remove the pan from heat and add the evaporated milk a little at a time, whisking constantly to prevent the sugar from seizing. When all of the evaporated milk has been added, incorporate the coconut milk and condensed milk in the same fashion.

3. Whisk the eggs, egg yolks, vanilla, and salt into the mixture. Divide the mixture among six 8-oz. ramekins, filling each one about three-quarters of the way.

4. Place the ramekins in a 13 x 9–inch roasting pan. Pour the boiling water into the roasting pan until it reaches halfway up the sides of the ramekins.

5. Place the pan in the oven and bake until the flan is just set, 45 to 50 minutes. The flan should still be jiggly without being runny. Remove from the oven, place the roasting pan on a cooling rack, and let cool for 1 hour.

6. Refrigerate for 4 hours before serving.

INGREDIENTS:

½	CUP SUGAR
2	TABLESPOONS WATER
12	OZ. EVAPORATED MILK
14	OZ. COCONUT MILK
14	OZ. SWEETENED CONDENSED MILK
3	EGGS
3	EGG YOLKS
1½	TEASPOONS PURE VANILLA EXTRACT
½	TEASPOON KOSHER SALT

MANGO CON CHILI PÂTE DE FRUIT

YIELD: 60 CANDIES / **ACTIVE TIME:** 25 MINUTES / **TOTAL TIME:** 3 HOURS AND 30 MINUTES

Putting the sublime combination of mango and chili into a candy turned out to be a fruitful gamble.

1. Line a baking sheet with a silicone baking mat and place a silicone candy mold on it. Place the pectin and a little bit of the sugar in a mixing bowl and stir to combine. Add the citric acid to the water and let it dissolve.

2. Place the mango in a saucepan and warm it to 120°F. Add the pectin-and-sugar mixture and whisk to prevent any clumps from forming. Bring the mixture to a boil and let it cook for 1 minute.

3. Stir in the corn syrup and remaining sugar, and cook the mixture until it is 223°F. The mixture should have thickened, and it should cool quickly and hold its shape when a small portion of it is dropped from a rubber spatula.

4. Stir in the lime zest and citric-acid-and-water mixture and cook for another minute or so. Remove the pan from heat, strain the mixture, and pour it into the candy mold.

5. Let cool for at least 3 hours before cutting into the desired shapes. Toss in the Tajín seasoning, sugar, and salt and enjoy.

INGREDIENTS:

3   TABLESPOONS APPLE PECTIN

20.1   OZ. SUGAR, PLUS MORE TO TASTE

1½   TEASPOONS CITRIC ACID

1½   TEASPOONS WATER

17.6   OZ. MANGO PUREE

3½   OZ. CORN SYRUP

1   PINCH LIME ZEST

TAJÍN SEASONING, TO TASTE

SALT, TO TASTE

ORANGE & COCONUT PANNA COTTA

YIELD: 4 SERVINGS / **ACTIVE TIME:** 30 MINUTES / **TOTAL TIME:** 4 HOURS AND 30 MINUTES

This tropically inspired panna cotta will keep you cool all summer long.

1. Place the gelatin sheets in a small bowl. Add 1 cup of ice and water until the sheets are submerged. Let the mixture rest.

2. Combine the heavy cream, coconut milk, confectioners' sugar, orange juice, orange zest, vanilla seeds, and half of the vanilla bean pod in a saucepan and bring to a simmer. Cook for 15 minutes, and then remove the pan from heat. Remove the vanilla bean pod and discard it.

3. Remove the bloomed gelatin from the ice water. Squeeze to remove as much water from the sheets as possible, add them to the warm mixture, and whisk until they have completely dissolved.

4. Strain the mixture into a bowl through a fine-mesh sieve and divide it among four 8-oz. ramekins, leaving about ½ inch of space at the top. Carefully transfer the ramekins to the refrigerator and chill until the panna cottas are fully set, about 4 hours.

5. Split the passion fruits in half and scoop the insides into a small bowl to remove their seeds and juice. Garnish the top of each panna cotta with about 1 tablespoon of passion fruit juice and seeds, and chill the panna cottas in the refrigerator until ready to serve.

INGREDIENTS:

4	SHEETS SILVER GELATIN
2½	CUPS HEAVY CREAM
1	CUP COCONUT MILK
4½	OZ. CONFECTIONERS' SUGAR
1¼	CUPS ORANGE JUICE
	ZEST OF 1 ORANGE
	SEEDS OF 1 VANILLA BEAN, POD RESERVED
6	FRESH PASSION FRUITS, FOR GARNISH

MANGO SHORTCAKE

YIELD: 1 CAKE / **ACTIVE TIME:** 1 HOUR AND 30 MINUTES / **TOTAL TIME:** 8 HOURS

Don't hesitate to serve the mango mousse on its own, or as the filling for a pie.

1. Preheat the oven to 325°F. Coat a 13 x 9–inch baking pan with nonstick cooking spray.

2. To begin preparations for the cake, sift the flour and ¼ cup of sugar into a mixing bowl. Set aside.

3. In the work bowl of a stand mixer fitted with the whisk attachment, whip the egg whites and salt on high until soft peaks begin to form. Reduce the speed to low and add the remaining sugar a few tablespoons at a time. When all of the sugar has been incorporated, add the vanilla, raise the speed back to high, and whip until the mixture holds stiff peaks.

4. Remove the work bowl from the mixer and gently fold in the dry mixture. Pour the batter into the prepared pan, place it in the oven, and bake until the cake is lightly golden brown and a cake tester comes out clean after being inserted, 20 to 25 minutes. Remove from the oven, transfer to a cooling rack, and let cool completely.

5. To prepare the mango mousse, place the gelatin sheets in a small bowl, and add 1 cup of ice and enough cold water to cover the sheets. In a small saucepan, bring the mango, confectioners' sugar, and lime zest to a simmer over medium heat. Immediately remove the pan from heat. Remove the gelatin from the ice bath and squeeze out as much water as possible. Whisk the gelatin into the mango mixture until fully dissolved. Let the mixture cool to room temperature.

6. Place the heavy cream in the work bowl of a stand mixer fitted with the paddle attachment and whip on high until soft peaks form. Fold the whipped cream into the mousse base.

7. Pour the mousse over the cake and use a rubber spatula to spread it evenly. Refrigerate for 4 hours.

8. To prepare the mango gelee, place the gelatin sheets in a small bowl, and add 1 cup of ice and enough cold water to cover the sheets. Place the water, mango, and sugar in a small saucepan and bring to a simmer over medium heat.

9. Remove the pan from heat. Remove the gelatin from the ice bath and squeeze out as much water as possible. Whisk the gelatin into the mango mixture until fully dissolved. Let the gelee cool to room temperature.

10. Pour the gelee over the mousse layer, and refrigerate the cake for 2 hours.

11. To serve, cut the shortcake into bars.

INGREDIENTS:

CAKE

½	CUP CAKE FLOUR
¾	CUP SUGAR, DIVIDED
6	EGG WHITES, AT ROOM TEMPERATURE
⅛	TEASPOON KOSHER SALT
½	TEASPOON PURE VANILLA EXTRACT

MANGO MOUSSE

4	SHEETS SILVER GELATIN
1¼	CUPS MANGO PUREE
2.6	OZ. CONFECTIONERS' SUGAR
	ZEST OF 1 LIME
1¼	CUPS HEAVY CREAM

MANGO GELEE

4	SHEETS SILVER GELATIN
½	CUP WATER
1¼	CUPS MANGO PUREE
2	TABLESPOONS SUGAR

MATCHA RICE KRISPIES TREATS

YIELD: 12 BARS / **ACTIVE TIME:** 15 MINUTES / **TOTAL TIME:** 1 HOUR AND 15 MINUTES

The earthiness of matcha is a perfect match for the sweetness of a marshmallow bar.

1. Line a 13 x 9–inch baking pan with parchment paper and coat it with nonstick cooking spray.

2. Fill a small saucepan halfway with water and bring it to a simmer. Place the marshmallow creme, butter, matcha powder, and salt in a heatproof mixing bowl, place it over the simmering water, and stir the mixture with a rubber spatula until the butter has melted and the mixture is thoroughly combined. Remove the bowl from heat, add the cereal, and fold until combined. Add the vanilla and white chocolate chips and fold until evenly distributed.

3. Transfer the mixture to the baking pan and spread it with a rubber spatula. Place another piece of parchment over the mixture and pack it down with your hand until it is flat and even. Remove the top piece of parchment.

4. Place the pan in the refrigerator for 1 hour.

5. Run a knife along the edge of the pan and turn the mixture out onto a cutting board. Cut into squares and enjoy.

INGREDIENTS:

12	OZ. MARSHMALLOW CREME
4½	OZ. UNSALTED BUTTER
2	TABLESPOONS MATCHA POWDER
¾	TEASPOON FINE SEA SALT
9	CUPS RICE KRISPIES
¾	TEASPOON PURE VANILLA EXTRACT
2½	CUPS WHITE CHOCOLATE CHIPS

SHAVED ICE WITH SWEET RED BEANS & FRUIT

YIELD: 2 SERVINGS / **ACTIVE TIME:** 10 MINUTES / **TOTAL TIME:** 10 MINUTES

The unique and tasty combination of shaved ice topped with red beans, chopped fruit, and condensed milk is found throughout the region. Countries in Asia experience heat and humidity for months at a time—some even year-round—and a variety of cooling snacks and desserts is a must. In Korea it's called patbingsu, and in the Philippines the variation of the dessert is called halo-halo.

1. Portion half of the shaved ice into two chilled bowls, and top the shaved ice with the sweet beans.

2. Drizzle ¼ cup of milk over the sweet beans in each of the two bowls.

3. Place the other half of the shaved ice into both bowls, building a mound of shaved ice in each bowl.

4. Arrange the fruit and mochi, if using, around each bowl of shaved ice.

5. Drizzle the condensed milk over the top and enjoy immedietly.

INGREDIENTS:

6 CUPS SHAVED ICE, FROM 4 CUPS FROZEN WATER

1 CUP SWEET RED BEANS (SEE PAGE 502) OR STORE BOUGHT

½ CUP WHOLE MILK, DIVIDED

2 CUPS HALVED STRAWBERRIES

½ CUP MANGO, KIWI, OR BERRIES

MOCHI, CUT INTO ½-INCH PIECES (OPTIONAL)

⅓ CUP CONDENSED MILK

CUSTARD ICE CREAM BASE

YIELD: 1 QUART / **ACTIVE TIME:** 30 MINUTES / **TOTAL TIME:** 5 HOURS

This rich custard base is the key to getting the most out of your other ingredients. Don't believe us? It's actually why French vanilla is recognized as its own flavor.

1. In a small saucepan, combine the heavy cream, milk, sugar, and salt and bring to a simmer over medium-low heat, stirring until sugar completely dissolves, about 5 minutes.

2. Remove the saucepan from heat. Place the egg yolks in a heat-proof mixing bowl and whisk them until combined. While whisking constantly, slowly whisk about a third of the hot cream mixture into the yolks. Whisk the tempered egg yolks into the saucepan.

3. Warm the mixture over medium-low heat, stirring constantly, until the mixture is thick enough to coat the back of a wooden spoon (about 170°F on an instant-read thermometer).

4. Strain the custard through a fine-mesh sieve into a bowl and let it cool to room temperature. Cover the bowl, place it in the refrigerator, and let it chill for at least 4 hours.

5. Flavor the custard as desired and churn it in an ice cream maker until it has the desired consistency.

INGREDIENTS:

2	CUPS HEAVY CREAM
1	CUP WHOLE MILK
⅔	CUP SUGAR
⅛	TEASPOON FINE SEA SALT
6	LARGE EGG YOLKS

PHILADELPHIA ICE CREAM BASE

YIELD: 1 QUARTS / **ACTIVE TIME:** 10 MINUTES / **TOTAL TIME:** 5 HOURS

An eggless ice cream base that will be slightly less creamy, but no less delicious.

1. In a saucepan, combine the cream, milk, sugar, corn syrup or honey, and salt and bring the mixture to a simmer, stirring until the sugar has dissolved.

2. Pour the mixture into a heatproof bowl and let it cool to room temperature. Cover it with plastic wrap and store in the refrigerator for at least 4 hours.

3. Flavor the ice cream base as desired and churn it in an ice cream maker until it has the desired consistency.

INGREDIENTS:

3	CUPS HEAVY CREAM
1	CUP WHOLE MILK
½	CUP GRANULATED SUGAR
½	CUP LIGHT CORN SYRUP OR ⅓ CUP HONEY
½	TEASPOON FINE SEA SALT

VEGAN ICE CREAM BASE

YIELD: 1 QUART / **ACTIVE TIME:** 15 MINUTES / **TOTAL TIME:** 4 HOURS AND 15 MINUTES

The natural creaminess of coconut milk allows vegans to not feel left out when it's time for a frozen treat.

1. Place the coconut milk, maple syrup, vanilla seeds, and salt in a blender or food processor and blitz until combined. Transfer the mixture to a bowl, cover it, and refrigerate for 4 hours.

2. Flavor the base as desired and churn in an ice cream maker until it has the desired consistency.

INGREDIENTS:

2   (14 OZ.) CANS OF COCONUT
     MILK

¾   CUP MAPLE SYRUP

     SEEDS OF 2 VANILLA BEANS

1   TEASPOON FINE SEA SALT

CHOCOLATE ICE CREAM

YIELD: 1 QUART / **ACTIVE TIME:** 30 MINUTES / **TOTAL TIME:** 9 HOURS

This may well be the best delivery system for the miraculous flavor of chocolate.

1. While the ice cream base is still warm, combine the cream and cocoa powder in a saucepan and bring to a simmer over medium-low heat.

2. Place the chocolate in a heatproof bowl and pour the warm milk mixture over it. Stir until melted and smooth.

3. Stir the melted chocolate mixture, crème fraîche, and vanilla into the base. Let the mixture cool to room temperature. Strain into a bowl through a fine-mesh sieve, cover the bowl, and store in the refrigerator for 4 hours.

4. Churn the base in an ice cream maker until it reaches the desired texture. Place the ice cream in an airtight container and freeze it for 4 to 6 hours before serving.

INGREDIENTS:

1	QUART ICE CREAM BASE
¾	CUP HEAVY CREAM
3	TABLESPOONS COOCA POWDER
4	OZ. CHOCOLATE, CHOPPED
¾	CUP CRÈME FRAÎCHE
1	TEASPOON PURE VANILLA EXTRACT

VANILLA ICE CREAM

YIELD: 1 QUART / *ACTIVE TIME*: 30 MINUTES / *TOTAL TIME*: 9 HOURS

While it has become synonymous with bland, or plain, using fresh vanilla beans will show you that this ice cream is anything but.

1. While preparing the ice cream base, halve the vanilla beans, scrape the seeds into the saucepan, and add the pods as well. When the base is ready, pour it into the heatproof bowl and let steep for 1 hour.

2. Remove the vanilla bean pods, cover the bowl, and place it in the refrigerator for 4 hours.

3. Churn the mixture in an ice cream maker until it is the desired texture. Place the ice cream in an airtight container and freeze it for 4 to 6 hours before serving.

INGREDIENTS:

1   QUART ICE CREAM BASE

2   VANILLA BEANS

COCONUT ICE CREAM

YIELD: 1 QUART / **ACTIVE TIME:** 30 MINUTES / **TOTAL TIME:** 9 HOURS

Don't hesitate to experiment with the amounts of sweetened and unsweetened coconut here until you find a ratio that produces the flavor you want.

1. While preparing your preferred ice cream base, add the coconut cream and toasted unsweetened coconut to the pot and proceed with the preparation as normal.

2. After removing the pan from heat, let the mixture steep for 1 hour.

3. Strain into a bowl through a fine-mesh sieve, pressing down on the coconut to extract as much liquid from it as possible. Cover the bowl and refrigerate for 4 hours.

4. Place the mixture in an ice cream maker and churn until it almost has the desired texture. Add the toasted sweetened coconut and churn for 2 minutes, or until it is equally distributed. Place the ice cream in an airtight container and freeze for 4 to 6 hours before serving.

INGREDIENTS:

1   QUART ICE CREAM BASE

1   CUP COCONUT CREAM

1   CUP SHREDDED UNSWEETENED COCONUT, TOASTED

½   CUP SHREDDED SWEETENED COCONUT, TOASTED

BANANA ICE CREAM

YIELD: 1 QUART / ACTIVE TIME: 30 MINUTES / TOTAL TIME: 9 HOURS

The pungent sweetness of the banana may be at its best when swaddled in layer upon layer of luscious frozen cream. The riper they are, the better, as they begin to pick up notes of vanilla, honey, and rum as they brown.

1. While the ice cream base is still warm, place all of the remaining ingredients, except for the crème fraîche, in a blender and puree until smooth. Stir the puree and crème fraîche into the base and let the mixture cool to room temperature. Strain into a bowl, cover the bowl, and store in the refrigerator for 4 hours.

2. Churn the base in an ice cream maker until it reaches the desired texture. Place the ice cream in an airtight container and freeze it for 4 to 6 hours before serving.

INGREDIENTS:

1	QUART ICE CREAM BASE
4	VERY RIPE BANANAS
2	TABLESPOONS SUGAR
1	TEASPOON FRESH LEMON JUICE
	PINCH OF FINE SEA SALT
½	CUP CRÈME FRAÎCHE

DRINKS

*B*artenders across Asia have devised countless creative ways to use local ingredients while keeping apace with the global craft cocktail movement. Whether it's fruits, teas, sake, or soju, if you're already cooking with it, why not add it to a tasty beverage?

GINSENG HONEY MILK SHAKE

YIELD: 1 SERVING / **ACTIVE TIME:** 2 MINUTES / **TOTAL TIME:** 2 MINUTES

Adding ginseng to drinks or food imparts a hint of spiciness while helping boost the immune system. This no-fuss shake is pleasurable to drink in the morning or after a meal.

1. In a blender, combine all of the ingredients and puree for about 1 minute, until smooth and frothy. Serve immediately.

INGREDIENTS:

1–2   OZ. FRESH GINSENG ROOT,
       THINLY SLICED

3   CUPS COLD MILK

5-6   ICE CUBES

1-2   TABLESPOONS HONEY

VIETNAMESE COFFEE

YIELD: 1 SERVING / **ACTIVE TIME:** 2 MINUTES / **TOTAL TIME:** 2 MINUTES

If you're a fan of strong coffee and creamy sweetness, this is the perfect caffeinated drink for you. It's typically prepared using dark-roasted Vietnamese coffee grounds; however, you can prepare it with your favorite brand.

1. Using a coffee press, brew the coffee; slightly bitter, strong-tasting coffee is what you want.

2. Once the coffee is brewed, pour it into a cup: for hot coffee, add 1 tablespoon of condensed milk to ½ cup of coffee; for iced coffee, add 2 tablespoons of condensed milk to ½ cup of coffee and pour over ice. Stir well.

INGREDIENTS:

6-8   TABLESPOONS GROUND
       DARK-ROAST COFFEE
       BEANS

2   CUPS WATER

       CONDENSED MILK, TO
       TASTE

SUJEONGGWA

YIELD: 8 SERVINGS / **ACTIVE TIME:** 10 MINUTES / **TOTAL TIME:** 1 HOUR

One way to keep warm during the harsh Korean winters is to enjoy a steaming cup of sujeonggwa; however, drinking it chilled is also popular. This persimmon-and-cinnamon punch is traditionally served during holidays like Chuseok, a moon festival that is viewed as the "Korean Thanksgiving." Having a cup after a heavy meal, like barbeque, is believed to benefit one's digestion.

1. In a pot, bring 2 quarts of water and the ginger to a boil and cook until all of the ginger flavor has been extracted.

2. In a separate pot, bring 2 quarts of water and the cinnamon sticks to a boil and cook until all of the cinnamon flavor has been extracted.

3. Combine the ginger water and cinnamon water, whisk in the sugar and honey, bring to a boil, and then remove from heat. Let cool.

4. Once cooled, add the persimmons, cover, and refrigerate overnight.

5. Serve chilled, garnished with the pine nuts.

INGREDIENTS:

4   QUARTS FILTERED WATER, DIVIDED

¼   LB. GINGER, SLICED

3   CINNAMON STICKS

1   CUP SUGAR

½   CUP HONEY

12   DRIED PERSIMMONS, PITTED AND SOAKED IN WATER FOR 1-2 HOURS

     PINE NUTS, FOR GARNISH

SOJU SANGRIA

YIELD: 6 SERVINGS / **ACTIVE TIME:** 10 MINUTES / **TOTAL TIME:** 10 MINUTES

Chef Brian's fusion of Korea's infamous spirit, soju, and a traditional Spanish sangria results in a light and fruity cocktail that can be enjoyed year-round. Be warned: soju is smooth and almost flavorless, and it can creep up on you.

1. In a large container, combine all of the ingredients, mix well, and refrigerate covered for at least 3 hours, and ideally overnight.

2. Serve in wineglasses with your preferred garnish.

INGREDIENTS:

1	(375 ML) BOTTLE SOJU
½	CUP DICED ASIAN PEAR
½	CUP GRAPES, CUT IN HALVES
½	CUP DICED MELON
½	CUP DICED APPLE
½	LIME, THINLY QUARTERED
1	(8 OZ.) CAN ALOE VERA JUICE
2	TABLESPOONS GRAND MARNIER
4	TABLESPOONS SIMPLE SYRUP, PLUS MORE AS NEEDED

TUMUGI COCKTAIL

YIELD: 1 SERVING / **ACTIVE TIME:** 2 MINUTES / **TOTAL TIME:** 2 MINUTES

The koji of the Tumugi and the lactic notes of the yogurt combine to create an aroma like the air of a sake brewery.

1. Add 2 large ice cubes to the highball glass.

2. Add the Tumugi, then the liqueur, and top with the ginger ale. Lift with a spoon to combine and garnish with a strip of orange peel.

INGREDIENTS:

⅔ OZ. TUMUGI

½ OZ. YOGURT LIQUEUR

SWEET GINGER ALE, TO TOP

YUZU MATCHA MARTINI

YIELD: 1 SERVING / **ACTIVE TIME:** 2 MINUTES / **TOTAL TIME:** 2 MINUTES

Grilled zest and a splash of juice are all it takes to tell your senses that this is a yuzu drink.

1. Add all of the ingredients to a cocktail shaker with ice, shake vigorously, and strain into a cocktail glass.

2. Garnish with a strip of grilled yuzu zest.

INGREDIENTS:

1½   OZ. VODKA

1   OZ. FRESH GRAPEFRUIT JUICE

1   BAR SPOON FRESH YUZU JUICE

1   BAR SPOON MATCHA POWDER

ADZUKI COCKTAIL

YIELD: 1 SERVING / **ACTIVE TIME:** 2 MINUTES / **TOTAL TIME:** 2 MINUTES

What says "Japanese after-dinner drink" more than adzuki beans?

1. Add all of the ingredients to a container and combine with a hand blender.

2. Pour the mixture into a Boston shaker, add ice, and shake briefly.

3. Double strain into a cocktail glass and garnish with a rose petal and edible gold leaf.

INGREDIENTS:

1⅓ OZ. ADZUKI BEANS

1 OZ. NIKKA YOICHI SINGLE MALT WHISKY

3 OZ. SOY MILK

1 BAR SPOON BROWN SUGAR SIMPLE SYRUP

THE JAPANESE COCKTAIL

YIELD: 1 SERVING / **ACTIVE TIME:** 2 MINUTES / **TOTAL TIME:** 2 MINUTES

This cocktail reverses the custom of serving green tea with wagashi confectionary, putting the wagashi flavors in the drink and the green tea on the side.

1. Add all of the ingredients, except for the salt water, to a mixing glass with ice, stir, and strain into a coupe.

2. Spritz with the salt water and garnish with a matcha-dusted warabi mochi.

JAPANESE MIX: Heat 500 ml of soy milk and 3 grams of agar agar and allow to dissolve. Add another 500 ml of soy milk, 1 liter of SG Kome Shochu, 100 grams of kinako (roasted soy flour), and 400 grams of molasses. Mix well, remove from heat, and refrigerate for 6 to 12 hours. Strain through a cheesecloth before using or storing.

MUGWORT SHOCHU: Combine 10 grams of dry mugwort and 1 (750 ml) bottle of SG Kome Shochu and steep for 24 hours at room temperature. Strain before using or storing.

INGREDIENTS:

- 1½ OZ. JAPANESE MIX (SEE RECIPE)
- ½ OZ. MUGWORT SHOCHU (SEE RECIPE)
- ½ OZ. | 15 ML WATER
- 1 BAR SPOON WASANBON SUGAR
- 1 SPRITZ SALT WATER

TIME'S ARROW II

YIELD: 1 SERVING / **ACTIVE TIME**: 2 MINUTES / **TOTAL TIME**: 2 MINUTES

With Suntory and *Star Trek*'s help, here's a terrific play on a Negroni/Boulevardier from what was downtown Napa's popular izakaya, prepandemic; unfortunately, it is no longer open. "I often find that affixing a suitable name to a cocktail is a challenge," says Andrew Salazar. "I want the title to say a little something about the drink without it sounding corny, pretentious, or ham-handed. A tried-and-true method I like to implement is using a cultural reference. Our initial cocktail list had a lot of allusions to different anime series. Since the base spirit of this cocktail is Toki, a Japanese whisky by Suntory, which translates to 'time,' I knew that I wanted to work around that idea. Recently, at the suggestion of a friend and colleague, I've been watching episodes of *Star Trek: The Next Generation*. There's a fun two-part episode called 'Time's Arrow' that is set (drumroll). . .in 19th-century San Francisco! Just a bit of fun trivia. This is the second iteration of this drink: hence, Time's Arrow II."

1. Combine all of the ingredients in a mixing glass with ice, stir, and strain into the Old Fashioned glass over a large ice cube.

2. Garnish with the Sesame & Citrus Candy (see recipe) or expressed orange peel.

SESAME-INFUSED TOKI: Add 1 cup of toasted sesame seeds to a 750 ml bottle of Toki Whisky and let stand for a couple of days before straining off the solids.

OLEO SALIS: In a bowl, combine the zest of 10 lemons and 10 oranges with ½ cup of kosher salt. Massage the mixture together (Salazar recommends wearing a latex glove) for a minute or so, and allow the salt to act on the peels overnight to extract the essential oils. In order to collect as much of the oils as possible, add 2 oz. of Toki Whisky to the mix. Stir thoroughly and strain off the resulting liquid. Be sure to press out as much as you can.

INGREDIENTS:

1   OZ. SESAME-INFUSED SUNTORY TOKI JAPANESE WHISKY (SEE RECIPE)

1   OZ. LUXARDO BITTER BIANCO

1   OZ. CARPANO BIANCO VERMOUTH

1   BAR SPOON OLEO SALIS (SEE RECIPE)

Continued . . .

SESAME & CITRUS CANDY

The expressed orange peel is a lovely garnish for Time's Arrow II. But this savory candy makes for an unforgettable garnish.

1. Measure out ½ cup of sugar. Add a small coat of the sugar to a saucepan over medium-high heat and wait for it to begin melting. Slowly and incrementally add more sugar to the spots in the pan where the sugar is liquefying. Once about a third of the sugar has been introduced, the pace can be increased as you add more sugar and begin to stir with a wooden spoon or heat-resistant spatula.

2. After all of the sugar has been converted into caramel, add 3 tablespoons of mixed toasted and black sesame seeds, and the zest of 1 lemon, zest of 1 orange, and ⅛ teaspoon of baking soda. Stir well to distribute all of the ingredients and incorporate the baking soda.

3. Once fully combined, pour the mixture onto a parchment paper–lined sheet pan. Use an offset spatula to spread the caramel in a thin layer across the sheet.

4. While still hot, sprinkle 1 teaspoon of Maldon sea salt over the surface.

5. After the caramel has cooled for approximately 1 minute, use a sharp knife to score the firm, yet slightly tacky, caramel candy in the shapes that you like.

6. Wait for the caramel to set fully before snapping along the score marks. Crosshatching in a simple rectangular pattern will yield the most usable pieces.

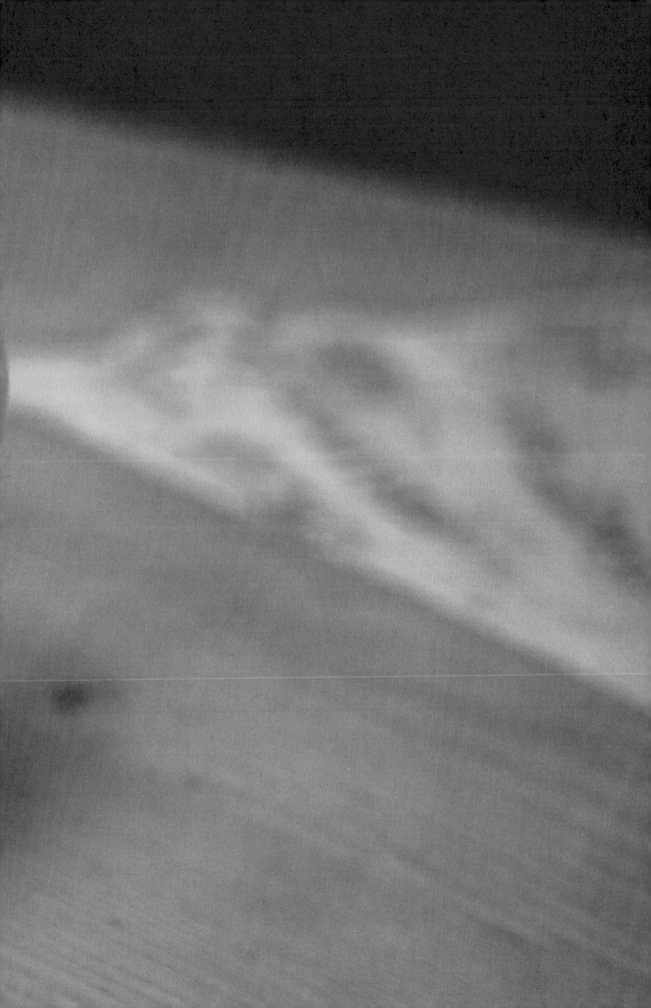

SHURA NO HANA

YIELD: 1 SERVING / ACTIVE TIME: 2 MINUTES / TOTAL TIME: 2 MINUTES

This extremely unique gin-shiso-watermelon cocktail, designed by Paper Plane bar manager Ryan Ota and co-owner George Laulouh, is a terrific example of creative edginess. The song might sound familiar, because it's played in *Kill Bill*. Most likely where you might have heard of it!" declares George Lahlouh.

1. Combine all of the ingredients in a cocktail shaker with ice, shake vigorously, and strain into a chilled coupe glass.

2. Float a fresh shiso leaf to garnish.

WATERMELON SYRUP: Juice a seedless watermelon. Using a 3:1 ratio of juice to white sugar, combine the juice and sugar in a container and stir vigorously. There shouldn't be any solid sugar granules left on the bottom of the container. After mixing thoroughly, strain through a chinois and store. It can be refrigerated for 7 to 10 days.

GALANGAL TINCTURE: Add 1 (750 ml) bottle of Everclear, 300 grams of fresh chopped galangal, and 34 grams of dried galangal to a blender and blend thoroughly. Add the mixture to a 1-gallon sealable bag, making sure to remove as much air as possible. Cook the bag in a sous vide machine at 130°C for 3 hours. After cooking, strain through a chinois, and then squeeze through a cheesecloth to remove all particulates. This will keep indefinitely in a glass jar stored at room temperature.

INGREDIENTS:

- 1½ OZ. ROKU GIN
- ¼ OZ. SIDETRACK SHISO LIQUEUR
- 2 OZ. WATERMELON SYRUP (SEE RECIPE)
- ½ OZ. FRESH LEMON JUICE
- 3 DASHES GALANGAL TINCTURE (SEE RECIPE)

RED TEMPLES

YIELD: 1 SERVING / **ACTIVE TIME:** 2 MINUTES / **TOTAL TIME:** 2 MINUTES

For this cocktail, Christian Suzuki uses shochu as the base, then takes the drinker for a wild yet elegant ride full of fruit, bitter, nuttiness, floral notes, and smoke. It's got it all in beautiful harmony. That seems fitting with the inspiration coming from the magnificent Sensoji Temple in the Asakusa district of Tokyo, which is Suzuki's hometown.

1. Muddle the strawberry in a mixing glass.

2. Add the rest of the ingredients to the mixing glass with ice, stir, and double strain into a rocks glass over ice (double straining this is important, to prevent any strawberry pieces from going into the cocktail).

3. Torch one end of a cinnamon stick for garnish.

INGREDIENTS:

1 STRAWBERRY

1 OZ. IICHIKO SAITEN SHOCHU

¾ OZ. CAMPARI

¾ OZ. AMONTILLADO SHERRY

¼ OZ. ST. GERMAIN ELDERFLOWER LIQUEUR

5 DASHES PEATED SCOTCH

CUCUMBER COLLINS

YIELD: 1 SERVING / **ACTIVE TIME:** 2 MINUTES / **TOTAL TIME:** 2 MINUTES

The Napa Valley is famous for its Cabernet Sauvignon—and its signature cocktail, Scott Beattie's Cucumber Collins. Beattie's invention here touches on many modern themes: local ingredients, a photogenic drink, and the resourceful use of ingredients (note how the huckleberries contribute to the pickled purple cucumbers).

1. Add the vodka, juices, and syrup to the short half of a mixing tin. Fill to the top with ice and seal it up.

2. Shake just a few times to mix, then unseal, leaving everything in the larger half.

3. Add the chilled soda water to the mixture, swirl it around a few times to mix, and then dump everything into a Collins glass.

4. Garnish with 5 thin cucumber slices, Pickled Purple Cucumber Slices (see recipe), and Pickled Huckleberries (see recipe). Pickled Huckleberries: Add 6 cups unseasoned rice vinegar, 2 cups mirin, and 2 cups cooking sake to a saucepan over medium-high heat and bring to a boil. When the liquid boils, add 3 cups granulated white sugar and stir to dissolve. Add 2 lbs. wild huckleberries and return to a boil. When the mixture reaches a boil, remove from heat and let cool. Strain off excess liquid and reserve for Pickled Purple Cucumber recipe. Refrigerate the the strained berries; they will last up to 1 month.

PICKLED PURPLE CUCUMBERS: Add 3/4 qt. reserved Pickled Huckleberries pickling liquid and ¾ qt. thinly sliced English cucumbers to a large container, cover, and refrigerate for 24 hours. The color should set after 24 hours. The cucumbers will keep for 2 months in the refrigerator.

INGREDIENTS:

- 1½ OZ. SQUARE ONE CUCUMBER VODKA
- ½ OZ. FRESH LEMON JUICE
- ¼ OZ. YUZU JUICE
- ½ OZ. SIMPLE SYRUP
- 1½ OZ. CHILLED SODA WATER
- 5 THIN ENGLISH CUCUMBER SLICES
- 5 THIN PICKLED PURPLE CUCUMBER SLICES
- 1 TABLESPOON PICKLED HUCKLEBERRIES

86 DIGNITY

YIELD: 1 SERVING / **ACTIVE TIME:** 2 MINUTES / **TOTAL TIME:** 2 MINUTES

The sweet-umami sensation of candy cap mushrooms is the core of this Japanese whisky cocktail created by Goose & Gander's bar manager, Emma Kreis. Ultimately, it's just a three-ingredient cocktail, but in reality, there are a half dozen different elements at play that make for a dignified, multilayered cocktail. Any restaurant and bar workers reading this will understand the inside joke of the cocktail's name—"86" is restaurant terminology for when an ingredient or a menu item runs out.

1. Rinse a Nick & Nora glass with the absinthe.

2. Combine the whisky, syrup, and lemon juice in a cocktail shaker with ice, hard-shake for approximately 30 seconds, and double strain into the glass.

3. Garnish with a lemon peel.

INGREDIENTS:

ST. GEORGE ABSINTHE VERTE, TO RINSE

1½ OZ. CANDY CAP BUTTER-WASHED SUNTORY TOKI JAPANESE WHISKY

1 OZ. SARSAPARILLA SYRUP

1 OZ. FRESH LEMON JUICE

SEA COLLINS .

YIELD: 1 SERVING / **ACTIVE TIME:** 2 MINUTES / **TOTAL TIME:** 2 MINUTES

The good folks at Oakland Spirits Company certainly have fun with their gin. The Automatic Halfshell Gin is a London Dry style, for which 200 Hog Island Sweetwater oysters are crushed in the distilling process. For this version of a Tom Collins, which is vividly inspired by the seaweed- and kelp-filled Northern California coast, the Oakland Spirits Company Automatic Sea Gin is the drink's briny anchor, packed with foraged nori, lemongrass, and some other elements of our coastal terroir.

1. Combine all of the ingredients, except for the soda water, in a cocktail shaker with a medium amount of ice, shake vigorously, and double strain into a Collins glass.

2. Top with the soda water and lightly stir with a bar spoon.

3. Garnish with 2 or 3 nori leaves, gently stirring the seaweed into the cocktail to create the appearance of tidal water.

SEAWEED-INFUSED HONEY: In a bowl, combine equal parts of the raw honey and water and mix well. Add the dry nori seaweed and let sit at room temperature for 7 days. Strain, making sure to extract all liquid/flavor from seaweed, and store. (Hog Island uses 1½ cups of seaweed per 1 liter of honey water.)

INGREDIENTS:

2   OZ. OAKLAND SPIRITS COMPANY AUTOMATIC SEA GIN

¾   OZ. SEAWEED-INFUSED HONEY (SEE RECIPE)

½   OZ. FRESH LEMON JUICE

½   OZ. FRESH LIME JUICE

4   DASHES CHAMOMILE TINCTURE

     SODA WATER, TO TOP

音響熟成
奄美黒糖焼酎
25度

奄美黒糖焼酎
Amami Kokuto Shochu Lento
れんと

本格焼酎

製造者：株式会社 奄美大島開運酒造
鹿児島県大島郡宇検村湯湾2924-2
フリーダイヤル 0120-52-0102

壷焼酎

さつま名産
本格焼酎

本格焼酎

THE ROBIN'S NEST

YIELD: 1 SERVING / ACTIVE TIME: 2 MINUTES / TOTAL TIME: 2 MINUTES

Michael Mina's partnership with two of Honolulu's top chefs, wife-and-husband team Michelle Karr-Ueoka and Wade Ueoka, provides a definitive Hawaiian regional cuisine dining experience 3,000 miles away from the Islands . . . in one of Downtown San Francisco's giant Salesforce office buildings (not the famous tall one).

1. Combine all of the ingredients, except for the cranberry juice, in a cocktail shaker with ice, shake vigorously, and strain into a hurricane glass.

2. Fill with crushed ice, top with the cranberry juice, and garnish with a candied pineapple wedge, maraschino cherry on a bamboo skewer, and umbrella pick.

INGREDIENTS:

1	OZ. SUNTORY TOKI JAPANESE WHISKY
½	OZ. PLANTATION O.F.T.D. (OR SIMILAR BLENDED OVERPROOF RUM)
½	OZ. TBT CINNAMON SYRUP
½	OZ. FRESH LEMON JUICE
¾	OZ. PINEAPPLE JUICE
1	OZ. TBT PASSION HONEY SYRUP
1	OZ. CRANBERRY JUICE

FARM & VINE

YIELD: 1 SERVING / ACTIVE TIME: 2 MINUTES / TOTAL TIME: 2 MINUTES

According to Niku Steakhouse bar manager Ilya Romanov, "This unique cocktail features a pantry full of ingredients that you typically find dusting up at a bar and rarely find a use for."

1. Combine all of the ingredients, except for the tonic water, in a cocktail shaker and shake without ice for 10 seconds. Add ice and hard-shake for an additional 10 seconds.

2. Add the tonic water to the tin and strain the contents into the Old Fashioned glass. Add a couple of ice cubes to keep the cocktail cold.

3. Garnish with a shiso leaf and Umeboshi Powder (see recipe).

SUGAR SNAP PEA SYRUP: Wash and juice 2 lbs. of sugar snap peas to yield 5⅓ oz. of snap pea juice. Add 4 oz. of water to a saucepan and bring to a boil. When the water boils, add 16 oz. of cane sugar and whisk until the sugar is fully diluted. Remove the pan from heat and let cool. Add the snap pea juice to the syrup and stir until fully incorporated. Bottle and use within 3 days.

UMEBOSHI POWDER: Using a dehydrator on a setting for vegetables, spread out the pitted and pickled umeboshi plums on a tray and dehydrate for 3 days. This will produce a perfectly dry plum, which can be ground into a powder and used to, in the words of Ilya Romanov, "add a salty-savory-funk note."

INGREDIENTS:

1 OZ. SVOL SWEDISH-STYLE AQUAVIT

¾ OZ. LA GITANA MANZANILLA SHERRY

½ OZ. FUSION NAPA VALLEY VERJUS BLANC

¾ OZ. FRESH LIME JUICE

¾ OZ. SUGAR SNAP PEA SYRUP (SEE RECIPE)

½ OZ. EGG WHITE

1 OZ. Q MIXERS ELDERFLOWER TONIC WATER

YINCHUAN

YIELD: 1 SERVING / **ACTIVE TIME:** 2 MINUTES / **TOTAL TIME:** 2 MINUTES

Known for producing rice, cereals, and oils, the Chinese city og Yinchuan enjoys beautiful natural scenery and favorable conditions for agriculture.

1. Place all of the ingredients, except for the hay, in a mixing glass filled with ice, and stir until chilled.

2. Strain into a rocks glass, filled with whiskey stones or other frozen stones.

3. Using a smoke gun filled with the hay, smoke the cocktail for 10 to 15 seconds.

4. Garnish with a sesame cracker and, if desired, an edible butterfly.

FAT-WASHED RAGTIME RYE WHISKEY: Place 1⅞ oz. of sesame oil and a 750 ml bottle of Ragtime Rye in a container, shake vigorously, and store in a cool, dry place for 24 hours. Freeze the mixture until the oil solidifies into a solid layer. Remove the oil and strain the whiskey through a cheesecloth before using or storing.

SICHUAN PEPPERCORN SYRUP (MAKES APPROXIMATELY 1½ CUPS): Place 9 oz. of water, 9 oz. of honey, and ¾ oz. of Sichuan peppercorns in a vacuum bag and sous vide for 6 hours at 120°F. Strain before using or storing. If you do not have access to a sous vide, place all of the ingredients in a saucepan and bring to a boil. Reduce the heat and let the mixture simmer for 20 minutes. Remove from heat, let cool, and strain before using or storing.

INGREDIENTS:

- 1⅜ OZ. FAT-WASHED RAGTIME RYE WHISKEY (SEE RECIPE)
- ¾ OZ. RED DATE TEA
- 1 TEASPOON SICHUAN PEPPERCORN SYRUP (SEE RECIPE)
- 1 TEASPOON CRÈME DE PÊCHE
- 3 DROPS VANILLA BITTERS

  HAY, FOR SMOKE GUN

FIZZ KAFFIR

YIELD: 1 SERVING / **ACTIVE TIME:** 2 MINUTES / **TOTAL TIME:** 2 MINUTES

A refreshing, sweet, and sour drink that was originally designed to satisfy guests who have a bit of a sweet tooth, via the fruity notes.

1. Add all of the ingredients to a cocktail shaker filled with ice, and shake vigorously until chilled.

2. Strain into a highball glass, and then add ice cubes.

3. Garnish with a lime wheel and maraschino cherry.

MAKRUT LIME LEAF-INFUSED GIN: Place 10 to 12 makrut lime leaves and a 750 ml bottle of gin in a large mason jar and stir vigorously for 1 minute. Let steep for 12 hours, and strain before using or storing.

INGREDIENTS:

- 1⅜ OZ. MAKRUT LIME LEAF-INFUSED GIN (SEE RECIPE)
- ½ OZ. PEAR BRANDY
- ½ OZ. GIFFARD CRÈME DE RHUBARBE
- 1 OZ. CRANBERRY JUICE
- ¾ OZ. FRESH LEMON JUICE
- 1 EGG WHITE

JAPANESE WHISPERS

YIELD: 1 SERVING / **ACTIVE TIME**: 2 MINUTES / **TOTAL TIME**: 2 MINUTES

This is a long, refreshing, and complex cocktail that uses only Japanese spirits to provide the punchy aromas. The other ingredients combat the high alcohol content with sweetness, citrus, and a thick texture, resulting in a concoction that is both subtle and satisfying.

1. Add all of the ingredients to a cocktail shaker containing no ice, and dry shake for 15 seconds. Add ice and shake vigorously until chilled.

2. Strain into a highball glass, and add the ice cubes.

3. Dust the rim of the glass with smoked paprika.

PASSION FRUIT CORDIAL (MAKES APPROXIMATELY 35 OZ.): Place 35 oz. of Boiron Passion Fruit Puree, 7 oz. of fructose, and 7 oz. of caster sugar in a mason jar and stir until the fructose and sugar have dissolved.

INGREDIENTS:

1⅜   OZ. SHOCHU

¾   OZ. SUNTORY TOKI WHISKY

1   OZ. PASSION FRUIT CORDIAL (SEE RECIPE)

1   EGG WHITE

⅞   OZ. CITRUS BLEND (EQUAL PARTS FRESH LIME AND LEMON JUICES)

ELECTRIC EARL

YIELD: 1 SERVING / **ACTIVE TIME:** 2 MINUTES / **TOTAL TIME:** 2 MINUTES

This psychedelic cocktail creates a balance between bitter flavors (from the Lady Grey-infused liqueur and grapefruit juice) and herbal freshness. Try to find and use the electric daisy too—it actually zaps your tongue.

1. Add all of the ingredients to a mixing glass filled with ice, and, using another mixing glass, utilize the Cuban roll method to mix the cocktail.

2. Pour the cocktail into the chosen glassware.

3. Garnish with a purple shiso leaf, LED ice cubes, and electric daisy.

SANSHO-INFUSED OXLEY GIN: Add ½ oz. of chopped sansho pepper to a 750 ml bottle of Oxley Gin, and let steep for 3 to 5 days. Strain before using or storing.

LADY GREY-INFUSED FORTUNELLA: Add 6 oz. of loose-leaf Lady Grey tea into a 500 ml bottle of Fortunella Golden Orange Liqueur and let steep for 30 to 45 minutes. Strain before using or storing.

GIBSON GRASS CORDIAL: Place 25 oz. of tonic water in a saucepan and bring to a boil. Add 1 small handful of each of the following: kukicha tea, prunella leaves, shiso leaves, eucalyptus leaves, chopped lemongrass, makrut lime leaves, lemon balm leaves, and lemon thyme leaves. Reduce the heat, and simmer for 15 minutes. Strain and add 26½ oz. of sugar to the mixture. Stir until the sugar has dissolved, and let cool completely before using or storing. The cordial will keep in the refrigerator for up to 1 month.

INGREDIENTS:

1¾	OZ. SANSHO-INFUSED OXLEY GIN (SEE RECIPE)
½	OZ. FRESH LIME JUICE
⅞	OZ. FRESH PINK GRAPEFRUIT JUICE
3	DASHES ELECTRIC BITTERS
2	TEASPOONS LADY GREY-INFUSED FORTUNELLA (SEE RECIPE)
1½	OZ. GIBSON GRASS CORDIAL (SEE RECIPE)
1	SPLASH SHISO VINEGAR

JAZERAC

YIELD: 1 SERVING / **ACTIVE TIME:** 2 MINUTES / **TOTAL TIME:** 2 MINUTES

Hidetsugu Ueno's Japanese Sazerac uses all local ingredients, including an absinthe from Kyoto, the high-proof Nikka Whisky from The Barrel, and a Nikka brandy. His homemade yuzu bitters bring the citrus notes, so there's no need for the traditional lemon peel garnish.

1. Rinse a Old Fashioned glass with the absinthe.

2. Place two large ice cubes in the glass and stir. Discard the top cube.

3. Add the remaining ingredients and stir until chilled. Remove and discard the remaining ice cube.

YUZU PEEL BITTERS: Peel a yuzu and dry the peel. Ueno places the peel in front of a fan for a day or two to get it to the proper level of dryness. Cram as much of the peel as possible into a jar and fill it with high-proof vodka. Let the mixture sit for 6 months. Strain before using or storing.

INGREDIENTS:

ABSINTHE, TO RINSE

1⅓ OZ. NIKKA WHISKY FROM THE BARREL

⅔ OZ. NIKKA XO DELUXE BRANDY

2 BAR SPOONS SIMPLE SYRUP

1 BAR SPOON YUZU PEEL BITTERS (SEE RECIPE)

SHISUI

YIELD: 1 SERVING / ACTIVE TIME: 2 MINUTES / TOTAL TIME: 2 MINUTES

Akinori Shibuya won the 2018 Suntory Cocktail Competition with this drink, designed to taste mizumizushii (rough translation: "dewy and fresh"). It's a great prelude to a meal by Aileron owner and chef Kiyohachi Sato, who makes excellent retro sandwiches, omelets, and pasta dishes. Sato began bartending half a century ago at the Imperial Hotel, but long ago passed cocktail duty to Shibuya.

1. Combine all of the ingredients with ice in a cocktail shaker, shake vigorously until chilled, and strain into the cocktail glass.

GINGER SYRUP: Add a peeled, 1-inch piece of ginger to a standard simple syrup after the sugar has dissolved and cook for another 5 minutes. Let cool, strain, and store in an airtight container.

INGREDIENTS:

- ¾ OZ. SUNTORY ROKU GIN
- ½ OZ. MISTIA MUSCAT LIQUEUR
- 2 BAR SPOONS FRESH LEMON JUICE
- 1 BAR SPOON GINGER SYRUP (SEE RECIPE)
- 1 BAR SPOON MATCHA LIQUEUR

GARDENING ORCHARD

YIELD: 1 SERVING / **ACTIVE TIME:** 2 MINUTES / **TOTAL TIME** 2 MINUTES

I t's citrusy, refreshing, and beautifully balanced, and it comes with a watering can of absinthe on the side. As you sip, you sprinkle the green fairy to your taste.

1. Squeeze the juice of the yuzu wedge into a Boston shaker and throw in the spent wedge. Tear the shiso leaf and add it to the shaker. Add the gin, liqueur, wine, lemon juice, and simple syrup and muddle.

2. Add a small scoop of crushed ice to the shaker, shake vigorously, and pour into a miniature bucket. Add more crushed ice and a straw, and garnish with a bean sprout. Sprinkle matcha powder and cinnamon over the cocktail.

3. Place the bay leaf in a miniature watering can, pour the light absinthe over it, and serve alongside the cocktail.

INGREDIENTS:

1	YUZU WEDGE
1	SHISO LEAF
1½	OZ. KA NO MORI GIN
2	BAR SPOONS YUZU LIQUEUR
2	BAR SPOONS WHITE WINE
2	BAR SPOONS FRESH LEMON JUICE
2	BAR SPOONS SIMPLE SYRUP
1	BAY LEAF, TOASTED
	LIGHT ABSINTHE, TO TASTE

BLACK CAT

YIELD: 1 SERVING / *ACTIVE TIME:* 2 MINUTES / *TOTAL TIME:* 2 MINUTES

Yomeishu is made in Nagano prefecture, where Yasuhiko Mizusawa grew up drinking it. The bittersweet herbal elixir is sold in drugstores as a remedy for fatigue, poor circulation, and gastrointestinal issues. That branding is why most bartenders ignore it, but the former Nippon Bartenders Association champion pairs it brilliantly with a whisky that also hails from Nagano prefecture.

1. Combine the ingredients with ice in a two-piece cocktail shaker, shake very briefly, and strain over ice into an Old Fashioned glass.

2. Garnish with a strip of orange peel.

INGREDIENTS:

1   OZ. MARS IWAI TRADITION WHISKY

½   OZ. YOMEISHU

½   OZ. WHITE PEACH LIQUEUR

1   BAR SPOON FRESH LEMON JUICE

KYOHO & EARL GREY MARTINI

YIELD: 1 SERVING / **ACTIVE TIME:** 2 MINUTES / **TOTAL TIME:** 2 MINUTES

Manabu Ohtake beat 10,000 other contestants to win the Diageo World Class contest in 2011, and was quickly tapped by the Palace Hotel Tokyo to helm their historic, moodily lit Royal Bar. Each month he introduces new cocktails, usually based around fresh fruit. Autumn is the season for sweet Kyoho grapes, which he shakes with Earl Grey leaves for a beautiful bergamot accent.

1. Add all of the ingredients to a cocktail shaker and muddle.

2. Add ice, shake vigorously, and strain into a chilled cocktail glass. Garnish with a Kyoho grape.

INGREDIENTS:

1⅓	OZ. CÎROC VODKA
7–8	KYOHO GRAPES
1	BAR SPOON LOOSE-LEAF EARL GREY TEA

PLUM COCKTAIL

YIELD: 1 SERVING / ACTIVE TIME: 2 MINUTES / TOTAL TIME: 2 MINUTES

The upmarket Futako Tamagawa suburb is home to a stunning bar in a converted wooden warehouse that looks as though it were plucked from the streets of Kyoto. Bartender Takashi Makishima, who actually was plucked from the old capital, makes classics and hyperseasonal fruit cocktails.

1. Juice the plums, straining the liquid through a cheesecloth.

2. Add the plum juice and the remaining ingredients to a Boston shaker with ice, shake vigorously, and strain into a cocktail glass.

*Sumomo, or *Prunus salicina,* are usually sold as Japanese plums, Chinese plums, or Asian plums in English-speaking countries.

INGREDIENTS:

2   SUMOMO PLUMS*

1   OZ. TANQUERAY GIN

1   OZ. ML CRANBERRY JUICE

1   BAR SPOON GRENADINE

GLASSWARE
COCKTAIL GLASS

TAMACHI

YIELD: 1 SERVING / **ACTIVE TIME:** 2 MINUTES / **TOTAL TIME:** 2 MINUTES

This clever, alcohol-free drink doesn't feel like a compromise at all.

1. Add all of the ingredients to a cocktail shaker with ice, shake vigorously, and strain into a coupe. Garnish with 3 drops of sesame oil.

SHISO CORDIAL: Place 200 ml of water, 200 grams of sugar, and 25 ml of vodka in a saucepan and warm over medium heat, stirring to dissolve the sugar. Using a wand lighter or a long match, flame off any remaining alcohol, remove the pan from heat, and add 20 shiso leaves. Steep for 1 hour. Stir in 1 gram of citric acid and strain before using or storing.

BUTTERFLY PEA WATER: Steep 1 cup of loose-leaf butterfly pea tea in 1 liter of hot water for 10 minutes. Strain before using or storing.

INGREDIENTS:

1½ OZ. SHISO CORDIAL (SEE RECIPE)

1⅓ OZ. FRESH LEMON JUICE

⅔ OZ. | 20 ML BUTTERFLY PEA WATER (SEE RECIPE)

BLOOD RED DIAMOND

YIELD: 1 SERVING / **ACTIVE TIME:** 2 MINUTES / **TOTAL TIME:** 2 MINUTES

Jameson Irish Whiskey ran a "farm-to-glass" cocktail contest in 2019, and former IT engineer Atsushi Nakamura won it with something that tastes like licking your fingers after a day of tilling fields—in a good way. It's earthy and juicy, made with potatoes and beets from his home prefecture of Saitama.

1. Add all of the ingredients to a mixing glass with ice, stir until chilled, and strain into a cocktail glass.

HOUJICHA HONEY WATER: Combine 1 part honey with 1 part brewed houjicha tea, and let cool before using or storing.

ROASTED SWEET POTATO JUICE: Preheat the oven to 400°F and roast 1 sweet potato until the flesh is tender, about 1 hour. Remove from the oven and scrape the sweet potato's flesh into a blender. Add 3 parts water and puree until smooth. Strain through a cheesecloth before using or storing.

INGREDIENTS:

- 1⅓ OZ. JAMESON IRISH WHISKEY
- ½ OZ. HOUJICHA HONEY WATER (SEE RECIPE)
- 2 BAR SPOONS ROASTED SWEET POTATO JUICE (SEE RECIPE)
- 1 BAR SPOON FRESH BEET JUICE

LAUGH

YIELD: 1 SERVING / ACTIVE TIME: 2 MINUTES / TOTAL TIME: 2 MINUTES

The Hotel New Otani Tokyo is a storied place, occupying what was once a feudal lord's estate. It appeared in the Bond movie *You Only Live Twice* as the headquarters of Osato Chemicals, and has hosted prime ministers, presidents, royals, and autocrats. The main bar has a menu with original cocktails spanning six decades, including gems like this from current bar captain Hiroki Yoshida, that would make his predecessors' heads spin. Yoshida says he found apple and lactic notes in Johnnie Walker Gold Label and amplified them with a bespoke juice and amazake, Japan's low-alcohol fermented rice drink.

1. Add all of the ingredients to a cocktail shaker with ice, shake vigorously, and strain into a cocktail glass. Garnish with a cinnamon-dusted dried rosebud.

AMAZAKE FALERNUM: Place 250 grams of amazake, 250 grams of sugar, 1 cinnamon stick, ¼ vanilla bean, ½ teaspoon of cardamom pods, ¼ teaspoon of whole cloves, 2 slices of lemon, and 2 slices of lime in a saucepan and bring to a simmer over medium heat, stirring to dissolve the sugar. Remove from heat, let cool completely, and strain before using or storing.

APPLE PIE JUICE: Place 300 ml of apple juice, ¼ teaspoon of cinnamon, and ½ vanilla bean in a saucepan and bring to a boil over medium-high heat. Cook until the mixture has reduced by half, and then remove from heat. Let cool completely, and strain before using or storing.

INGREDIENTS:

- 1⅓ OZ. JOHNNIE WALKER GOLD LABEL RESERVE SCOTCH WHISKY
- ⅔ OZ. AMAZAKE FALERNUM (SEE RECIPE)
- ½ OZ. APPLE PIE JUICE (SEE RECIPE)
- 1 BAR SPOON FRESH LEMON JUICE
- 1 BAR SPOON LOOSE-LEAF RUBY ORANGE TEA
- 1 DASH BOB'S ORANGE & MANDARIN BITTERS

YAKUMI PENICILLIN

YIELD: 1 SERVING / **ACTIVE TIME:** 2 MINUTES / **TOTAL TIME:** 2 MINUTES

Yakumi translates as "condiments," and Koji Esashi balances four of them in a spicy, liberal interpretation of the Penicillin.

1. Place all of the ingredients in a container and use a hand blender to combine.

2. Strain the mixture into a cocktail shaker, add ice, and shake vigorously.

3. Strain into a Old Fashioned glass and garnish with a myoga leaf.

INGREDIENTS:

1½ OZ. MEZCAL

½ OZ. FRESH LEMON JUICE

1 BAR SPOON HONEY

1 SLICE FRESH GINGER

½ MYOGA BUD

1 PINCH FRESH WASABI

JAPANESE NEGRONI

YIELD: 1 SERVING / ACTIVE TIME: 2 MINUTES / TOTAL TIME: 2 MINUTES

The combination of Campari, Martini & Rossi Bitter, and houjicha creates a softer, more natural bitterness than you get with Campari alone.

1. Build the cocktail in an Old Fashioned glass containing an ice ball and stir, slowly, putting air in the drink without melting the ice.

2. Sprinkle houjicha leaves onto the top of the ice ball. Use enough to give a nose, but not so much that it slides into the drink.

HOUJICHA VODKA: Add 15 grams of loose-leaf houjicha tea to 1 (750 ml) bottle of vodka and steep for 2 days. Strain before using or storing.

INGREDIENTS:

- ⅔ OZ. HOUJICHA VODKA (SEE RECIPE)
- ⅔ OZ. MANCINO ROSSO VERMOUTH
- 2 BAR SPOONS CAMPARI, CHILLED
- 2 BAR SPOONS MARTINI & ROSSI BITTER, CHILLED

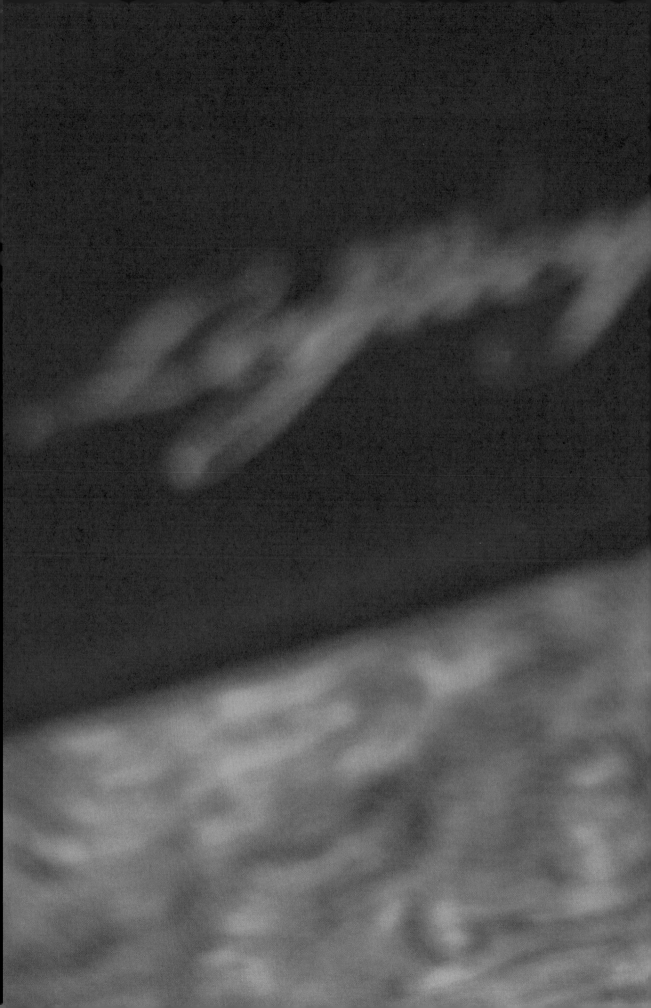

MADAME L'OSIER

YIELD: 1 SERVING / **ACTIVE TIME:** 2 MINUTES / **TOTAL TIME:** 2 MINUTES

The dessert counterpart to the Monsieur L'Osier (page 620) is opulent and indulgent.

1. Add all of the ingredients to a cocktail shaker with ice, shake vigorously, and strain into a coupe.

INGREDIENTS:

1⅓   OZ. COGNAC

2   BAR SPOONS GREEN TEA
      LIQUEUR

2   BAR SPOONS CREAM

BROWN & BLACK HIGHBALL

YIELD: 1 SERVING / **ACTIVE TIME:** 2 MINUTES / **TOTAL TIME:** 2 MINUTES

Kana Arai makes a cold-brew houjicha and runs it through a soda siphon to make a highball that pairs superbly with the curries her bar is famous for. She says she chose the tea to suit the smoky notes in the Scotch.

1. Add the whisky, sugar cube, and bitters to a chilled highball glass and muddle.

2. Add ice and top with the houjicha soda.

HOUJICHA BITTERS: In a bowl, combine 7 grams of loose-leaf houjicha (pan-roasted green tea) and 90 ml of Johnnie Walker Black Label Blended Scotch Whisky and let rest for 2 hours. Strain through a coffee filter and store.

INGREDIENTS:

- 1⅔ OZ. JOHNNIE WALKER BLACK LABEL BLENDED SCOTCH WHISKY
- 1 BROWN SUGAR CUBE
- ½ TEASPOON HOUJICHA BITTERS (SEE RECIPE)
- 3⅓ OZ. HOUJICHA SODA

SATOYAMA OLD FASHIONED

YIELD: 1 SERVING / ACTIVE TIME: 2 MINUTES / TOTAL TIME: 2 MINUTES

The taste of the forest, quite literally. Yoshihiro Narisawa adds a complex woody tone to the whisky by infusing a fistful of wood shavings; the infusion hits its peak around the 2-week mark.

1. Place the brown sugar in an Old Fashioned glass and moisten it with the club soda.

2. Add the bitters and ice. Add the Satoyama Hibiki and stir until chilled. Garnish with a slice of yuzu.

SATOYAMA HIBIKI: Add the lindela, oak, and cedar shavings, twigs from a cinnamon tree, and sansho pepper to 1 (750 ml) bottle of Suntory Hibiki Whisky. Steep for about 2 weeks. Strain before using or storing. Garnish with a slice of yuzu.

INGREDIENTS:

2   BAR SPOONS BROWN SUGAR

     CLUB SODA, AS NEEDED

3   DROPS VANILLA BITTERS

1½   OZ. SATOYAMA HIBIKI (SEE RECIPE)

APOTHECARY GIMLET

YIELD: 1 SERVING / ACTIVE TIME: 2 MINUTES / TOTAL TIME: 2 MINUTES

Why would you use lime when you have sudachi, a tart, green Japanese citrus fruit? And if you ever find shell ginger leaf, it adds a wonderful green note that elevates a Gimlet.

1. Use a mortar and pestle to grind the berries and leaf.

2. Add the mixture to a Boston shaker. Add the remaining ingredients and ice, shake vigorously, and strain into a cocktail glass.

3. Garnish with a sudachi wheel and shell ginger leaf.

INGREDIENTS:

20	JUNIPER BERRIES
¼	SHELL GINGER LEAF
2	OZ. OKUHIDA VODKA
⅔	OZ. FRESH SUDACHI JUICE
2	BAR SPOONS SIMPLE SYRUP

LAPSANG SOUCHONG

YIELD: 1 SERVING / **ACTIVE TIME:** 2 MINUTES / **TOTAL TIME:** 2 MINUTES

" I got tired of being a sommelier, a middleman between the creator and the customer," says Yushi Ando, who once poured wines at Joël Robuchon's restaurant in Tokyo. Ando wanted to create flavors, so in 2018 he opened The Standard. His menu has a section for drinks made using a coffee siphon, including this smoky, resinous tea cocktail.

1. Place all of the liquids into the bowl of a coffee siphon. Place the remaining ingredients in the upper chamber, and gently brew for 2 minutes. Pour into a Hot Toddy glass.

NOTE: Only metric measurements are used in this recipe, to honor its precision.

INGREDIENTS:

60	ML GIN
11	ML CALVADOS
15	ML SIMPLE SYRUP
180	ML WATER
13	G APPLEWOOD CHIPS
11	G ALMONDS
8	G ORGANIC LOOSE-LEAF LAPSANG SOUCHONG
1	LEMON PEEL
1	ORANGE PEEL
1	SLICE APPLE
1	PINCH FRESH ROSEMARY

SENCHA GIN TONIC

YIELD: 1 SERVING / **ACTIVE TIME:** 2 MINUTES / **TOTAL TIME:** 2 MINUTES

The Sencha Gin Tonic has become a modern Japanese classic, but no one makes it better than the bartenders at Mixology Salon. Owner Shuzo Nagumo says it's important to use fukamushi ("deep-steamed") tea, which is sweeter, deeper, and smoother than ordinary sencha. And skip the citrus garnish, it clashes with the tea.

1. Place three rounded-off ice cubes in a tumbler. Rinse the cubes with the club soda and strain.

2. Pour the Sencha Gin evenly around the glass and between the cubes. Add the tonic, making sure to pour onto the gin, not the ice, and gently stir.

SENCHA GIN: Place 1 tablespoon of loose-leaf sencha tea in 1 (750 ml) bottle of gin and steep for 1 day. Strain before using or storing in the refrigerator. Nagumo recommends Bombay Sapphire, Tanqueray, or Roku, and says to avoid gins with dominant citrus notes.

INGREDIENTS:

CLUB SODA, AS NEEDED

1 OZ. SENCHA GIN (SEE RECIPE)

2.8 OZ. FEVER-TREE TONIC WATER

ROASTED RUM MANHATTAN

YIELD: 1 SERVING / **ACTIVE TIME**: 2 MINUTES / **TOTAL TIME**: 2 MINUTES

Two long-aged spirits, two vermouths, and some roasted green tea make for an after-dinner sipper with a long and layered palate.

1. Add all of the ingredients to a tasting glass and stir without ice. Add the mixture to a mixing glass, add ice, and stir once.

2. Strain into a cocktail glass and garnish with a griottine or black cherry.

HOUJICHA RUM: Place 1 tablespoon of loose-leaf houjicha tea in 1 (750 ml) bottle of Ron Zacapa Centenario 23 Rum and let steep overnight. Strain before using or storing.

INGREDIENTS:

- 1½ OZ. HOUJICHA RUM (SEE RECIPE)
- 1 BAR SPOON DANIEL BOUJU XO COGNAC
- ½ OZ. CARPANO ANTICA FORMULA SWEET VERMOUTH
- 1 BAR SPOON CARPANO PUNT E MES VERMOUTH

MONSIEUR L'OSIER

YIELD: 1 SERVING / **ACTIVE TIME:** 2 MINUTES / **TOTAL TIME:** 2 MINUTES

The vivid green color is a throwback, but the taste is timeless. .

1. Add all of the ingredients to a cocktail shaker with ice, shake vigorously, and strain into a cocktail glass.

INGREDIENTS:

1⅓ OZ. GIN

2 BAR SPOONS GREEN TEA LIQUEUR

2 BAR SPOONS FRESH LIME JUICE

MISTER NINE

YIELD: 1 SERVING / *ACTIVE TIME:* 2 MINUTES / **TOTAL TIME:** 2 MINUTES

In the postwar years, the Golden Gai district was a warren of brothels and black-market shops, but the prostitutes left long ago and bartenders moved in. For cocktail fans, the pick of the bunch is Suzu Bar, opened in 2014 by a family that runs the tonkatsu restaurant Suzuya in a nearby red-light district. The signature bar snack is, naturally, a tonkatsu sandwich.

1. Build the cocktail in an Old Fashioned glass containing one large cube of ice, and garnish with the bay leaf.

JASMINE-INFUSED GIN: Combine 1 teaspoon of loose-leaf jasmine tea with 700 ml of gin and steep for 1 minute. Strain before using or storing.

INGREDIENTS:

1 OZ. JASMINE-INFUSED GIN (SEE RECIPE)

½ OZ. BOURBON

½ OZ. ST-GERMAIN

POTATO STOCKING

YIELD: 1 SERVING / **ACTIVE TIME:** 2 MINUTES / **TOTAL TIME:** 2 MINUTES

This clever riff on the Silk Stocking calls for sweet potato shochu where the tequila usually goes, and amazake in place of the cream. Creator Katsuyoshi Chikazawa says the Moriizou brand of shochu works best, but any quality potato shochu will do.

1. Add all of the ingredients to a cocktail shaker with ice, shake vigorously, and double strain into a coupe.

INGREDIENTS:

- 1 OZ. SWEET POTATO SHOCHU
- ¾ OZ. WHITE CRÈME DE CACAO
- ⅓ OZ. AMAZAKE
- 1 DASH LUXARDO

L.I.T.

YIELD: 1 SERVING / **ACTIVE TIME:** 2 MINUTES / **TOTAL TIME:** 2 MINUTES

Sure, it's catnip for tourists, but the L.I.T. (Lost In Translation) cocktail is also a great low-alcohol option in the Cosmopolitan family. Beverage manager Yasukazu Yokota says he wanted to create something with the same sweet-sour balance as the movie, much of which was filmed in this hotel.

1. Add all of the ingredients to a cocktail shaker with ice, shake vigorously, and strain into a cocktail glass.

INGREDIENTS:

1⅓	OZ. DAIGINJO SAKE
⅔	OZ. CRANBERRY JUICE
2	BAR SPOONS PEACH LIQUEUR
2	BAR SPOONS SAKURA LIQUEUR
2	BAR SPOONS FRESH LIME JUICE

TAIKOH

YIELD: 1 SERVING / **ACTIVE TIME:** 2 MINUTES / **TOTAL TIME:** 2 MINUTES

Nobuo Abe was running Bar Capri at the Hotel New Otani when the sister-in-law of a famous tea master asked him to create a cocktail for a conference she was organizing there. He combined three of the most auspicious Japanese ingredients—matcha, sake, gold leaf—into something light, sweet, bitter, and delicately tart. The tea master gave the drink its name, which means "aroma of moss."

1. Add all of the ingredients to a cocktail shaker with ice, shake vigorously, and strain into an Old Fashioned glass filled with ice.

2. Garnish with the edible gold leaf.

INGREDIENTS:

1⅓ OZ. SAKE

¾ OZ. GREEN TEA LIQUEUR

1 BAR SPOON MATCHA

2 BAR SPOONS FRESH SUDACHI OR LIME JUICE

SHUNGYO

YIELD: 1 SERVING / **ACTIVE TIME:** 2 MINUTES / **TOTAL TIME:** 2 MINUTES

Back in the 1980s, Kazuo Uyeda would create seasonal menus featuring drinks of varying strengths. This one from the fall of 1982 was filed under Strong. The name means "spring dawn"; hence the cherry blossom petal garnish.

1. Add all of the ingredients to a mixing glass with ice, stir until chilled, and strain into a cocktail glass.

2. Garnish with a cherry blossom petal.

INGREDIENTS:

1	OZ. SMIRNOFF VODKA
½	OZ. SAKE
1	BAR SPOON GREEN TEA LIQUEUR

THE TIME

YIELD: 1 SERVING / **ACTIVE TIME**: 2 MINUTES / **TOTAL TIME**: 2 MINUTES

In 2017, the Imperial Hotel held a staff contest to design a cocktail for Frank Lloyd Wright's 150th birthday. The great architect had designed an earlier incarnation of the hotel, and remnants of his work decorate the hotel's storied Old Imperial Bar. Chief bartender Nobuaki Sogawa beat more than 30 rivals with a superb recipe combining American and Japanese ingredients for a tart, juicy cousin of the Manhattan.

1. Add all of the ingredients to a cocktail shaker with ice, shake vigorously, and strain into a cocktail glass.

2. Garnish with red and green ume and gold powder.

*Sogawa sprays the ume garnish with gold powder. When he places it in the drink, the gold floats to the surface.

NOTE: Only metric measurements are used in this recipe, to honor its precision.

INGREDIENTS:

- 18 ML WOODFORD RESERVE BOURBON
- 12 ML DRY SAKE
- 30 ML UMENOYADO ARAGOSHI UMESHU

TRENCH 75

YIELD: 1 SERVING / ACTIVE TIME: 2 MINUTES / TOTAL TIME: 2 MINUTES

Bar Trench's riff on a French 75 was intended as a seasonal special but proved too popular to drop.

1. Place the gin, lemon juice, and Honey Syrup in a cocktail shaker with ice, shake vigorously, and strain into a coupe. Top with the sake and garnish with a lime wheel.

HONEY SYRUP: Place 1 cup of honey and 1 cup of water in a saucepan and warm over medium heat, stirring until emulsified. Remove from heat and let cool before using or storing.

INGREDIENTS:

1   OZ. NIKKA COFFEY GIN

½   OZ. FRESH LEMON JUICE

2   BAR SPOONS HONEY SYRUP (SEE RECIPE)

1   OZ. SHICHIKEN SPARKLING SAKE

BAMBOO LEAF MARTINI

YIELD: 1 SERVING / ACTIVE TIME: 2 MINUTES / TOTAL TIME: 2 MINUTES

Can you really call a cocktail a "martini" if it has whisky in it? One thing is certain, this is a distinctly Japanese cocktail.

1. Take the bamboo leaf and cut a small incision along the axis of the leaf. Take one end of the leaf and pull it through the incision to make a "cup." Place the leaf cup in a cocktail glass.

2. Fill a mixing glass with ice, add white crème de menthe, and swirl to rinse; discard the excess.

3. Add the whisky, water, and bamboo leaf syrup. Stir to chill and strain into the leaf cup in the cocktail glass.

4. Squeeze a small wedge of yuzu lightly outside the leaf cup to add an accent to the cocktail.

INGREDIENTS:

1	BAMBOO LEAF
	WHITE CRÈME DE MENTHE, TO RINSE
1⅓	OZ. TAKETSURU PURE MALT WHISKY
⅔	OZ. SOFT WATER
1	TEASPOON BAMBOO LEAF SYRUP

GLASSWARE
COCKTAIL GLASS

GARNISH
SMALL YUZU WEDGE

TATAMI COCKTAIL

YIELD: 1 SERVING / ACTIVE TIME: 2 MINUTES / TOTAL TIME: 2 MINUTES

Tatami is a type of mat used as flooring in Japan, which is where you might end up after too many of these delicious drinks.

1. Combine the the pineapple juice, simple syrup, apricot brandy, and lemon juice in a cocktail shaker and set aside.

2. Combine the whisky and crème de cacao in a mixing glass and set aside.

3. Dip the lemongrass stalks into the bottle whisky and set aside.

4. Add ice to the shaker, shake lightly, and double strain into a cocktail glass.

5. Carefully float the liquid in the mixing glass on top.

6. Ignite the lemongrass and shake to extinguish. Place the singed lemongrass stalks in the cocktail and garnish with a twist of lemon.

INGREDIENTS:

1	OZ. PINEAPPLE JUICE
⅓	OZ. SIMPLE SYRUP
1	TEASPOON APRICOT BRANDY
1	TEASPOON FRESH LEMON JUICE
½	OZ. SUNTORY YAMAZAKI 12-YEAR WHISKY
1	TEASPOON DARK CRÈME DE CACAO
2	(3 TO 4 INCH) STALKS LEMONGRASS

RAINY SEASON

YIELD: 1 SERVING / **ACTIVE TIME:** 2 MINUTES / **TOTAL TIME:** 2 MINUTES

Pickled plums, umeboshi, add a sweet tartness to this drink that is brighter than the name suggests.

1. Combine the whisky, lemon juice, and cucumber in a blender and puree until smooth. Add the umeboshi and blend some more; add the simple syrup and puree to incorporate.

2. Add a small handful of ice and puree; repeat, adding ice and pureeing until achieving the consistency of a smoothie.

3. Spoon into a Nick & Nora glass and garnish with a sprig of mint.

INGREDIENTS:

1⅓ OZ. SUNTORY HIBIKI
     12-YEAR WHISKY

1   TEASPOON FRESH
     LEMON JUICE

4   CUCUMBER SLICES

½   TEASPOON UMEBOSHI

⅓   OZ. SIMPLE SYRUP

JAPANESE RED PINE HIGHBALL

YIELD: 1 SERVING / **ACTIVE TIME:** 2 MINUTES / **TOTAL TIME:** 2 MINUTES

Kyogi is a paper-thin sheet of wood commonly used to serve food.

1. Using a bar spoon, gently muddle the mint and crème de menthe in a wine glass; discard most of the liqueur.

2. Roll up a sheet of kyogi and insert it in the glass, so that it lines the inside; pull one end up so it sticks out of the glass.

3. Place two large ice cubes in the glass, add the whisky, and top up with the soda water.

4. Garnish with a bamboo leaf, if desired.

INGREDIENTS:

FRESH MINT LEAVES, PREFERABLY JAPANESE

1 SPLASH WHITE CRÈME DE MENTHE

1 SHEET KYOGI

1½ OZ. SUNTORY YAMAZAKI DISTILLER'S RESERVE WHISKY

SODA WATER, TO TOP

GLASSWARE
RIESLING GLASS

GARNISH
BAMBOO LEAF (OPTIONAL)

GREEN BREEZE

YIELD: 1 SERVING / **ACTIVE TIME:** 2 MINUTES / **TOTAL TIME:** 2 MINUTES

The name of this drink delivers, thanks to the multiple sources of mint and the refreshing bubbles from the tonic and soda.

1. Using a bar spoon, gently muddle the mint and crème de menthe in a conical highball glass; discard the liqueur.

2. Carve an ice sphere; the diameter should be such that the ice sphere sits in the glass without touching the bottom.

3. Add the whisky, then just enough tonic water so that the mixture covers the bottom of the ice sphere.

4. Top up with the soda water. Spank a few mint leaves and use as a garnish.

INGREDIENTS:

	FRESH MINT LEAVES
1	SPLASH WHITE CRÈME DE MENTHE
1	OZ. SUNTORY HAKUSHU 12-YEAR WHISKY
	TONIC WATER
	SODA WATER, TO TOP

GRAIN MARKET

YIELD: 1 SERVING / **ACTIVE TIME:** 2 MINUTES / **TOTAL TIME:** 2 MINUTES

Blackish-purple in color, and sometimes almost black, Kyoho grapes have large seeds, juicy flesh, and a high sugar content. If you cannot source them, Concord grapes are a suitable substitute.

1. In a cocktail shaker, crush the grapes with a muddler.

2. Add the whisky and Madeira, along with ice, shake vigorously, and double strain into a cocktail glass.

INGREDIENTS:

6–7 KYOHO GRAPES (OR CONCORD GRAPES)

1½ OZ. NIKKA COFFEY GRAIN WHISKY

⅔ OZ. MEDIUM-SWEET MADEIRA

MAPLE MARRIAGE

Yuzu, a citrus fruit native to parts of Asia, has a distinctive floral flavor. If you cannot source it, a Meyer lemon is a good substitute.

1. Combine the whisky, maple syrup, yuzu juice, and egg white in a cocktail shaker and mix with a hand blender.

2. Add ice to the shaker, shake until frothy, and strain into a coupe.

3. Carefully add the bitters to the foam's surface in a circular pattern; use the tip of a toothpick to connect the droplets.

4. Garnish with a strip of yuzu peel, if desired.

INGREDIENTS:

1⅔ OZ. ICHIRO'S MALT DOUBLE DISTILLERIES WHISKY

⅓ OZ. MAPLE SYRUP

⅓ OZ. YUZU JUICE

1 EGG WHITE

8 DROPS GINGER BITTERS

FOREST FLAVOR

YIELD: 1 SERVING / ACTIVE TIME: 2 MINUTES / TOTAL TIME: 2 MINUTES

If you are striving for authenticity when making this drink, use a Japanese mortar, a suribachi, and a wooden pestle, a surikogi.

1. Thoroughly muddle the sage leaves with a mortar and pestle. Add the whisky and muddle some more; add the honey and lime juice and muddle some more.

2. Transfer to a cocktail shaker, shake with ice to chill, and double strain into a highball glass over ice.

3. Top up with the club soda, stir gently, and garnish with a sage leaf.

INGREDIENTS:

4   FRESH SAGE LEAVES

1½   OZ. SUNTORY HAKUSHU DISTILLER'S RESERVE WHISKY

⅓   OZ. HONEY

⅓   OZ. FRESH LIME JUICE

      CLUB SODA, TO TOP

JAPONISM

A guinomi is a sake cup of a specific size, larger than others, that perfectly suits this cocktail. Shiro-an is a sweet white bean paste.

1. In a bowl, whisk the egg white until foamy.

2. In another bowl, beat the yolk, shiro-an, and matcha powder until combined.

3. Add the egg white foam to the yolk mixture and whisk a bit more to incorporate. Add the whisky and sake and whisk to incorporate.

4. Transfer to a cocktail shaker, shake with ice, and double strain into a guinomi.

INGREDIENTS:

1   EGG, SEPARATED

1   OZ. SHIRO-AN*

2   TEASPOONS MATCHA POWDER

1½ OZ. FUJI-SANROKU 50° NON-CHILL FILTERED WHISKY

⅔   OZ. DRY SAKE

AROMATIC CHICHIBU

YIELD: 1 SERVING / ACTIVE TIME: 2 MINUTES / TOTAL TIME: 2 MINUTES

Here's an innovative way to keep a cocktail cold. You might want to practice the presentation a few times before wowing guests.

1. Combine all of the ingredients in a mixing glass filled with ice, stir, and strain into a Burgundy wineglass.

2. Fill a stemless cocktail glass with crushed ice and place the bowl of the wineglass on the bed of ice.

INGREDIENTS:

1⅓	OZ. ICHIRO'S MALT CHICHIBU THE PEATED CASK STRENGTH WHISKY
⅔	OZ. BÉNÉDICTINE
⅓	OZ. SWEET VERMOUTH
⅓	OZ. FRESH BLACK CURRANT PUREE
1	TEASPOON FERNET-BRANCA

APPENDIX

BASIC RECIPES

STOCKS

Depending on dietary needs, ingredients on hand, and personal preference, it is always good to have solid stock recipes close by.

TIPS:
1. Stocks can stay in a freezer for up to six months.

2. Don't be intimidated by large quantities of stock, as the same amount of time is required, it is always best to make a larger quantity and save some for the future.

VEAL, BEEF, OR LAMB STOCK

YIELD: 6 QUARTS / **ACTIVE TIME:** 30 MINUTES / **TOTAL TIME:** 6 TO 7 HOURS

Veal bones make a smoother, lighter stock than pure beef bones. However, beef bones are a more readily available (and cheaper) option. If you are making a lamb stock, try to use half beef or veal bones and half lamb bones, as lamb bones provide a pungent, often overpowering flavor.

1. Preheat oven to 350°F.

2. Lay the bones on a flat baking tray, place in the oven, and cook for 30 to 45 minutes, until they are golden brown. Remove and set aside.

3. Meanwhile, in a large stockpot, add the oil and warm over low heat. Add the vegetables and cook until any additional moisture has evaporated. This allows the flavor of the vegetables to become concentrated.

4. Add the water to the stockpot. Add the bones, aromatics, peppercorns, salt, and tomato paste to the stockpot, raise heat to high, and bring to a boil.

5. Reduce heat so that the stock simmers and cook for a minimum of 2 hours. Skim fat and impurities from the top as the stock cooks. Cook until the desired flavor is achieved, around 4 to 5 hours.

6. When the stock is finished cooking, strain through a fine strainer or cheesecloth. Place the stock in the refrigerator to chill.

7. Once cool, skim the fat layer from the top and discard. Use immediately, refrigerate, or freeze.

INGREDIENTS:

10	LBS. VEAL, BEEF, OR LAMB BONES
½	CUP VEGETABLE OIL
1	LEEK, TRIMMED AND CAREFULLY WASHED, CUT INTO 1-INCH PIECES
1	LARGE YELLOW ONION, UNPEELED, ROOT CLEANED, CUT INTO 1-INCH PIECES
2	LARGE CARROTS, PEELED AND CUT INTO 1-INCH PIECES
1	CELERY STALK WITH LEAVES, CUT INTO 1-INCH PIECES
10	QUARTS WATER
8	FRESH SPRIGS PARSLEY
5	FRESH SPRIGS THYME
2	BAY LEAVES
1	TEASPOON PEPPERCORNS
1	TEASPOON SALT
1	CUP TOMATO PASTE

CHICKEN STOCK

YIELD: 6 QUARTS / **ACTIVE TIME:** 20 MINUTES / **TOTAL TIME:** 6 TO 7 HOURS

A good homemade chicken stock should be good enough to eat on its own. As with most stocks, the longer they cook, the more flavorful they become, so feel free to increase the cooking time. This recipe will work with most poultry.

1. Preheat the oven to 350°F.

2. Lay the bones on a flat baking tray, place in the oven, and cook for 30 to 45 minutes, until they are golden brown. Remove and set aside.

3. Meanwhile, in a large stockpot, add the oil and warm over low heat. Add the vegetables and cook until any additional moisture has evaporated. This allows the flavor of the vegetables to become concentrated.

4. Add the water to the stockpot. Add the chicken carcasses and/or stewing pieces, the aromatics, the peppercorns, and the salt to the stockpot, raise heat to high, and bring to a boil.

5. Reduce heat so that the stock simmers and cook for a minimum of 2 hours. Skim fat and impurities from the top as the stock cooks. Cook until the desired flavor is achieved, around 4 to 5 hours.

6. When the stock is finished cooking, strain through a fine strainer or cheesecloth. Place stock in the refrigerator to chill.

7. Once cool, skim the fat layer from the top and discard. Use immediately, refrigerate, or freeze.

INGREDIENTS:

10	LBS. CHICKEN CARCASSES AND/OR STEWING CHICKEN PIECES
½	CUP VEGETABLE OIL
1	LEEK, TRIMMED AND CAREFULLY WASHED, CUT INTO 1-INCH PIECES
1	LARGE YELLOW ONION, UNPEELED, ROOT CLEANED, CUT INTO 1-INCH PIECES
2	LARGE CARROTS, CUT INTO 1-INCH PIECES
1	CELERY STALK WITH LEAVES, CUT INTO 1-INCH PIECES
10	QUARTS WATER
8	FRESH SPRIGS PARSLEY
5	FRESH SPRIGS THYME
2	BAY LEAVES
1	TEASPOON PEPPERCORNS
1	TEASPOON SALT

FISH STOCK

YIELD: 6 QUARTS / **ACTIVE TIME:** 20 MINUTES / **TOTAL TIME:** 3 HOURS AND 30 MINUTES

White fish works best for this recipe, as other types of fish tend to add extra oil to the stock and overpower the delicate balance of flavors. However, if you're making a thickened or creamed soup, you can stray from that recommendation, as salmon stock is divine in those types of dishes.

1. In a large stockpot, add the oil and warm over low heat. Add the vegetables and cook until any additional moisture has evaporated. This will allow the flavor of the vegetables to become concentrated.

2. Add the whitefish bodies, the aromatics, the peppercorns, the salt, and the water to the pot.

3. Raise heat to high and bring to a boil. Reduce heat so that the stock simmers and cook for a minimum of 2 hours. Skim fat and impurities from the top as the stock cooks. As for when to stop cooking the stock, let the flavor be the judge, typcally 2 to 3 hours total.

4. When the stock is finished cooking, strain through a fine strainer or cheesecloth. Place the stock in the refrigerator to chill.

5. Once cool, skim the fat layer from the top and discard. Use immediately, refrigerate, or freeze.

INGREDIENTS:

½ CUP VEGETABLE OIL

1 LEEK, TRIMMED AND CAREFULLY WASHED, CUT INTO 1-INCH PIECES

1 LARGE YELLOW ONION, UNPEELED, ROOT CLEANED, CUT INTO 1-INCH PIECES

2 LARGE CARROTS, CUT INTO 1-INCH PIECES

1 CELERY STALK WITH LEAVES, CUT INTO 1-INCH PIECES

10 LBS. WHITEFISH BODIES

8 FRESH SPRIGS PARSLEY

5 FRESH SPRIGS THYME

2 BAY LEAVES

1 TEASPOON PEPPERCORNS

1 TEASPOON SALT

10 QUARTS WATER

VEGETABLE STOCK

YIELD: 6 CUPS / **ACTIVE TIME:** 20 MINUTES / **TOTAL TIME:** 3 HOURS

This stock is an excellent way to use up leftover vegetable trimmings you're loath to throw away. However, it's best to avoid starches like potatoes and colorful vegetables like beets, as these will make the stock cloudy or add an unwanted tint. This stock is an ideal replacement for any of the meat stocks in this book.

1. In a large stockpot, add the oil and the vegetables and cook over low heat until any additional moisture has evaporated. This will allow the flavor of the vegetables to become concentrated.

2. Add the aromatics, water, peppercorns, and salt. Raise heat to high and bring to a boil. Reduce heat so that the soup simmers and cook for 2 hours. Skim fat and impurities from the top as the stock cooks.

3. When the stock is finished cooking, strain through a fine strainer or cheesecloth. Place the stock in the refrigerator to chill.

4. Once cool, skim the fat layer from the top and discard. Use immediately, refrigerate, or freeze.

INGREDIENTS:

2	TABLESPOONS VEGETABLE OIL
2	LARGE LEEKS, TRIMMED AND CAREFULLY WASHED
2	LARGE CARROTS, PEELED AND SLICED
2	CELERY STALKS, SLICED
2	LARGE ONIONS, SLICED
3	GARLIC CLOVES, UNPEELED AND SMASHED
2	FRESH SPRIGS PARSLEY
2	FRESH SPRIGS THYME
1	BAY LEAF
8	CUPS WATER
½	TEASPOON BLACK PEPPERCORNS
	SALT, TO TASTE

MUSHROOM STOCK

YIELD: 6 CUPS / **ACTIVE TIME**: 20 MINUTES / **TOTAL TIME**: 3 TO 4 HOURS

You can use any mushroom you have on hand in this stock, so feel free to tailor your choice to the dish you have in mind. The trick to a great mushroom stock is to cook down the mushrooms beforehand to reduce their liquid. This cuts down on cooking time and helps concentrate the flavors.

1. In a large stockpot, add the oil and mushrooms and cook over low heat for 30 to 40 minutes. The longer you cook the mushrooms, the better.

2. Add the onion, garlic, bay leaves, peppercorns, and thyme and cook for 5 minutes.

3. Add the wine, cook for 5 minutes, and then add the water.

4. Bring to a boil, reduce heat so that the stock simmers, and cook for 2 to 3 hours, until you are pleased with the taste.

INGREDIENTS:

2   TABLESPOONS VEGETABLE OIL

3   LBS. MUSHROOMS

1   ONION, CHOPPED

1   GARLIC, MINCED

2   BAY LEAVES

1   TABLESPOON BLACK PEPPERCORNS

2   FRESH SPRIGS THYME

1   CUP WHITE WINE

8   CUPS WATER

ANCHOVY STOCK

YIELD: 3 QUARTS / **ACTIVE TIME:** 15 MINUTES / **TOTAL TIME:** 2 HOURS AND 30 MINUTES

With three ingredients from the sea, this stock has a deep tidal umami that is perfect for seafood and vegetable dishes.

1. In a stock pot, combine the water, kombu, mushrooms, and anchovies and let stand covered at room temperature for 1 hour.

2. Uncover, bring to a simmer, and cook for 45 minutes to 1 hour; if cooked for too long, the stock will turn bitter.

3. Turn off the heat, add the bonito flakes, and let steep for 15 minutes.

4. Using a cheesecloth or superfine strainer, strain the stock and cool.

5. Refrigerate for up to 3 days.

INGREDIENTS:

1	GALLON COLD WATER
2	8-INCH KOMBU SQUARES
5	DRIED SHIITAKE MUSHROOMS
10-12	DRIED LARGE ANCHOVIES, HEADLESS AND GUTTED
2	CUPS BONITO FLAKES

PASTAS

Store-bought pasta is easy, but making your own is much tastier, and fun. If you have the time, be sure to include fresh noodles in the myriad recipes that call for them in this book.

CHINESE EGG NOODLES

YIELD: ABOUT 1 LB. / **ACTIVE TIME:** 45 MINUTES / **TOTAL TIME:** 2 HOURS

This noodle is a staple of recipes like lo mein and chow mein, as well as many Asian soups. It is incredibly easy to make and, of course, delicious.

1. Mix the flour and salt together in a large bowl. Add the eggs and mix until a floury dough forms. Add the 3 tablespoons of water and continue to mix until you almost cannot see any remaining traces of flour. If you find, even after adding the water, that your dough is still very floury, add more water, 1 tablespoon at a time, and continue mixing it with your hands until the dough starts coming together more easily. Start kneading the dough in the bowl with your dominant hand. Continue kneading in the bowl until a smooth ball forms; this may take about 10 minutes. Wrap the dough tightly in plastic wrap and let rest at room temperature for 40 to 50 minutes to allow the gluten in the dough to relax.

2. Unwrap the dough and place it on a lightly floured work surface. Using a rolling pin, begin "beating" the dough, turning it over after every 10 whacks or so. Continue doing this for 6 minutes. Then, shape the dough into a ball, cover with plastic wrap, and let rest at room temperature for another 30 minutes.

3. Return the dough to the work surface (no need to flour again). Cut it in half and wrap one half in plastic wrap to prevent drying. Roll the other half into a large, thin sheet about twice the length and breadth of the length of your rolling pin (you should be able to almost see your hand through it). Lightly flour both sides of the sheet of dough and then fold the sheet of dough twice over itself to create a three-layered fold (like a letter).

4. Using a very sharp knife, slice across the roll into evenly spaced strands. You can make them as thin or thick as you'd like. As you cut the dough, be sure to hold the knife perpendicular to the surface and lightly push the newly cut strip away from the roll with the knife to completely separate it. Continue until you have cut the entire roll, then lightly dust the slivered noodles with flour to prevent any sticking. Transfer the noodles to a parchment-lined baking sheet, shaking off any excess flour if necessary. You can leave them nested or unspool them according to your preference, as they will unravel and straighten once boiled. Repeat with the remaining dough. Cook in a pot of boiling, salted water for 3 to 4 minutes, or cover and refrigerate for up to 1 day.

INGREDIENTS:

2   CUPS ALL-PURPOSE FLOUR, PLUS MORE FOR DUSTING

1   TEASPOON SALT, PLUS MORE FOR THE PASTA WATER

2   LARGE EGGS, LIGHTLY BEATEN

3   TABLESPOONS WATER, PLUS MORE AS NEEDED

UDON NOODLES

Japanese udon noodles are best when homemade, as the packaged versions lack some of the chewiness and bulk of the fresh variety.

1. Stir the water and salt together in a small bowl until the salt dissolves. Put the flour in a large bowl and make a well in the center. Add the salted water in a stream while stirring the flour. Once all the water has been added, begin working the dough with your hands to incorporate all the flour. If the dough is too dry, add water in 1-teaspoon increments until the dough sticks together.

2. Transfer the dough to a work surface that you have dusted very lightly with the potato starch or cornstarch. Knead the dough with the palm of your dominant hand, turning it 45 degrees with each pressing, until the dough becomes uniformly smooth and slowly springs back when pressed by a finger, about 10 minutes. Cover the dough tightly with plastic wrap and let rest for 1 to 2 hours to relax the gluten.

3. Cut the dough into two pieces. Set one on a lightly dusted work surface and wrap the other in plastic wrap to prevent drying. Pat the piece of dough into a rectangular shape and, using a lightly dusted rolling pin, roll the dough into a ⅛-inch-thick rectangle. Lightly dust the dough and then fold it twice over itself to create a three-layered fold, as you would a letter.

4. Using a very sharp knife, slice the roll into ⅛-inch-wide strands. As you cut the dough, be sure to hold the knife perpendicular to the surface and lightly push the newly cut strip away from the roll with the knife to completely separate it. Continue until you have cut the entire roll, then lightly dust the slivered pasta to prevent any sticking. Transfer the noodles to a parchment-lined baking sheet, shaking off any excess starch if necessary. Repeat with the remaining dough. Udon noodles quickly turn brittle and break when handled, so cook as soon as you finish making them.

5. To cook the udon, cook for about 1 minute in a pot of boiling, salted water, until they are tender but still chewy.

INGREDIENTS:

- ¼ CUP WARM WATER, PLUS MORE AS NEEDED
- 1 TEASPOON FINE SEA SALT
- 2¼ CUPS CAKE FLOUR OR FINELY MILLED "00" FLOUR

  POTATO STARCH OR CORNSTARCH, FOR DUSTING

DUMPLING WRAPPERS

All of these doughs are used in recipes in this book, but you can fill them with anything you like.

BASIC DUMPLING WRAPPERS

YIELD: 32 WRAPPERS / **ACTIVE TIME:** 35 MINUTES / **TOTAL TIME:** 2 HOURS AND 35 MINUTES

Dumplings are some of the most versatile foods on the planet. Steam them, boil them, deep-fry or panfry them—the results will have your guests coming back for seconds (and thirds).

1. Place the flour in the mixing bowl of a stand mixer fitted with the paddle attachment. With the mixer running on low, add the water in a steady stream. Beat until the dough just holds together, adding water in 1-teaspoon increments if needed.

2. Place the dough on a flour-dusted work surface and knead until smooth and elastic, about 5 minutes. Wrap tightly in plastic wrap and let rest at room temperature for 2 hours.

3. Cut a resealable freezer bag at the seams so that you have two squares of plastic. Place the dough on a flour-dusted work surface and cut it in half. Cover one half with plastic wrap and roll the other into a 1-inch-thick log. Cut the log into 16 pieces. Dust each piece with flour, cover with plastic wrap, and press down gently until the rounds are ¼ inch thick.

4. You will want the filling prepared before starting on this step, as the dough sticks together better when it has not been exposed to the air for too long. Place the disks between the two squares of plastic and press down with a rolling pin until they are ⅛ inch thick. Transfer to a flour-dusted work surface and fill the wrappers as desired or freeze, in layers separated by parchment paper, for up to 1 month.

INGREDIENTS:

2   CUPS ALL-PURPOSE FLOUR, PLUS MORE FOR DUSTING

¾   CUP JUST-BOILED WATER, PLUS MORE AS NEEDED

CRYSTAL DUMPLING WRAPPERS

YIELD: 18 WRAPPERS / **ACTIVE TIME:** 35 MINUTES / **TOTAL TIME:** 35 MINUTES

These beautiful dumplings have a limited shelf life, so it's best to have your filling prepared ahead of time.

1. Cut a resealable freezer bag at the seams so that you have two squares of plastic and set aside. Place the wheat starch and cornstarch in a heatproof bowl. Add the boiling water and oil. Using a rubber spatula, stir the ingredients until a loose dough forms. Turn the dough out onto a work surface dusted with wheat starch and knead until it is smooth and slowly bounces back into place when pressed with a finger. This should take about 10 minutes.

2. Roll the dough into a 1½-inch-thick log. Cut it into 18 equal pieces, dust them with wheat starch, and cover with plastic wrap. Press down lightly on the pieces to create a disk that is roughly ¼ inch thick. Place the disks between the two squares of plastic and press down with a rolling pin until they are ⅛ inch thick. Dredge any disks that feel sticky with wheat starch, place on a parchment-lined baking sheet, and fill as desired.

INGREDIENTS:

1	CUP WHEAT STARCH, PLUS MORE FOR DUSTING
½	CUP CORNSTARCH
1¼	CUPS BOILING WATER
1	TABLESPOON GRAPESEED OR SAFFLOWER OIL

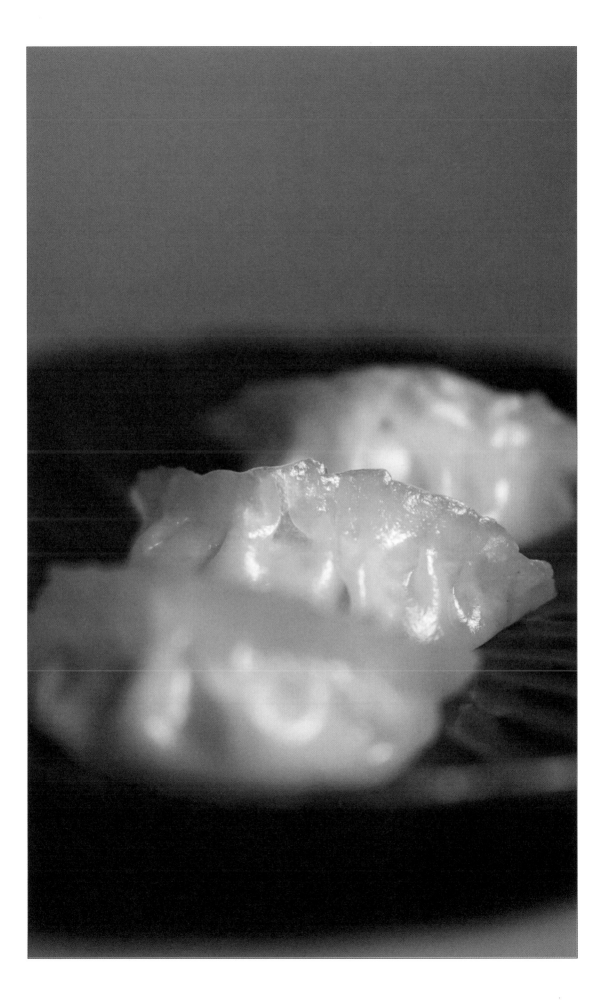

WONTON WRAPPERS

YIELD: 48 WRAPPERS / **ACTIVE TIME:** 1 HOUR / **TOTAL TIME:** 3 HOURS

Wonton wrappers can be used to make wontons or other preparations that require a thin, delicate wrapper. They can also be fried for a crisp, satisfying appetizer or garnish.

1. Place the water, egg, and salt in a measuring cup and whisk to combine. Place the flour in the bowl of a stand mixer fitted with the paddle attachment. With the mixer running on low speed, add the egg mixture in a steady stream and beat until the dough holds together. Add water or flour in ½-teaspoon increments if the dough is too dry or too wet, respectively. Fit the mixer with the dough hook and knead at medium speed until the dough is soft, smooth, and springs back quickly when pressed with a finger, about 10 minutes. Cover the dough tightly with plastic wrap and let rest for 2 hours.

2. Cut the dough into three even pieces. Working with one piece at a time (cover the others tightly in plastic), shape the dough into a ball. Place the dough on a flour-dusted work surface and roll it out until it is ½ inch thick. Feed the dough through a pasta maker, adjusting the setting to reduce the thickness with each pass, until the dough is thin enough that you can see your hand through it. Place the sheets on a parchment-lined baking sheet.

3. Dust a work surface with cornstarch and cut the sheets into as many 4-inch squares or 3-inch rounds as possible. Pile the cut wrappers on top of each other and fill as desired, or cover in plastic wrap and refrigerate for up to 3 days.

INGREDIENTS:

- ¼ CUP WATER, PLUS MORE AS NEEDED
- 1 LARGE EGG
- ¾ TEASPOON KOSHER SALT
- 1½ CUPS ALL-PURPOSE FLOUR, PLUS MORE AS NEEDED
- CORNSTARCH, FOR DUSTING

BAOZI WRAPPERS

YIELD: 16 WRAPPERS / **ACTIVE TIME:** 45 MINUTES / **TOTAL TIME:** 1 HOUR AND 30 MINUTES

Baozi reside in the delectable space between steamed buns and potstickers.

1. Place the yeast, water, and oil in a small bowl and let stand until foamy, about 10 minutes.

2. Place the sugar, salt, baking powder, and flours in a food processor and pulse for 15 seconds to combine. With the food processor running on low speed, add the yeast mixture and keep it running until it comes together as a slightly tacky dough. Place the dough on a flour-dusted work surface and knead until it is smooth, about 3 minutes. Place the dough in a bowl greased with vegetable oil, cover with a kitchen towel, and let rise in a naturally warm place until it has doubled in size, about 30 minutes.

3. Place the dough on the flour-dusted work surface, cut it in half, and roll each half into a log. Cut each log into eight pieces. Roll each piece into a 4" circle and fill as desired. Cover the unrolled pieces of dough with a kitchen towel so that they do not dry out. To cook the filled baozi, follow the instructions in Step 3 on page 111.

INGREDIENTS:

1 TABLESPOON INSTANT YEAST

1½ CUPS WATER, AT ROOM TEMPERATURE

¼ CUP VEGETABLE OIL, PLUS MORE AS NEEDED

¼ CUP SUGAR, PLUS 1 TEASPOON

½ TEASPOON KOSHER SALT

4 TEASPOONS BAKING POWDER

2 CUPS ALL-PURPOSE FLOUR, PLUS MORE FOR DUSTING

2 CUPS BREAD FLOUR

GUIDE
TO
INGREDIENTS

Adzuki beans: Loaded with fiber, protein, and antioxidants, these small red beans are grown throughout East Asia and are typically prepared to be sweet, though they are used in both sweet and savory recipes.

Banchan: Literally translated from Korean as "side dishes" this is the collective term used to refer to a wide range of small dishes served alongside a typical Korean meal.

Chinkiang vinegar (also known as Chinese black vinegar): Made from fermented black sticky rice or glutinous rice, and sometimes from a combination of rice with sorghum and wheat, this vinegar is malty, deeply flavorful, a bit sweet, and less acidic than many vinegars.

Dasida powder: Created in Korea during a time of financial hardship, this seasoning powder was meant to impart the flavors of meat and seafood when such ingredients were hard to come by; today it is used to enhance such flavors in recipes.

Doenjang: Similar to miso in that it is made from fermented soybeans and salt, unlike miso this Korean paste does not contain rice or other grains, and its texture more closely resembles that of chunky peanut butter.

Fernbrake (also known as bracken fiddleheads): A spring delicacy in Korea when this fern—colloquially referred to as "beef of the mountain"

for its high protein content—is picked and prepared fresh, it is typically found dried and when used in recipes soaking it is called for; the banchan gosari namul is one of the most common uses for fernbrake.

Fish sauce: Salted and fermented shrimp or krill gives many Southeast Asian dishes their funky umami. Don't let the smell put you off; using it adds a dynamic, and essential, flavor component.

Five spice powder: This Chinese spice blend has been used for centuries and typically contains Szechuan peppercorns, fennel, star anise, cloves, and cinnamon; the blend often also includes other ingredients like ginger, nutmeg, licorice, and orange peel.

Gochukaru: The smoky-sweet spiciness of this chili powder made from sun-dried chilies is one of the defining flavor elements of Korean cuisine, and also contributes to the red coloring of so many dishes.

Gochujang: There's a reason this Korean paste of red chilies, fermented soybeans, and glutinous rice has become so popular of late—it is delicious, not overly spicy, and can be used to punch up the flavor of pretty much anything.

Hoisin sauce: This dark, sweet, and salty ingredient is made from fermented soybean paste mixed with garlic and chilies and is traditionally used in marinades and sauces, particularly in Cantonese-style cooking.

Hondashi powder: This Japanese soup stock powder can be thought of like instant dashi.

Kamaboko: This Japanese seafood product is processed by forming various pureed white fish and flavoring elements into a steamed cake or loaf; it is sliced and eaten both cold and hot.

Kansui powder: If you want to make ramen noodles with the same flavor, texture, and color of those from your favorite restaurant, this is an essential ingredient: a mixture of sodium car-

bonate and potassium carbonate that makes the noodles alkaline.

Kecap manis: Palm sugar or jaggery gives this Indonesian soy sauce its sweet, molasses-like consistency.

Kombu: This edible kelp imparts umami in many Japanese recipes, including dashi.

Lap cheong: Made with pork and pork fat, this Chinese-style of dried, hard sausage is seasoned with rose water, rice wine, and soy sauce.

Maltose: This thick golden syrup, which can become hard at room temperature, is a secret ingredient in traditional Chinese cooking; it is what gives char siu its glossy look.

Masago: Smelt roe; it has an almost sandy texture and a briny flavor.

Michiu rice wine: This style of Chinese cooking wine has about 19.5% alcohol and is most commonly used in poultry dishes.

Mirin: This Japanese rice wine is like sake, but sweeter and with a lower alcohol content.

Miyeok: Also known by its Japanese name, wakame, this edible seaweed has a high content of calcium and iodine; its flavor is slightly sweet and is mostly used in soups and salads.

Mochiko flour: Unlike rice flour, which is made from non-glutinous, long-grain white or brown rice, mochiko flour is made from glutinous short-grain sticky rice.

Oyster sauce: As the name implies, this dark, thick, and savory seasoning sauce is made from oyster extract; the most common brands found in markets also include sugar, thickening agents, and MSG.

Ponzu: This sweet and citrusy Japanese dipping sauce typically includes rice vinegar, mirin, kombu, bonito, soy sauce, and yuzu.

Umeboshi/umezu vinegar: The brine from pickled plums (umeboshi) is mixed with salt and red shiso leaves to make this tart Japanese seasoning.

Shichimi togarashi: Colloquially known as "Japanese seven spice," this earthy and spicy seasoning typically contains sansho pepper, hemp seeds, sesame seeds (white and/or black), ginger, dried yuzu peel, red chili pepper, and nori.

Somyeon: Also known by its Japanese name, somen, these thin wheat flour noodles are pleasantly chewy when cooked.

Tare: Meaning "seasoning" or "sauce" in Japanese, this is an essential component of ramen and this concentrated seasoning mixture can be made in any number of ways (see pages 222, 226, 229).

BOK CHOY AND NAPA CABBAGE

Bok choy, aka pak choi, is a type of cabbage originally from south China. It is mild and sweet, consisting of a crunchy stalk and a leafy top. It is most often used in a stir-fry and takes very well to almost any sauce as well as simple seasonings. In markets, you will find a large bok choy with dark green leaves and a smaller version with lighter-colored leaves and stalks. The larger bok choy is considered the true bok choy and the smaller is often referred to as Shanghai or "baby" bok choy. When a recipe calls for bok choy, you can use either.

The cultivation of bok choy in China dates back as far as 5 CE. It is very popular throughout Asia and is widely grown in Japan, Malaysia, the Philippines, and Indonesia. It was brought to Europe in the mid-18th century and is also now commonly found in Europe and U.S. markets. European chefs often pair it with fish since its delicate taste does not overwhelm.

Napa cabbage is thought to be the natural cross of a turnip and bok choy and has been cultivated in China since the 15th century. Like bok choy, it is popular throughout all of Asia and has become a market staple from Korea to Singapore. I had always assumed the name meant it was grown in Napa, California, but in fact it comes from the Japanese word *nappa,* which refers to the leaves of any vegetable. Though this cabbage has a tighter head than bok choy, the flavor and uses are similar, as it has a mild cabbage flavor with lots of crunch. They are similar enough that in Chinese, Napa cabbage is called *da bai cai,* which means "big white vegetable," and bok choy is simply *bai cai* or "white vegetable."

Napa cabbage is especially important in Korean cuisine as the main ingredient in kimchi, the fermented vegetable pickle that is widely considered the national dish of both North and South Korea. There are many variations on kimchi, but one of the most common renditions contains Napa cabbage, daikon radish, chilies, scallion, ginger, and garlic. Koreans consider Napa cabbage such an important crop that extensive research has gone into plant breeding, and in the 21st century 880 varieties of it were registered by the Korea Seed and Variety Service. Kimchi, like fermented foods in general, has gained popularity in the States as well, and plenty of chefs have capitalized on its ability to put some kick into sandwiches, soups, and just about anything else it is added to.

Napa cabbage and bok choy are typical of other cabbage types in their growth habit; they prefer cool weather with plenty of water, but not too wet and not too cold. In the U.S., they are a feast for many types of pests, especially flea beetles, which don't kill the plant but put unsightly little pinholes in the leaves. These pests are managed in organic farming by putting hoops along the row and then a fabric cover over the hoops that lets in light and water but not pesky bugs. Since I am a huge fan of bok choy, I included it as part of the crop list my first year of farming. I thought I would attempt the season without the row cover but discovered I had a thriving population of flea beetles that were very appreciative of the food I provided them. Henceforth, the beetles were cut off from their favorite meal by the row covers, and I had very nice, whole heads of choy. If you see pristine-looking organic bok choy in the market, know that that it is some very pampered cabbage.

CABBAGES

Cabbage has found its way into kitchens across the globe, with each culture putting their own imprint on this adaptable vegetable. The cultivation of cabbage dates back to 4000 BCE in China and over 3,000 years ago in Europe. As explorers moved about, they brought it with them since it stores well, is very nutritious, and provides essential vitamin C to prevent scurvy. Once brought to a new region, it was incorporated into local cuisines. When considering which country has the best cabbage recipes, I'm at a loss. Eastern Europe loves a good braised cabbage. Koreans turn it into kimchi. Indians incorporate it into curries, and the Chinese use it in stir-fry. Americans are crazy for coleslaw and Germans are famous for sauerkraut. This incomplete list of the various uses of cabbage shows just how versatile it is.

It grows best in cool weather and fertile soil. China produces the most by volume, but Russia wins the prize of consuming the most per capita. Worldwide production in 2014 was 71.8 million tons. Red and green heads taste largely the same; choose one based on the color you would like. Savoy cabbage has a similar taste, but the wrinkled leaves are slightly softer. Napa cabbage is somewhat different and is covered in the section on bok choy (see pages page 709).

Tab. 24.

Brassica capitata alba, et viridis.
Ital. Cauolo Bolognese. Gall. Chou

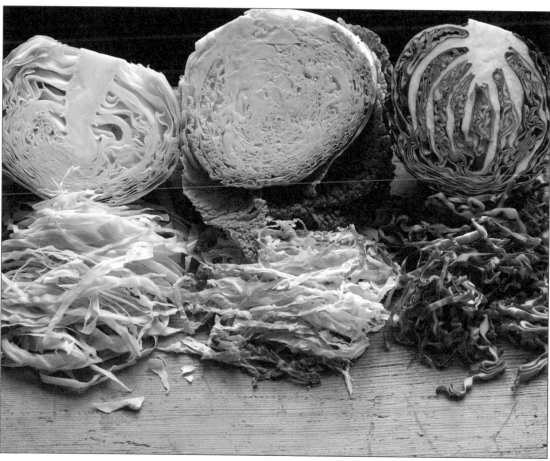

EGGPLANT

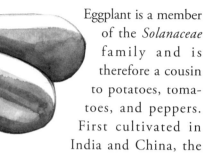

Eggplant is a member of the *Solanaceae* family and is therefore a cousin to potatoes, tomatoes, and peppers. First cultivated in India and China, the bulbous fruit got its name from the fact that early cultivars were small and white and resembled eggs hanging about the garden. When Arabs brought eggplant to Europe and Africa at the start of the 15th century via trade routes, it was met with skepticism, rumored to be poisonous (as was the tomato) and cause insanity. Traders must have been aware of the old adage that "sex sells" because they soon created a reputation for the fruit of being an aphrodisiac. The rumor persists to this day, and the veg has been popular ever since. African and South American cultures were more welcoming to the eggplant. Thomas Jefferson introduced eggplant to America; it is likely that the white and purple varieties he lists in an 1812 journal entry were grown from seeds collected by Jefferson in France or brought from Africa by the slaves who were responsible for Monticello's abundant gardens. Today, there are now numerous cultivars of every shape and color available in temperate and tropical regions.

Cooking with eggplant can be a challenge because of its spongy texture. When cooking it in a pan, it seems like it can absorb an unlimited amount of oil and still be in danger of burning. For this reason, when sautéing, try to keep the flame medium-low and stir often. Another option for Italian varieties is to brush with oil and then grill or bake. You can still achieve some nice browning without ending up with an oil-saturated mess.

Asian types, also known as Japanese or Chinese eggplant, have a sweeter, less fibrous flesh. Though they take well to stir-frying, they are lovely steamed and doused with a tangy sauce. The texture becomes melt-in-your-mouth tender, and their mild flavor is a good platform for bold Asian sauces such as ginger, fermented black bean, and soy. Even when I switched from commercial farming to a small kitchen garden, I always made space for Asian eggplants because they are not always available in local markets and I had to ensure I had access to some.

China is by far the largest producer of eggplant, growing almost 60 percent of the world's supply. It is such a popular ingredient there that a traditional adage states that a woman must have 12 eggplant recipes if she is to be eligible for marriage.

Eggplant is available year-round but will be at its freshest in late summer. The two most popular types that can be found in American markets are Italian and Asian. Look for fruits that are firm with no dents. Among the Italian varieties, you will find black, white, striped, and green types, all of which have a similar flavor and texture. Asian varieties tend to be long and slender and usually come in purple, but there are also white and green ones. You may be able to find the small, round Thai varieties that are commonly used in stir-fries and can be green, orange, and purple. Thai eggplants have more seeds than other types and are best cooked over high heat in a frying pan or simmered for a long time in a soup.

GARLIC

Where and when to cook with garlic is like asking where and when one should use butter: anytime, anywhere. Nearly any dish, save for the most delicate, includes a clove or two of garlic to give it backbone. Whether in a marinade or tossed straight into the pan, garlic imparts a sweet, rich, umami flavor and aroma that draws people into a kitchen. Americans didn't always embrace this allium and it wasn't in common use in home kitchens until the 1940s (save for the Italians, Chinese, and other communities whose cuisines knew better). We now consume about 260,000 tons (about 2 pounds per person) annually, and it is impossible to imagine modern American cuisine without it.

Garlic is thought to come from central Asia, and its use in both food and medicine dates back several thousand years. It was found in King Tutankhamun's tomb and was a well-known part of the diet of Greek and Roman soldiers. Explorers spread it worldwide, and now it is an integral part of cuisines from Brazil to Vietnam.

Today, garlic is an important commodity but is also at the center of some strife for farmers. The majority of the world's garlic is grown in China. The Chinese not only use it prolifically in cooking but also believe in its medicinal qualities. In the past several decades, China has been part of a trade war over garlic with the U.S. and the European Union. Several countries accused China of dumping huge quantities of cheap garlic on their markets, making it difficult for local growers to compete. In 1994, the U.S. enacted a whopping 377 percent tariff on Chinese garlic to protect U.S. production, most of which is grown in California, Oregon, and Nevada.

Along with politics, a fungal disease called white rot is a serious problem that is popping up in garlic-growing regions. It is a nasty pathogen that can remain in the soil for up to 40 years, even without a garlic or onion host to keep it alive. If a farmer's field is infected, they would have to stop growing garlic or onions all together.

There are German, Chinese, Russian, Spanish, and American-developed varieties of many different sizes, colors, and degrees of pungency. Customers were always surprised to see that there was more than the plain white variety they found in the supermarket. It is a crop well-suited to Vermont and is fairly easy to grow and market. Like potatoes, garlic is grown from garlic; you split the heads into individual cloves and plant the best of them to keep the quality high.

There are a few things to remember about cooking with garlic. Keep in mind that it has a high oil content and burns easily. Burnt garlic can make a dish taste bitter, so keep an eye on it and turn down the heat or add the rest of

your ingredients when you notice it starting to brown. It may be counterintuitive, but garlic is at its mildest when it is freshly harvested. The longer it has cured, the more intense the flavor. Garlic should be a team player and, when used raw, more than one makes it a prima donna. For dishes where it is cooked, such as in soups or stir-fry—don't hold back. Cooking mellows its zing but adds a sweet, robust flavor to any savory dish.

JICAMA

Jicama is a crunchy, sweet tuber that is excellent in cold salads and stir-fries. Native to Mexico and Central America, it is often eaten with chili powder and lime juice as a snack. Spaniards brought jicama to Asia, where it is also popular in Indonesia, the Philippines, Malaysia, and Singapore. Given its similarity to water chestnuts it is a natural for stir-fries and curries.

Jicama is in the legume family and produces long vines with bean-type pods. It requires at least nine months of hot weather to grow, making it only suitable for cultivation in the tropics. While the tuber is completely benign, the top portion of the plant is poisonous. The seeds contain the compound rotenone, which is used to kill fish and insects. But jicama has been consumed in Mexico since the days of the Aztec empire. It is harvested in the fall and is ready in time to be used in important Mexican holidays such as the Day of the Dead and Christmas.

Include jicama in salads anywhere a carrot would be appropriate. It is also a great choice for a crudités platter since, unlike other white fruits and vegetables, jicama will not oxidize and turn brown. You must always peel the tubers, not only because the skin is tough but also because they are often treated with wax to keep in moisture. A knife is more effective than a peeler for this job.

MUSHROOMS

The topic of edible mushrooms is vast. The majority of mushrooms consumed in the United States are white or button mushrooms (*Agaricus bisporus*). These were originally discovered in the 1920s, a mutant of the common brown mushroom that we know as the portobello or cremini. The white ones had a "cleaner" look to them and they have dominated the market ever since. Brown portobellos made a comeback in the 1980s, in part because they grow large caps that are excellent for grilling. *Agaricus* types are grown in soil, usually composted manure, in large grow houses under controlled conditions.

Many of what we call "wild" mushrooms are grown on wood, either whole logs or sawdust blocks. Among these are oysters, shiitakes, maitake, and lion's mane, all of which can be grown by farmers, using some type of wood as a substrate, with a good degree of success. Then there are the truly wild ones that have thus far eluded cultivation: morels, chanterelles, black trumpets, porcini, the ethereal truffles, and so many more. Many have tried to domesticate these, and some have claimed success; it is possible to purchase a grow kit for porcini (*Boletus edulis*), and some entrepreneurs are "planting" spores in orchards in anticipation of commercial-sized crops. But generally, one must go to the woods at the right time of year, under the right conditions, with a reliable field guide, to get the real thing.

China produces the largest portion of mushrooms worldwide, followed by Italy, the US, and the Netherlands. Poland is the fifth-largest producer, but they rank first in passion for them; their mushroom industry is growing larger every year. Mushroom hunting, for Poles,

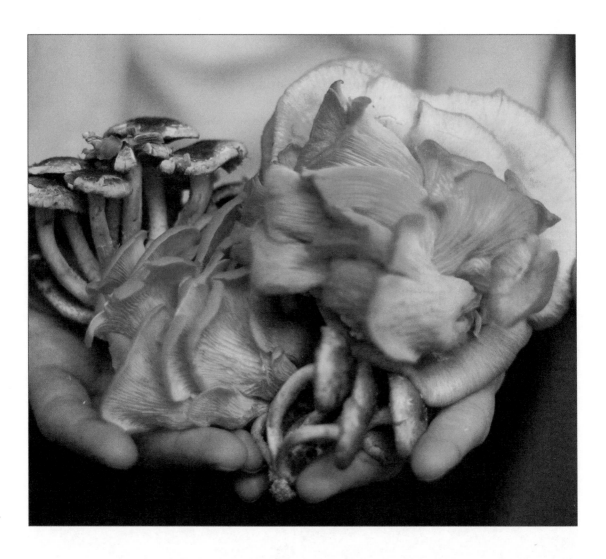

is a national pastime, enjoyed as a family out-ing, much like apple picking is for Americans. If you have considered looking for wild mush-rooms yourself, please be extra careful, as there are fatalities from poisonous mushrooms every year. Varieties such as *Amanita bisporigera*, aka, the Destroying Angel, which causes liver and kidney failure, are as much a part of the land-scape as choice edibles.

Fresh mushrooms are available year-round and, if you are lucky, your local market may carry oysters and shiitake. The white button mushroom gets a bad rap for being dull, but it can be plenty tasty if it is cooked properly. Por-tobellos are similar in flavor to the white mush-room but get more attention for their large size.

Dried mushrooms are excellent flavor boosters. One of the secrets of a really rich mushroom soup is to add dried porcini along with fresh mushrooms. Just make sure the dried ones are well chopped (once reconsti-tuted), as the texture can be tough. Chinese cuisines use dried, pickled, and canned mush-rooms in their soups and stir-fries, and you can discover many different types of mushrooms in Asian markets.

When cleaning them, it is heresy among mushroom lovers to even speak of rinsing them under water, and the general advice is to brush off any dirt with a towel. If the mushroom is really dirty, it is better to rinse them with water just before cooking than suffer grit in your dish. Any water that was absorbed by the mushroom will be cooked off if you immediately put it in a hot pan, but definitely do not soak them or wash them well in advance.

Capsicum fructu subrotundo, ventricoso dulci in summitate tetragono.
Ital. Peperoni di Spagna grandi, e dolci. — Gall. Poivre d'Inde ou de Guinée

PEPPERS

Both bell peppers and chili peppers are of the species *Capsicum annum*. The only difference is that chili peppers contain capsaicin, a compound that sets your tongue on fire. They are also one of the few vegetables that is commonly used as a spice. All peppers start green and then can eventually turn red, yellow, orange, purple, brown, and white. Members of the nightshade family, they are related to tomatoes, potatoes, and eggplant and are native to Mexico, Central America, and South America. Cuisines across the planet have embraced peppers, particularly in areas where spice is prized, like India and Southeast Asia.

China is the world's largest grower by volume, but the US imports most of its peppers from Mexico. Within the States, the majority of peppers are grown in California because they need a long period of warmth to reach maturity. In 2017, the US grew approximately 1.6 million pounds of bell peppers, with the crop valued at $642 million. Total chili pepper production in 2017 was 4.7 million pounds, valued at $143 million.

Fresh peppers are moderate contributors to the American diet. On average we consume 11.4 pounds of sweet peppers and 7.7 pounds of chili peppers per person, per year. They are excellent in salads, contributing not only sweetness and crunch but a nice array of colors as well. They are also part of the Cajun Holy Trinity, which consists of onion, celery, and bell peppers; crawfish etouffee, gumbo, and jambalaya all start with this trio.

Peppers figure more prominently in other countries' cuisines as a spice, like in Mexico, Hungary, and Turkey. The chili powder that one finds in the store, more often than not, is a blend of ground chilies and other spices such as cumin. Chipotles are dried and smoked jalapeño peppers that either come powdered, in whole form, or canned in adobo sauce. The canned version is highly recommended because both the pepper and the sauce are useful in recipes. Ancho chilies are dried poblanos that are used for similar purposes as a seasoning. All of these types are described as "mild heat," but spice is a very subjective thing. There are hundreds of other varieties of chilies from Mexico, many of which can be found in powdered form.

Less familiar to Americans are types of paprika from Hungary. While Americans think of paprika as a spice that goes on deviled eggs and some potato recipes, in Hungary it is integral to many regional dishes, the most famous of which is goulash. Paprika is so important in Hungary that there are at least seven different grades to choose from, such as "delicate," "exquisite delicate," and "pungent exquisite delicate." Smoked paprika (also found in Spain and known as pimenton) is also a terrific seasoning that adds a rich, smoky flavor to dishes but not a lot of heat, allowing you to taste the herbal notes of the pepper.

Another pepper seasoning that is just starting to make waves in the US is Urfa biber, commonly called the Black Urfa pepper. Grown in the Urfa region of Turkey, it looks like a big, red poblano. After harvest, the peppers are laid in the sun and then put under plastic or tarps at night to preserve some of the oils and moisture. The result is a semi-dry flake that is quasi-cured and has incredible, rich flavor reminiscent of tobacco. It goes on anything from grilled meat to roasted vegetables. It was introduced to our household last year, and now my husband puts it on everything.

Fresh peppers are available year-round but will be the best locally at the end of the summer. Look for firm ones with thick walls. Don't wash them until you are ready to use them and keep them cool in the fridge until then. The seeds of sweet bell peppers are always removed before using; just cut the pepper in half and pull out the seed ball out with your fingers. Hot chilies are served with or without seeds, but it is a myth that this is where all of the heat comes from. In fact, it is the ribs, or white pith, that contains the most capsaicin, with some also in the walls of the peppers. The seeds pick up heat from their proximity to the ribs but are not inherently hot. If you want to reduce the heat of a chili pepper, cut out the white pith, but be aware there is still some in the walls.

RADISHES

Early spring is a bonanza for greens, but it doesn't produce too many vegetable superstars, with the notable exception of asparagus. If you approach a farm stand, there may be one pop of color in all that green: radishes. They are commonly found in salads or relegated to a supportive role, whether as a garnish or in spring rolls or sushi. Often, it is just a decoration. A little investigation into the life and times of the radish, however, reveals that it can do wondrous things. It can provide important vitamins, improve soil, produce vital oils, and even inspire an entire festival. The radish, as it turns out, has some gravitas.

Radishes were domesticated in Europe in pre-Roman times and today are consumed worldwide. In Europe and the Americas, we grow the common short-season radish, which comes in shades of red, purple, black, and white. They are a cinch to grow, taking only 25 days from seed to harvest. The only restriction in their production is that they become intensely bitter in the heat, making them spring- and fall-only crops.

In Asia, the longer-season daikon radish can be used raw, cooked, or pickled. We can also thank China for the watermelon radish, which has a plain white exterior that belies a stunning center of bright pink. Its Chinese name is xin li mei, which translates to "in one's heart beautiful." A crosswise slice of watermelon radish is so visually arresting, it will elevate almost any dish just with its color.

All types of radishes are good sources of vitamin C, folic acid, and potassium. In addition, they are fat-free and provide a long list of micronutrients such as magnesium and copper. As well as being food for humans, it turns out that the radish is a good producer of oil and a remarkable soil improver. The oilseed radish, as its name would suggest, was developed for oil production. The seeds contain nearly 48 percent oil by weight, which is inedible to humans but may be a potential source of biofuel. More recently, the oilseed radish was discovered to be a good cover crop. A cover crop is meant to improve the soil by suppressing weeds, increasing biomatter or nutrients, or breaking up compacted soil. Farmers will seed overworked crop land with radishes, and their long taproots will bust through hard-packed dirt and then expand, breaking up the soil and allowing air and water to pass through. In addition, the taproots can reach as deep as 16 inches into the soil and capture nitrogen that is inaccessible to shorter-rooted crops. The farmer will let the radish die over the winter or till it under, making the nitrogen available for the next crop. Because of their speedy growth, radishes are also good at squeezing out weeds.

In Oaxaca, Mexico, the radish has, in fact, become a superstar to the extent that there is an entire festival dedicated to it. *Noche de Rábanos* or "Night of the Radish" is celebrated December 23. Farmers let their radishes grow to 2 feet in length and use these enormous roots to sculpt scenes depicting the Nativity or important moments in Oaxacan history. The competition is held in the main square with elaborate displays and prizes. Noche de Rábanos might not improve the radish's culinary reputation, but let's review: soil improver, potential biofuel, medium for divine inspiration. A little respect for the garnish, please.

SCALLIONS

Scallions may be as taken for granted as radish or parsley, considered little more than homely garnish. But, like dry towels, you'd miss them if they weren't around. Consider the classic dish of Peking duck. The traditional presentation is the roasted duck meat, wrapped in a thin pancake, topped with plum sauce and chopped scallions. The scallions may seem like they are thrown in for color, but if you took them out of the dish, it would not be half as good. Yellow onions would be too strong, and chives would not make themselves known. The middle ground of oniony flavor from scallions offers the perfect counterpart to the sweet sauce and fatty duck. There is no substitute.

Scallions are integral to salsas, nachos, salads, scallion pancakes, miso soup, yakitori, and too many Chinese and Korean dishes to count. There are so many culinary situations where an onion is too much, but you need a bit of onion flavor—scallions are the solution.

There is some confusion with the name, in that some people refer to scallions as shallots. To be clear, scallions are long, green shoots with a small white (sometimes purple) bulb that grows underground. They are grown in clusters and grow for a relatively short time until harvest (about 60 days). Shallots are a different plant, which creates a red bulb that is harvested like an onion and takes an entire season to reach maturity (over 100 days). Scallions are also called spring onions, green onions, table onions, salad onions, tubular onions, onion sticks, long onions, baby onions, precious onions, yard onions, gibbons, and syboes. (the Scottish name for the vegetable).

Good-quality scallions are available year-round. Look for bunches that have dark green tops and firm, white tips. If you are lucky, you may run across the purple variety at a farmers market; the flavor is the same as white, they are just extra-pretty. When ready to use them, cut off the roots as close to the end as possible and rinse well under cold water, pulling off any wilted or yellowing leaves. You can use practically the whole plant from white tips to the tops of the greens, trimming off only the very last inch.

SEAWEED

If you feel like all of the veggies in the produce section shelf are same old, same old, perhaps you should consider expanding your culinary repertoire to include seaweed. Though many coastal communities feature seaweed in their diets, it is still not part of mainstream fare in most of the States outside of Japanese restaurants. This may be changing, as cooks are learning of the versatility of both fresh and dried versions. There is also a nutritional and environmental benefit to consuming seaweed. Seaweed advocates are trying to give it an image makeover and rebrand it as "sea vegetables," but if enough people give it a try and discover how good it is, that may not be necessary.

Nearly all of the seaweed varieties that are edible come from the ocean, not freshwater sources. The most common types to end up on a plate are kelp, dulse, wakame, kombu, nori, Irish moss, sea palm, hijiki, and arame. Obviously, finding the dried versions, especially of kombu, nori, wakame, arame, or hijiki, is easier than fresh unless you live near a coast.

Nori is the flat, black sheet of seaweed used for rolling sushi and wrapping the Japanese rice balls called onigiri. You can also slice it and add it as a garnish to a salad. Kombu is most commonly used to make dashi, a Japanese broth. Wakame comes as dried black slivers that are often used in miso soup. When using them, be aware that a few dried strands will expand considerably, so go easy unless you want an all-seaweed soup. Hijiki and arame are used in everything from soups to salads.

Fresh seaweed is gaining traction as a commercial crop and may tick a lot of boxes that concern today's consumers, including sustainability and nutrition. There has been a movement to start farming kelp along the Eastern seaboard as a hedge against dwindling fish stocks. It is among the most sustainable agricultural projects in existence. Seaweed farmers put out lines planted with kelp seedlings in late fall, when recreational boating and commercial fishing is mostly done. The kelp grows quickly and is ready to harvest in April. Not only does it not require inputs (fertilizer, pesticides) or take up any land, but it absorbs excess nutrients like nitrogen and carbon that are causing problems in our coastal regions and effectively cleans the water. The kelp itself (*Sacharima latisima*) is delicious and very versatile to cook with.

Suzie Flores Douglas of Stonington Kelp Co. is one such kelp farmer who sets her lines off the coast of Connecticut. Her operation is only two years old and she is still learning, but in her first year she harvested 2,500 pounds of kelp and expects to expand her site. Seaweed is used in a variety of applications, and when asked where the kelp may end up, she offered a list of potential clients that would make a land farmer green with envy. Her yield goes direct to chefs; is used as animal feed and fertilizer; and is also used in the cosmetics and biofuel industries. Ideally, though, she would like to see it used primarily for food.

When I asked how she cooks with it, she said she puts it in everything, as one can consume it both cooked and raw. Raw kelp has a briny flavor and a crunchy-chewy texture. The taste of cooked kelp is very mild, so you can integrate it into a dish like lasagna and it won't change the flavor, but it adds loads of nutrients. Since Suzie has young children, she sneaks it into many of their meals. She also dries and pulverizes it, then uses it as a salt substitute.

At this point, marketing is everything. Getting chefs to incorporate it into their menus and encouraging broader awareness in the general public is essential to launching seaweed as the next big thing. Introducing a new food to the public is often more about psychology than appealing to taste buds; consumers need to change their perception of seaweed from

"slimy stuff you step on" to "delicious food." The taste is all there—we just need an attitude adjustment. A nonprofit group called Green-Wave exists to help those already involved with the fishing industry start kelp operations and find markets, as well as promote the new food. "Aqua farmers" know that public education will be key to their success. "We are very much at Step 1 in the process," says Douglas.

Finding edible seaweed is a matter of location. Dried seaweed is available in most supermarkets in the section with Asian food, and you can also order a wide variety online. Fresh seaweed is harder to come by; not only is its dis-

tribution limited but it is also highly seasonal. Frozen kelp can be found online under the name of Ocean Approved, which sells pureed kelp frozen into cubes meant for smoothies, sauces, soups, or anywhere you'd like a nutritional boost. They also sell frozen strips of kelp to be used for seaweed salad. The aqua farmers are doing their best to get their product to influential chefs, so if you see it on a menu, give it a try, knowing that you are in the hands of an expert who has experimented with it and is presenting it in a dish that he or she feels highlights its best qualities.

SEITAN

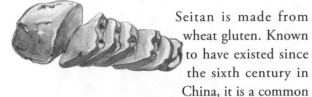

Seitan is made from wheat gluten. Known to have existed since the sixth century in China, it is a common ingredient and source of protein in cultures across Asia. Used most often in China, Japan, Vietnam, and North America, it has a texture similar to meat and has several different monikers in English, including "wheat meat." Like tofu, it has a very mild flavor that makes it a good platform for bold sauces and spices.

Seitan is made by adding water to wheat flour to activate the gluten. The mixture is then rinsed repeatedly to remove any starch, leaving behind a mass that is pure gluten. It has a satisfying, chewy texture that makes for a good replication of meat, if that is the effect you are going for. Seitan has a character and taste of its own that is mild but quite good. That said, if you are trying to coax carnivores into cutting back on animal consumption, seitan is a good option for a meat-like component. Mock duck, for instance, is seitan hopped up on flavoring agents like soy sauce and MSG.

While other vegetarian processed foods like tofu come in standard blocks, seitan comes in a variety of forms, which may explain why it is not more commonly used: cooks are baffled by it. In China, it is sold fried, steamed, and baked, with each iteration used in a different way. Fried seitan is put in soups, whereas steamed seitan is often shaped like a sausage, dyed pink, and referred to as "mock ham." Baked seitan, kao fu, is spongy in texture and is prized for soaking up savory sauces in stir-fry. In Japan, it is sold raw, formed into different shapes such as maple leaves, and steamed. It is also available "dry baked," taking on the appearance of bread.

In the States, it is sold mostly precooked with flavoring added. Some brands, like Tofurkey, combine wheat gluten with tofu to make an amalgam meat-like substance that simulates deli meats, bacon, patties, and steaks. You can also make seitan yourself using vital wheat gluten, which comes in powder form, combined with umami-rich seasonings like garlic powder and nutritional yeast (see page 743). Once you have created a dough, it can be shaped into any form you like and cooked, making for many recipes that pose as meatloaf, meatballs, sausages, and cuts of meat.

Seitan is low in calories and very high in protein (21 grams per 3 oz. serving) making it a healthy muscle-builder. It should be noted that it is pure gluten, so is not a good option for the gluten-intolerant. But if soy is your allergy, then this one is for you. Asian markets and health food stores will likely have the widest variety of premade seitan, as well as vital wheat gluten.

HOMEMADE SEITAN

YIELD: APPROXIMATELY ½ LB. / **ACTIVE TIME:** 15 MINUTES / **TOTAL TIME:** 45 MINUTES

If you can't find premade seitan or don't care for the options in your local market, it is easy to make at home with the purchase of some unusual ingredients. You will need to find vital wheat gluten, which is wheat flour that has been stripped of any starch and dried. Health food stores or stores that specialize in baking will likely carry it, but you can also order online from King Arthur Flour or Bob's Red Mill. Nutritional yeast is the same species of yeast used for making bread and beer but has been deactivated. In other words, it is not "alive" and cannot be used for leavening or fermenting; rather, it is meant to be used as a seasoning. It has a cheesy, nutty taste that is terrific on popcorn and other savory dishes. You can look for it in the bulk spice section at your local supermarket or order it online. Once you have made a batch of seitan, you can cut it to suit your recipe and cook as you would meat or tofu.

1. In a mixing bowl, mix the gluten, yeast, and garlic powder until blended.

2. Incorporate the stock or water and soy sauce a little at a time until a dough forms. If it is too dry, add extra stock or water. Knead the dough for a few minutes until it feels elastic and all of the ingredients are thoroughly incorporated. Divide into two pieces and shape into round disks.

3. Bring a pot of stock, water, or a combination of the two, deep enough to cover the dough, to a boil. Put the disks in the pot and reduce heat to a simmer. Poach for 30 minutes. Turn off the heat and let cool in the pot.

INGREDIENTS:

1	CUP VITAL WHEAT GLUTEN
¼	CUP NUTRITIONAL YEAST
1	TEASPOON GARLIC POWDER
½	CUP VEGETABLE STOCK (SEE PAGE 684) OR WATER, PLUS MORE FOR POACHING
1	TEASPOON SOY SAUCE

TOFU

Tofu is most commonly described as being devoid of flavor, but that is its most useful attribute. True, it is not going to alight great culinary passions on its own, but consider it a platform for the flavor you are really craving, such as soy sauce, sriracha, or curry. It is the boneless chicken breast of the vegetarian world: a nice substrate on which to show off the character of bolder players around it. Don't think of tofu as bland—think of it as a flavor train.

Tofu has been in the Chinese diet for 2,000 years and is also commonly used in the rest of East and Southeast Asia. In China, it is called *doufu*, which means "beans that are fermented," but Americans adopted the Japanese pronunciation. Benjamin Franklin was among the first Americans to take an interest in tofu, which is revealed in his letters to his dear friend John Bartram in the 1700s. In their correspondence, he mentions a "cheese" made from "Chinese garavances (soybeans)" and is clearly fascinated by the process. Franklin was a trendsetter, but it would take another 200 years for tofu to break into the culinary scene in the New World. It wasn't until the late 1900s that it began to become familiar to Western cooks, both in Asian and vegetarian dishes.

Franklin likely referred to it as cheese because the method of making tofu is similar to dairy-based cheese. To create tofu, a coagulant, either a salt or acid, is added to boiled soymilk, and the liquid binds into curds. The curds are pressed into a cake, which can vary in firmness depending upon how one wants to use it. Unpressed tofu, called *sun dubu*, is served like a porridge and is not commonly seen outside of Asian communities. The slightly firmer silken tofu comes in a block but is very soft and is often used for smoothies, in pastries, or as a substitute for eggs. The types most commonly seen in the West are firm or extra-firm tofu, which have had most of the moisture pressed out of them. These two types are easier to cut into cubes that hold their shape in a stir-fry or soup. Due to their lower moisture content, they are also good candidates for baking and frying. There are several other iterations such as processed tofu, thousand-layer tofu, stinky tofu (its real name), fermented tofu, and freeze-dried tofu if you are inclined to take a deep dive into the topic.

Tofu is an important source of protein for vegetarians. Unlike many other vegetable-sourced proteins, it is a complete protein, meaning it contains all nine essential amino acids. One cup of boiled soybeans contains about 29 grams of protein, which would make Popeye chuck his can of spinach and grab a bowl of mapo tofu for lunch. It is also gluten-free, which makes it the best option for vegetarians with an allergy to wheat products.

Its mild flavor makes it adaptable for a variety of dishes. One can embrace its mild nature and use it in a classic miso soup, allowing the tofu cubes to highlight the complex but delicate taste of white miso. It is also a good filler for dumplings, giving a springy texture to mix in with the vegetables of Tofu-Filled Momos (see page 125). Tofu can also be a an oasis in spicy dishes, giving your palate a refuge from fiery peppers.

YU CHOY

Yu choy is life-saving. Just when you've had your umpteenth panfried dumpling or forked another plate full of dough-crusted General Tso's chicken into your mouth, a beautiful plate of simple greens comes out of the kitchen and is placed on the middle of the table. You have no idea what to call these greens other than "Chinese vegetables," but their cleansing taste is a miracle. They have that subtle mustard-green tang, though they are somewhat sweeter, and the leafy parts taste like spinach. It doesn't really matter what they are called, they are the perfect antidote to the indulgent meal you just consumed too much of.

Yu choy is part of the brassica (cabbage) family and is a close cousin to gai lan, also known as Chinese broccoli. Their appearance is nearly identical. The only differences are that yu choy has yellow flowers whereas gai lan has white ones, and yu choy is sweeter than gai lan with more tender stalks. If you cannot name the delicious dish that shows up on your table at the Chinese restaurant, don't feel too bad, because no one else seems to have settled on a name either. It is also referred to as green choy sum, cai xin, choisum, you cai, cai hua, yai tsoi, flowering white cabbage, mock pak-choi, or false pak-choi. This may be because yu choy is used widely throughout Asia and has adopted different names depending on where it is being eaten.

Yu choy is native to China but is now shipped around the world to cater to Asian communities. Like others in the cabbage family, it prefers cool but not cold weather. Only taking about 40 days to maturity, it is one of the few greens that is harvested while it is flowering. (Most vegetables are too tough once they start flowering and are harvested in the bud stage, like broccoli or asparagus, or before flowering, like kale.)

This particular green cooks up quickly and is best served with a simple preparation. It has also bucked the trend of roasting by being so tasty when simply steamed. You can readily find it in the produce aisle of Asian markets. Ask for yu choy, and if that doesn't work, consult the list of alternative names above.

TECHNIQUES

FILLING AND SHAPING WONTONS

When working with wonton dough, you want to leave it covered until you're going to use it. When you are ready, lay a few wrappers out on your work surface and place your filling in the center. Dip your finger into some water and wet the edge of the wonton wrapper—not too much water, or the dough will become sticky and unworkable. Take two opposite corners and lift until they meet. Secure with a little pinch, and then lift the two remaining corners, one at a time.

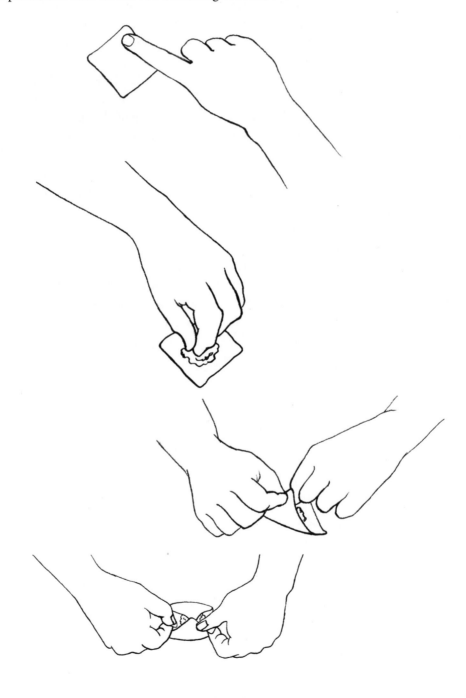

TOMATO CONCASSE

Boil enough water for a tomato to be submerged and add a pinch of salt. While it is heating, prepare an ice bath and score the top of the tomato with a paring knife, taking care not to cut into the meat of the tomato. Place the tomato in the boiling water for 30 seconds, or until the skin begins to blister. Carefully remove it from the boiling water and place it in the ice bath. Once the tomato is cool, remove it from the ice bath and use a paring knife to peel the skin off, starting at the scored top. Cut the tomato into quarters, remove the seeds, and cut according to instructions.

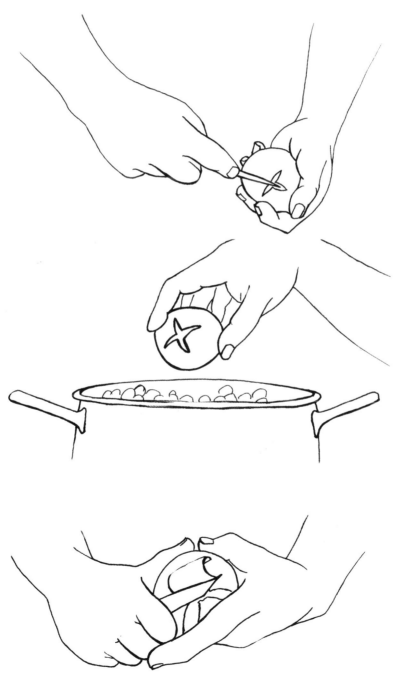

CONVERSION TABLE

WEIGHTS

1 oz. = 28 grams

2 oz. = 57 grams

4 oz. (¼ lb.) = 113 grams

8 oz. (½ lb.) = 227 grams

16 oz. (1 lb.) = 454 grams

VOLUME MEASURES

⅛ teaspoon = 0.6 ml

¼ teaspoon = 1.23 ml

½ teaspoon = 2.5 ml

1 teaspoon = 5 ml

1 tablespoon (3 teaspoons) = ½ fluid oz. = 15 ml

2 tablespoons = 1 fluid oz. = 29.5 ml

¼ cup (4 tablespoons) = 2 fluid oz. = 59 ml

⅓ cup (5 ⅓ tablespoons) = 2.7 fluid oz. = 80 ml

½ cup (8 tablespoons) = 4 fluid oz. = 120 ml

⅔ cup (10 ⅔ tablespoons) = 5.4 fluid oz. = 160 ml

¾ cup (12 tablespoons) = 6 fluid oz. = 180 ml

1 cup (16 tablespoons) = 8 fluid oz. = 240 ml

TEMPERATURE EQUIVALENTS

°F	°C	Gas Mark
225	110	¼
250	130	½
275	140	1
300	150	2
325	170	3
350	180	4
375	190	5
400	200	6
425	220	7
450	230	8
475	240	9
500	250	10

LENGTH MEASURES

¹⁄₁₆ inch = 1.6 mm

⅛ inch = 3 mm

¼ inch = 1.35 mm

½ inch = 1.25 cm

¾ inch = 2 cm

1 inch = 2.5 cm

IMAGE CREDITS

CONTRIBUTORS

BRAIN HUSKEY

Top Chef Season 11 alumnus Brain Huskey was born in the early 1980s to Korean immigrant parents and his childhood experiences in the kitchen with his mother and grandmother set him on his culinary path. Growing up in Southern California and cooking all over the world exposed Huskey to myriad flavors from different cultures. This exposure is what has defined his unique style and approach to cooking. Before opening his own restaurant, Huskey helped launch several prominent restaurants in the Los Angeles area. Today he is the chef and owner of The Jetty in Corona del Mar, California.

VANESSA CECEÑA

Vanessa Ceceña, a daughter of Mexican immigrants, grew up in San Diego, California, along the US-Mexico border. She writes about life on the border, migration, and about the intersections between food, policy, and community. As a transfronteriza, her writing is influenced by her bicultural identity and travels in Mexico and Asia, giving her work a transnational flair. Vanessa received her master's degree in Social Work from USC and an undergraduate degree in International Development Studies. The early years of her career were spent working alongside Oaxacan indigenous communities, where she was taught the importance of food and language as a tool for cultural preservation. In 2015, Vanessa received an award from the Society of Professional Journalists, San Diego chapter, for her piece on deportation and family separation. When she isn't eating or writing, she can be found on the dance floor, dancing salsa and bachata.

JIM SULLIVAN

Jim is a graduate of the Art Institute of California's culinary program and a self-taught photographer. His work has a strong focus in the culinary field as well as portraiture and lifestyle. His publications range from *Food and Wine* to *Leica Camera* and *Art Culinaire*. His clientele ranges from Californios, Michelin-starred restaurants, Birdie G's, and Liholiho Yacht Club. When he isn't traveling for work, he can be found in Southern California spending time with his family and their little French Bulldog, Mochi.

INDEX

ABOUT CIDER MILL PRESS BOOK PUBLISHERS

Good ideas ripen with time. From seed to harvest, Cider Mill Press brings fine reading, information, and entertainment together between the covers of its creatively crafted books. Our Cider Mill bears fruit twice a year, publishing a new crop of titles each spring and fall.

"Where Good Books Are Ready for Press"

Visit us online at

cidermillpress.com

or write to us at

PO Box 454
12 Spring St.
Kennebunkport, Maine 04046